The "Insight Travel Library" is the
collector's hardcover edition of the *Insight Guides* series
by APA Publications

INSIGHT
TRAVEL LIBRARY

Indian Wildlife

ISBN: 0-245-54904-8.

Indian Wildlife

DESTINATION: INDIA

DESTINATION: NEPAL

DESTINATION: SRI LANKA

Edited by Samuel Israel *and* Toby Sinclair

Executive Editor: Bikram Grewal

Designed by V. Barl

Illustrated by Klaus Geisler

Directed by Hans Johannes Hoefer

APA

PUBLICATIONS

The *Indian Wildlife* title has the distinction of being a double milestone in Apa Publications' list of travel books. It was the first of the *Insight Guides* special theme titles in Apa's Great Adventure series in 1986. Now, it is again the initial title in Apa's new collection of large format books, the hardcover edition *Destination* series. These books are specially designed collector's editions, featuring new graphics, more pictures and updated text. By virtue of its enlarged format, *Destination: Indian Wildlife* also offers a liberal sprinkling of impressive double page photographs.

The editorial team assembled by Apa's Singapore-based founder and publisher **Hans Hoefer** is a well-balanced one. **Samuel Israel** is a book publishing editor of long standing and former Director of the National Book Trust, India. **Toby Sinclair**, whose working life started in a leading British publishing house, was some years ago driven by wanderlust and love of wildlife to Nepal and India, to work as an organizer of wildlife and mountain tours. After some years as a company manager in the area of travel and communication, he has returned to publishing and book distribution. Besides photographs, Sinclair contributed the piece on the Mudumalai National Park and has compiled and written the very comprehensive Travel Tips. **Bikram Grewal** is now head of Dass Media, an Indo-British enterprise that provides representation and promotion services in India for several major British publishers. His earliest job was leading and guiding hunting trips in the jungles of eastern India.

He thus belongs to the tribe of big-game-hunters-turned-conservationists.

For expert coverage of two major parks in Nepal, Chitwan and Bardia, the editors' obvious choice was **K. K. Gurung** who, since the late 1970s, has been professionally involved in adventure tourism in Nepal. Educated as a biologist, Gurung is a naturalist by profession, working with the well-known Tiger Tops organization as Director, Special Projects. He is the author of *Heart of the Jungle* which he illustrated himself with exquisite line drawings. Examples of his photographic studies of nature and wildlife are to be seen in the present volume. Gurung has also penned the articles on Observing Wildlife and the Indian Rhinoceros.

Sri Lanka is dealt with by **Ravindralal Anthonis** who was Colombo Editor for *Insight Guide : Sri Lanka*. Anthonis is Honorary General Secretary of the Wildlife and Nature Protection Society of Sri Lanka and has served on several official committees concerned with wildlife and conservation in the country.

Dr Kamala Seshan, geographer on the staff of the National Council of Educational Research and Training, New Delhi, opens this guide with a survey of physical and climatic conditions governing the distribution of animals and birds on the subcontinent.

Royina Grewal, writer on travel and matters cultural, and currently in charge of research for *Sanctuary*, India's leading journal devoted to wildlife and conservation, discusses traditional regional attitudes to and beliefs about wild animals, and their expression in various forms.

Bittu Sahgal provides a general survey of the current wildlife situation in the region in both its positive and negative aspects and the prospect it faces. Sahgal, as editor of *Sanctuary*, producer of wildlife films, wildlife photographer and treasurer of the Bombay National History Society, is able to take the full subcontinent into his sweep. Sahgal freely gave his time and knowledge in assisting the editors and also placed the excellent Sanctuary Picture Library at their disposal.

Kaushalya Ramdas teaches at the Centre for Cultural Resources & Training in Delhi. In addition to her article on the forest regions of the Indian subcontinent, Ramdas also wrote about some of the mammal species not covered in detail by the other articles.

H. S. Panwar is currently Director of the India Wildlife Institute, Dehra Dun. He has also been Director of Project Tiger, and prior to that, Director of Kanha National Park, and is well suited to write authoritatively about the glory of the tiger and also about Kanha, one of its major homes in India.

J. C. Daniel wrote the chapter on Lions, Leopards and Lesser Cats. This veteran Indian naturalist has been active in the field for 35 years and more. Currently Curator, Bombay Natural History Society, he is one of the editors of its journal and author of some 50 scientific papers on a very broad range of subjects. He also rediscovered the golden gecko in the Tirupati Hills of South India after it had been unsighted for 114 years.

Dr D. K. Lahiri Choudhury has combined his duties as Professor and Head of the Department of English at Rabindra Bharati University in West Bengal with years of study of the Asian Elephant, on which he has written extensively.

Dr M. K. Ranjitsinh who contributed the section on Deer, Antelopes and Bovines, is a senior Indian administrator who is currently Joint Secretary to the Government of India in the Department of Environment, Forest & Wildlife in the Ministry of Environment and Forests. He has written extensively on wildlife and environment. In recognition of his service to conservation, he was awarded in 1979 the Order of the Golden Ark, a decoration instituted by Prince Bernhard of the Netherlands, first president of the World Wildlife Fund (WWF).

Kunal Verma, who wrote on Primates; The Dog Family, Hyenas and Bears; and on Kaziranga and Manas National Parks, is a young journalist who divides his time between writing general interest features for the Associated Press, and wildlife-related articles for *Sanctuary* and other magazines, and wildlife photography and film-making with Sanctuary Films. Born into an "army family," he spent many of his growing years in remote parts of India where his acquaintance with wildlife and nature was direct and intimate.

Rom and **Zai Whitaker** co-authored the section on Reptiles. Rom is the founder of three major institutions concerned with reptiles, the Madras Snake Park, the Madras Crocodile Bank, and the Irula Snakecatchers Co-operative. He is the author of several scientific papers and a book on Indian snakes. With his wife Zai, he takes photographs and makes films for Eco Media, a Madras-based company. Some of their photographs are

Hoefer

Israel

Sinclair

B. Grewal

Gurung

Anthonis

Seshan

Daniel

included in this guide. Zai is a writer and journalist mainly in the field of popular natural history. Working on her third film with Rom provided fresh material for their article on Periyar National Park.

Zai's father, **Zafar Futehally**, one of India's leading ornithologists, contributed both the general introduction to the birds of the subcontinent and also a handy reference guide to those most frequently seen by the visitor. His contribution to popular education on conservation and wildlife through his writing has received international recognition. Futehally was Honorary Secretary and later, Vice President of the Bombay Natural History Society.

Kailash Sankhala, who wrote on life in the desert, has led expeditions to the salt desert of the Rann of Kutch, the icy desert of Ladakh and the sandy desert of the Thar, the Great Indian Desert. His published works include *Tigerland; Tiger; The Story of the Indian Tiger; Wild Beauty; and Garden of the Gods—Bird Sanctuary, Bharatpur.* Sankhala also contributed some striking photographs to this volume.

Dr E. G. Silas is senior Indian marine biologist. He has participated in several national and international fishery and oceanographic expeditions, either as member or leader. His major scientific contributions are on tuna, bill fish and related species, squid, cuttlefish and octopus, and endangered marine species such as whales, dolphins, dugongs and sea turtles.

Joanna Van Gruisen has lived in Sri Lanka, Nepal and India since 1978, working first as a wildlife photographer and later also as cinematographer with husband **Ashish Chandola**. Her 14 months filming "New Hope for the Hangul" in Dachigam made her an obvious choice both for the article on this national park and the piece on Wildlife of the Himalaya. She has filmed in Sagarmatha National Park, Nepal, and in Manas Tiger Reserve. As a still photographer, Van Gruisen has also made a substantial contribution to this guide. She and Chandola have been of great help to the editors through all stages of the preparation of this volume.

As Honorary Warden, Corbett National Park and as the producer of a film on the park, natural-history consultant **Brijendra Singh** is well qualified to present it to readers of this guide. He, like a number of other conservationists, started as a hunter and has in recent years trapped (not killed) three man-eating tigers and one man-eating leopard and has had to shoot a rogue elephant.

In the case of Dudhwa National Park, we are fortunate to have an article by **Arjan Singh,** the person who was almost singlehandedly responsible for getting it established and who has been associated with its development ever since. In recognition of his pioneering work, he was awarded the WWF International Gold Medal for 1976. His books include *Tiger Haven, Tara—A Tigress* (the story of how a motherless cub was trained for life in the wild and then freed), *Prince of Cats*, and *Tiger! Tiger!*

Gillian Wright has been based in India for several years, working as a researcher for TV documentaries. She collaborated with Mark Tully and Satish Jacob of the BBC in the writing of *Amritsar: Mrs Gandhi's Last Battle.*

She is a regular visitor to the Keoladeo and Bandhavgarh National Parks about which she writes with intimate knowledge and great sensitivity.

Divyabhanusinh is one of India's talented wildlife amateurs whose knowledge and authority in the field matches those of the professionals. Divabhanusinh is a hotelier by profession, being Vice President (Operation), North, in charge of eight hotels of India's oldest major chain, Indian Hotels Co. Ltd., the celebrated Taj groups. As a life member of the Bombay National History Society, he served on its governing body from 1977 to 1982. Ranthambhore, Sariska and Gir are parks he knows intimately.

Ullas Karanth is a graduate in mechanical engineering who, after seven years as an engineer, switched to agricultural/forestry farming and then, in 1984, to wildlife studies as a profession instead of as the hobby it had been. Karanth is now Research Officer at the Centre for Wildlife Studies, Mysore and is well equipped to write on Nagarahole and Bandipur National Parks.

In addition to the contributors mentioned above, a number of other persons deserve thanks for their assistance and encouragement. **Dr Shelton Atapathu**, Director, Department of Wildlife Conservation, Sri Lanka, greatly assisted Ravindralal Anthonis in the preparation of the section on Sri Lanka. **Dr J. Fox** of the Indo-U.S. Snow Leopard Project provided, at short notice, the splendid shot of the rare snow leopard appearing on pp. 98. **Dass Media Pvt. Ltd.**, under the supervision of **Surit Mitra**, made a number of their facilities and supporting.

services available to the editors; **Dr Sarah Israel** assisted throughout in checking copy and proofs; **Dr Shobita Punja** helped in checking factual information; and **Parminder Kaur Sabharwal, Jessy Mathew** and **Estella Dickson** provided secretarial and typing services. Others who were helpful in various ways, too numerous to mention are **Ashish Madan, Lakshmi Sinclair, Nikhat Grewal, Lisa Choegyal**, Director, Tiger Tops, Kathmandu, **Durgi** and **K.K. Singh** of Handhavgaroh Jungle Camp, **Colonel John Wakefield, Vira Mehta, S. K. Kandhari, P.G. Ramachandran, Roshmi Raychaudhuri, Madhu Saghal, Ajit Grewal** and **Mohan Chawla**.

—Apa Publications

Verma

R. Whitaker

Z. Whitaker

Van Gruisen

Brijendra Singh

Arjan Singh

Wright

Divyabhanusingh

IINTRODUCTION AND MAPS

MAPS

FEATURES

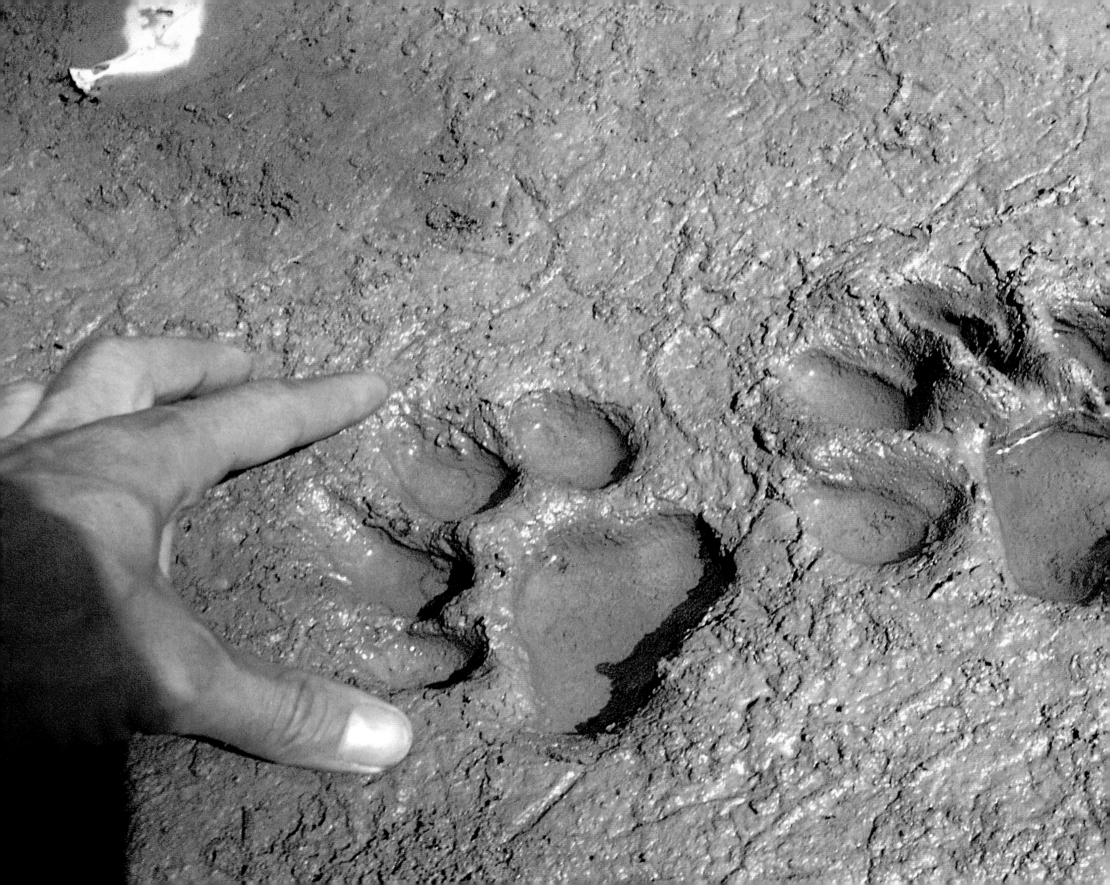

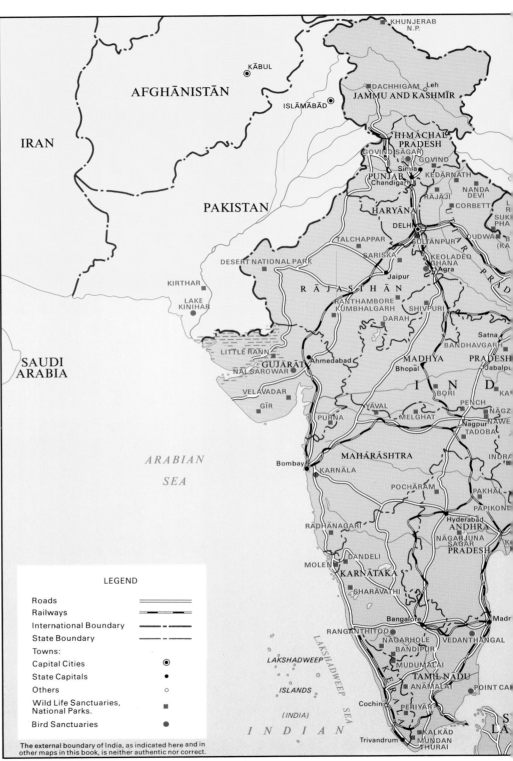

AFGHĀNISTĀN

IRAN

PAKISTAN

SAUDI
ARABIA

KĀBUL

ISLĀMĀBĀD

KHUNJERAB
N.P.

DACHHIGAM   Leh

JAMMU AND KASHMĪR

HIMĀCHAL
PRADESH

GOVIND SĀGAR   GOVIND

KEDĀRNATH

PUNJAB
Chandigarh

RĀJAJI

NANDA
DEVI

HARYĀNA   CORBETT

DELHI

SULTĀNPUR

TALCHAPPAR

SARISKA

KEOLADEO
GHANA   Agra

DESERT NATIONAL PARK

Jaipur

KIRTHAR

RĀJASTHĀN

RANTHAMBORE
KUMBHALGARH   SHIVPURI

LAKE
KINIHAR

DARAH

Satna

BANDHAVGARH

LITTLE RANN

GUJARĀT
NAL SAROWAR   Ahmedabad

MADHYA   PRADESH

Bhopal   Jabalpu

VELĀVADAR

BORI

IN   D

GĪR

YĀVAL

PENCH

NĀGZ

PURNA   MELGHAT

Nagpur   NĀWE

TADOBA

ARABIAN

SEA

MAHĀRĀSHTRA

INDR

Bombay

KARNĀLA

POCHĀRAM

PAKHĀL

PĀPIKOND

RADHĀNAGARI

Hyderabād   ANDHRA

NĀGĀRJUNA
SĀGAR   PRADESH

MOLEN

DANDELI

KARNĀTAKA

SHARĀVATHI

Bangalore   Madr

RANGANTHITOO

NĀGARHOLE   VEDANTHANGAL

LAKSHADWEEP   BANDIPUR

MUDUMALAI

LAKSHADWEEP
ISLANDS

TAMIL NĀDU

ANĀMALAI   POINT CA

(INDIA)

Cochin   PERIYĀR

KALKĀD

INDIAN   MUNDAN
THURAI

Trivandrum

S
LĀ

LEGEND

Roads	
Railways	
International Boundary	
State Boundary	
Towns:	
Capital Cities	◉
State Capitals	●
Others	○
Wild Life Sanctuaries, National Parks.	■
Bird Sanctuaries	●

The external boundary of India, as indicated here and in
other maps in this book, is neither authentic nor correct.

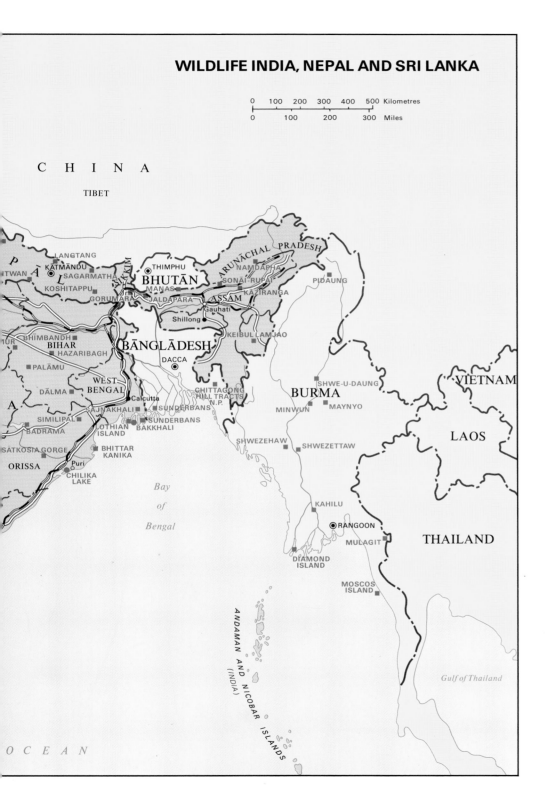

WILDLIFE INDIA, NEPAL AND SRI LANKA

0   100   200   300   400   500 Kilometres

0   100   200   300   Miles

A RICH ARRAY

This guide is planned to serve a dual purpose: to acquaint the reader/user with the wildlife picture in the region it covers, and to provide a practical guide for visitors making a wildlife tour of the region, both at the planning stage and then on the ground during the tour itself.

The first part of the guide that immediately follows therefore provides the broad background in which the region's wildlife lives and can be observed; the current wildlife situation and prospects in the light of local attitudes and traditions; and an eminently practical article on the art and practice of observing wildlife.

India, Nepal and Sri Lanka have much in common, but also a fascinating diversity; and in the case of India, a rich diversity even within its national frontiers. Though so close to the tip of the Indian peninsula, Sri Lanka, thanks to the narrow strip of ocean between the two countries, has some unique features in terms of nature of habitat and species. Even among birds that have the capacity to fly over the narrow Palk Strait, while many are common to both countries, some, from either side, just refuse to cross.

This guide presents this diversity in broad spectrum. The tiger, the elephant and the unique Indian rhinoceros get separate treatment, as also the very special Himalayan and desert habitats. Others are grouped for coverage under headings such as Primates, Birds, Reptiles etc.

· ·

Preceding pages: contemplating the vastness of Everest Park; wild apricots in autumn, Kashmir; view from Chitwan; early morning, Corbett National Park; painted storks, Bharatpur; tiger tracks in Chitwan; and *left*, Langur river.

A VARIETY OF HABITAT

Forests and wildlife with a wide variety of trees and animals are found in the subcontinent. From the early days of the great King Ashoka, trees and forests have received protection. Though the Mughals cared more for their well-laid-out gardens than for forests, there is evidence that the now arid dusty ravines of the Chambal were (during the days of Akbar) a rich dense forest with elephants.

Today, given the protection of the forest reserves, we can still see glimpses of the wildlife of India in places like Simplipal, Ranthambhore, Kanha and Mudumalai. Every state of the Indian Union has a sanctuary which protects the special animals of the area. This is only natural since India's unique climate and landscape support typical animals in each region.

India and its neighbors constitute a unique subcontinent. Though it is in the tropics, it differs in climate from all the other countries of this belt, whether it be Sudan or Brazil, because it has an exclusive monsoon climate. Sri Lanka to its south, just 8° north of the Equator, provides a totally different botanical region. In Sri Lanka there is a dry, almost desert-like landscape in the north, giving way to a small scattered savannah in the central region and a luxuriant equatorial rain forest to the south.

The Seasons: In India the sanctuaries where the animals are best seen in winter, October to March, are those of Assam at Manas for wild buffalo and at Kaziranga for rhinoceros; in Kashmir at Dachigam for the now almost extinct Kashmir stag; in Kerala at Periyar for elephant and bison; and in Rajasthan for birds at Keoladeo Ghana (Bharatpur).

The summer and monsoon months of March to July are ideal for visiting the wildlife sanctuaries at Bandipur in Mysore to see the bison; Kanha and Shivpuri in Madhya Pradesh for swamp deer and tiger; Mudumalai in Tamil Nadu for elephant and reptiles; Hazaribagh in Bihar for the mahua-eating bears; Gir forest for the Indian lion; and the Corbett National Park and the other sanctuaries of Uttar Pradesh for tiger and panther.

Given the startling fact that in the last 300 years the two-horned rhino of the Sunderbans have disappeared, as have the Indian cheetah, golden eagle and the pink-headed duck, it is not surprising that the Kashmir stag, musk deer, blackbuck and wild buffalo face the same fate if these are not sought, cared for and studied.

Following the monsoons is the cool dry February, the most delightful time of the year in India. The air masses pouring across the east flow around the Himalaya as a herald of the ensuing drought which will last till the monsoons return in the following year.

Plants, animals and birds generally breed in September and nest through the monsoons when an abundance of insect life is found. The red-eyed koel migrates to West Malaysia as if to herald the monsoon there.

Woodlands: The forests of the Indian subcontinent, from the Himalaya to the Andamans, range from the tropical, moist evergreens to deciduous trees. The evergreens here are

broadleaved and do not have conifers. These evergreen forests indicate almost 80 inches (200 cm) of rainfall in the area whereas the deciduous forests indicate definite wet and dry seasons.

In the latter type of forests, what is striking is that all the animals and birds are smaller since the temperatures are higher. Climbing mountains here is also rewarding with the quick change in weather and vegetation and increasing size of all the animals. Even at 3500–7000 feet (1000–2100

. . . .
Above, **Himalayan River gorge and *right*, the effects of deforestation.**

meters), rainfall is never less than 300 inches (760 cm) a year and temperatures are between 64°F (18°C) in winter and 88°F (31°C) in summer. Higher up, there are the moss forests with a dense dark bush of low trees covered with orchids, ferns and rhododendrons which grow amidst the moss cover.

The poet, Subramania Bharti, describes this land of India in a poem as

A land of mountains
crowned with peaks of sapphire blue;
and of ambrosial water in all its
brooks and pools
a land of lovely woods and trees
of clustering fruit and of groves
dense with trees with
cool luxuriant leaf.

Within the high Himalaya there are distinct

lofty mountains are treeless and in Ladakh turn into a stony desert due to the area being in the rain shadow of the Himalaya. These cold deserts merge into green meadows with scrub beyond the tree line. To these meadows the Gujjar herdsmen lead their sheep and mules every summer. Come winter, they quickly descend to the warm tropical forests of the Siwaliks, to sit out the cold winter months.

Himalayan Gamut: The eastern Himalaya in sharp contrast does not have any species of pine. The temperate forests occur immediately above the tropical forests of the Ganga plain. These temperate forests are dense, and fed by the monsoons. Above 5000 feet (1500 meters), there are oak, laurel, maple and birch, and on the higher slopes of the Dhaulagiri and eastern Himalaya, the brightly colored rhododendrons.

homes are to be seen these have to be visited separately in the *terai*, and the middle and inner Himalaya, both in the western and eastern parts. An ideal place to see the entire gamut of Himalayan natural environment is in the mountains and valleys of Nepal. This 500-mile (800-km) stretch east of the Karakoram between Afghanistan and Burma is known as the Nepal Himalaya and has a large number of high peaks, including Everest. Besides the mountainous regions, the Nepal Himalaya include the *terai*, the Himalayan foothills, the dry Khatmandu valley with tropical and subtropical climate, and the high alpine meadows of the inner Himalaya.

The *terai* in Nepal, as also the Indian part of the Himalaya, gets less rain than the foothills. However, in this area, up to 8000 feet (2450 meters) there are dense forests of deciduous trees

thick and dense and in the spring are a burnished red. These forests have cinnamon, magnolia, chilauni, chestnut, birch and plum trees. The branches of the trees are covered with mosses and a variety of woody climbers entwines them.

Higher, between 6500 and 11,500 feet (2000 and 3500 meters) are the moist temperate, purely coniferous forests. The other trees here are spruce, deodar, fir, kail, oak, maple and birch. These pine and oak forests have tree ferns along the shaded banks of the river. Nearer the tree line, juniper and rhododendron (the national flower of Nepal) grow, and below are the belts of fir and hemlock trees which lie between the moist temperate and alpine forest belts. These are the forests where the much poached musk deer roam with the protected blue sheep and bharal. In the fir forests, the red panda is sought after for its

differences in the vegetation and wildlife. From Kashmir to Bhutan and Nepal are distinct tropical forests of the area known as the *terai* where usually a single major species of tree is found — the sal. Higher up along the slopes, these temperate forests, unlike those of Europe or eastern United States, do not have conifers but are forests of oak, juniper, the stately deodar, maple, birch, pine, chestnut and spruce. These forests too are usually of single species and a very distinct forest line separates them from the Alpine meadows of the Inner Himalaya. These

· ·
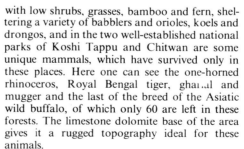
***Above**, alpine forest and **right**, early morning on a sandy riverbank.*

The wildlife of the lofty Himalaya presents typical examples of how, in cooler climates, animals become larger and more long-haired. The chinkara stag, blackbuck and barking deer wander through these evergreen forests and on the higher slopes is the bear which is friendly and easily taught tricks. Racoons and swamp buffaloes are also common here. The eastern Himalaya, being wetter, has exotic flying foxes and the oriental squirrel with three stripes on its back caused, it is said, by the loving caress of the god Rama. The famous Indian mongoose also abound in these jungles. The treeless slopes of the northern mountains have moles, hares and the antelope or bharal. Though none of these animals are facing extinction, their habitats are fast being eroded and if their interesting natural

with low shrubs, grasses, bamboo and fern, sheltering a variety of babblers and orioles, koels and drongos, and in the two well-established national parks of Koshi Tappu and Chitwan are some unique mammals, which have survived only in these places. Here one can see the one-horned rhinoceros, Royal Bengal tiger, gharial and mugger and the last of the breed of the Asiatic wild buffalo, of which only 60 are left in these forests. The limestone dolomite base of the area gives it a rugged topography ideal for these animals.

Between 2200 and 3200 feet (670 and 970 meters) are the temperate forests. These are on the wet foothills of the Himalaya which get a lot of rain from the monsoons. These closed, evergreen forests have short, stout trees. The crowns are

skin but today is rarely seen. It is said that here the yeti, the link between man and his monkey ancestors, is sometimes spotted. The gorgeous monal pheasant with a multi-colored tail is also found here.

Higher, nearer the snow line, are the alpine meadows where, between large patches of white, ice-covered ground, are huge swathes of pink, blue, white, scarlet and gold — fields of potentillas, anemones, aconites, edelweiss, saxifrage and gentians, which push their way through mud and melting snow. In the warmer valleys, the celitis tree droops with orchids up to late October, before the icy winter winds freeze the valley. This is the land of the sherpas. The wildlife reserves of Langtang and Sagarmather are ideal examples of such landscapes. The latter is at an altitude of 10,000 feet (3050 meters). Here the musk deer, tahr, red panda and the snow leopard are found, whereas in the foothills wild boar and black bear live in the coniferous forests.

The Khatmandu valley itself is an extension of the Gangetic plain and has a subtropical climate. The old sal forests were quickly cut down and today one sees just stretches of flat ground covered with a carpet of green paddy, the monotony broken only by a pagoda or a village.

On the Plains: Descending from the Himalaya to the legendary battlefields of the Ganga plain, there is a distinct difference in the vegetation of the Satluj basin and the Gangetic plain. Whereas that of the former is a dry thorn scrub, the rich plains of the Ganga have tropical vegetation now changed to rice fields. Traveling upstream, at the mouth of the Ganga is the dense coastal forest. In

and Assam. North Bengal and the slopes of the Assam Himalaya along the mighty Brahmaputra are the home of the deer and the water buffalo with swept-back horns; in the denser forests, the elephant and the single-horned rhino roam, with the macaque occupying the green rain-forest canopy. In the dense undergrowth are the reptiles. The birds too are of a great variety, with teals, sarus cranes, swans and ducks.

The entire Ganga plain has a changing variety of vegetation from monsoon forests to open savannah country in the west. The water holes or perennial pools of water in these areas are visited by all the animals in summer when the rivulets dry up. These savannahs because of the open forests and low trees support many grass-eating animals like elephant, sambar deer, wild boar and specially the chital deer which can be seen grazing

panther are also common where there is some vegetation, as at Sariska and Ranthambhore. In the open grasslands with dry scrub, single-humped camels and spotted deer, held sacred by the sages, wild monkeys and flamingos with their sinuous necks who fly away by summer, are common.

The Gangetic plain is now more cultivated than wild, but it still has a wide variety of wildlife. Tiger and panther, gerbil, antelope and the black and gray gazelle are still seen in the forests of the *terai*.

The Deccan Plateau: Southward, over the peninsula, flanked by the Western Ghats, there is a dry interior. The west coast is separated from this dry interior by the wet *ghats* which get all the rain, letting none through to the interior. Like southern Sri Lanka, the west coast, North

teak (unmistakable because of its broad leaves and straight trunk). In these areas, the sal of the Gangetic plain is replaced by teak up to the Godavari river.

The plateau areas of Karnataka and interior Andhra are in the rain shadow of the Western Ghats and therefore dry. Here sandalwood forests flourish. These deciduous forests extend over the plateau from Jhansi to Orissa, westward up to Travancore in Kerala to the south and east of Nagpur in central India. In these forests, elephants and tigers are seen. In the denser forests of the wetter east, near Orissa, are the forests of Ranchi (in Bihar), and here lemur, pangolin (scaly anteater), sloth bear, elephant and gaur live in the secluded forests with the porcupine and laughing hyena. These forests have satin wood, the Indian redwood, and toon trees intermingling

these wet swamps of the east, the exotic Sunderbans with the mangroves — tall standing roots through which boats weave their way — is an ecosystem with a delicate balance of sea and land animals. Spikes stick out of the muddy ground absorbing air from the inner, submerged roots. The sindri (*Heritiera minor*), goran (*Griops roxburgliana*), gewa (*Excoccaria agallocha*), dhundal (*Carapa ohovata*) and kewa grass love this salty marsh. The water-logged delta of the Ganga between the Damodar and the Hooghly full of *kana* (blind) rivers is now being rapidly urbanized but once was the home of the alligator and turtle and the gateway to tiger country.

The entire area of the middle and lower Ganga Plain has tropical evergreen forests which extend up the slopes of the eastern Himalaya

in herds at Kanha or in the *chaurs* of the Corbett.

The western plains of the Ganga, around Delhi and Jhansi and near the Siwaliks till the black cotton soil of the Malwa, have sisoo and khair forests. These small-leaved thorny acacias with black wood are used for making furniture and carvings with exquisite designs depicting dense, evergreen forests of long ago. A landscape dotted with trees in stretches of open, fallow land is seen everywhere between Delhi and Jhansi and in southern Rajasthan. This is a tribal homeland where sal and babul forests are being specially cultivated today.

The drier parts of India are an open zoo. The Gir forest of Gujarat is the home of the yellow-maned Indian lion which, unlike its African counterpart, looks like a big kitten. The tiger and

Kanara, Coorg and the Annamalai hills have deciduous forests with lofty trees and a dense undergrowth which has a variety of ferns. These cool green forests on the mountainsides are luxuriant and shed their leaves at different times of the year. In May and June, before the onset of the monsoon, every tree has a different variety of orchid.

Visiting these forests of the Nilgiris and the Western Ghats one can see lion-tailed macaque, langur, brown mongoose, civet cat and spiny mouse. The higher slopes have exotic birds.

The Chota Nagpur and Ranchi plateau has a zone of humid areas on the east and southwest. These have some evergreen forests but most are deciduous with tendu, the yellow-gold-flowered amaltas, axelwood, khair, kel and the ubiquitous

with the sandal. These deciduous forests have substantial populations of cobra and other poisonous snakes as well as other reptiles. Near the coast in northern Orissa is the spectacular inland saltwater lake of Chilka. In the vicinity of this vast area of shallow water are a wide variety of terns, and kingfishers, and in the murky green waters lives the gharial, the Indian crocodile.

In Bandipur and Nagarahole in Karnataka the tropical moist deciduous forests have a lush vegetation which hides more than it reveals and the animals are small and swift. The tall trees favor

. . . .
Left, **elephant grass in *terai* habitat and *above*, riverine forest, Assam.**

monkeys and snakes and a variety of climbers among plants like betel. The dense undergrowth hides tigers, and provides food for the sure and soft-footed elephant.

Rain Forests: Distinct from these dry forests are the tropical moist, deciduous forests of Malabar and coastal Kerala. As in the central part of Sri Lanka and the eastern hills of Arunachal Pradesh and Mizoram, this area has teak. At a lower level these tall trees are accompanied by the shorter simal (silk cotton), amla and rosewood trees. The undergrowth is of bamboo and climbers like pepper. In the ravines and the shaded slopes are thickets of trees and shrubs and the blue-flowered strobilanthus. Elephants and a great variety of snakes and exotic birds live in these rain forests. The Silent Valley, with over a hundred varieties of butterflies, and the Mudumalai hills, with their

Jeweled Isle: An island at the southern tip of the subcontinent or, more truly, a sparkling dewdrop in the Indian Ocean, the emerald island, Sri Lanka, has a distinct natural environment. Though influenced by the same monsoons as India, the general physical structure of Sri Lanka makes for its different natural environments. To the south are the hills and upland belt which give way to the coast. This massif has a plain on its summit, the Nuwara Eliya. The northern part of the island, including the well-known peninsula of Jaffna, is a plain of sedimentary rock partly covered with sand.

The north and east of the island are dry but the west coast is an area of contrasts. The southern portions are rain forests which merge northwards into savannah-like vegetation and soon there is palm and sand.

steamy like the rain forests of the plains. Their thickly wooded areas open out into park-like meadows.

The rolling, treeless grasslands on the old laterite rocks now worn to a coarse red soil are called *patanas*. The browns of the Indian plateau reoccur and the thin vegetation supports a variety of birds like lapwings, flycatchers, jungle fowl and mynah with yellow bands like sunglasses. The absence of any large mammals in these grasslands is compensated by the reptiles, including the poisonous cobra and Russel's viper. Crows of course carouse about and a common sight in the villages is a conference of crows near the drying food grains. The Ruhuna National Park and Wilpattu National Park still preserve *patana* country; the rest is now rice fields and rubber plantations.

The flame tree in bloom in March; the large-eyed loris peering through sweet-scented gardenias; equatorial jungles with rhododendron; the unforgettable landscape — a parapet of mountains in the upland country (the *dagoba*) hanging over patches of forest and the rice fields of the *patana* land, each image giving a glimpse of the total glory. The Jaffna coast leaves a haunting memory of the singing fish of Batticoloa and the palmyra-fringed coasts shielding a dusty interior.

A Rich Collection: In the 247 sanctuaries and 55 national parks of India there is every possibility of being able to see a variety of animals typical of the environment. The popular resorts of the east are those of Namdafa in Tirap, Mizoram, where the snow leopard can be still seen; the Manas Wildlife Sanctuary for the Indian one-horned rhinoceros; and the Marudhar Sanctuary where

shimmering lakes, are fascinating hideouts for the small animals and the monkeys. The Malabar civet cat and the stripe-necked mongoose are typical animals of the west coast jungles, not to mention the giant lobsters and prawns in the Arabian Sea.

Northwards along this coast and in the Indian Ocean archipelagoes of the Andaman and Nicobar and Lakshadweep islands are the great reefs and volcanic islands of the subcontinent. A variety of animals and plant species survive here without ever having been disturbed by man.

• •
Above, **coastal landscape, Yala National Park, Sri Lanka and** *right,* **chinkara, an elusive Indian antelope in the Thar Desert, Rajasthan.**

The wet tropical forests are luxuriant and at the floor of the forest it is dark because the tall canopy of treetops cuts off the light. Since all the food, the flowers and fruits are in the tall canopy, most animals live at that height, like the monkey, shrew, pangolin and lemur. Flying foxes live on those 90-feet (30-meter) tall treetops. The forest floor has only plant food and is usually full of decaying matter. Here elephants, sambar deer, lorises and palm squirrels are found.

From the central hills flow 16 rivers. These hills are jagged peaks with fertile valleys and waterfalls. At over 7000 feet (2100 meters) on the Horton Plains is "World's End" where a sheer precipice drops to 5000 feet (1500 meters) below, and from where can be seen the sea some 40 miles (65 km) away. These jungles are not hot and

The palm-lined coast is broken here and there by coral reefs, sand-banks and shoals. Off the coast are islands, the largest of which have wild horses which are descendants of those domesticated ones brought there by the Portuguese.

The ocean waters have a variety of prawns and the big sea turtle. The hawksbill turtle is much hunted for its shell, sought after for making combs and boxes. The climbing fish which are able to climb trees and the flower parrot fish that lives near the coral reefs are unique to the Sri Lankan coast. The most remembered experience of these coconut-lined beaches is, of course, the singing fish which produce a hum as if to keep company with the chirping birds.

This small island, this gem-laden country has a charm and variety out of all proportion to its size.

tiger and leopard can be seen. Descending to the Ganga plain, notable sanctuaries are those at Govind Pashu Vihar, the Nanda Devi sanctuaries where Himalayan wildlife is seen and the Rampur and Chandra Prabha Sanctuaries at Banda and Varanasi where tropical grassland animals can be seen.

In the plateau, Karnala at Raigad for birds and the great Indian bustard sanctuary at Ahmadnagar are unique. This Sharawathy Valley in Shimoga has the largest species-wise collection of animals of the plateau. Unique for their own reasons are the sanctuaries at Idukki and Mudumalai. Apart from these, the offshore islands of Lakshadweep and Andamans are themselves environments still preserving a landscape fast disappearing elsewhere.

ANIMALS IN MYTHOLOGY, ART AND FOLKLORE

Seldom has any culture been so deeply and so ᵃsistently associated with animals and trees as t..ᵃt of Hinduism and Buddhism which are shared by India, Nepal and Sri Lanka. Religious belief, mythology and folklore combined to invest them with a sanctity that was reiterated throughout history and endures even today. This was the basis for the continued abundance of artistic representation and this brought to the depiction of animals a range of significance and association that encompassed the diversity of Indian culture.

Traditions of animal worship, originating in primitive fear and the need to propitiate those that presented danger to or served man still linger, especially in tribal areas, while other potent zoomorphic forms have been absorbed into the Vedic pantheon and ascribed varied degrees of consequence. Such was the apotheosis of animals that they were even woven into Buddhist and Jain myths.

The abiding sacredness of animals was rooted in a deep sense of identification. This was derived from the Hindu-Buddhist theory of transmigration, according to which the soul moves back and forth between different modes of existence — animal, human and suprahuman. This was extended by the corresponding belief that all forms of life partake equally in the universal life force, a belief that was reinforced by Buddhist and Jain teachings. These religions also introduced the concept of *ahimsa* (non-violence), prohibiting harm to any living being.

Disparate beliefs coalesced. Animals in Hindu and Buddhist art became eloquent symbols, closely related to the evolution of culture in the subcontinent. The cosmic zoo of Indian tradition, then, was presented with awe, reverence and empathy. The sacerdotal import of animal images dictated that the highest skills be brought to their depiction. Styles varying from the spontaneous vitality of primitive art, to the technically more sophisticated art forms, were all distinguished by their excellence. This grew out of an understanding of the essential character and significance of the subject and a close familiarity with every nuance of movement and behavior of the animals depicted. Despite the evolution of iconographic conventions, a tremendous variety in presentation was achieved by individual craftsmen. Depictions varied from the highly stylized to the most naturalistic.

A prolific delineation of animals is to be seen on seals and other objects of the Indus Valley Civilization (2500 B.C.). Although the bull and elephant appear to have been particularly popu-

lar, the rhinoceros, tiger, antelope and a flying eagle with a snake in its talons were crafted with a skill that contrasts with the comparatively perfunctory execution of the human figure. A terracotta monkey or a faience squirrel, although without sacred connotations, were as cunningly carved as any icon.

With the advent of the nomadic Aryans, the emphasis shifted to their anthropomorphic gods. The sanctity of animals was maintained through myths investing them with divine parentage. Brahma, the creator, himself assumed animal forms to beget the earth's creatures. His consort became a cow, he a bull, and from their union sprang horned cattle. Thus all manner of creatures were created. Other gods, demigods, and even demons also took on animal forms. The status of animals was enhanced in the mythology of Vishnu, the preserver, third member of the Hindu Triad in which he appears in incarnations (*avatars*), once as a fish (*Matsya*), once as a tortoise (*Kurma*), and once as a boar (*Varaha*), to save the world at various points in its precarious existence. Vishnu as a boar lifting the earth on his tushes is a favorite theme in art. A particularly fine example is the Udaygiri relief of around 400 A.D.

Several ancient animal deities were also incorporated into the new pantheon. Half-animal and half-human deities evolved, melding old idols

with Aryan gods. Ganesh, the elephant-headed god of wisdom and plenty, hailed as the remover of all obstacles, is a major and exceedingly popular deity. He is invoked at the start of all rituals and before any major undertaking. He was absorbed into the mainstream of Hinduism as a son of Parvati, consort of Shiva, the destructive aspect of the Triad. Various myths developed to establish this relationship. The most common has it that the goddess formed Ganesh from her sweat and appointed him guardian of her chambers. When Shiva sought to enter, Ganesh, unaware of his identity, barred his way and was beheaded by the enraged god. Subsequently, Shiva promised to replace his severed head with that of the first creature he found which was an elephant.

Other archaic animal deities were also closely associated with major Hindu gods. The Naga or

snake, a powerful folk idol, became an important element in the iconography of both Shiva and Vishnu; images of the former prominently display a serpent around his neck. The latter is often depicted reclining on the endless coils of the serpent Ananta, upon whom, indeed, the world is said to rest. Krishna, a human incarnation of Vishnu, is regularly represented sheltered by the multiple hoods of the snake-demon Kaliya.

Sacred animals also became the mounts (*vahanas*) of various Hindu gods. Symbolizing or complementing the energy or character of the deity, they came to be integral to iconography and were always depicted with the deity. Among the early Aryan gods to receive mounts were Agni (fire) whose *vahana* was a goat, Varuna (water) naturally mounted on a crocodile, Vayu

(wind) appropriately astride an antelope, and the Moon riding the heavens on a deer.

Carnivores, the dreaded enemy of man and his cattle, came to be the mounts of the Goddesses Durga and Kali. Their ferocity and strength was an obvious accessory to their destructive and demonic aspect and established their supreme power.

Herbivores on the other hand, were associated with male gods. Nandi, the bull, *vahana* of Shiva, reflected his legendary virility. Deer, consistently associated with Brahma, were also represented with Shiva who is frequently depicted holding a deer to signify his status as Pashupati, Lord of the Beasts. Vishnu soars above the earth on Garuda, the golden eagle-hawk, who is swifter than the wind and the sworn enemy of snakes. He has the head, wings and talons of a bird but the body of a man. A sense of power and strength is always evident in depictions of Garuda.

Brahma's mount is the *hamsa*, variously interpreted as a swan or goose. The bird was later also associated with Saraswati, the goddess of learning. Its veneration was believed to ensure success in every enterprise. Apart from its depiction with the deity, the *hamsa* also frequently adorns lamps, symbolizing the goddess's capacity to dispel the darkness of ignorance. Kartika, god of war, has a peacock for his *vahana*. This apparently incongruous relationship has been traced to the

• •

Left, **Indus valley seal (2000B.C.) depicting proto-Shiva as protector of animals and *above*, Naga stones, Banswara, Rajasthan.**

bird's formidable ability to destroy snakes. Indra, king of the lesser gods and lord of rain, rides the elephant Airavata. Also allied with Laxmi, goddess of prosperity, elephants were frequently sculpted or painted pouring the "fertilizing waters of life" over her. Referred to as Gaja (elephant) Laxmi, this motif, considered most auspicious, was widely represented.

The river goddesses, Ganga and Yamuna, were appropriately mounted on a tortoise and a crocodile respectively. The fish, symbol of fertility, as were all aquatic creatures, was related to the god of love, Kama, and often emblazoned on his banner. His consort, Rati (passion), was usually represented with a parrot. Commonly portrayed in erotic sculpture, this bird also indicated the mood of love. The demon Mahiasura, whom even the gods were unable to subdue, assumed

the form of a bison.

Some animals acquired a semi-divine status in recognition of their noble qualities and faithful service to the epic hero and god-king Rama. Monkeys gained respect as constituting the army that helped Rama defeat the demon king of Lanka, Ravana. Hanuman, his langur general, renowned for loyalty and valor, is venerated as one of the seven immortal heroes. A celibate, he is also believed to have originated the custom of *mantra* repetition. Considered the master deity of all spirits, he is propitiated in exorcism rites still
· ·

Above, Lion Capitol of an Asokan pillar, the emblem of the Goverment of India and *right*, the boar incarnation of Lord Vishnu, Bandavgarh National Park, Madhya Pradesh.

prevalent in rural India. In temples dedicated to Hanuman, the deity is represented as a brave warrior (Vira Hanuman) in various threatening stances, while in Rama temples he becomes a *dasa* (servant), assuming a supplicatory or servile posture. Jambavat, king of the bears, is also remembered for his assistance to Rama in the Lanka war.

Buddhist myths too reiterate the sanctity of animals. Stories of the Buddha's progress towards enlightenment through a series of births as various creatures accentuated their significance. The Buddha himself is said to have sought refuge from the bickering of his disciples among animals who served him with devotion. The elephant, in particular, was highly regarded and credited with presaging the divine conception.

This was also embodied in Jain myths, where

Mahavira's mother dreamt of a four-tusked elephant when she conceived the savior. Similarly, Mayadevi, mother of the Buddha, dreamt that a white elephant entered her womb. This episode is often sculpted in friezes on Buddhist shrines, particularly at Barhut and Sanchi. The sanctity of the elephant, and its depiction in the arts, increased as it became a symbol of the Buddha, who is said to have descended to earth as an elephant. Consequently, it was frequently represented to signify the Enlightened One.

The snake is another folk deity connected with Buddhist iconography, where the Buddha is often portrayed sheltered by the multiple hoods of the King and Queen of Snakes. Symbolizing the Buddha's first sermon at the Deer Park near Sarnath, deer captivated Buddhist sculptors.

They are frequently depicted on Mauryan abacuses with other animals associated with the Buddha, including the elephant and the swan. The latter is another favorite image for its legendary discerning judgement.

Buddhist Jataka stories dwell on the noble qualities of various species which are held up as examples to man. These stories are part of a huge collection of allegorical animal fables which include the well-known compilations, the Hitopadesha and the Panchatantra.

Consistent literary references brought new aesthetic dimensions to animal forms. Animal imagery in the Vedas establishes the natural animate world as an immediate frame of reference. These later developed into lyrical, poetic similes, where even the ideal of female beauty was seen as reflecting, and indeed derived from, nature. The creator, it is said, took the best from nature and formed woman. This was the basis for extravagant similes that became the idiom of subsequent writings in which a woman's eyes are likened to a gazelle's, her black hair to a swarm of bees, her walk to a swan's, and so on in a wealth of delightful parallels.

Extremely sympathetic were writings on the deer. Its gentle ways and simple habits were described and contrasted to the unhappy mores of the world. The devotion between the doe and stag has also been sung by the bards and idealized. The deer was considered so sacred that, according to Manu, an ancient Hindu law-giver, a place where deer wander unhindered is holy. Considering it most auspicious, ascetics in meditation sat on a chital or a blackbuck skin.

Hunting of both was naturally frowned upon.

Secular traditions also evolved around animals, reinforcing old beliefs and introducing new levels of meaning to their representation in the arts. Ancient beliefs associating the elephant with life-giving water led to the custom of coronation waters being poured over a king by a female elephant. An ancient ritual to invoke rain, involved anointing an elephant with sandalpaste and then taking it in procession through the town.

Admiration of the elephant's size and strength led to secular associations with royalty. A story of the subservience of an elephant to the renowned king Chandragupta confirmed his destiny as emperor of the universe. When the king was preparing to meet Alexander's generals, a magnificent wild elephant knelt before him. Chandragupta mounted the beast and won many battles guided by its wisdom. Royal processions and battle scenes frequently depicted in the arts were crowded with splendid elephants. The elephant also became a favorite decorative motif set among floral patterns to enhance form and structure or was used in striking temple friezes. It was also a favorite device for architectural ornamentation, adorning pillars and cornices. A stylized version of the elephant's trunk often formed brackets.

Another popular theme, later conventionalized, depicts the proverbial conflict between the elephant and the lion. While the former stands for the defeated but powerful enemy, the lion, as Lord of Beasts, represents the victorious king and the lion image was consistently associated with sovereignty.

Primitive customs, like those requiring combat with a lion or a tiger to prove manhood or establish kingship, were later substituted by the symbolic act of a king stepping on a tiger or lion skin. Secular depictions of the great cats, including the famous lion capital of Ashoka and other depictions of lions in the quadrant position, represent not violence but strength and power. While this representation is stylized, a group of lions at Mahabalipuram is most lifelike. Lion and tiger hunts were also popular subjects and were executed with skilled realism. Later, conventionalized lion-heads were commonly used as architectural ornaments.

Monkeys, revered for their association with Rama and Hanuman are also frequently represented. A remarkable sculpture, also at Mahabalipuram, depicts a female nursing her baby, while the male busily picks fleas from her coat.

The peacock's ability to foretell rain by dancing at the first appearance of clouds, as well as its prolific breeding, associated it with fertility. This led to its association with the goddess and its continuing veneration as an aspect of the Earth Mother. The bird's legendary killing of snakes, seen as destruction of evil, augmented its signifi-

cance and led to its frequent depiction with a snake in its talons. It is also connected with Krishna, who always wears peacock plumes, and is often represented with peacocks to signify a sanctified or an idyllic situation. The enormous decorative possibilities of the peacock were, naturally, fully exploited by ancient architects.

Worshiped as an incarnation of the goddess Parvati, consort of Shiva, the kokil or cuckoo is venerated by women during a month-long festival held every 20 years. Its presence and also its soothing call are associated with languorous summer days. The pigeon and the owl are said to be messengers of Yama, god of

• •
Above left, *(clockwise)* **elephant panel, Ellora Western India; ram's head on 17th-Century cannon, Daulatabad fort, Maharashtra; modern pavement poster art, Bombay; and 19th-Century drawing of Ceylon blue magpie.** *Right*, **18th-Century hunting camp.**

death. The vulture and other birds of prey are also considered of ill omen although they are sometimes presented with the goddess in her destructive aspect. Said to be the most unclean of birds, the crow is associated with the goddess of ill luck, Alakshmi. It is, however, somewhat redeemed by recognition of its loyalty to its own kind and by the belief that the crow carries food offerings to one's ancestors. Artistic conventions bring it a new significance with the popular theme, often expressed in miniature painting, that the crow heralds the arrival of the beloved to the anxiously waiting maiden. Stories of the conjugal devotion of various birds, including the sarus crane, the brahminy duck and others, made them appropriate accessories in scenes of love.

Representations of animals and birds reached new heights of excellence in miniature paintings inspired by the Mughal Emperor Jahangir. These were initiated by his insatiable interest in the "strange" fauna of India, which he ordered be painted "so that the amazement from hearing about them may be increased." In compliance, several animal and bird studies were executed by Mansur, a master-painter of the imperial atelier. A host of others were painted by artists in Delhi as well as the provinces, creating a unique collection of exquisite animal and bird paintings. Stripped of all spiritual or mystic overtones, these portraits were painted realistically, with a naturalist's eye and are characterized by a minute and unprecedented attention to detail. This was made possible through techniques, both imported and indigenous, that were refined by generations of great painters. Brush strokes were so fine that each hair and every feather were individually etched, minutely detailed and shaded with amazing exactitude. Hunting scenes, also frequently drawn, were equally distinguished by naturalism and rendered subtle nuances of movement and muscle.

Provincial and local schools inspired by the imperial nucleus, presented birds and animals with similar care. However, as several of these were established in Hindu kingdoms, or at least areas of considerable Hindu influence, old associations were revived. Animals and birds in these miniatures were again imbued with religious meaning and poetic allusions. They became important aesthetic accessories, used to reinforce theme and heighten mood. Thus, dancing peacocks established that the painting was of the rainy season. The kokil indicated summer, deer, a gentle romantic mood, a crow, the imminent return of a lover, and so on in a plethora of possible combinations of religious and popular beliefs, mythology and literary conceits.

Tribal lore and art introduced a new dimension as it was based in a living tradition of animal worship. It was also molded by widespread surviv-als of totemism which involved the worship of various species and taboos associated with them. An enormous and varied body of folktales evolved. Some postulated theories of the origins of different species. Others established the sacredness of cult and totem idols and dwelt on their beneficial or intimidating aspects. Simple but telling stories of a culture that moves easily between the animal, the human, and the divine worlds, they are products of people who live close to nature. In some origin legends, humans marry animals, giving birth to various species. The tiger, for example, was one of a pair of twins born of a miscegenous marriage. Although the animal was subsequently killed by its human counterpart, all carnivores were created from its bones. Other stories suggest that primates were originally men, degraded due to some moral failure.

There is the tale of the lazy boy whose step-mother turned him out. He later became a monkey. A Naga story tells of a man's in-laws fleeing to the jungle in shame as they were unable to perform a task he had set them. The men became mynas and cried *kyon kyon*, while the women smeared rice flour on their foreheads and cried *woko woko*, becoming the gibbon with the distinctive white forehead.

Other stories reflect attempts to comprehend the ways of nature. Tigers, for example, were created because men were too fearless. However, the cats soon made it unsafe for the people to even collect wood. Accordingly, the gods instructed tigers to restrict their killings, which is why they attack humans only sometimes. The Konds of Orissa explained the destruction of their crops by elephants in a myth where elephants, "originally just like dogs," were badly treated by the tribe. They complained to the gods and were transformed, after which they consistently ravage Kond fields in revenge.

Various art forms developed to depict animals and birds. Expressing veneration and appreciation, they were also attempts at propitiation and dominance. Tribal dances imitating the movements of different species are still current and are performed by dancers wearing appropriate masks and headdresses. The crafting of these is still an important and vital art. Other crafts continue to create age-old animal forms in terra-cotta, wood, wire and even straw. Some are potent ritual objects and votive offerings, while others just convey admiration and affection for the animal world. Although most are stylized, they are yet imbued with an instinctive knowledge of form and the innate sympathy of a people who live close to nature. These features, typical of all animal depictions in Indian art, whether in painting or in sculpture, tell a moving if intricate story of a people with an innate, possibly unique empathy with the animal world.

WILDLIFE OF THE INDIAN SUBCONTINENT

Deep in the jungle gloom a striped predator lurks. Programed by instincts genetically implanted millions of years ago, the cat waits patiently for a herd of spotted deer to make their way through tall grass towards a nearby water hole. Barely one in 10 attempts to kill will be successful, but because of sheer persistence, such odds work in favor of the hunter. Contrary to popular belief, success depends less on speed and power, more on stealth and ambush. In all probability a young, weak or careless deer will fall prey to the tiger. The fascinating drama between predator and prey has gone on uninterrupted for years and has been responsible for the perfection in nature which so moves and inspires us.

Rich Diversity: Unique, still mysterious, and forever fascinating, the natural history of the Indian subcontinent remains largely unstudied and its natural wealth little appreciated. Geological events that took place millions of years ago created an incomparable diversity of ecosystems. In the north the legendary snow-capped Himalayan ranges house rare and elusive creatures such as snow leopard, musk deer, ibex and pheasants of all descriptions. The Thar, also called the Great Indian Desert, sprawls between India and Pakistan in the northwest and supports a surprising variety of hardy plants and animals, several found nowhere else on earth. Towards the east, bordering Bhutan, Bangladesh and Burma, cloud forests and swamps shelter life forms ranging from tigers, elephants, rhinos and gibbons to the largest moth and some of the rarest orchids in the world. The lower slopes and foothills of the Himalaya, clothed in verdant coniferous forests and grasslands, are the last refuge of several endangered plant and animal species. The great floodplains of the Indus, Ganga and Brahmaputra rivers, though radically altered by man's agricultural life-style, are still among the most fertile areas in the world. The Western Ghats, an ancient chain of hills running from north to south, fringing the western coast of India, are perhaps the last hope for some of Asia's densest rain forests. In the scrub and grasslands of the Deccan Plateau, naturalists have recently rediscovered Jerdon's double-branded courser, a ground bird which was presumed extinct for nearly 80 years. Running all along the peninsula's coastline are some of the world's finest and most indiscriminately exploited coral formations, sand bars and mangroves. Off the southern tip of India, Sri Lankan forests thrive even as they provide naturalists with several fascinating pointers towards the evolution of life on earth. That leopards managed to colonize Sri Lanka, for instance, while tigers never reached its shores, indicates that the island separated from the Asian mainland before the spread of the tiger from Central Asia to the north Indian plains. Many unanswered questions, however, still lie hidden in the mists of prehistory, wrapped in the many marvels and mysteries of the natural world.

Eden Besieged: For long, Africa has been regarded as the Mecca of wildlife. Justifiably so, but in recent years the natural wealth of the Indian subcontinent has begun to offer naturalists, tourists and researchers a fascinating alternative to the once-dark continent. Tropical Asia, after all, probably houses the richest diversity of life forms on the face of the earth. And the Indian peninsula might well be considered the cornerstone of this Eden — an Eden, unfortunately, under siege from one-fifth of humanity.

In 1271 A.D. a young adventurer departed from his native Venice on a voyage of discovery. Among the other incredible stories he related in his "Book of Marvels," he spoke of a wondrous land filled with curious animals, like elephants, rhinos and great striped cats. That land was India. The man was Marco Polo. Incredibly, more than a thousand years before Marco Polo discovered the riches of India, Emperor Ashoka, who then ruled most of this vast region, had realized the value of its natural wealth and passed edicts to protect it. But that was still an age when man had need to "conquer" nature to carve an acceptable niche for himself in a hostile world. Yet, somehow, the awe and respect for natural systems, on which the very existence of the Indian people has always been dependent, prevailed. Animals have always played an important role in the daily lives of Indians. Regional mythology, religion and even social mores are entwined with rituals which involve the deification of plants, animals and the elements.

It was only when the British took over the subcontinent, that development first began to take a serious toll. Vast Burmese teak forests were razed to fabricate ships and homes for the Empire. Uncounted natural habitats were destroyed to obtain vital cash crops such as tea and cotton. The land was ripe for the taking and had never really been managed. Quite obviously, neither was it left to its own excellent devices as it had been for millions of years. The exploitation had begun in earnest.

Those who fervently hoped that independence would reverse the trend towards poor land use were mistaken. After 1947 the face of the Indian subcontinent began to undergo its most drastic change. The people were poor, and their leaders

filled with a genuine desire to "give" their wards something, anything to fill their empty and resource-starved lives. The only freely available commodity was land. No one thought of the disastrous consequences of converting wild grasslands and forests to pastures or industrial dumpyards. India, Pakistan, Bangladesh, Nepal and Sri Lanka are all currently reeling under the stress of shortsighted past decisions. And, in spite of knowing better, today's managers often continue to opt for minor political gains, using land as a tragic medium of barter to appease an unknowing people. The resultant havoc caused by nature's response to bad land management — floods, droughts and famines — is too well known to merit further comment.

The fact that representative pockets of wild habitats survive on the subcontinent today has

the entire subcontinent was as rich and productive as these oases of restraint and tolerance.

In such havens, the sight of thriving ecosystems provides a glimpse into the way things were, before the evolution of man. The profusion of life is truly staggering as lianas, vines, fungi and animals of every description are seen living out their threatened existences, oblivious of the inexorable press of humanity around them. These isolated green vaults are now zealously protected as a result of our newly awakened understanding of the consequences of environmental imbalances. But for vast areas it is already too late. The malaise has taken a firm grip of the land and many once verdant expanses have forever been reduced to dust.

What is likely to strike most visitors to the many reserves in the region is the stark contrast

pected. It's not that the surviving jungles are thinly populated, but that most creatures, which have mastered the art of camouflage and deception over millennia, are virtually impossible to spot unless you know what to look for. With the help of an experienced guide, however, a moving twig becomes a praying mantis, part of a tree stump takes wing to reveal itself as a roosting nightjar, or, with some luck, an imperceptible movement in the grass turns out to be none other than that of the tiger.

At one time "tigerland" comprised virtually the whole Indian subcontinent. Fearing no animal, the great cats colonized every imaginable habitat, from the lower slopes of high mountains, to desertified scrub lands, rain forests and swamps. Positioned at the apex of the food chain, tigers managed to carve a secure niche for themselves

other animals that shared the tiger's domain.

Elephants, perhaps more than any other animals, typify the man-animal conflict in India. The large beasts require vast ranges in order to survive. Their daily requirement of green fodder can exceed 450 lb (200 kg) per day. Plantations, hydel projects and jungle clearances have so totally fragmented their habitats that elephants, which once roamed virtually contiguous forests, must now contend with existence in small pockets, and when they do try to migrate to distant pastures they come into conflict with man, most often with disastrous results for both. The problem of habitat degradation is compounded by man's ancient yearning for ivory. Even today, despite stringent laws, elephants regularly fall victim to poachers who often use poison and pit traps to bring down their quarry,

Death of the man eater.

very little to do with man's realization of the worth of his natural heritage. Rather, credit is due to the inborn resilience of plants and animals which have evolved near perfect survival techniques after living for millions of years in a hostile environment. To understand how blessed the region once was, one needs merely travel to reserves such as Kanha or Bandhavgarh in Madhya Pradesh, Ranthambhore in Rajasthan, Manas in Assam, Chitwan in Nepal, Wilpattu in Sri Lanka, and the Sunderbans in West Bengal. At one time

· ·
Left, Mughal Emperor Akbar hunting, from the 16th-Century *Akbar Nama. Above*, late 19th-Century shoot, United Provinces and *right*, end of a shoot, 1935, Chitwan Nepal.

between the outside and inside of protected places. Almost without exception, the approach roads are barren and, often, a sense of apprehension creeps in, as you begin to wonder what lies in store. The moment you enter, say, the Periyar Tiger Reserve, however, the apprehension vanishes as you are transported to a primeval peace so familiar to anyone whose soul is stirred by the outdoors.

Stripes and Ivory: But there is a fundamental difference between the wildlife experience of the Indian jungle and that found in Africa. To begin with, tropical jungles are dense and most often visibility is fairly restricted. All too often visitors, lured to India by tourist brochures which promise exciting "tiger safaris," are therefore, disappointed to see fewer animals than they ex-

while still allowing adaptable predators such as the leopard and several lesser cats to co-exist. With the arrival of *Homo sapiens* all this changed. Having learned to alter the environment to suit his own convenience, man began to make inroads into virgin jungles, slashing and burning in his frantic haste to convert hostile habitats into hospitable havens. Over a period of time, having established his dominion over the natural world, he began to hunt for pleasure. Persecuted for their skin and for the illusion of bravery surrounding shikar, tigers reacted by altering their life-style. The once proud predators which hunted by day, turned to the security of nocturnal life to avoid humans. And, as people's numbers began to swell, the tiger retreated deeper into the jungle. A similar fate befell most of the

wiping out entire families.

Conservation: Fortunately, in recent years, the Indian government has taken a more progressive attitude towards the protection of wild animals. There is no doubt that execution still lags far behind intention; however, as a policy, the authorities have come down hard on known traders, poachers and exploiters. Consequently, India is probably the last hope of survival for the one-horned rhino, the great Indian bustard, the gharial (a fish-eating crocodile) and a host of other highly endangered species, many endemic to the subcontinent. Moreover, recognizing that knowledge is the first step towards protection, sterling organizations such as the Bombay Natural History Society (BNHS) are being partially funded by the government to carry out field natural-history projects to evolve management strategies for wild habitats. Through such pioneering efforts the strands of relationships between life forms and the habitats they live in are slowly being pieced together. Avifauna and hydrobiological studies are helping us to understand the critical needs of birds which migrate to the subcontinent from distant nesting grounds in Siberia, Afghanistan, Tibet and China. The thriving wintering grounds of such birds, like Rajasthan's famous Keoladeo Ghana National Park (Bharatpur) and Tamil Nadu's Point Calimere Sanctuary, where the BNHS has permanent research stations, are fine testimonials to well-executed conservation action. In the ethereal atmosphere of these wilderness areas it is easy to forget the ecological problems that beset the subcontinent as a whole.

eastward to Assam, organized treks, river rafting and wildlife viewing facilities are emerging, as private and government agencies gear up to meet the new influx of adventure-seekers from all over the world. The Royal Chitwan National Park in Nepal has become a routine stopover for all categories of tourists. Here, in fact, private enterprise has shown how easy it is to capitalize on the simple joys of nature. Visitors are given very basic but well-designed creature comforts and the rest is left to nature. Excursions into the forest are arranged on elephant back, one of the most satisfying and effective ways to view animals such as the great one-horned rhino and the tiger. Trained guides and four-wheel drive vehicles are also on hand to help visitors to get a "feel" of the habitat in the shortest possible time. Varying degrees of creature comforts are available in virtually every

Consider the fate of those exquisite islands of Lakshadweep some 200-400 km west of the Kerala coast. Terms such as "tropical island paradise" are wholly inadequate when describing the pristinity of such areas. To cater to and exploit the tourist potential of the coral formations, some misguided enthusiasts have suggested that a channel be blasted through the ring of corals to admit large ships capable of carrying thousands of tourists. The resultant death of living corals, as unfettered tides pour sand on the reefs, will probably cause the ecosystem to be destroyed within a decade, but that is not the concern of those who wish to boost tourism during the tenure of their charge. Some well-advertised treks to the mountains are no better. The Valley of Flowers and the Nanda Devi Sanctuary in the Himalaya have suffered

mangrove trees and coral reefs, nature's erosion barriers, continue to be brutalized in the name of industrial development. In Rajasthan the animal husbandry department busily distributes goats and sheep in villages where the social forestry department distributes saplings. The result? No saplings and, eventually, no goats and sheep either! The animals consume all available fodder in sight and are soon sold for their meat when they start damaging croplands.

As the list of such absurdities grows, the effects take on more sinister dimensions. In Madhya Pradesh for instance, the Bhopalapatnam and Inchampalli dam projects threaten to inundate 420,000 acres (170,000 hectares) of land, including prime forests within the Kutru National Park, the only wild buffalo habitat in the country outside the northeast. In the process

Wildlife and Tourism: There is no doubt about it. Natural India awaits discovery. Despite the lack of sophisticated tourist infrastructure, the heat and humidity, people are drawn back to the forests which Kipling immortalized. In any event, the secret for visitors lies in knowing what to expect and in understanding that the privilege of stepping into a pure and untouched world is a reward in itself. Actual animal sightings, fortunately on the increase each day as protection lends security to once shy creatures, must be viewed as a lucky bonus.

Recognizing the tourist potential of wildlife, the governments of India, Nepal and Sri Lanka have gone out of their way to cater to the basic requirements of nature lovers. From Kashmir and Ladakh, through the Garhwal Himalaya and

wilderness of India. And, in some of the more remote locations, where comforts fall short, the basic hospitality of locals can be depended upon for a simple meal and a place to bunk down. One need be armed with little more than mosquito repellents, water purification tablets, a sleeping bag and a basic love for nature.

These trends towards wildlife tourism, domestic and foreign, are to be welcomed; for there is no better way to communicate the worth of a country's natural wealth than to allow others to experience it first-hand.

The question conservationists and naturalists are asking today, however, is whether our besieged natural areas can withstand the trauma of uncontrolled tourism. Though sometimes exaggerated, such fears are often well founded.

more on account of uncontrolled tourism and indisciplined mountaineering expeditions than any other single cause.

As usual, only a few unscrupulous groups give tourism a bad name. To counter such problems, rigid controls, such as trekking permits in Nepal and supervised excursions into Indian national parks and sanctuaries, have been introduced in recent years, largely at the behest of enlightened mountaineers and wildlife tour operators. Nevertheless, short-term objectives still often need to be contended with.

Conflicting Policies: Examples of environmental bankruptcy are even more rampant outside the corridors of tourism. In Kerala the state government spends around Rs. 400 crores ($3.5 million) a year to prevent shore erosion. Yet

of siphoning power for distant industries, more than 70,000 tribals will also be displaced. They will then have to be "resettled" in camps, to become a permanent drain on the exchequer.

Saving the Land: With so many different languages it is almost impossible to communicate conservation's universal message without distortion. "In a land where people are dying," say some naive (and some not so naive) politicians, social workers and businessmen, "they want to save forests and animals!" But the people of the

· ·

Left, spiny lizard about to be cooked to extract "medicinal" oil and *above*, electrified dummy to discourage man-eating tigers; Sunderbans, West Bengal.

subcontinent are as directly dependent on the health of the land as the birds and animals of the forest. Saving the land is saving the people. And we cannot save wild habitats without saving the gardeners of our Eden. Once this reality is accepted, everything else will follow.

This then is the region — bountiful lands occupied by hard-pressed people. Fortunately, however, signs of renewed awareness are emerging. Slowly, very slowly, opposition to environmentally ill-advised plans is mounting — two classic examples being the saving of Silent Valley's rain forest in Kerala from the jaws of a hydel project, and the famous "Chipko" movement, where women in the Garhwal Himalaya prevented contractors from exploiting already degraded forestlands. Other successes, such as the protection of nests of the rare black-necked

Ganga of its chemical and organic pollutants are under way. The race to restore sanity and save the land is on.

Project Tiger: In retrospect, the turning point for Indian conservation was probably the forced acceptance in the late 1960s that the tiger was destined for extinction. Following an international appeal to save one of the world's most magnificent beasts, Project Tiger was launched in 1972. The first step was to abolish tiger shikar. The second was to save its vanishing home. Choosing habitats as far removed from each other as the Sunderbans in Bengal, Corbett in U.P., and Periyar in Kerala, the authorities decided that the only long-term way to save the tiger was to save its forests. In the process, innumerable other animals received protection, including the Asian elephant and the great Indian one-

plants and invertebrates that have been saved within the 15 tiger reserves. By any measure, Project Tiger must be seen as one of Asia's most successful conservation sagas and the tiger a symbol of the health of the Indian jungle.

Local Pressures: Though the situation is considerably better than it might have been, the trials and tribulations of India's wilds are far from over. Despite increased awareness, the rate at which the overall forest acreage is dwindling is nothing short of alarming. Domestic and industrial wood consumption far exceeds the regeneration capacity of existing forests. At the turn of the century a full 40 percent of the subcontinent was under natural cover. Satellite pictures indicate we are now down to around seven or eight percent. And "developers" seem unable to answer the straightforward question conservationists ask:

called *bakarwals* ask vociferously whether the hangul, a highly endangered deer, is more useful to the people than their wool and meat bearing livestock. In Dudhwa, U.P., farmers cry themselves hoarse for the blood of tigers. In Bharatpur, Rajasthan, villagers cannot understand why water is diverted for wild birds which raid their crops when their own fields are parched. In Orissa fishermen are dumbfounded by laws which protect turtles, only to let them return in their millions to the open sea. In Assam, tea estate owners still occasionally shoot elephants to protect their cash crops. In Gir, the last 200 lions are constantly under threat from Maldharis who poison them in retaliation for cattle lifting.

Conservationists have come to the conclusion that the way to reduce such hostility on the

crane, the declaration of Pirotan as India's first marine national park and the increase in sightings of the great Indian bustard, speak volumes for the resolve of forest officers and their staff who must often place their lives at risk in the course of their work. With increasing frequency, enlightened public figures have also begun making their views on the degradation of the environment known. At the behest of the Prime Minister of India, an ambitious wasteland development program has been instituted and plans to cleanse the

• •
Above, hill women returning with a day's collection of fuelwood and *right,* contrast between unprotected and protected forest, Kathmandu Valley, Nepal.

horned rhinoceros. Since 50 percent of the Project's funds were met by the Central Government, the states were able to protect tiger reserves better than ever before and the results are there for all to see more than a decade later. The presence of the tiger in its chosen habitat indicates that the ecosystem is vibrant and the number of tigers in Indian jungles has increased from less than 2000 in the early 1970s to 4005 in the 1986 survey. Dry deciduous habitats such as Ranthambhore and Sariska have received a new lease on life. The hard ground barasingha of Kanha have recouped their dwindling numbers. In Manas, Assam, a score and more endangered animals such as the hispid hare and the pygmy hog have been retrieved from the brink of extinction. No one can even begin to estimate the number of

"If we cannot look after and protect even eight percent of our land, what chance of survival can there be for the remaining 92 percent?"

Having reduced their once verdant lands to scrub, villagers now turn to forests to meet their daily requirement of fuel and fodder. To win elections, politicians often make unrealistic promises to their electorate, thus creating friction between park managers and locals. Another major problem, of course, is that of man–animal conflicts. Cattle lifting, crop destruction and occasional man killing incidents are genuine and very serious problems, but incidents are often blown out of all proportion and a frenzy is whipped up to pressure the authorities to give in to the demands of the local people.

In Dachigam, Kashmir, nomadic graziers

periphery of protected places is to improve the socio-economic standards of people who fringe forests. This, however, is easier said than done. Attempts to introduce stall feeding of cattle, or to improve their bloodstock have failed because there is simply no spare cash available for even the smallest investment. Even plans for the large-scale introduction of new, smokeless *chulas* (ovens), which can reduce a household's fuel consumption by over 30 percent, did not work, because villagers are unable to pay the one-time cost of around Rs. 30.00 ($2.50) per *chula*. Meanwhile, rural women are forced to walk more than a thousand miles (1,600 km) each year in search of head loads of wood; after nearly 40 years of independence, India has still not hammered out a national fuel wood policy. Con-

sequently, 50 percent of the domestic fires in some of the country's largest cities are fed by wood! Even as sporadic social forestry efforts meet with success, natural forests are literally being transported to the cities to vanish in smoke.

Hopeful Signs: The Indian subcontinent's wildlife and its fledgling conservation movement are nevertheless poised on the verge of a tremendous renewal and, in spite of several setbacks and hurdles, there is every reason to feel optimistic for the future. A major contributive factor has been the credibility of the press which has pitched its considerable might behind the efforts of rational conservationists in the past few years. The government-controlled television network have responded admirably as well and promise to deliver conservation education directly to millions of people in the coming years.

hunting, it would be wise to remember, however, that several existing parks and sanctuaries have survived the plow and axe only because they were once protected as hunting preserves by influential hunters, including maharajas and viceroys, in years gone by.

Today, for the benefit of tourists, orientation centers manned by qualified, experienced staff, have been set up in the more prominent parks such as Chitwan, Dachigam, Kanha, Corbett and Bharatpur. Here proper orientation, with the help of audio-visual aids, ensures that visitors have meaningful nature experiences, while simultaneously promoting compatibility between the objectives of conservation and tourism. With such a wide variety of habitats to choose from on the subcontinent, tourists can tailor their experiences to suit individual needs. They can

Meanwhile the forests of the subcontinent offer unique opportunities of escape from the pressures of urban living to adventure-seekers from all over the world. The gun has been replaced by the camera and this is as it should be, for while there is nothing wrong with hunting *per se*, there is no way that wildlife can survive the crossfire between habitat destruction and shikar. In the light of the sentimentality that often clouds rationality when it comes to the subject of

also pack diverse experiences into relatively short trips if they are so inclined. Where else in the world, after all, could a person travel from snow leopard and ibex country (Ladakh), to a hot desert (Thar), to a coral paradise (Pirotan), to **savannah grasslands** (the *terai*), to deciduous forests (Bandhavgarh), to mangrove swamps (Sunderbans), to a primeval rain forest (Silent Valley) — all without crossing a single international boundary?

As the deer and the tiger play out their destinies in the forests of the night, an onerous burden falls on man, the newest animal of all. A simple twist of fate has led us to assume the responsibility of guards to nature's domain. Whether the earth and its bounty survive our inexperienced stewardship, only time will tell.

· ·
Left to right, **lichen-draped rhododendron forest, central Nepal; the region boasts a spectacular range of insects; and hoardings at entrance to Kanha National Park, Madhya Pradesh.**

OBSERVING WILDLIFE

To most people, the word *jungle* conjures up images of dense, lush tropical forest with torrential rainfall, huge trees festooned with creepers, and infested with dangerous animals, snakes and insects. In its Sanskrit origins, the word *jungle* denotes any wild country, untamed land, a wilderness. How many trees grow on it and how tall, and what and how many creatures live in it, makes no difference. The semi-arid thorny scrub of Yala in Sri Lanka is no less a "jungle" than the steaming jungle of Manas in Assam in Eastern India.

At the outset, it should be pointed out that, although the Indian subcontinent harbors a great variety of wildlife, the large assemblies of animals seen so often in the African bush are not seen here. Most jungles of the Indian subcontinent are thick and dense, with poor visibility. Animals living in such closed environments are generally shy and retiring, and live in small scattered groups, or even as solitary individuals.

Perhaps it is also necessary to explain why so many more birds than mammals are seen. Mammals are largely nocturnal, retreating into their hideouts during the day, and are usually silent. On the other hand most birds are diurnal, not so shy of man and quite vocal. Moreover, there are far more birds than there are mammals — India alone has about 1200 species of birds against 350 species of mammals. So, while spotting a hundred species of birds in a day is not unusual, a mammal list of even 10 species is considered good. But the mystique and the romance of exploring the jungle here, perhaps for this very reason, is greater than anywhere else in the world.

Your Safari Kit: Your most invaluable companion while on a wildlife safari is a good pair of medium-size compact binoculars. For general purposes, 7x or 8x magnification is adequate, but for bird-watching 10x magnification is better as it brings out details of plumage clearly — so vital for positive identification. Many rare sightings have been missed because binoculars were not easily at hand. So carry your binoculars round your neck, and use them constantly to scan the area around you. You will be surprised how much more you will see if you do.

Another essential item is a three-yard (three-meter) tape measure, preferably the spring coil type, with both centimeter and inch calibrations,

· ·

Left to right: **otter and wader tracks on riverbank; and radio-tracking tiger.**

to measure anything of interest — dimensions of a den, the size of a track, the height of a claw mark on a tree, for example.

To record your observations, you will need a small notebook in which you may also want to sketch things of interest. Do not forget to mention the name of the place, time and date. In time, in this notebook you will have put together an amazing variety of information.

When to Look for Animals: A national park or reserve is a living museum of nature's creations — landscapes, rock formations, waters, plants and animals. But unlike in an art or historical museum where objects are on display, here you have to seek out your animals. You have to know where they live, when they move about, how to attract and approach them.

Not unlike men, animals are creatures of habit and have distinct daily and seasonal patterns of activity. An understanding of these patterns increases our chance of seeing them. The frequency of wildlife sightings in national parks and reserves varies, depending on the time of year. The Indian subcontinent is affected by the monsoons (in some areas twice a year), which influences the pattern of vegetation growth and the availability of food and water. This in turn affects the distribution and behavior of animals. Since the vegetation is overgrown and lush during, and for a few months after, the monsoon, these are not the best months for wildlife viewing in most national parks. Generally, the best times are from February to May. During these months the trees are often bare and the undergrowth dead or regenerating, so visibility is considerably improved. Since there is also a general scarcity of water, the animals concentrate near sources of water. In places where annual grass burning is still practiced, such as in Chitwan and Bardia in Nepal, regrowth of grasses attracts large concentrations of herbivores, who in their turn attract predators.

However, the time of year you choose to visit a park will also depend on what you are looking for. By "best months" is usually meant those in which one is most likely to see large mammals which are the main attraction of most national parks and reserves. But in Chitwan, for instance, the best months for seeing birds are February – March, for mammals March–May, for insects and for the lush jungle June–September, and for crocodiles, who come out of water to bask in the sun, October–February. The marshes of Bharatpur present a magnificent spectacle of breeding birds during August, September and October.

There are rewards for the nature lover at every hour of the day and night, but for watching mammals you have to follow their daily cycle of activity. They are mostly nocturnal and remain active for two–three hours after sunrise. A night drive can be a very rewarding experience, but is not permitted in most parks and reserves, and rightly so. Animals should have at least some time to conduct their lives without human intrusion. Around 10 a.m., animals retreat for rest and lie in hiding, giving the impression during midday and in the early afternoon that the jungle is devoid of life. But they resume their activities around 4 p.m., filling the jungle with life and activity.

Your safaris are therefore best organized during the early mornings and late afternoons. In the winter, afternoon safaris are better as there is often a thick mist in the morning.

Monkeys, like men, are creatures of the day. They are up early and feed for a few hours before their midday siesta, when they sit around contentedly on the ground or in trees. They resume feeding activity in the afternoon and by sundown are ready to go to sleep. Langurs are noisy feeders and not only their calls but also their jumping from branch to branch make a loud noise, so their presence can be detected from a distance.

Where to Look for Animals: Animals are most conspicuous when they are feeding or at play and the most likely spots to observe such activities are grassy meadows, the edge of forests, at salt licks or near water holes. Herbivores have to feed daily for several hours, and the heavyweights, such as rhino and elephant, have prodigious appetites and may spend 15–18 hours a day feeding, thus making themselves very conspicuous.

Open grass meadows and river banks are the favorite grounds of hoofed animals, where the short grasses provide them nourishment. For them the tall grasses are often inedible and therefore of little value, except as shelter. In a forest thick with trees and scant grass, hoofed animals will usually be thinly spread but leaf-eaters, such as langurs, are usually common. Recently burned patches of grassland and forest attract deer, antelope, wild boar, gaur, buffalo, rhino and other herbivores who come for the new succulent grasses.

Most mammals have to drink at least once, if not twice, a day. In areas where water is plentiful, such as the floodplains of Chitwan, Manas and Kaziranga, animals are evenly spread out. But in places where water is localized, as in the Siwalik hills of northern India and Nepal, mammals usually stay close to water, especially during the afternoon when they come to drink. In arid areas with scant rainfall, water is in short supply during the summer before the rains, so this is the time to look for animals near the few remaining sources of water. Predators often lie up, in cover, near a

water hole and take their chances on the prey species that wander within range. Which also explains why herbivores are so nervous when approaching these spots.

Large animals also use water for cooling their bodies. In the steaming months of May and June, tigers lie in secluded pools in the jungle, and elephant, rhino, buffalo and wild boar also have favorite spots to wallow in the water or mud.

Mammals also visit salt licks regularly to replenish their body stocks of vital minerals. Over the years, salt licks become well known to the animals living in the area, and elephant, rhino, gaur, deer, monkeys and others come to them from time to time. A salt lick may be part of a hillside, a patch of earth or clay, or buried in the bed of a spring, lake, river or stream.

How to Conduct your Safari: Dress comfortably, in clothes that permit easy movement, and avoid wearing bright colors that make you conspicuous. Jungle-green, khaki, beige camouflage are preferred for tropical and subtropical environments, but in the Himalaya, where snow is present, light neutral colors may be most suitable. The idea is to blend with the surroundings so that you do not unnecessarily announce your presence from a distance.

Animals are very wary of the human voice. So, in order to get close to them, absolute silence is essential. Walk lightly and, unless in the mountains, avoid heavy boots; sneakers, or running shoes are best.

Animals living in closed environments have an exceptional sense of smell and will detect and avoid human scent. While stalking animals, it is therefore important to stay downwind of them or you will give your presence away sooner than you think, especially if there is a gentle breeze. For the same reason avoid wearing perfumes and, if using insect repellant, choose the kind that smells the least. Also, no smoking, please.

Move slowly, as this gives you more time to look around and you are less conspicuous to the animals, thereby permitting you to approach closer to them. Walking slowly is also safer. A hasty step might bring you face to face with a rhino, gaur, elephant, or tiger — encounters of a kind that is best avoided. In South India, which has a good population of poisonous snakes, it pays to look where you step. Even while in a vehicle, a slow drive gives you the time to scan the area around you.

Most times the animals will spot you first and disappear without your knowing it. There are far more human sightings by animals than animal sightings by humans. Occasionally you will know that you have been spotted when you hear or see animals bounding away. They may even give an alarm call which will convey a warning to other creatures. But if you spot them first you should move cautiously, using every bit of cover to your

advantage, freezing every time they look in your direction. A deer or antelope will soon get your wind and will try and pinpoint you with its nose, eyes and ears.

Some animals are inquisitive and may even come towards you. But under no circumstances should you stalk or go close to large carnivores and other potentially dangerous animals. Most animals will retreat at the sight of man but the large animals may have good reason not to. A leopard or bear may be guarding her cubs, for example. Under these circumstances they are likely to warn you with a noisy snarl before you come too close. If you do not heed that, it is at your own risk.

Some drivers and guides, in the heat of excitement, will take you dangerously close to potentially harmful animals. Or perhaps because

Radio-tracking tiger, Smithsonian Tiger Project, Chitwan, Nepal.

you want a close-up photograph. This kind of drama should be discouraged as casualties are likely to occur if you violate the personal space of wild animals and make them feel vulnerable. In a national park or reserve their welfare comes first and disturbing, harassing or unnecessarily provoking them is taboo.

On a nature walk, keep your senses on the alert. Most animals blend extremely well with their environment. The spotted fur of the leopard breaks its contours and is invisible in the light and shadow of the jungle. Even the giant elephant merges with the gray tree trunks and the undergrowth. But don't get obsessed with seeing animals: the imagination can play tricks and you may start "seeing animals" that are not there. A rock on the mountainside may become a black bear! And a black bear a rock!

Two ways to maximize your chances of seeing animals are:
- to watch them from a hide or blind, locally known as a *machan*, where you wait for them to come near you while you are hidden from their view; and
- to actually go out in search of them by vehicle, elephant, boat, or on foot.

This may sound simple, but to get the best results requires deep knowledge of the wilds and its denizens.

Machan: A *machan*, as explained, is a hide or blind in a tree or on the ground. When on the ground it resembles a hut with several peepholes to look out from. They are best made from local materials — trees, bamboo, grass, leaves, stone, or mud. A good temporary or mobile *machan* can be made of canvas or burlap stitched to size, with custom-made windows and exit door. It can easily be put up with the help of sticks or its own set of aluminium poles. It should be jungle-green or light brown in color or with camouflage pattern to break its outline. Such a collapsible *machan* is essential to the wildlife photographer. The idea of a *machan* is to become so inconspicuous that animals come close to you without detecting your presence. In this respect, a tree *machan* has the advantage that, apart from providing a better lookout point, human scent disperses from it more rapidly into the upper air than from a ground *machan*.

In an area where wind or breeze is a constant factor, especially during the mornings and afternoons when you are most likely to use a *machan*, it is best sited downwind from where the animals appear. A *machan* must also not stand out from the surrounding landscape if animals are to approach it without much hesitation. If situated in a thick jungle, it is usually hidden and camouflaged by foliage; if in an open area, it may be so placed as to appear to blend with a natural structure such as a termite mound or rock outcrops.

A *machan* usually overlooks a natural water hole or a salt lick (either or both may be artificially created if necessary), and occasionally open ground with a long view. Unless water is plentiful in the area, *machans* overlooking water holes are very productive for spotting animals. Smaller animals such as porcupine, can be attracted by regularly leaving some potatoes and other vegetables on a spot frequented by them during the night. Carnivores, such as tiger and leopard, can be baited by using a chunk of meat or by tying a buffalo calf or goat in their path.

But, whatever the advantages of *machans*, from them you can only hope to see the animals that chance to come by. When you go out in search of them, whether by landrover, on elephant back, by boat, or on foot, in full view of the animals that you seek, while you have the freedom to look for them in the most likely spots, you also run the risk of announcing your presence and warning them away.

Safaris by Landrover and Elephant: For some unknown reason, most wild animals seem quite indifferent to the sight and sound of a vehicle and during the night the headlights seem to mesmerize them. In fact, it is amazing how close you can get to some animals by vehicle. As the sound of the engine does not seem to bother most animals, it is best to keep the engine running as this not only drowns human noises but also ensures speedy escape if your subject happens to be big and angry. Animals may accept the presence of your vehicle, but this does not mean that they will continue to "cooperate" if you step out of the vehicle. Why animals should tolerate such an alien object and bolt at the sight of man, no one knows. Perhaps vehicles, although strange, do not seem dangerous to them, whereas they have a long history and tradition of the need to avoid man.

Vehicles have the advantage that you can cover a large area in a relatively short time. Tracks in the parks are rough and you may need to cross streams, rivers and muddy places and they give you quick and easy access to the best spots for viewing animals. But vehicles will only take you where there are roads and since driving on roadless tracks is usually not allowed in most national parks, you will have to resort to other means — elephant, boat and walking.

Elephants have long been used for hunting, and more recently for forestry operations, wildlife management and wildlife watching. Nepal and India must be among the few Asian countries to employ elephants for wildlife tourism.

Elephants have the advantage that they can go to places where no vehicle, boat, or man on foot can go. They will climb up hillsides, negotiate steep banks, and walk through marsh, swamp and thick jungle. In fact, were it not for the elephant, tall grasslands, like those found in Chitwan and Kaziranga, would be so much more difficult to explore safely. Elephants, however, dislike and avoid deep rivers and strong currents and quicksands. They give you a feeling of security and, although they are quite timid by nature, few animals will attack them. Rhino and tiger have been known to, under provocation, but perched on the *howdah*, 10 feet (three meters) from the ground, you are quite safe. The only disadvantage is that elephants move slowly and therefore you can only cover a small area in each outing.

Despite the human smell and noise, most animals tolerate people on elephants. In fact, even the keen-nosed wild elephant will allow a man on a domesticated elephant to approach and sometimes even mingle with the wild herd. (In Mela Shikar, men on trained elephants display much daring in capturing wild elephant by actually mixing with them and cleverly sneaking behind the chosen candidate for capture and chaining it with a noose. It will then quite happily follow the domestic elephant — with a little encouragement.)

Elephants with their keen nose constantly pick up smells left by other animals. Being the largest creature in the Asian jungle, they will ignore most animals but they have an instinctive dislike of large carnivores. If such an animal is nearby, an elephant might resist going towards it, but it will show no fear of an immobilized (drugged) tiger or a dead one. It also dislikes going close to gaur, buffalo and rhino.

Signs in the Jungle: Wildlife observation may be direct, when you actually see the animals in their natural state, or indirect, when you "observe" their presence or passage by their spoor, scats, shelters, smells, sounds and so on. The jungle is full of such signs but their interpretation is not simple; therefore only the most obvious are mentioned here.

Look for markings on trees in the jungle. Deer rub their antlers against small trees, usually to clear their velvet, and leave distinct marks of injury. And depending upon how high the marks are from the ground, one-four feet (30–120 cm), you can make a good guess as to which deer species was responsible for it. In rhino country, rhino rubbing posts are frequently encountered. They are usually three-five feet (about 1½ meters) above the ground on a sloping tree trunk or stump. From regular use, the rubbed area becomes smooth and devoid of bark, often with a coating of mud. In elephant country, trees with stripped bark, uprooted trees, and twisted branches betray their presence. Bears and leopards leave distinct claw marks on the trees they climb, and tigers habitually rake their claws on trees, leaving deep gashes, sometimes with fragments of claw in them. Other cats also indulge in this form of marking/cleaning.

A forest floor littered with fresh fallen leaves and twigs indicates the feeding activity of langurs. Chital often take advantage of this "free lunch" and follow the monkeys who feed in the treetops.

In the jungle all kinds of cavities and holes may be seen in rock, on the ground and in trees. These are often shelters or dens used by a variety of animals and birds. Most carnivores live in burrows. They either dig these themselves or appropriate existing holes and cavities. Porcupine warrens are elaborate systems of tunnels under the ground usually with two or more entry and exit points. They are often recognized by the gnawed horns, bones and antlers lying at the entrance.

Wild boar rootle the ground for food and leave tell-tale patches of loose upturned earth. Sloth bears dig up termite mounds at their bases and suck up the insects. These diggings may be three feet (one meter) deep, and sometimes even larger craters may be excavated by them in search of choice food.

Elephants have an exceptional nose and where water is scarce will locate subsurface water, dig a hole with their forefeet and drink the clear water that collects at the bottom. Other animals use these "water holes" after the elephants have left.

Otters live in burrows with an underwater entrance although their living chamber is above the water level. Their burrows are usually at the bases of trees, among the roots. Even large carnivores like brown and black bears hibernate in cavities during the winter. Contrary to popular belief, tigers and lions do not live in caves or dens, although occasionally they may use them as shelter. Tiger "dens" are usually very secluded spots in the forest or tall grass where they are least likely to be disturbed.

A common sight on most steep river banks are holes used as nests by the sand martin. Bee-eaters and kingfishers also nest in burrows. The tailor bird stitches a nest out of one or more leaves, and the weaver makes a graceful nest hanging from a branch. The most interesting nest is made by the giant hornbill. The male seals his mate in a hole in a tree, using a plaster of clay and debris, leaving a small opening through which he feeds her. When the chicks hatch and are large enough, the wife breaks open the wall and emerges. The couple then replaster the opening and continue to feed the chicks through a hole until they are ready to come out, when the wall is broken once again, and the family set out into the jungle.

The shape, size, color and smell of mammal droppings can give clues to which animals live in the jungle. Local tribals and trackers are often very knowledgeable about droppings. The contents of herbivore droppings give useful indications of the plant species eaten, and carnivore droppings of the species of prey consumed. Exceptionally, you may find something particularly interesting, such as the claws of tiger cub or leopard in tiger droppings.

Some animals, such as civets and weasels, habitually defecate at "latrines" and, in time, large piles are formed. Large quantities of wolf droppings may be found near its den. Rhinos also have dung piles which, after months, even years, of use become huge accumulations. Some animals, such as the red fox and the otter, defecate at prominent spots, such as on stones, a fallen branch, or on top of a mound. Birds of prey, herons and owls, regurgitate matter from their mouths. These distinct pellets, consisting of bone, feather, hair and other indigestible matter, are often found in large numbers below a favorite perch or roosting site.

The sounds in the jungle often give clues to the identity of the animals producing them. With training and long experience you learn to recognize the sounds of most birds and mammals. In fact, identification of a bird is sometimes easier from its call than from its sighting, and elusive birds, such as cuckoos, are far more often heard than seen. Birds of the night, such as owls and nightjars, are difficult to recognize but have very distinctive calls, making it possible to identify them instantly.

The roar of a lion, the alarm call of a sambar, the trumpeting of an elephant, the whistle of a wild dog, are all sounds betraying their identities. Some sounds will tell you more. The bugling of a hundred barasingha stags will tell you that their rutting season is on. If you hear rhino huff and puff, snort and grunt, thundering about in the tall grass, and then a peculiar whistling sound, you know that two rhinos have had a dispute; or perhaps a male is chasing a reluctant female. The alarm call of a peafowl or a deer often indicates the presence of a tiger or leopard. The rhesus will bark agitatedly and the langur makes the distinctive call (*kha-ko, kha-ko-kha*) which almost invariably means tiger or leopard.

Carcasses of the kills of large predators are often betrayed by vultures, crows and blue magpies. By mid-morning, the vultures riding the thermals in the sky spot the carcass or the excitement of crows, and are attracted to it, and within the hour dozens of vultures descend on the carcass out of the sky. If you see vultures heading in a particular direction and follow them you will certainly come upon a dead beast or its remains.

Approach a carcass with caution, especially if the vultures are in the nearby trees or on the ground at a distance. This often indicates that a large carnivore is nearby. Hungry tigers can be possessive of their kills and, although they usually retreat at the sight of man, they might not.

Tracks around the kill will indicate which carnivore or scavenger has been feeding on it. Leopard and tiger kills may be distinguished by the size of canine punctures and the gap between them, these being always larger and wider in the case of a tiger. The tiger begins to eat from the hind-quarters, the leopard from the stomach or chest. The tiger's feeding is quite clean, with the alimentary canal left unpunctured, but the leopard is a messy feeder. Leopards usually take their kills into trees, especially when in open areas, in order to protect them from other predators and scavengers. Tigers, on the other hand, stay near the kill for up to several days, depending upon the size of the carcass, and will resent intrusion and often rush at the vultures and manage to kill one or two. In order to hide the carcass from competitors, the tiger covers it with earth, twigs and other debris. Lions are communal feeders and usually finish the kill in a single sitting and so do not need to guard or stay near it.

Tell-tale Tracks: All terrestrial animals leave impressions of their feet on the ground as they go about their business. A good tracker, by looking at the tracks and trail (a sequence of tracks), can often tell the species, age, sex and speed with which the animal was moving.

Primitive tribal groups, who still supplement their diet by hunting, are very knowledgeable about the natural history of their area and have the knack of reading tracks and other signs with accuracy. A reliable interpretation of the signs in the wild gives them clues as to where to put traps, what kind of traps and what bait to use at what time of year and day.

Roads, banks of rivers and lakes, the seashore and snow are the best places to look for tracks. But not all tracks reproduce faithfully and in fact those made by the same animal may look different, depending upon the hardness of the ground and the gait of the animal at the time. In deep mud and soft sand or snow the tracks are indistinct and larger than life, whereas on harder ground they are more realistic and show details of the contours of the feet. If the animal is running, the tracks will show a slide mark towards the direction of travel, the slide being more pronounced on soft ground. The toes or hooves will often splay for better traction and the impact itself will cause the tracks to be larger. In deep snow or sand a running animal will leave quite unrecognizable tracks.

An early morning walk is the best time to study tracks as at that time they are fresh and well preserved. As the day wears on, tracks are gradually obliterated by the action of the elements, and by the activities of man.

In an Indian jungle the most conspicuous tracks are those of the tiger and by following a fresh tiger trail you can learn about its doings of the previous night. Track one with the help of a professional tracker or guide and you will be amazed at the information he will be able to infer on the animal that made them. From the size of the tracks he will perhaps infer that it is a male and, if he has tracked tigers regularly in that area, even identify which male. Soon you will be shown where the tiger sat for a while, where he started to run, and began to stalk. From time to time, you will scent a strong musky smell and a closer examination will reveal that the tiger has been marking his trail with a spray of urine.

Here the tiger has scraped the ground with his hind paws and defecated, leaving evidence of what he has eaten. Halfway down the road his trail mixes with those of a female and as the tracks of both are equally fresh, we know they were together. Tracking, if expertly done, will sometimes lead to the animal itself, its kill or den.

When you see a track you may want to sketch it, but this is easier said than done. A simple method is to use a rectangular plate of glass 8″ x 12″ (20 cm x 30 cm), in a wooden frame, the molding of which is about a quarter inch above the surface of the glass. When you place this tracer flat on the ground over the track, the glass will be slightly raised and the track will remain intact. Now with a medium-point black felt pen and with your eyes vertically over the track, trace its outlines on the glass exactly as you see them. Then trace the track from the glass on to thin tracing paper, and you have a permanent record of a track, lifesize.

In a national park or reserve, ideally, nothing should be removed. Even such seemingly valueless things as antlers on the forest floor, or a dead log, have their role in the scheme of nature. In a way they are as much a part of the jungle as the deer and the tree that shed them. The antler will provide minerals to porcupines, rodents, etc., and the deadwood will sustain a number of insects. Later, when the antler and the deadwood have disintegrated, they will return the minerals to the soil. And so, in a cycle of life and death, nature in all its glory should survive intact as we see it in the jungle.

[For guidance on Wildlife Photography, see "Guide in Brief" at the end of this book.]

• •

Left to right: scientist monitoring tranquilized tiger; and tropical rainforest.

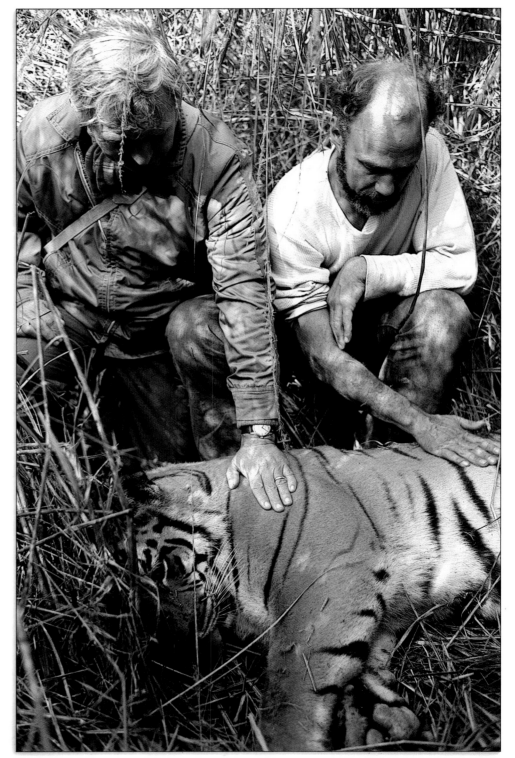

Today, with a renewed emphasis on environment protection, forest development has, like many other matters of ecological significance, become a focal point of activity. Forests were greatly valued in ancient India. Everyday life was closely connected with nature; kings protected forests and ascetics retired to them for peaceful meditation in their quest for salvation (*moksha*). Emperor Chandragupta Maurya, as early as the 3rd Century B.C., had forests classified as those used for religious purposes and others to be exploited commercially. He also allotted some forest areas for hunting. Forest offenses and careless deforestation were punishable by death. During Emperor Ashoka's reign (3rd Century B.C.), several species of trees were identified for protection. The abundant evidence of natural forms in the Indian art of this period reflects a great affinity with nature.

Alexander is said to have used Indian timber for building ships in the 4th Century B.C. For many centuries Indian wood was exported to Persia and Arabia, but this commercial activity was on a very small scale compared to the immensity of India's then forest resources and had no noticeable effect on the extent of forest cover. Hundreds of years later, in Mughal times, there was a great deal of hunting in the forests of North India. Nevertheless, although the Mughals had no positive interest in conserving forests, they did not harm or denude them. At the turn of the 19th Century, however, the British developed a keen interest in the valuable woods of the Indian jungle. Some of the ships in Nelson's fleet at Trafalgar had been built by the famous Bombay shipbuilders, the Wadias, teak replacing the English oak. Trees yielding prized wood like sandalwood, rosewood, satinwood and ebony were felled for commercial purposes, doing great damage to India's forest wealth.

Despite steps taken by the British in the early 19th Century to regenerate forests, in the long run they encouraged agriculture at the expense of forests rather than as complementary to them. This short-sighted policy did immense damage.

Since independence, the Indian Government's New Action Plan for Forestry has declared 33.33 percent of the whole land area of the country (60 percent on the hills and 20 percent in the plains) as reserved for forests. However, this has not

prevented further extensive encroachments on India's forest cover (now less than 9 percent in India) and unless firm and effective action is taken soon, the future does seem grim indeed. The situation in Nepal is equally serious. Destruction of forests there has resulted in frequent landslides and bare hillsides. In Sri Lanka, the situation is better, though also critical.

Natural Vegetation: An immense variety of flora is found in South Asia. In fact, due to climatic diversity in the subcontinent, it covers a whole range of types of vegetation regions from swamp and thorn forests to alpine forests. The amount of

rainfall and average temperature, the topography, soil conditions and altitude are the major factors that affect the vegetation of a region. Clean-cut lines demarcating each type are naturally impossible, and there are many areas where a mixture of types of vegetation is seen. The overlapping of types occurs both on the mountains and in the plains. Nevertheless, India can be divided into broad phytogeographical zones.

The Deccan: This region, otherwise known as the Deccan Plateau, comprises Tamil Nadu, Andhra Pradesh, a large part of Karnataka, Madhya Pradesh, Orissa, and parts of Maharashtra and Gujarat. Even within this peninsular area, the differences in annual rainfall cause variations in the natural vegetation.

. . . .
Left, rhododendron, Nepal and *right*, Himalayan flowering shrub.

In the southern portions, consisting of hilly terrain, the annual rainfall is 34–40 inches (86–100 cm) whereas in the northern parts of the Deccan the rainfall increases to 56 inches (142 cm). Dry deciduous forests rich in teak (*Tectona grandis*), known for its excellent timber, is the dominant variety. Other large trees like mahogany (*Swietenia*), Indian rosewood (*Dalbergia*), *Terminalia* and *Chikrassia* also grow here. These trees have abundant foliage and are of majestic dimensions, often growing to great heights and spreading wide. The sandalwood tree (*Santalum*), with its fragrant wood, is particularly common in Karnataka. This tree is slender, with small leaves and tiny fruit. The wood in the living tree has no scent, yet the dry wood has a strong fragrance.

Intermittent patches of color break the

trees in some areas — using the host tree for support and to gain access to sunshine, not living off the tree as parasites do.

In the northern stretches of the Deccan, sal (*Shorea robusta*) forests extend from Madhya Pradesh to Orissa, and present a totally different picture. Sal trees are straight, compact and tall, with rounded leaves, and grow close together, forming stretches of homogeneous forests in continuous belts for many miles.

In those areas of the Deccan where rainfall is lower, the vegetation changes to scrub forests. The hardy trees here are, to a large extent, thorny and well adapted to dry climatic conditions. The mixed population of trees consists of *Zizyphus, Acacia, Capparis, Balanites, Euphorbia, Flacourtia, Prosopis* etc., forming thinly wooded forests.

Coastal Areas: These form a striking contrast to

prolific vegetation, many shrubs, climbers, epiphytes, bamboo and ferns grow in abundance. These thick-set jungles have been utilized by man in several ways. *Hevea* and *Ficus elastica* yield rubber, while ebony (*Dyospyros*) and toon (*Cedrela*) are good timber sources. The species common here are *Dipterocarpus, Artocarpus,* sandalwood (*Santalum*), red sandalwood (*Pterocarpus*), nutmeg (*Myristica*), Alexandrian laurel (*Calophyllum*), *Michelia, Ternstroemia, Mimusops, Hopea* and *Sterculia*. Coconut palms (*Cocos*), talipot palms, thick shrubbery and climbers complete the scene of tropical splendor.

In most areas of the west coast region where rainfall is relatively low (60–80 inches / 150–200 cm), vegetation is sparse and consists mainly of deciduous trees. These shed their leaves annually and remain bare after leaf-fall. Mountain ebony

(25–50 cm) in Rajasthan to 25–30 inches (64–76 cm) in the Punjab. The area suffers from extremes of temperature and low himidity. Winter can be harsh and summer equally unpleasant, with blistering heat and hot winds. The soil has a high percentage of salts and is sandy. A large part of Rajasthan is covered by the Thar Desert, and shifting sand-dunes cause desertification. On the fringes of the desert the vegetation is typically xerophytic, adapted to dry surroundings — their long roots penetrating deep below the earth's surface and enabling the plants to avail of subsoil moisture. Such vegetation requires very little water and can survive in extreme climates and tolerate harsh soil conditions. In order to prevent evaporation the leaves are small, stems greatly reduced, and the pores on the leaf-surfaces few in number.

• •
Above, wild iris and ***right***, the rhododendron forest, Helambu, Nepal.

monotony of vast expanses of forestland. The flame of the forest (*Butea frondosa*) is a burst of pale orange when in bloom, while *Bauhinias* and *Lagerstroemias* are laden with delicate white, pink and mauve blossoms in the flowering season. *Cassia fistula* with its shower of pale yellow flowers and *Cassia nodosa*, which has pink inflorescences, are exotic flowering trees that dot these forests.

Many forests have a mixture of *Acacia, Dillenia,* red sandalwood, *Odina, Grewia, Buchanania* etc. Many epiphytic orchids adorn the

the forested areas although lying in close proximity to them. Here, there are long stretches of coastline with symmetrical coconut palms that bear a rich yield of coconut. Further inland in the coastal plain jackfruit and mango trees are plentiful along with tamarind. In some pockets of the Deccan coast, near the river estuaries, mangroves, typical of wet marshy areas, are common.

The **west coast region** comprises the Western Ghats and extends from Gujarat in the north to Kerala in the south. It has, in places, an annual rainfall of over 100 inches (250 cm). Its natural exuberance is apparent in its rich forests and lush tropical vegetation. The **tropical evergreen forests** are remarkable for their luxuriant growth of trees, both tall and medium-sized, which do not as a rule shed their leaves annually. To add to the

(*Bauhinia*), teak, *Dalbergia, Adina, Lagerstroemia, Terminalia* and *Grewia* form an assortment of trees of many sizes, some with beautiful flowers and others with high-quality wood. Characteristic of this area is bamboo (*Bambusa*), which grows in dense clumps. The bamboo here is very long and has a large girth. It is used in house building and furniture making.

In the higher ranges of this region, tucked away in comparatively smaller areas, are temperate evergreen forests with *Michelia, Eugenia, Ternstroemia* etc.

Dry Lands: In sharp contrast to the green West Coast Region is the **Indus Plain**. This phytogeographical region covers parts of Indian Punjab, Rajasthan, and most of Pakistan. Annual rainfall varies from a low 10–20 inches

Along the riverbanks there is abundant subsoil moisture although the soil is sandy. Where there is black saline soil there is no vegetation at all. The **desert thorn forests** of this area consist mainly of *Prosopis, Salvadora oleoides* and *Caparis*. These grow in isolated clumps. *Acacia, Tamarix, Albizzia lebbek, Morus alba* and flame of the forest are the mixed varieties that constitute such forests. Arabian grass, saltwort and seablite grow where there are salt tracts. The undergrowth consists of thorny shrubs.

Dune scrub which differs from the forest vegetation also resists desert conditions and is characterized by stunted trees and bushes with adaptive thorns. This vegetation is found in southern Punjab and Rajasthan. The only tree found here is *Acacia jacquemontia*. Sandy alluvial deposits are found on the banks of the rivers of this region. Dominant here are forests consisting mainly of species like *Acacia catechu* and *Dalbergia sissoo*. Poplars (*Populus*) and *Tamarix* occur here and there.

On the whole, the "Indus region" consists of hardy plants that can protect themselves against trying weather conditions.

Gangetic Plain: The vegetation of the **Gangetic Plain** slowly changes from that of the Indus Plain since the rainfall increases gradually as one moves eastwards. This region can be divided into three parts. The upper, dry sub-region extends from Punjab to Allahabad in Uttar Pradesh. It receives 20–40 inches (50–100 cm) of rainfall annually. *Peganum, Acacia, Moringa, Prosopis, Tecoma, Rhus* etc., and some palms are found in this sub-region. The vegetation is still quite sparse in the

area and, where the soil is alkaline, *Salvadora* is common. This region also has grasslands or savanahs interspersed occasionally with *Bombax*, Butea, Zizyphus and *Randia*.

In the lower Gangetic Plain which stretches from Allahabad to West Bengal, the rainfall is 76–100 inches (190–250 cm). *Mangifera, Artocarpus, Ficus, Areca, Borassus, Phoenix, Lagerstroemia, Pterospermum, Bombax, Polyalthia* and *Casuarina* grow commonly in the area. The vegetation grows more abundant and many different aroids begin to occur. Aquatic plants, several types of grasses and sedges abound in the vicinity of lakes and small reservoirs.

The third part of the Gangetic Plain is an unusual area forming the vast **Sunderbans** around the delta of the Ganga in both India and

Bangladesh. Characteristic of this region are interconnected waterways and marshy swamps. The sea makes its way into the land through a number of creeks. The **tidal swamp forests** of the delta region cover an area of 6000 sq miles (15,500 sq km), the largest stretch of swamp forest in the world, most of it lying in Bangladesh. The area is thick with evergreen trees and shrubs typical of mangrove or littoral forests, which thrive in the saline water washed in with the tide. Typical mangrove trees like *Rhizophoras, Ceriops, Kandelia* and *Bruguiera* are prolific in the area. Of the 36 species of mangrove trees found in the Sunderbans, *Avicennia officinalis* is the largest. The little swampy islands found here and there are covered with savannah grass. Palms like *Nipa fruticans, Phoenix paludosa,* coconut palms and cane (*Calamus*) occur extensively. Elephant

grass and screwpine grow near streams, ponds, swamps and canals. The vegetation is thick and many species bind the mud and prevent it from being washed away. Ferns and orchids are also found here. The flora of the Sunderbans is of great interest to the botanist, the infinite variety and uncommon growth conditions making it exceedingly attractive for study. The forests of this area give economic support to the people —firewood and timber being the most important products.

Assam Region: The northeastern region of India is exceedingly wet and humid. Annual rainfall varies from 110 inches (280 cm) in the Garo hills to 510 inches (1300 cm) at Cherra Punji. On the whole it averages at a high 80 inches (200 cm). The region does not experience large fluctuations

of climate. The temperature is mild and ranges between 86°F and 68°F (30°C and 20°C). The hills, however, are much colder. Humidity is between 80 and 90 percent. The torrential Brahmaputra river flows right through the Assam Valley, spreading its rich alluvial deposits on the banks. The soil is extremely fertile and all these favorable conditions together result in extraordinarily rich and lush vegetation, making some pockets of Assam the world's richest in flora. Hills and plains have an abundant supply of water and are covered with uninterrupted forests.

The **tropical evergreen** or **rain forests** extend from northeast Arunachal Pradesh to Darrang district in Assam. They also occur in Nowgong and Cachar districts in Assam and most of the Khasi hills in Meghalaya. The peculiarity of these

forests is their three-tier structure. The top tier looms over the rest and consists of isolated, tall, evergreen or deciduous trees which grow to a height of around 150 feet (46 meters). The most common species among them are *Dipterocarpus macrocarpus, Artocarpus, Chaplasha, Tetrameles* and *Terminalia*, each growing tall and handsome, with spreading branches and abundant foliage. The middle tier consists of several medium-sized trees growing up to a height of about 80 feet (25 meters). *Colophyllum, Mesua, Amoora, Cinnamomum, Phoebe, Machilus* and *Duabanga* form the mixed middle layer. *Ficus elastica, Michelia, Magnolia* and *Schima* are also found. The ground tier consists of shrubs and climbers, orchids, aroids and ferns that cover every inch of land.

The pine forests of the Khasi hills, however, are devoid of the brush that gives the forest elsewhere its dense cover. Other trees present here mixed with pine are oak (*Quercus*), *Pieris*, chestnut (*Castanopsis*) and birch (*Betula*). In other areas, yew (*Taxus*), spruce (*Picea*), silver fir (*Abies*), deodar or cedar (*Cedrus*), *Tsuga*, cypress (*Cupressus*) and juniper (*Juniperus*) occur. Pines, yews and *Tsuga* are the few varieties that survive at very high altitudes.

In the lower Assam Valley, in the Garo hills and North Cachar hills, there are sal forests which are mainly of the deciduous type. Scrub forests also occur here and are dotted with colorful trees like *Lagerstroemia, Cassia fistula, Bombax, Sterculia* and others like *Schima wallichii, Careya arborea, Dillenia, Kydia, Albizzia, Gmelia, Alstonia,* Walnut, *Terminalia*

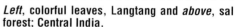

Left, colorful leaves, Langtang and *above,* sal forest; Central India.

and *Dalbergia*.

In certain parts of this belt, the forests are strikingly different, as they are pure sal forests, consisting of a variety peculiar to the region (*Shorea assamica*) which grows to a height of 100 feet (30 meters). These unmixed sal forests present a beautiful and eye-catching picture.

In the dry regions of Cachar, forests are heterogeneous, consisting of *Dipterocarpus, Adina, Bombax, Stephegyne, Ficus* and *Cassia nodosa*. Bamboo and several grasses are common. Colorful flowering shrubs provide an attractive ground

cover — white *Coffea bengalensis*, blue *Strobilanthes*, white and yellow *Mussaenda* and scarlet-red *Holmskioldia*.

Assam is unique and is unparalleled in the variety and richness of its forest wealth. In the swampy regions of the Assam valley, aquatic and semi-aquatic grasses and aquatic ferns of many varieties are prominent. The flowering plants that occur commonly are *Euryale, Alpinia,* water lilies (*Nymphaea*), lotus (*Nelumbo*). Among the trees, *Barringtonia, Cephalanthus,* and some *Ficus* species are seen here.

Another variation in the vegetation of Assam occurs in the low-lying areas which have very little rainfall. Along the riverbanks are very tall grasses, whereas the dry lands have short and sturdy varieties.

In the foothills of the Bhutan range, extending from Goalpara district to Darrang district, are the **riparian forests** that grow along large streams and are composed mainly of two tree varieties, *Acacia catechu* and *Dalbergia sissoo*. The few mixtures are mostly of *Duabanga, Bombax, Trewia, Barringtonia, Salix, Anthocephalus.*

In the northeast region, there is another interesting occurrence among the flora — carnivorous plants and parasites abound. Over four hundred species of orchid and innumerable varieties of fern, and even fern trees, are special to this region.

Himalayan Flora: The vast area covered by the magnificent Himalaya mountain range lies to the extreme north of India and includes Bhutan, Nepal and parts of Pakistan. On the basis of climatic conditions, the Himalaya can be divided into three fairly distinct regions: the **eastern Himalayan region**, extending from the Arun Valley in East Nepal to the Mishmi hills of Arunachal Pradesh, has an average precipitation of 120 inches (300 cm) a year. The next division, namely the **central Himalayan region**, is demarcated by a sharp decrease in rainfall, and comprises chiefly Nepal and Eastern Uttar Pradesh in India. The third division, the **western Himalayan region**, originates in Peshawar in Pakistan, where the annual precipitation is 20 inches (50 cm) and extends in a southeasterly direction towards the Kumaon hills in Uttar Pradesh, with the precipitation increasing gradually to approximately 40 inches (100 cm) in Kumaon. It is, however, important to note that it is the altitude, determining the temperature of an area, that is the most important factor contributing to regional variations in the Himalayan flora. Because of this, the three divisions mentioned, can, in turn, be split up into zones, according to differences in altitude, running in a northwest to southeast direction across the whole expanse of the Himalaya. These divisions and zones, however, often do not have well-defined boundaries, due to an inevitable overlapping of vegetation types.

The **tropical zone,** with rainfall of 40–60 inches (100–150 cm), lies south and east of the Himalayan foothills, and is locally known as the *terai* region. The thick forests of the *terai* can be divided into two types, according to variance in rainfall — areas having an annual rainfall of over 100 inches (250 cm) support evergreen forests, whereas deciduous forests are found in regions where the rainfall is sparse.

The **temperate zone** of rainfall 60–140 inches (150–350 cm) is otherwise called the **coniferous zone** due to the predominance of conifers. This zone has abundant flora and exhibits decrease in vegetation with increase in altitude.

North of the coniferous zone lies the **alpine zone** where the highly unconducive temperature and rainfall (140–180 inches/350–450 cm) conditions support only a meager plant cover. This region stretches from above the tree line to the permanent snow line.

The eastern Himalaya is populated with varied and profuse flora. Over 4000 species of flowering plants and a few hundred varieties of ferns make it a richly vegetated area. Amongst the conifers, the predominant species are many varieties of pine (*Pinus khasya, P. excelsa, P. longifolia*). Himalayan silver fir, junipers, *Podocarpus* and *Picia* are also common varieties. Growing abundantly here are several species of rhododendron adorned with flamboyant blossoms. *Berberis, Impatiens, Saxifraga,* and Himalayan poppies are a few examples of the numerous flowering plants of this region. Adding to the lush vegetation are orchids, bamboos, palms, epiphytes and creepers.

abundantly here are several species of rhododendron adorned with flamboyant blossoms the common conifers are found in many varieties of pine and juniper. *Pinus longifolia, P. excelsa* and *P. gerardiana* are the predominant varieties of pine, while *Juniperus communis* and *J. recurva* are the common junipers. The mixed species found in this region are *Abies pindrow,* cypress (*Cupressus torulosa*), deodar (*Cedrus deodara*), *Picea morinda* etc. The exuberant growth in the east formed by rich flowering plants, orchids, palms and bamboo is far from being equalled in the western region. The variation in the two regions is apparent in the fact that the epiphytes and creepers that form an important part of the eastern forests are quite insignificant numbers here, whereas grasses and leguminous plants are comparatively common due to the drier climatic conditions. Although rhododendrons are found here, the number of species is considerably less than in the eastern Himalaya. *Rubus, Rosa, Prunus, Pyrus, Ranunculus* etc., form the vegetation of the upper reaches.

The tiger, unlike the lion, is a predator that relies on cover for success in hunting. Again, unlike the lion, it leads a solitary life. The only associations that occur are between male and female during the short courtship period and, of course, the long association between a mother and her cubs, till the latter grow and they can fend for themselves. Young siblings, on parting company with their mother, may sometimes stay together in an area for a few months, but soon tensions develop among them which break up the company. Socialization is extremely rare and is generally limited to a young adult occasionally visiting its mother who is now caring for her next litter. Such a gathering may take place at a kill, but is invariably shortlived, a day or two at the most.

The parental care and upbringing of the young is the responsibility of the mother alone. This solitary way of life and the stalking or ambushing strategy of hunting is the only way food can be secured by a large predator in a forest environment or one with plenty of other forms of cover, such as the tall, dense reeds of the *terai* grasslands. Communal hunting by a large predator, as in the case of lions, depends upon fair visibility and lack of obstructions, a situation not available in a closed forest environment. It is for this reason that the tiger and lion are mutually exclusive in their distribution, the two having adapted themselves to forest and savannah environments respectively. The past and the present distributions of the tiger and lion in the Indian subcontinent, where alone both the species occur, bear testimony to this.

Habitat and Population: Having originated in Siberia, as suggested by fossil evidence, the tiger found its best home in the Indian subcontinent. It is a truly Asian animal and science recognizes eight subspecies, two of which (the Caspian and Balinese) are already extinct. The other six are the Siberian, Chinese, Indo-Chinese, Indian, Sumatran and Javan. Body-size diminishes as the distribution advances from the cold Siberian scrub thickets to the multi-tiered evergreen forests of Java and Sumatra. On the Indian subcontinent the tiger is at home in a variety of environmental situations, from the high-altitude, cold, coniferous Himalayan forests to the steaming mangroves of the Sunderbans delta, from the swampy reedlands of the *terai* to the rugged,

scorched hills of the Indian peninsula, and from the lush, wet evergreen forests of the northeast and the south to the scrub-thorn arid forests of Rajasthan.

An estimate placed the population of tiger in India at the turn of the 19th Century at 40,000. While this could be an exaggeration, the present plight of the tiger became evident when, in 1972, an all-India tiger census revealed that a population of only 1800 had survived. The history of the decline of the tiger is the pathetic story of the shrinkage and ravaging of the Indian wilderness, pressed forward by the thoughtless onslaught of demographic pressures that followed the promptings of immediate expediency and failed to take account of the doubtful sustainability of the changed land use.

The hunters of yesteryear regarded the tiger as the symbol of India's wilderness. Its savage beauty and might and its ability to melt into the forest like a phantom, not only whetted the hunter's spirit of adventure but also provided the base for countless juicy *shikar* stories. But ecologically also, the tiger justifies itself as reflecting in its own level of welfare the health of the country's wilderness. The tiger is the ultimate consumer in the complex food web in many of the forest ecosystems of India. The soil fertility in these ecosystems rests on the micro-organisms that decompose the plant and animal residues to form humus. The diverse vegetation so supported is the food of a thriving community of herbivorous insects, birds and mammals and also helps to conserve the soil and enhance water flow. Among the terminal carnivorous users of this productivity, the tiger stands at the head. Conservation of the tiger in its natural environment can be achieved only by total conservation of the wilderness based on an ecosystem approach, as has been established by India's Project Tiger. Truly, therefore, the status of the tiger in India is the index of success, as a whole, in conservation of its wilderness.

Fortunately, spurred on by Project Tiger, India is now involved in a massive conservation effort covering over 300 national parks and sanctuaries accounting for over 12 percent of the country's total area under forests. A very large number of these protected areas harbor the tiger. Thanks to these measures, according to the all-India tiger census of 1984, their number has gone up to 4000.

Cunning Predator: Even in areas of prey abundance, the tiger has to work hard for its food since all its prey species have highly evolved systems of self-preservation which the tiger must

Preceding page, an adult male enjoying the afternoon at Rathambhore Tiger Reserve and *left,* tiger as often observed.

beat. The ungulates, the hoofed herbivores, which constitute the main food of the tiger, have a highly developed sense of smell and reasonably keen senses of sight and sound. Whether living singly (as the sambar do) or in herds (like the chital, nilgai and gaur), they are constantly vigilant as they move, forage or rest. Herd security and leadership is provided by the matriarchs who keep a close watch while the herd is foraging or resting. They constantly shift their muzzle to face the breeze in order to catch scents and funnel their ears in different directions to catch sounds. On apprehension of danger, the first alarm is signaled by stamping a forefoot. If, on further assessment, the danger seems real and imminent, a vocal alarm is sounded. Finally, the matriarch provides the lead and the herd drifts, scampers or bolts. Different species of deer have their distinctive alarm calls which are heeded by *all* the prey species. Langur and monkeys, from their superior position on trees, also constantly observe and notify the presence and movements of predators by calling out in alarm. In order to beat their vigilance, the tiger takes to stalking behind cover, treading silently. It approaches its quarry against the direction of the breeze so as to avoid detection by smell.

A young tigress once sat on a high rock in a clearing in a sal forest for over half an hour. Hearing the mating call of a chital stag, it became alert and sensed the direction of the call by funneling its ears, but did not move. When the call was repeated after a couple of minutes, it gently got down from the rock and moved very slowly towards the chital which were about a hundred yards (100 meters) away. Her movements could be discerned only from a slight quivering of the bush. The stag kept calling, intermittently. The tigress took 35 minutes to come within 20 yards of the small chital herd. Then, in a split second, in a couple of lightning leaps, she pounced on the stag, killed it instantly and dragged it further into the bush.

On yet another occasion a limping tigress was offered a tethered buffalo calf to help her tide over her temporary disability. The buffalo was walked to within 246 feet (75 meters) of the tigress, being herded there by three elephants. It was then tethered to a bush in full view of the tigress. The buffalo, however, remained ignorant of the tiger's presence. As soon as the elephants and the park staff moved away, the tigress who was already on sharp alert, moved in an outflanking stalk, taking cover of shrubs and grass clumps. Her movements, observed from elephant back, had to be seen to be believed. Stretching her body in a low posture her advance was in the slowest possible slow motion, carefully taken silent measured strides, zig-zagging so as to remain in cover. She took more than 20 minutes to cover those 60 yards, and when she came to

within about 15 yards, she waited for almost two minutes behind a grass clump, the buffalo still oblivious of the tigress's presence. Then in a lightning outburst she was on the buffalo's neck, burying her sharp long canines into it. The buffalo could not even emit a shriek and fell to the ground under the weight of the tigress. She clung to the poor quarry for well over two minutes, until all movement ceased and the buffalo died of suffocation. The tigress herself was exhausted. She sat panting beside the kill for half an hour, went to take a drink of water and began to feed only an hour later.

A tiger usually takes its quarry from behind, laying its chest on the back of the animal, grabbing the neck in its canines, sometimes bracing a forearm on the forelimb of the quarry and trying to pull it down by their combined

• •
Above, tiger with langur kill, Rathambhore, Rajasthan and *right*, tigers often cool themselves in water and mud.

weight. As the prey falters and falls, the tiger usually gives an upward jerk to the neck and is sometimes able to break the spinal cord, killing the prey instantly. Alternatively, a common method is to keep the prey pressed under its weight and hold onto its trachea, preventing breathing. Even experienced *shikaris*, having often seen tigers in this posture, believe the tiger to be sucking the blood of its victim. This cannot be true because its long canines and short lips do not allow the tiger, and most other feline and canid predators, to create a vacuum in their

mouth to enable them to suck. It is for this reason that all cats and dogs, even to drink water, have to lick and lap.

The tiger's formidable and sharp retractile claws play a significant role in capturing and holding on to its quarry. A mighty swipe of the forearm is sometimes used to stop a fleeting animal or to kill very small prey like monkey or peafowl. The tiger starts feeding from the rump and hind legs and, as the stomach cavity of its kill is opened, by a neat surgical operation, the tiger removes the intestines and the stomach and then feeds on the fleshy organs in the cavity. It does not feed on the rumen and the viscera. Its rasping tongue enables it to remove flesh from the large bones and proves useful in clean and complete utilization of the food secured. Depending on the size of its kill, the tiger may feed on it for four to

five days, without taking note of the stink of the putrefying meat. By the end, it may have fed on all the flesh, small bones, skin and hair. As a matter of fact the hair acts as roughage and helps in digestion.

The tiger's choice of quarry is hardly by species, it is, rather, by size, the bigger the better. With very large prey, e.g. the gaur or the buffalo, the tiger goes for the subadults. When a mother is training her cubs, regardless of size, many monkeys and langur are killed — the only form of communal hunting seen among tigers.

Tigers are powerful swimmers and are in full command in the difficult tidal-swamp and mangrove habitat of the Sunderbans, where they feed a lot on fish, sea-turtles and water monitors, in addition to chital and wild pig.

Occasionally the tiger gets a windfall. Once in Kanha, a massive gaur bull easily more than a ton in weight became sedentary, lounging around a water pool in a dry stream bed, foraging on the grass growing there. Its movements were seemingly constrained by old age, because there were no visible signs of disease or injury. For over a fortnight the bull was observed at the pool, its ambit progressively shrinking. It was photographed from the ground with a tripod-mounted camera. Every day, the pugmarks of a young tigress resident in the area were seen in the vicinity. One day from these marks, it was evident that the tigress had even stalked and approached the bull. It was apparent, however, that the tigress was not able to muster up the courage to attack the huge gaur which might have snorted and scared away the tigress with his formidable horns.

Finally, one evening, the bull became stationary at the edge of the pool and did not move at all even at the passage of vehicles on the road barely five yards from the pool. Early next morning the bull was gone, dragged by the young tigress some 50 yards away into bamboo thickets, up above the six-foot (two-meter) high bank. From the marks on the carcass, it was evident that the helpless bull was brought down by hamstringing and was probably dragged up the bank even before it died. After a week, when the kill was abandoned by the tigress and her two six-month-old cubs, there was still plenty of food left for the scavengers. The amazing side of the episode is the evidence it provides of the enormous strength of the tigress — she probably weighed no more than 330 pounds (150 kg) whereas the bull surely weighed over a ton.

A tiger may feed on an average size kill (e.g. chital) for a day or two and then may not hunt for two or three days. It usually hides its kill under cover and tries to remain nearby to protect it from scavengers, particularly vultures who, once they detect it may descend in hordes and polish off the kill in half an hour if the tiger is not around. An average-size tiger may kill up to three average-size prey every two weeks or about 80 every year. Depending upon the quality of habitat, a tiger would need a base population of 300 chital to sustain itself without upsetting chital demography.

Devoted Mothers: Tiger cubs are tiny, blind and helpless when they are born. But a tigress is a loving mother and brings up her cubs with great care and effort. Despite this, usually only two make it to adulthood from a normal litter of six. Until they are about three months old, the cubs are not allowed to trail the mother and food is brought to them. Their lair has to be frequently shifted, because if detected, they may be killed by other predators and scavengers, and even by rival male tigers. They are trained and disciplined to be quiet while the mother is away on hunting errands. A carefully worked out scheme of vocalization further guides the cubs to lie low or to respond and come out to meet the mother. Their first lessons in hunting consist of learning to pounce on their mother's tail, which she shifts to dodge them and playing hide and seek with her. They learn to stalk by searching for mother who hides under cover and practice by stalking each other. Training hunts take place in bushy cover during daytime, pursuing deer fawns, langurs or monkeys foraging on the ground. The cubs are taught to keep clear of man, the most crafty of all predators.

A tracker employed in a park once went surveying for water holes during the dry season. As he peered over a pool from a *nullah* bank, he was charged by a young tiger. The height of the bank allowed him just enough time to scramble up a slanting tree on the bank. From there he could see the young tiger's mother with two more cubs, lying in yet another pool nearby. The cubs were about a year old and too grown up for the tracker's comfort. The young tiger repeatedly came charging up the thick slanting stem, but could not reach the man. The mother beckoned the cub by calling, and when he did not give up, she got up and moved towards the cub. Thereupon the young tiger thought it prudent to obey and joined his mother. All the four then disappeared in the bush and the man safely walked back to the park headquarters to recount the tale, which was verified from clear pugmarks on the ground and claw marks on the tree stem.

Survival of the Fittest: Social organization among tigers varies with the quality of habitat in a given area, the determinant of quality being the relative abundance of prey and optimum hunting cover. In a high-prey-density area, the territorial definition of land tenures is prominent. In such an area, the dominant males occupy very extensive territories, as large as 20 to 40 sq miles (50 to 100 sq km). Up to three or even five females may occupy mutually exclusive sub-territories within a large male territory. The females in such an organization are assured of food supply for themselves and their progeny and, in return, owe allegiance to the territorial male. This also affords protection to their cubs from rival males as the territorial male meticulously demarcates and jealously guards his territory against rivals. Such a high-prey-density area in a region thus serves as the main natal area with most of the breeding taking place there. Moving radially away from the natal area, as the prey-density declines, the territorial definition also becomes less rigid.

The young cubs stay under the care of the mother for anything from 1½ to 2½ years, whereafter they are compelled to leave the natal area. But a young tiger is seldom able to find a place in the adjacent medium-prey-density areas because of their firm occupation by either the past-prime adults recently thrown out from the natal area, or the pre-prime adults preparing to find a foothold there.

Thus a young tiger dispersing from the natal area may be required to travel far and may, in fact, remain transient in the low-prey-density peripheral area for a long time. If contiguous tiger habitats are available, such a dispersing sub-adult may never return to its natal area and may in fact join another nearby population, thus ensuring the exchange of genes so essential to the viability of the population of a long-ranging, major predator like the tiger.

Males demarcate their territory by spraying scent with their urine on prominent trees on their territorial boundaries. They also often deposit their scent on the underside of the drooping branches of low bushes. This way the scent lasts longer, preserved from excessive evaporation or from being washed away by rain. Another and simultaneous way of marking territory is to make scrapes on the ground and tree trunks with the paws and then to deposit a foul-smelling secretion from the anal gland. These markings are intelligible to the other tigers and are recognized. Territorial integrity is further maintained by frequent patrolling.

The females also mark their territories in the same manner, but not as frequently or meticulously. The intensity of scent markings by a female becomes very high when she is in estrus and ready to have a mate. Her physiological condition is advertised by this scent and helps attract the males. The courtship period usually spreads over a week or 10 days, but the actual mating period may be only two to three days, during which copulation is frequent. Such prolonged association of the courting pair is necessary among cats in whom ovulation is promoted by frequent copulation. The gestation period in the case of the tiger is short, being about 105 days. Because the tigress, even during the terminal days of her pregnancy, has to hunt for herself, nature has ensured that her pregnancy does not disable her from doing so. It is for this reason that the gestation period is so short, the foetal size at birth small, and the stage of development of the cubs, when they are born, rather low. In order to provide against likely losses in rearing from this low developmental stage at birth, the litter size tends to be large — up to six.

Both the males and the females occupying the natal area are prime members of a population

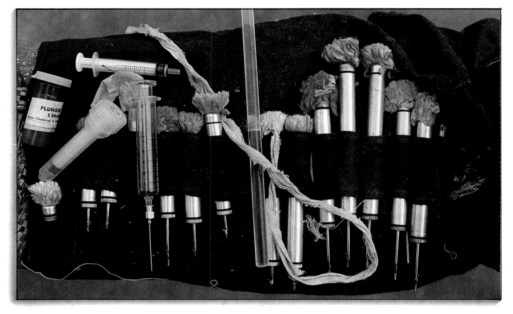

Tranquilizing darts used in research.

wounds may not heal and may eventually cause death after a few days or even weeks. However, tigers are generally able to heal all their wounds by licking them. Where direct licking is not possible, they manage to reach the spots and and such occupancy of prime habitats by prime adults is indeed a corollary to the axiom, "survival of the fittest." This ensures that only the best animals of both sexes are able to breed. Expectedly, therefore, confrontations take place among dominant tigers, particularly males, in order to establish supremacy and possess a territory. Such confrontations may range from a skirmish to a serious fight, depending upon the match between the contenders. All-out fights are by no means uncommon and very serious and deep wounds may be sustained. Such grievous

apply saliva by first depositing it on one of the limbs, usually a forearm, and then wiping the injury with the limb. It is those injuries on which saliva cannot be applied and those that are too deep and grievous, that prove fatal. Usually, in the natal area a wounded tiger may be helped by another tiger, mate by the mate and mother by young.

In one case, a huge territorial male was observed over the carcass of an only slightly smaller male he had killed in an encounter. The former cannibalized and persisted on the kill for four days, in much the same manner as he might persist over a herbivore kill. The intriguing aspect was that the killing was not made by the conventional method. No canine marks were seen on the neck or the nape of the carcass. It appeared that the smaller male had intruded into the territory of

the larger male in the belief that the latter was away from the intruded segment of its territory. But the presence of the smaller male was probably advertised to the territorial male by the alarm calls of langur or the deer and this alerted the territorial male and brought him out in search of the intruder. Suddenly confronted with the territorial male, the intruder may have offered submission which the territorial master was not magnanimous enough to accept. He probably therefore took the intruder by surprise by holding his head between his forepaws and twisting his neck with a vicious jerk, snapping the spinal cord.

Even subadult males are not tolerated and there have been numerous other recorded instances of half-grown cubs having been killed and partly eaten by the territorial male. Tigers are also known to kill and eat leopards. However, such internecine fights should not be regarded as being in quest of food, even though the killed animals may have been eaten. It should also not cause excessive worry in terms of loss of a member of a rare and endangered species. In nature, this is the only means of auto-regulation of the population of a supreme predator.

Cattle-lifters and Man-eaters: Tigers are often maligned for their aberrant behavior, reflected in their lifting cattle and sometimes killing and eating man. Though such behavior cannot be tolerated, invariably it is disturbance or damage

Above, resting after a meal and *right*, clawing tree to sharpen nails.

to the tiger or its habitat that induces or compels it to act in such a manner. As already mentioned, the tiger, by training and instinct learns to avoid man. However, when a wildlife habitat is degraded, causing a reduction in the population of natural prey, tigers are driven to occasionally taking cattle. This may lead to conflict between man and tiger and there may be situations when, while being chased away from a livestock kill, a hungry tiger launches an attack on man to prevent such deprivation. A few such instances may embolden a tiger to take to man-killing and

man-eating. Also, there are sometimes attempts by people to avenge livestock killing by shooting tiger. Often such attempts only end in wounding or injuring a tiger who, partly out of vengeance, and partly because of its inability to kill free-ranging wild prey because of the injury, goes for cattle or even man.

In a policy statement, the Government of India has permitted destruction of proven man-eaters, while providing compensation to owners of the cattle killed. At the same time, attempts are under way to rehabilitate habitats for the tiger both in the protected as well as in other forest areas.

Identification: Each tiger has a pattern of stripes and facial markings unique to itself and individuals can thus be identified. While such identifications, by visual or photographic confirmation, are usually employed in long-term behavioral studies in a given area to great advantage, counting tigers by this method is not practicable in large areas. The tiger's partiality to cover, its nocturnal habits, unpredictable movements and generally secretive behavior do not allow repeated sightings or photography, especially of all individuals in an area. The standard and practical method of counting tigers is to identify individuals by their pugmarks — a method equally capable of near mathematical accuracy. Features in a pugmark, e.g. the shape and relative size of the right, left or bottom lobe of the pad, the top edge of the pad, the relative sizes and placings of the toes with respect to the pad and several other features vary from tiger to tiger. An individual can be identified from a study of a combination of these features unique to itself,

ascertained replicably, from frequent tracings of pugmarks recorded in the field.

Conservation of the wilderness has come to stay in India, accepted on ecological merit and endorsed by the traditional values of aesthetics, culture and religion. Important statutory, regulatory and restorative measures have benefited a host of species and their habitats in a number of tiger reserves, national parks and sanctuaries. Some of the best places to see the tiger are Kanha and Bandhavgarh in Madhya Pradesh, Ranthambhore in Rajasthan, and Corbett and Dudhwa in Uttar Pradesh. Other unique tiger habitats with a fair chance of encountering one on excursion are Manas and Kaziranga in Assam and Nagarahole and Bandipur in Karnataka.

Nepal, like India, has taken remarkable strides

in wildlife conservation. Its Royal Chitwan National Park is a fine example of tiger conservation in action.

Family Meal: An account of a night-long observation, in the light of a full moon, of a tigress caring for her young would be an apt epilogue to this essay on the tiger. A well-hidden sambar kill by a tigress was located along a *nullah* in Kanha. A makeshift, thatch hideout was erected across the *nullah*, about 50 yards from the bush where the sambar carcass was lying hidden. Nothing remarkable happened until two hours after dark, when the copious chital alarm calls signified the approach of a predator. The tigress appeared in the *nullah* bed some 15 minutes later, heading towards the kill. After inspecting her kill, she sat alongside the bush for

another 15 minutes — a picture of beauty, moonlight glinting in her bright eyes—apparently assessing the security environment for her cubs. She then rose and disappeared into the forest. An hour and a half later, sambar and barking deer alarms were heard in the distance. The tigress reappeared on the scene in another half an hour and patrolled the *nullah* bed up and down for about 15 minutes. Then, standing near the bush where the sambar carcass lay, she gave two short, low calls. Presently came an equally short and muted response, apparently from the cubs. The tigress then again went into the forest and reappeared at the edge 10 minutes later. Having reassured herself after a brief survey of the scene she beckoned the cubs by a barely audible call.

Two very young cubs, the size of a large domestic cat, came out and skirted around the mother, rubbing themselves on her flanks, as if nudging her to take them to the kill. The tigress then went inside the bush and dragged the kill out and took a few bites, not so much as to feed but to expose fresh tender flesh for the cubs to eat. The cubs fed on the carcass for about 15 minutes whereafter the tigress again helped them, by opening up fresh meat. After a little while, the cubs having satiated themselves came to the mother. She licked them as if demonstrating to them how to clean themselves. The cubs then indulged in a bit of cleaning by themselves. Later they became very playful and the three engaged in a mutual display of affection by licking, rubbing and fondling each other's bodies. The mother would beat her tail from one point to the other and the cubs would pounce on it and try to grab it. Occasionally the cubs would come up on the low branches of the trees on the bank and then jump down into the sand below. Such play went on for most of the night. In the early hours, the tigress herself fed on the carcass for over an hour and intermittently the cubs joined her. At least an hour before sunrise, the tigress disappeared into the jungle with the cubs, and until sunrise there was nothing more to it. As the morning sun peeped over the tree line, the moist sand in the *nullah* provided evidence in its markings of the love of a devoted mother for her offspring.

* * * * *

Tiger Population: India is the only country that undertakes an annual census of its tigers. In 1986 the figure was 4015, which compares favorably with 1800 announced in 1972. The figures from other countries are largely guesswork. The Bengal tiger and Indo-Chinese tiger are both found in Burma (the Irrawaddy river is supposedly the divide). The Balinese tiger is extinct; the Caspian tiger is probably also extinct; the Javan tiger is reduced to a few individuals. The total world tiger population is estimated at anything between 6200 and 8600.

LIONS, LEOPARDS AND LESSER CATS

The **Indian** or **Asiatic Lion** (*Panthera leo persica*) is the lion which has figured in history, distributed as it was within historic times from Southern Greece in the northwest to Palamau, Bihar, in India in the east. Separated from the African and the recently extinct Barbary lion by the breadth of the Sahara, the Indian, West Asian or the Persian lion, the common name depending on its area of occurrence, disappeared by the beginning of the 20th Century from all areas of its distribution except the Gir Forest in Saurashtra, Gujarat, in India. The disappearance of open grass and scrub forestlands under the

plow, the increase in pastoralism, better arms for the hunter and the subsidence of political turbulence and settlement of human communities throughout its erstwhile range of distribution was the main cause of its wide-ranging extinction.

The Indian lion is a shaggier creature than the more well-known African lion. The coat and the belly fringe are denser, and the elbow and tail tuft longer. A character which is invariably present in the Indian lion is a distinct belly fold. In size, the average measurements compare favorably with that of the African lion. The record Indian lion measured 9′ 7′ (2.92 meters) as against the 10′ 7′ (3.23 meters) for the African lion. However, the Indian lions measured are from a tiny fraction of territory when compared with the extensive range of the African lion.

Though in general habits and behavior the Indian lion differs little from the African, there is one significant difference which is perhaps the key to the survival of the small population presently living in the Gir Forest. This vital behavior pattern is the tolerance of man by the Indian lion. During the several decades that lion and man have lived together in the forests of the Gir there have been remarkably few wilful instances of aggression by the lion. Although they avoid inhabited areas during the day they are remarkably fearless of man and will permit his near approach before moving off with dignity. Living with the lions in the Gir are the Maldhari and Rabbari herdsmen of cattle and buffaloes whose *neses* or villages bear a close resemblance to African villages, with their thorn *bomas* to keep lions out. Lions live largely on the cattle of these forest villages rather than the wild ungulates such as the sambar, chital, nilgai and wild boar. They also take whatever they can kill including goats and camels.

The Gir lion is a gregarious creature and prides often hunt in concert to separate and drive the selected prey to other members of the pride lying in ambush.

Males often live in pairs, the association is usually of long standing; instances are known of such pairs being seen together for several years. The Indian lion has not been sufficiently studied to understand the territorial system occurring among the prides.

During the day, the lions lie up in cover near a water hole or stream or in the shade of spreading banyan trees or within the dense cover provided by the evergreen Carissa which stand out in summer as islands of green in the starkly desolate forest of bare and gaunt trees. They come out to hunt at dusk, skulking near the outskirts of the villages as the cattle are driven home, to try and pick a stray cow or buffalo. Often the male spends much of the night roaring. The females are much more circumspect. Lions, however, are noisy animals, especially when mating. October and November are the main mating months and the cubs are born in January and February.

The Gir Forest, the last home of the Asiatic lion is itself a relict, being the only patch of extensive forest in the Saurashtra Peninsula. As the only forest of any extent in Saurashtra, it is of considerable importance not only as the home of the lion but also for its effects on the climate and water table of the surrounding districts.

The Gir Forest, to which the Indian lion had finally retired by the turn of the century, was situated in the princely state of Junagadh before India became independent. Without any doubt the continued survival of lions is due to the protection given to them by the Nawabs of Junagadh. At the end of the 19th Century, poaching and uncontrolled shooting had brought the lions to the verge of extinction and it was believed that not more than 20 existed. The Nawab's government then placed a strict ban on shooting which was enforced rigidly. At a much later date a limited quota of never more than three in a year were permitted to be shot at the discretion of the Nawab. The protection measures were wonderfully successful and the number of lions increased to a remarkable extent. A census held in 1936 gave a count of 287 animals. Censuses in subsequent years indicate that the Gir holds a population of not less than 175 and not more than 275 lions. The protection

• •
Left, family at pool and *above,* on the prowl.

received by the lions has been continued even more rigorously since India became independent.

The lion was for a period of time the national animal of India and still continues to be a national animal from its presence on the nation's crest, the lions of Ashoka.

The **leopard** or **panther** (*Panthera pardus*) is probably the most successful model of a predator. The known distribution within recent times was enormous, covering the whole of Asia from Asia Minor to the Caucasus to Manchuria and Amurland and reaching south to the islands of Indonesia and almost the whole of Africa south of the Sahara. That it is still not uncommon over a substantial portion of this range is a testimonial to the survival capability of the leopard. In size it is much smaller than the other

two big cats of the Indian subcontinent, the lion and the tiger, with which it coexists. It is thought to be a more primitive and earlier type than the lion and the tiger, and like them migrated into India from the north. Fossil remains have been recovered from central and southern Europe. It obviously entered India well before the tiger and before Sri Lanka separated from the mainland as it occurs there too.

The coat and color of the leopard are distinctive. The ground color is of varying shades of grayish or whitish buff, the underside of the body white, with a white patch on the otherwise black ear. The pattern of the coat consists of solid black spots on the head and upper neck, outer side of the limbs and belly. Elsewhere rosettes of varying size occur. In some areas, notably in the high-rainfall areas of the Western Ghats and eastern India, **black leopards** are not uncommon. Cubs of the normal and black or melanistic form may occur in the same litter.

In size, leopards are considerably smaller than the lion and the tiger, the largest male hardly exceeding 7′ 9′ (2.36 m) in total length with a maximum weight of about 179 lb (80 kg). The female is much smaller in length and weight, a foot (30 cm) less in total length and about 75 lb (34 kg) less in weight. The wide distribution and the ability to adapt to different environments has resulted in several races of the leopard being described from different habitats. Among these are six races from the Indian subcontinent.

Although the habitats differ, the habits of the leopard throughout its range are more or less the same. The most successful and adaptive among the larger cats, the leopard lives in all types of habitats from open country with rocky outcrops to thick forests. The environs of villages and even the environs of large cities such as Bombay (if it has a forest nearby) hold leopards. They have adapted to man's habits and, though they live on his domestic stock, remain invisible to the untrained and searching eye. Catholic in diet, they eat anything they can kill from crabs to cattle and can be a pest in the neighborhood of villages and towns, living on domestic stock and being particularly fond of taking dogs. Monkeys are another favorite food and are often killed as

The call of the leopard heard more often during the breeding season is distinctive, being three or four short bark-like roars very like the sound that a saw makes on wood. Leopards breed right through the year. The pairs stay together up to and after the cubs (two to four in number) are born. The gestation period is slightly over three months. The leopard is now a completely protected species in India, largely to protect it from the commercial exploitation of its skin by the fur trade.

The **snow leopard** (*Panthera unica*), the gray ghost of the snows, occurs along the length of the Himalaya from Kashmir to Arunachal Pradesh. An exclusively high-altitude leopard, it rarely descends below 7000 feet (2130 meters) in winter and in summer frequents the fringes of the snow line, the pasture area of its normal prey, the

endangered. It is on the fully protected schedule of the Indian Wildlife Protection Act.

The **clouded leopard** (*Neofelis nebulosa*) is a wide-ranging species being distributed from Nepal in the west to south China and south and east to Borneo. However, it is still a rare and little-known species. A dark gray or ocherous-colored cat, it is marked with bold-black or dark-gray blotched patches giving a clouded pattern and hence the popular name clouded leopard. The face has the cheek stripes seen among many of the smaller cats. It is equal in size to a small leopard, measuring up to 6′ 5″ (two meters) in total length and weighs up to 45 lb (20.5 kg). A feature peculiar to the clouded leopard is the proportionately enormous development of the upper canines which present the nearest approach among the living cats to the massive tusks of the

The **marbled cat** (*Felis marmorata*) is another widely distributed cat of eastern India, ranging in distribution from Nepal to Borneo. The marbled cat, as its name implies, has a marbled coat pattern made up of dark blotches more or less lined with black. The face has the usual cheek stripes. The general body color varies from gray to earthy or yellowish-brown of varying intensity; white or tawny below. It is slightly larger than a domestic cat being about three feet (one meter) in total length, half of which is the tail. The marbled cat is a forest animal, at home in trees, and feeds on small mammals and birds. Very little is known of this elusive cat.

The **leopard cat** (*Felis bengalensis*) is more widely distributed than the three cats described earlier, occurring as it does throughout the whole of Southeast Asia, from Baluchistan in the west

• •
Above, the rare leopard cat, Dachigam, Kashmir and *right*, leopards are good climbers.

they panic and seek safety on the ground. For its size, the leopard is quite powerful and often carries its prey up a tree to store, probably to prevent other stronger predators from appropriating the kill. Apart from man, the leopard's natural enemies are other carnivores such as the tiger, wild dog and hyena. There are instances of leopards being killed and eaten by python and the mugger crocodile. Leopards are a deadlier menace than the tiger when they become man-eaters, particularly from their greater boldness and knowledge of the habits of man.

wild goats and sheep of the Himalaya. It has perhaps the most beautiful coat among the cats. It is gray above with a buff or cream tint, and has gray-centered black rosettes on the body and spots on the head. In winter the coat is dense and the tail bushy. It is smaller in size than the leopard of the plains, hardly exceeding 6′ 8″ (two meters) in total length. Very circumspect in its habits, the snow leopard is seldom seen though it does become troublesome to herders of domestic stock. The high position of the eyes on the head permits it to peep over a rock without exposing itself to its alert natural prey of bharal and ibex. Its habits are little known. The breeding season is in spring and two to four cubs form a litter. The pelt of the snow leopard is in high demand and commercial exploitation has made the species

extinct saber-toothed tiger. An inhabitant of dense forests, it is supposed to live on prey up to the size of the smaller deer. Nothing has been recorded of its breeding habits in the wild but it has been bred in captivity.

The **golden cat** (*Felis temmincki*) has a peculiar distribution, one species occurring in the west and central African forests, and another in the forests of Nepal to South China and south to Sumatra and Java. The color of the coat varies from dark brown to red to nearly gray with a distinct stripe pattern on the cheeks. About four feet (1.22 meters) in total length, including a comparatively short tail, it is next in size to the clouded leopard. It is a forest and hill-area cat of eastern India capable of killing animals up to the size of small deer. Little is known of its habits.

to Manchuria and Korea in the north to Borneo and the Philippines in the south. Curiously enough, it does not occur in Sri Lanka. The leopard cat looks like a miniature replica of its namesake; spots of black replacing the rosettes. The ground color varies from whitish, creamish-white buff, ocherous-buff to ashy gray. It is about the size of a domestic cat, being just under two feet (60 cm) in total length, more than half of which is the tail. A forest cat, it is not uncommon. It feeds largely on birds and small mammals and in the vicinity of forest villages, is an inveterate poultry stealer. The young, three to four in a litter, are born in the first half of the year. Its beautiful coat is a coveted item for the fur trade and the species is now fully protected under the Wildlife Protection Act.

The **rusty-spotted cat** (*Felis rubiginosa*) is closely related to the leopard cat but is smaller in size and has no markings on the tail. The spots on the body are ferruginous and the ground-color is fawn-gray. This cat was thought to be peculiar to south peninsular India with a race in Sri Lanka. Recently it has been reported from Kashmir. It frequents fairly open country as well as forests. An excellent climber, it feeds on birds and small mammals and is known to take poultry. A litter consists of two to three kittens born in the hollow of a tree or in a cave or burrow among rocks.

The **fishing cat** (*Felis viverrina*) is a stocky, medium-sized cat with a tail shorter than its head and body length. The general body color varies from dark olivaceous-tawny with gray flanks to nearly ashy-gray. The stripes on the nape and

with a 10″ (25 cm) tail, and about a foot (30 cm) in height at the shoulder. The general body color is yellowish with distinct black spots; the tail is banded with black distally. The desert cat is a race of African wild cat which is widely distributed in Africa, and southwestern and Central Asia to North India. In India it occurs in the deserts of Ladakh and Rajasthan and the drier areas of Kathiawar. It has been reported as far south as Puné. Adapted to life in desert conditions, it is nocturnal and spends the day underground in burrows dug by it, emerging at dusk to hunt. It lives largely on rodents, but when necessary can subsist on insects, reptiles etc. The gestation period is about one and a half months and a litter is of two to three kittens. The female alone cares and fends for the young.

Pallas's cat (*Felis manul*) is a small one, about

and Mediterranean, North Africa through Iran to the Indian subcontinent and Sri Lanka, and through Burma to Indo-China. There is a distinct spinal crest of hairs and a small pencil or tuft of hairs on the ears. The general body-color is gray to tawny to deep brown. Ear tips may be black. The two stripes on the foreleg are distinctive. Three races have been described from India. In size they range up to 2½ feet (75 cm) in body length with a tail half the length. The maximum weight recorded is 19.8 lb (9 kg). The most familiar among all the Indian wild cats, it is very adaptable and occurs in habitats ranging from the vicinity of human dwellings to the densest forest. It often hunts during the day and is a swift and powerful predator, being exceedingly strong for its size. Though catholic in diet, it lives largely on small mammals and birds. It breeds during

the size of gazelles. The caracal breeds once a year but has no fixed breeding season. Litter sizes vary from two to six. Caracals when taken young are easily tamed and they used to be trained for hunting in the past.

The **lynx** (*Felis lynx*) is primarily a cat of the palaearctic zoogeographic region, the fringes of which extend into India in Kashmir and the Western Himalaya. The Himalayan race, *isabellina*, also occurs in Outer Mongolia, North China and the Russian Pamirs. Other races of the species occur in the tundra and boreal zones of Europe and North America. The lynx is a medium-sized cat with a very short tail and powerfully developed legs. The Himalayan race is pale isabelline in color, lacks a pattern of spots and, unlike in other races, the pads of its feet are not covered by hair in winter. The ears are

head, and the spots on the body and base of tail, and the bands on the tail, are black. Widely distributed in Southeast Asia, it prefers marshy habitats and its distribution is therefore patchy. In the Indian subcontinent it occurs in the Indus Delta, Keoladeo Ghana Sanctuary at Bharatpur, Rajasthan, coastal backwaters, estuaries and swamps of the southern maritime states and of West Bengal. It is very adept at fishing and is also powerful enough to kill sheep, calves, dogs and large snakes. The litter is usually of two kittens. The cat apparently does not have a fixed breeding season.

The **desert cat** (*Felis libyca ornata*) is believed to be one of the progenitors of domestic cats. Slightly larger in size than the domestic cat, the average size is about 20″ (50 cm) in body length

the size of the domestic cat, is peculiar to the arid high altitudes of Ladakh in India. Elsewhere it occurs in Pakistan and Central Asia. Its appearance is distinctive, the head being flat with widely spaced ears. The fur is dense and soft, with a grizzled or buff appearance and the tail, black-tipped and banded. The face is strikingly marked and the animal appears as if it is wearing a bandit's mask of black and white. Little is known of the habits of this high-altitude desert cat. It is said to live largely on the mouse-hare, rodents and ground-dwelling birds. Its call is said to resemble the yelping bark of a small dog.

The **jungle cat** (*Felis chaus*) differs from the cats so far described in being longer in the leg, and with a short tail. It is widely distributed, ranging from the Caucasus to the Middle East

the early months of the year. Three to four kittens form a litter and the coats of these young ones are faintly spotted.

The **caracal** (*Felis caracal*) is a handsome, lithe, graceful, medium-sized cat occurring throughout Africa, except in forested areas, and from the Middle East to northern India. The color varies from pale sandy-fawn to reddish brown or dark gray. The pointed ears are black above, frosted with white, white on the inside, and with pencils or tufts of black and gray hairs. Its tail is short, about 9″ (22 cm), its body length is about 29″ (74 cm) and its shoulder-height is about 16″ to 18″ (40–45 cm). It weighs up to 40 lb (18 kg). Incredibly agile, it is capable of knocking over several birds from a flock of pigeons which it has charged and is capable of killing animals up to

Left, **jungle cats are found throughout India and** *above,* **the fishing cat is rarely seen.**

pointed and tufted as in the caracal and the lower cheek has a fringe of long hairs. The body length is about 34″ (85 cm) and it stands about 20″ (50 cm) at the shoulder and weighs about 35 lb (16 kg). An uncommon animal, the Himalayan lynx is a resourceful hunter and feeds on a variety of prey ranging from young ibex to voles. It has an unusual habit for a cat: hiding or burying for future use portions of the prey it cannot eat at a sitting. The young are born in late spring or early summer, the gestation period being about two months. The litter size varies from two to four.

THE ASIAN ELEPHANT

Zoologists put the **elephant** in the "order" *Proboscidea*, the natural group of animals with a proboscis or trunk as their distinguishing physical feature. Delving back into Earth's history, scientists have identified 352 members of this order which now survives in two genera, each represented by a single species, the African elephant (*Loxodonta africana*) and the Asian or Indian elephant (*Elephas maximus*). While the African elephant has at least one recognized subspecies, there is no unanimity among specialists on the question of subspecies of Asian elephant. According to one taxonomic classification, the *forma typica* for the Asian animal is the Sri Lankan species; and there are three subspecies of the animal, one found in Sri Lanka, one on the Asian mainland extending to Burma and adjoining territories, and one in Sumatra. Some would find a fourth subspecies in West Malaysia. However, scientists working in the field in Sri Lanka did not find any significant morphological difference between the Sri Lankan and the mainland elephant.

To most people, particularly from the west, the elephant and India are inseparable. For an Indian, the elephant is a part of his history, tradition, myths and culture and, in many outlying areas, very much a part of his way of life. In northern Bihar and eastern Uttar Pradesh it is still the most coveted status symbol among the landed gentry; in South India there is no temple of any importance without its elephant; for some tribes in Arunachal Pradesh in northeast India, it is just another domesticated animal which lives as a part of the household, serving its owner in many capacities, including that of a plow-animal.

It is difficult to say exactly when the art of capturing and training wild elephant was mastered in India. For at least three thousand years in India the elephant has been in the service of man; yet, most of these animals have been taken from the wild, and subsequently tamed and trained to serve man. They have seldom been bred for the purpose of developing a domestic strain. This is where the elephant is unique and different from all other domesticated varieties of animals and birds. A certain number of calves are born to domesticated cow animals living in forest conditions, usually but not exclusively sired by wild bulls; but their number is insignificant, at least in India, compared to the number culled from the wild. In fact, in India, animals taken from the wild are preferred to those born in captivity, as the former have a better temper and are more amenable to training. Strange, but true.

There is enough evidence to suggest that, historically, the elephant had a very wide distribution in India. During the Indus Valley civilization (3rd to 2nd millennium B.C.) when, as available evidence suggests, the western part of the subcontinent had not yet been desertified, elephants were probably ubiquitous all over the land, barring the higher reaches of the Himalaya and the coastal salt-water mangrove swamps. Even in the Himalaya, evidence of casual visits by elephants has been noticed at a height of 10,500 feet (3200 meters) in recent times.

Today, the Asian elephant is considered an endangered species. The distribution of wild elephant in India is limited to four widely separate geographical zones: South India (in Kerala, Karnataka and Tamil Nadu; very recently a small group has found its way into Andhra Pradesh, much to the amazement and understandable consternation of the local people who had never seen a wild elephant before); Central India (in Orissa, Bihar and the adjoining southern part of West Bengal); North India (in the sub-Himalayan tracts of Uttar Pradesh); and northeast India (in Arunachal Pradesh, Assam, Meghalaya, Mizoram, Nagaland, Tripura and the northern part of West Bengal; a few come into Manipur from Burma seasonally). Apart from India, Nepal and Sri Lanka, wild elephants are found in Bangladesh, Burma, China, Indonesia, Kampuchea, Laos, Malaysia (including Sabah), Thailand and Vietnam. In Nepal, the few elephants that survive keep to the sub-Himalayan belt of forests. In Sri Lanka they are confined mostly to the forests of the eastern and northern provinces.

This fragmentation of the once-compact geographical range of the elephant in the subcontinent (Pakistan has no elephants) is a direct result of drastic shrinkage of habitat. Elephants make large demands on their environment, an adult animal of average size consuming something like 450 lb (200 kg) of green fodder a day, and probably wasting an equal amount in the process. A degraded habitat, therefore, cannot sustain elephant.

Indicators of Ecological Health: It has few natural enemies. Elephant calves are jealously guarded by their mothers and tigers seldom have the opportunity to take them. Even more rare, but not unknown, are instances of adult animals being attacked and killed by tiger. But these cases are noteworthy only because of their rarity.

· ·

Tusker, Yala National Park, Sri Lanka.

Lesser predators like the leopard, do not, of course, count in the context of the elephant. By and large, therefore, elephant is truly an apex species, indicators of the health of their habitat, mostly tropical forests, but also some limited areas of subtropical forests. A habitat which is good for the elephant is also good for its associate species, the sambar deer (*Cervus unicolor* Kerr), the spotted deer (*Axis axis* Erxleben), the barking deer (*Muntiacus muntjak* Zimmermann), and so on, which in their turn keep predators like the tiger or the leopard happy. When the forest is good for these animals, the ecosystem is doing all right, which means the water-regime is right, and so also is the condition of the soil; it is, therefore, also good for man and the environment in general.

The elephant is a slow-growing species: the

gestation period is between 19 to 21 months. Given the best living conditions, it has been estimated that the interval between two calvings is about four years. On the other hand, it is a long-living animal. The first calf is generally born to a female elephant around the age of 14 or 15 years. Instances of much younger cows calving are not unknown. And they can go on calving till the age of 60 or more. The longevity of the elephant in the wild is largely a matter of conjecture. The average life-expectancy of a healthy animal is assumed to be around 70 to 80 years. The long reproductive period of the female of the species is a cushion against temporary setbacks suffered by a population due to natural calamities like extreme drought conditions (not a common happening in those Indian forests where the

elephant now survives), or epidemic diseases like anthrax. This long life-expectancy combined with the fact that elephant are extremely adaptable in their preference of habitat—they thrive in all kinds of tropical forests except in dry scrubland and desert (which do not put off the African elephant), and salt-water mangrove—helps to explain why it has managed to survive in sizable number despite a massive destruction of its habitat: the latest estimate of their number for the whole of India is 16,500 to 21,300. Sri Lanka has an estimated wild elephant population of 2500 to 3000, and Nepal of about 50.

The elephant's is a matriarchal society. The leader of a group is a female, usually the oldest, the largest, and the wisest of the lot. This is also called the family group which consists of a nucleus of two or three mature cows, subadult

• •
Periyar National Park in Kerala is one of the best places for viewing elephants.

animals still moving with their mothers, and calves. The basic unit consists of a cow with its unweaned calf. The size of such a family group can vary from three to 10 or more in number. Sometimes, in some particular season, especially when elephant are on the march, moving from one area of forest to another, several family groups come together to form what can be termed a "herd." They usually split up into smaller units once they settle down in any particular area for foraging. One such famous elephant herd in Manas Tiger Reserve in Assam numbers more than 140 animals. Subadult male

animals, when they approach adulthood, are expelled from the group. This is taken to be nature's protection against inbreeding.

The nature of the relation of mature old bulls of reproductive age to these family groups is a matter that has caused a lot of controversy. We now know a lot more about the social behavior of the African elephant than previously, thanks to the researches of Iain Douglas-Hamilton and others since the 1960s. We still lack such quantified research data for the Asian species. It seems, however, that the same group-behavior pattern prevails for both the African and the Asian species. As with the African animal, the adult male of the Asian species seems to lead a free, unattached existence, sometimes forming loose "bachelor parties" of their own, called *maljuria* in northeast India. An adult male goes into a herd when a cow comes into estrus, and leaves the group when the period of mating, which can last for a week to 15 days or more, is over.

Ivory, through the ages, has been a thing of irresistible attraction to man. This has made the species peculiarly vulnerable in our era of breech-loading rifles. Fortunately, the female of the Asian species, unlike its African counterpart, does not carry ivory, and a good percentage of the male elephants in northeast India are tuskless (called *makna* locally) and hence do not attract ivory-poachers.

How big do they come? There is no currently accepted standard of judging the bigness of an elephant except by its height. The traditional method of measuring the height of an elephant, following the practice with horses, is at the withers. The average height of an African male elephant is around $10\frac{1}{2}$ feet (3.20 meters) at the withers, the very tall going up to 12 feet (3.65 meters) or even slightly more. With the Asian animal, it's an exceptionally large animal, when the male approaches 10 feet (three meters). The average height of the adult Asian female elephant would be eight to $8\frac{1}{2}$ feet (2.43 to 2.59 meters).

Elephants "Never Forget": How intelligent is the animal? Many tantalizing stories circulate about the alleged sagacity of the beast, and extravagant claims are sometimes made regarding its intelligence. Most experienced naturalists dismiss these claims. However, of all animals in the service of man, this is the only one which continues to be taken from the wild. Its ability to learn quickly is proverbial. A really well-trained animal can respond to about 40 command words. Using instruments is supposed to indicate intelligence. That elephants scratch themselves with sticks which help them to reach inaccessible areas of their body is well-known. Recently it was observed that elephants were breaking down energized fences with branches of trees, often collected from some distance away, seemingly

specifically for the purpose.

The elephant's long memory is probably not just a tall yarn. There is an authentic account of a tusker running away to the forest, and then returning to its stall four years later, not having forgotten in the meanwhile a single one of the 40-odd command words it had been taught in its years of domestication.

Which is the most dangerous animal in the Indian forests? Barring such aberrant creatures as the man-eating tiger or leopard, undoubtedly it is the elephant. Docile zoo animals or circus animals performing tricks can give a very false impression of the animal in its natural state. Unquestionably, it is the King of the Forest, before whom all animals, including man, must give way. Not surprisingly, Kipling made *Hathi* (elephant) the keeper of the law of the jungle at a time of exceptional stress, a terrible drought, and made Sher Khan the tiger slink away from its wrath after attemtping some petty transgressions. There is nothing more magnificent (and more dangerous) in the forests of Inida, nothing that will give a greater thrill, than an encounter on foot with a lone 10-foot tusker in full *musth* (an elephant with its temporal glands secreting, when the Asian male elephant tends to become psychologically unbalanced and, sometimes, aggressive).

A good photograph of an elephant in the wild is worth the time and patience (and caution) it demands: for the Asian elephant is largely a forest-dwelling animal and one has to be lucky to see it in the open in good photographic light. For viewing and photographing wild elephant, Sri Lanka has some splendid sites, particularly in Wilpattu (also famous for its leopard), Ruhuna, Yala, Gal Oya and Lahugala. In July–September in Lahugala, one can see as many as a hundred elephant or more grazing out in the open. In India, wild elephant can be seen in Manas (Assam), Dalma and Palamau (Bihar), Bandipur and Nagarahole (Karnataka), Periyar (Kerala), Mudumalai (Tamil Nadu) and Corbett (Uttar Pradesh).

Talking of wild elephant one must not forget elephants in captivity, the way most of us know them. The annual dazzling show of elephants in the historic city of Kandy in Sri Lanka during the 10-day festival of Perahera in August deserves special mention. For 10 successive nights a procession of gorgeously caparisoned elephants parade the narrow streets of the ancient royal city, the chief pride of which is the Maligawa, the temple which houses the sacred tooth of the Lord Buddha. During the concluding nights of the festival over a hundred elephants take part in the processions.

In India, the Dussehra procession in Mysore which features elephants, and the temple elephants of South India in general and Kerala in particular are noteworthy.

THE INDIAN RHINOCEROS

One misty morning in Chitwan National Park, southern Nepal, a magnificent male rhinoceros feeds nonchalantly in a lake. Occasionally, he submerges almost completely as he grazes on aquatic plants on the lake bottom. Suddenly, he pricks up his ears, perhaps on hearing the human intruder. He rushes out of the water grunting angrily, and disappears into the tall grass. Such a sight can now be seen in only a few other places on the Indian subcontinent, mainly in Kaziranga in the eastern Indian state of Assam. Small numbers of rhinos still survive in some other areas also.

Only a few hundred years ago the Indian rhinoceros (*Rhinoceros unicornis*) ranged over all of the grassy floodplains of the Indus, Ganga and Brahmaputra rivers. Mongol invader Timur, during his conquest of Delhi in 1398, and later, Babur, the founder of the Mughal empire in India in 1526, hunted rhinos in northern India. But the rhino's habitat was also suitable for human settlement, and was gradually turned into farmland. By the turn of the 20th Century the Indian rhino was fast heading towards extinction.

Because of excessive hunting for sport and poaching, by 1908 such prime rhino habitats as Kaziranga in Assam had only a dozen or so rhino left. It was only when hunting was stopped and immediate protection afforded to the area that the rhino showed signs of recovery. Kaziranga was declared a game sanctuary in 1926 and renamed Wildlife Sanctuary in the late 1940s. In 1950 Chitwan in Nepal had the largest concentration of this animal anywhere, with 800 to 1000. But, again, as a result of indiscriminate deforestation and poaching during the next 20 years their numbers fell to about 100 at the close of the 1960s. Chitwan was declared a Rhinoceros Sanctuary in 1962 and gazetted a National Park in 1973, but the killing of the rhinos in the park stopped only in 1976, when a contingent of the Nepalese Army was entrusted with the task of combating poaching. The rhino has since staged a comeback, and there are now about 1200 in Kaziranga and 400 in Chitwan, with about 100 in a half dozen other areas.

Appearance: With its deeply folded thick skin, studded with rivet-like tubercles on the shoulders, flanks and hindquarters, the Indian rhino appears armor-plated, which even sparked off

. . . .
Left and right, **the Indian rhinoceros is now confined to a few parks in Assam, West Bengal, Bihar and Nepal.**

myths that it was bullet-proof. Its massive build, its peculiar hide, its short stumpy legs, its huge head and the horn (actually a mass of densely matted hair) on the top of its snout, gives one the impression of a truly prehistoric beast. Which is not far from the truth as the rhinoceros has changed little in the last million years.

The Indian rhino averages about 5.5 feet (1.6 meters) at the shoulder and weighs 4000 lb (1820 kg). Gray in color they look jet black when wet, but may appear whitish, or whatever the color of the wallow, once the mud dries on their skin. Adult males may be differentiated from the

females by their larger size, their more pronounced skin folds on the neck, their genitals being visible from behind, and by horns that are usually thicker at the base and often broken or split at the tip (the horn of the female is usually slender and unbroken). The horn averages eight inches (20 cm) in length, but may be longer. Adult females may also be recognized by the presence of their accompanying calves.

To a casual observer, all rhinos look alike, but to a naturalist, a nick in the ear, a scar on the flank, a notch in the fold or a split in the horn is a definite mark of each beast.

Other Rhinos: Altogether there are five species of rhinos, two in Africa and three in Asia. African rhinos, both the **black** (*Diceros bicornis*) and the **white** (*Ceratotherium simum*) have two long horns, set one behind the other. The **Sumatran rhino** (*Didermocerus sumatrensis*) has two smaller horns, often thick stubs. The **Javan rhino** (*Rhinoceros sondaicus*), like the Indian species, has a single horn, usually less than six inches (15 cm) long. Both the Sumatran and Javan rhinos roamed eastern India until the end of the 19th Century, but have since disappeared.

Habitat: Floodplain grassland interspersed with marsh, swamp and lake, and the adjoining riverine forest, are the favored habitat of the Indian rhino. They prefer to feed on short grasses and seek shelter in thick stands of tall grass, sometimes 20–25 feet (six–eight meters) high.

Although largely grazers, Indian rhinos will also browse leaves from shrubs and trees and, when near farms, will supplement their diet with crops which they habitually raid at night. They

are fond of water and will spend hours wallowing. Besides cooling their huge bodies, the swamps and lakes also provide them with nourishing food in the form of aquatic plants.

Behavior: Rhinos occasionally feed and wallow in scattered groups of up to 10 or so, but they are solitary by nature and normally confine their movements to a small area of 0.3 to two sq miles (0.75 to five sq km). This, therefore, is their home range which meets most of their requirements of food, water and shelter. Males may have to wander farther for mates.

When two rhinos meet, ritualized behavior, a series of displays and postures, involving curling of lips and baring of sharp tushes, accompanied by snarls and grunts, usually decides who is dominant and violence is avoided. But at times

only physical battle will settle the dispute. These fights are noisy, and sometimes lengthy affairs, and can lead to serious injury; in rare instances, losers are mortally wounded. The horn is not their chief instrument of attack; their razor sharp tushes are, which can cut an opponent's hide without difficulty.

Male rhinos become sexually mature at about 10 years old, females a few years earlier. During courtship, violent encounters between the male and the female usually ensue and after much noisy chasing of the female by the male, mating finally takes place. Mating takes long, for up to an hour or more, the female sometimes dragging the male about, while still mounted.

After a gestation period of 16 to 16½ months, a calf (exceptionally two) is born. At birth they are pink and weigh about 130 lbs (60 kg). The

• •
The rhinoceros calf is dependent on its mother for protection against the tiger.

mother and the calf will stay together for three to four years. Meantime, the mother will probably have mated again and be ready to produce another young. Rhinos live for up to 50 years.

Rhinos usually avoid humans, but anyone straying too close to one, cornering one, or threatening a mother with calf, had better watch out. It will usually warn an intruder with an angry snort, but sometimes it will charge, occasionally without any provocation. Human casualties from rhino attack are not uncommon. Most charges are displays of threat, stopping short of the target, but a rhino will, on occasion,

press home its attack.

Signs: Rhinos leave distinct three-toed spoor on the ground, squarish in shape but not quite as large as those of the elephant. From constant use a large network of rhino trails is formed in the grassland, often forming "tunnels" through the thick grass. They also have favorite rubbing posts: a low overhanging branch, a sloping tree trunk or a stump. From regular rubbing, a distinct smooth patch is left, often coated in mud.

In rhino country, large piles of dung, known as middens, are common. These are accumulations from months, even years of use. The dung pile probably serves to inform other rhinos about an individual using a particular area. In the past poachers used to take advantage of this habit of the rhino to hunt them. They would either dig and conceal a pit on the approach path to the dung pile, or they would lie in wait for them in a nearby tree and dispatch them with a muzzle-loader gun.

Myth, Medicine, Masculinity: Rhinos have long been regarded as magical beasts surrounded by strange myths, and early Europeans have confused them for the fabled unicorn. In fact, for hundreds of years, until the late 18th Century, rhino horn was imported into Europe as unicorn horn and used as a potent drug. In medieval Asia, cups were carved out of rhino horn — often with exquisite designs on them — in the belief that the liquid in such a cup would froth, or that the cup itself would split in two, if the liquid contained a poison, thus warning and saving the life of the intending drinker.

The medicinal value of rhino horn is recognized even today and smart modern pharmacies in the East proudly display medicines containing rhino horn and other rhino products, as cures for numerous ailments, notably as a fever-depressant. Contrary to popular belief in the West, the Chinese do not use rhino horn as an aphrodisiac; only some Indians do. In Nepal it has no medicinal significance but a bowl made of rhino horn (or hide) is used to offer libations during the Hindu memorial ceremony of *shraddha*. And were it not for the incredible value placed upon this protuberance, the rhino's future would perhaps have been more secure.

Whether or not the horn has the ability to cure disease and enhance sexual capacity is a matter of debate but it does fetch good money. Indian rhino horn is considered the best and a pound (0.45 kg) of it may be* worth US$9,000 in Bangkok or Mandalay, although the primary poacher gets only a small percentage of its eventual price. However, he still makes more than if he were to toil on the land for one to three years. Because of desperate poverty, ignorance and unemployment, the poacher finds it worth his while to take risks, although, if prosecuted, he is imprisoned and fined. Some businessmen

resort to subterfuge and have tried to hoodwink the Hong Kong dealer with rhino horn look-alikes made out of bamboo roots!

In India and Nepal, every part of a rhino is used: skin, horn, hooves, flesh, bone, penis, the internal organs and even blood, urine and dung. They are believed to cure diseases, ward off evil spirits, reduce labor pains, bring good luck, ensure good harvest, improve health and, above all, one's sex life! No part of a rhino is waste. So, when a dead rhino is found, its horn (if there), hooves and skin are taken into government custody and the local people rush to the carcass with gusto. In no time all is gone. To those who do not understand conservation, a rhino is more useful dead than alive. Apart from satisfying their medicinal and superstitious needs when dead, live rhinos are a menace to their farms and a threat to their lives and livelihoods.

The Future: In terms of increasing rhino numbers, Kaziranga and Chitwan may be viewed as successes. But this has also increased the conflict between rhino and man. Rhinos, like elephants, have no natural predator other than man—although calves are sometimes eaten by tigers—and with continued protection their numbers are likely to exceed the natural carrying capacity of the parks. This will have to be carefully monitored by the park managements.

Biologically speaking, the more rhinos the better, but socio-economically, it is counter-productive to antagonize the farmer as his support is vital for the long term future of the rhino and other wildlife. Already crop damage by rhinos is considerable; very chronic in some areas. In Chitwan a rhino fence (consisting of a deep pit) in the Sauraha area met with limited success. Fencing off national parks and reserves sounds good theoretically but has practical limitations. Putting up heavy-duty fences on the floodplains will not only be very expensive but will also involve constant repairs.

Political disturbances in Assam slackened park vigilance in Kaziranga for some years and over a hundred rhinos were poached in the first half of the 1980s. In Chitwan, however, because of stringent protection, rhino poaching in the park is almost nonexistent.

Although the future of the Indian rhino now seems secure, it is still a matter for anxiety that this rare and endangered creature should be confined to so few habitats. To place the eggs in more baskets, so to speak, a few rhinos from Assam were released in Dudhwa National Park in Uttar Pradesh in 1984 and a few more were brought in from Chitwan a year later. In early 1986 a few rhinos from Chitwan were released in Bardia, in far west Nepal. These translocation projects are an insurance against the possibility of random extinctions. Only time will tell how the rhino will fare in their new homes.

Africa is universally accepted as the world's greatest haven for wildlife. Few are aware that, of the six greatest cats in the world belonging to the genus *Panthera*, India has five species to the African continent's two; and has eight species of deer and three species of wild ox to Africa's one each. In fact no country in the world, not even Russia, possesses the number of distinct species of cervids that India has.

The largest and the most widely spread of the Indian deer, the **sambar** (*Cervus unicolor*), has the widest distribution of all deer in the world, extending from Saurashtra to Taiwan and the Philippines, and from the Himalaya to Laos and Borneo, Sumatra and Sri Lanka. Yet nowhere does the species reach the same proportions in body and antlers as it does in India. The largest antlers, including the record specimen of 50 inches (127 cm), come from the Vindhya and Satpura ranges of Central India. A large stag may stand 59 inches (150 cm) at the shoulder and weigh 660 lb (300 kg).

Essentially not gregarious in behavior and mainly nocturnal and wary in the major portion of its area of distribution, the sambar has become common, confiding and diurnal in parks and sanctuaries where it has been adequately protected, and Sariska and Ranthambhore National Parks in Rajasthan would be about the best places in the world to see and photograph them by daylight. The Betla Tiger Reserve in Bihar, the Melghat and Taroba National Parks in Maharashtra, Bandhavgarh and Satpura National Parks in Madhya Pradesh, Nagarahole National Park in Karnataka and Periyar National Park in Kerala are other excellent places to see sambar. They also occur in the Gir forest, in Corbett and Dudhwa, Manas and Kaziranga and in fact in most forested parts of India, excepting the mangrove, and extend up to 9800 feet (3000 meters) in the Himalaya.

The larger stags are usually solitary, except during the rut, which extends from November to January. The antlers are shed from March to May and the animal goes into molt, often assuming a very ragged pelage. New antlers begin to grow soon after shedding, but during this period the stags are secretive and rarely seen. The most often seen sambar group is one or more hinds with their progeny of different years.

They are a preferred prey species of the tiger and are widely preyed upon by the wild dog

• •

Hangul or the Kashmir stag is found only in a few areas in Kashmir.

(*Cuon alpinus*). However, the greatest threat to their survival, apart from the common factor of habitat destruction, is their susceptibility to bovine diseases, contagion contracted from India's ubiquitous livestock. The sambar population of Sariska was severely ravaged some years ago by an epidemic disease.

Survival for the Sangai? At the other extreme of the scale — in rarity as well as in the restricted area of occurrence — is the **Manipur brow-antlered deer** (*Cervus eldi eldi*), the most endangered wild animal in Asia. The smallest in both body and antler development of the three subspecies of this deer (the other two being the Burmese thamin and the Thailand subspecies), the Manipur deer, locally called the **sangai**, was from historical times confined to the vale of Manipur. Adapted to the grassland-forest mosaics, the most productive ecological entities of Asia, the sangai were driven to extinction by man in their preferred habitats. Till World War II, however, they were still not uncommon in the swamps where the survivors had sought refuge. They had adapted to their semi-aquatic existence by developing elongated hooves and hard and hairless posterns which assisted them in their movements in the morass and floating islands, and which are a distinguishing feature of this subspecies.

The intrusion of the Japanese army into Manipur in the war—their westernmost advance, followed by Indian independence, augured unsettled times for the sangai and an end of the princely patronage which had previously protected it. Being in close proximity to human settlements, the sangai were doomed, and by 1951 they were believed to be extinct. However, E.P.Gee, a pioneer of the conservation movement in India, located a small, surviving population of the deer in a remote swamp at the southern end of the Logtak lake. A unique ecosystem, consisting of a contiguous floating mass of dead and living grass, the 11-sq-mile (28-sq-km) area of the Keibul Lamjao was estimated by Gee to hold about 100 sangai.

The nature of the swamp, where the floating morass supported the weight of the deer with their long hooves and specially adapted gait of small hops (which had earned them the nickname of dancing deer from Gee) — but on which man sank to his waist every few steps, made a true ground survey of their numbers almost impossible. In 1972, a gross estimate, based on a sample survey, placed the sangai population at 50. It was only when, for the first time, a helicopter survey was carried out in 1975 that the grim position became evident. There were only 14 Manipur brow-antlered deer left in the wild — 5 stags, 6 hinds and 3 fawns. In 1978, 23 animals were counted; in 1984 the tally increased to 51. But still there are far more sangai in captivity than there are in the wild and searches have not revealed any area really suited to their rehabilitation in a second home in the wild. Thus, the survival of the wild sangai is as yet irrevocably linked with the fate of the miniscule Keibul Zamjoo National Park. Almost the only chance that a visitor has of seeing this most graceful deer in its natural environs is to quietly punt a dugout canoe with a pole over a specially cleared water channel to the Pabot Hill, a feature within the park, and from the elevation of this lookout point observe the animal.

Standing a little over three feet (a meter) at the

of population in the Ganga-Brahmaputra and Central Indian grasslands. No deer species in India has suffered such a drastic decline of habitat as the barasingha. It survives today only in fragmented herds, frequently wide apart and often small. There was a period in the 1960s when there was despair about the future of this elegant deer, especially the southern race in Central India. Effective protection, especially the creation of parks and sanctuaries in its remaining habitats, has yielded good results and the decline of the barasingha has not only been halted, but in many places it has made a good recovery.

Divided into three subspecies — *C.d. duvauceli*, the nominate race occurring today mainly in Dudhwa National Park, Kanchanpur Sanctuary and the Pilibhit forests of U.P., with a relict population close to Hastinapur near Meerut and

in early autumn. They are almost exclusively grass grazers, another manifestation of their grassland adaptation, but fortunately they are not prone to crop-raiding which has been the bane of many a herbivore. They frequently wade into water to eat the sedge-grasses, sometimes immersing even their heads. With the approach of winter the barasingha emerge from their khaki-saffron coat to the rutting pelage of dark brown. The stags, standing about 50 inches (127 cm) at the shoulder and weighing approximately 400 lb (180 kg), lose the velvet of their antlers, develop a swollen neck and ruff characteristic of many a deer species in the same situation. The antlers, 12 or more — pointed in an adult (hence the name, *bara* = twelve; *singha* = horns) — are usually more polished and hence lighter colored in the northern and eastern races than in the

in numbers, coupled with a high rate of reproduction and ecologic adaptability, has enabled it to attain its current safe status. In the Andaman Islands, where it was introduced less than a hundred years ago, it had assumed pest proportions. It is found from the Gir forest in the west to Manas in the east, and from the Himalayan foothills to Point Calimere Sanctuary in the south. Chital, of all the south-Asian deer, also has the greatest tolerance to human proximity. In many a national park and sanctuary they seek the safety of human habitations at night —often moving amongst the tourist huts — as a precaution against predator attack.

Being both a browser and a grazer, chital prefers grassland-forest borders. In the vast grassland *chaurs* of Corbett and *maidans* of Kanha national parks, both very favored habi-

shoulder and weighing about 200 lb (100 kg), the stag sangai is much larger than the hind. They are a very handsome deer, turning dark chocolate-brown in the rutting season from their ocher-fawn pelage during the molt. Their most notable physical feature is the unique formation of their antlers, which form a continuous arc from the highly developed brow-tines to the main beam of the antler, without the angular junction over the pedicle characteristic of all other deer antler formations. Hence the name brow-antlered deer.

Costly Specialization: The **barasingha** (*Cervus duvauceli*) is another deer which has paid the price of its specialized adaptation to alluvial and riparian grasslands so coveted for agriculture by man. Gregarious, and living in favorable habitats, the barasingha in the past attained great density

a sizable herd in Kanchanpur Division of Nepal; the eastern race *C.d. ranjitsinhi*, now confined to Assam and there almost only to Manas and Kaziranga; the southern or Central Indian race, *C.d. branderi* to Kanha and Indravati National Parks in Madhya Pradesh — their total world population would be between four to five thousand. In Kanha, their numbers have increased from 66 in 1968 to approximately 500 at present and this park is the best place to both view and photograph them. Dudhwa and Kaziranga are two other excellent areas to watch this deer.

In Assam and Uttar Pradesh the barasingha continues to remain almost exclusively partial to its grassland habitat, remaining even in the open meadows in the noonday summer sun. In Central India they do move into the sal forests, especially

southern. Grass is thrashed and a deliberate attempt is made to carry grass tussocks on the antler rack to give it more impressive proportions. Wallowing in mud and "bugling" are other manifestations of the rut, the call being a hoarse braying not dissimilar to that of a donkey. The stags are not territorial and the male hierarchy and dominance of the master stag is achieved more by display than actual combat.

Spotted Beauty: The **chital** or **spotted deer** (*Axis axis*) is amongst the most widely distributed and common of the larger wild mammals of the Indian subcontinent. Indeed, it is also one of the most ornamental, and unlike many other spectacular ungulates both sexes sport an exquisite pelage, and that too throughout the year.

Its watchful and alert behavior, seeking safety

• •
Left to right: musk deer is sought for its scent glands; a group of brow-antlered deer (the world's rarest) of Manipur; and a magnificent display of blackbuck, Velavadar, Gujarat.

tats, they congregate in great numbers and in the Kanha central *maidans*. In early July when the chital rut is at its peak, about 4000 chital have been seen milling around in an area of barely four sq miles (10 sq km). Their numbers in Kanha increased from about 8500 in 1973 to 14,500 in 1985. Bandipur in Karnataka, Taroba in Maharashtra, Palamau in Bihar, Barnawapara in Madhya Pradesh, Chila in Uttar Pradesh, Sariska and Ranthambhore in Rajasthan are other protected areas notable for their chital concentrations.

A daily drink or two is essential for chital and they are never found too far away from water. But of the larger species of Indian deer, chital is the one which does not wallow when in rut — as if it were loth to soil its dainty coat. The rutting period of the chital is also less defined and there are always some stags in hard antlers throughout the year, a factor contributing to its prolific propensity. The rutting stags thrash saplings, strut and emit harsh, bellowing calls.

They have a symbiotic relationship with the common langur (*Presbytus entellus*), congregating beneath the feeding monkeys for pickings falling to the ground. Primates have been seen riding the back of a chital. The chital and the langur are the most frequent and first notifiers of the presence of predators, the shrill, musical

The rutting of the hog-deer occurs in autumn, earlier than that of most other deer of the plains, and consequently the antlers are also shed earlier in early spring, the deer then assuming a lighter colored coat on which the spots are visible more distinctly.

When disturbed, hog-deer dash off with a characteristic lumbering lope, head slung low and stretched out, the long tail raised to reveal the white underside as a danger-flag.

Once to be found from the grassbeds of the Indus in Sind to Assam, and beyond to Indo-China in the east, it was restricted to the Indo-Gangetic-Brahmaputra valleys in the Indian sub-continent. Today in India it occurs sporadically in the Jumna and Ganga highgrass *khadars*, along the *terai* and *dooar* grasslands from Uttar Pradesh to Arunachal Pradesh, in suitable high

barking deer carries both tushes and a unique pair of antlers. These grow from a pair of elongated skin-covered pedicles, which themselves appear as an extension of two elevated ribs or ridges that so prominently mark the forehead of the deer. The antlers have a short brow-tine, but the main beam is then not bifurcated in its journey upwards and then inwards. But it is the tushes that are the weapons actually used.

Solitary, shy and secretive, restricted in their movements and often confined to small home ranges, barking deer are seen in ones and twos, often mere **fleeting** glimpses. The best and frequently the only method of photographing them is to watch over a water hole or salt lick. Their alarm call is barely distinguishable from the barking of a village dog; their mode of escape not dissimilar to that of the **hog-deer.**

barely a foot (30 cm) high, whose male members carry small dagger-like tushes, the mouse deer is not a true deer, having only three compartments to its stomach and belonging to the family *Tragulidae.* Its present range extends from the heavily forested regions of the Western Ghats, through eastern Madhya Pradesh, to the sal forest belt of southern Bihar and Orissa. Even smaller, more solitary, evasive and cryptic than the barking deer, the mouse deer is rarely seen except with the aid of a powerful light at night.

Elegant Antelope: Africa is the continent for antelopes, with a multitude of species from the magnificent greater kudu to the tiny dik dik. But with the exception of the sable, there is no antelope that can really match the male **blackbuck** (*Antilope cervicapra*) for its color-combination and elegance, the matching proportions of its

• •
Above, **the mouse deer, the region's smallest.**
Right, **nilgai or blue bull, Asia's largest antelope, Ranthambhore, Rajasthan.**

whistle-calls of the deer often interspersed with the harsh, staccato barks of langur marking the march of the tiger.

Though preyed upon by both the tiger and the leopard, in many parts of its habitat it is the wild dog which is the chital's main predator.

Closely related to chital is the **para** or **hog-deer** (*Axis porcinus*), a squat, rotund deer adapted once again to riverine grasslands. The stags carry a three-point antler formation, like those of the chital and the sambar, but with the inner, top tine curved characteristically downwards.

grasslands and lowland **grassland-forests** on both banks of the Brahmaputra, and in Manipur.

High floods take a heavy toll of the hog-deer in Kaziranga. But the numbers recover fast and this park is the best place to see and photograph the animal in India; Corbett being the other. Dudhwa in Uttar Pradesh, Jaldapara in West Bengal, and Manas and Orang in Assam are other protected areas where hog-deer are prominent.

Shy Tush-bearers: A primitive member of the Cervidae family, the **barking deer** (*Muntiacus muntjac*) represents the transition phase of the deer family, from oversized canines or tushes as weapons of offense and defense, to antlers which serve the same purpose. While the musk deer and some other species elsewhere carry tushes, the

Found in heavy forested regions from the Himalayan pines and firs to the southern tip of the Western Ghats near Kanyakumari and from the Satpura Hills in Western Central India to Arunachal Pradesh and Nagaland and beyond, barking deer can be seen in most of the protected areas in this vast region. Yet none can be called an ideal place to view them. In Nagarahole and Bandipur in Karnataka, Nagjhira and Melghat in Maharashtra, Satpura and Bandhavgarh in Madhya Pradesh, Rajaji and Dudhwa in Uttar Pradesh, Manas in Assam, and Simlipal in Orissa, to name a few, the chances are better than in other places.

Closely related to the hornless, tush-bearing deer is the **chevrotain** or **mouse deer** (*Tragulus meminna*). A diminutive, speckled-gray creature,

horn shape and length to its body size. There are few animals that one can truthfully describe as exquisite. The male blackbuck in his chocolate-black rutting pelage, strutting stiff-legged, with face upraised and horns swept back, is one such. It is also an animal truly representative of India, having evolved in this subcontinent and having become extinct in the wild except in India and on the **India-Nepal border**. It is one of **the swiftest** animals in the world and a herd traveling at 50 miles (80 km) per hour for a distance of over a kilometer has been clocked.

Dominant herd males are intolerant of the presence of other mature males and male blackbuck maintain territories, often very small and in close juxtaposition to each other. Aggression is mostly confined to strutting displays, but sparring, jousting and chasing are not infrequent. There is, however, rarely any serious injury, evolution having provided in the convoluted horn-shape of the bucks, as it has provided in the branching antler-tines of stags, a locking mechanism that prevents an animal from making a fatal thrust. The pre-orbital glands exude a strong-smelling musky secretion which is rubbed on grass stems or tree boles if they are available. Horns are thrashed on vegetation and if none is available, as is sometimes the case in blackbuck country, on the bare ground.

Pure white blackbuck are not uncommon, though this occasional lack of pigmentation appears to be more common in Saurashtra.

Blackbuck were perhaps the commonest wild animal in India prior to independence. Being in close proximity to human habitations, living in

Noradehi and Kanha in Madhya Pradesh, the last having a small herd in a unique habitat; Vetnoi in Orissa; Point Calimere in Tamil Nadu and Rane Bennur in Karnataka.

Frisky Gazelles: Even more independent of water and moisture content in food plants than the blackbuck, the **chinkara gazelle** (*Gazella gazella*) has a wider range of distribution than the antelope in arid lands. They are also at home in rolling hills and scrub forest, and being less prone to raid crops and living less in agricultural areas in the proximity of man, the rout suffered by the gazelle, though drastic, has not been as complete as that of the blackbuck. The decline of the chinkara and the blackbuck in the past two centuries has been a major contributory factor in the decline and final extinction of the cheetah (*Acinonyx jubatus venaticus*) in the subcontinent.

propensities it has been left unmolested in areas of Hindu predominance, and Muslims have been hired on occasions to get rid of them. Its flesh is still taboo to the Hindus.

Occurring in small groups from Jammu and the Punjab to Karnataka and Saurashtra to Bihar, the nilgai prefers open forests and scrubland, though where persecuted they have moved into heavier cover. Living mainly in areas where the tiger is absent, and the leopard rarely being able to tackle them, man has been their main predator in the present and recent past.

Sariska and Ranthambhore in Rajasthan, Panna and Shivpuri National Parks in Madhya Pradesh, Paneli in Gujarat, and the more open-forested protected areas of Maharashtra and Andhra Pradesh are the best places to view the nilgai.

the Barda and Gir forests of Gujarat, extending eastwards to Bihar. It is another very difficult animal to photograph in the wild.

It is interesting to note that the only other known ruminant to have possessed four horns, the Sivatherium, whose fossils are found in the Siwalik hills, also occurred in India and was the largest known ruminant.

Wild Oxen: The tallest, sleekest and, colorwise, one of the most striking of the 11 species of the subfamily *Bovinse* or wild oxen that survive in the world today, the **gaur** (*Bos gaurus*) is also, next to the wild **yak** (*Bos grunniens*), the best adapted to hilly terrain. It is also currently the least endangered of the Asiatic wild bovines.

Preferring dense forests away from human habitations and livestock, quite content to confine itself to its beloved bamboo thickets and

open, easily approachable habitats and raiding croplands as they did, no animal in the subcontinent has suffered such a steep decline in numbers, and reduction in areas of occurrence, as has the blackbuck. There were hardly any parks or sanctuaries which held blackbuck populations prior to the 1970s. They survived in isolated pockets, particularly in Rajasthan and Gujarat, almost entirely due to the religious sentiments of the local people, notably the Bishnois and the Valas. According to one estimate there were once some 4 million blackbuck on the subcontinent. Today, the estimated number is around 25,000. The foremost places to view the blackbuck are the Velavadar National Park in Gujarat with a population of about 2000; Talchapar, Gajner, Doli, and other Bishnoi areas in Rajasthan; Bagdara,

Less gregarious than the blackbuck (groups of over a dozen are rare), chinkara tend to keep within definite home ranges. They are in a constant state of animation, black tail wagging, ears twitching, heads frisking one way and the other. Chinkara are presently met with in goodly concentrations in the Desert National Park and the Bishnoi areas of Rajasthan, and Kunu Sanctuary and Panna National Park in Madhya Pradesh.

Blue "Cow": The **nilgai** (*Boselaphus tragocamelus*), the largest of all Asiatic antelopes, has been fortunate. Firstly, it possesses an insignificant pair of horns which is no real trophy for the hunter. But what is more important, its somewhat physical resemblance to cattle has earned it the name *blue cow* and the religious sanction that goes with it. Despite its serious crop depredation

Unique Antelope: The only animal in the world to possess four horns, the **four-horned antelope** (*Tetraceros quadricornis*) is the smallest antelope in Asia, being about two feet (60 cm) high and weighing about 35 lb (16 kg).

Exclusive again to the Indian subcontinent, the animal possesses a pair of short anterior horns with a pair of sharp-pointed longer posterior horns that can be used as rapiers.

Preferring patches of grassland amidst forests and open forests with a grassy understory, the **chousingha**, as the four-horned antelope is commonly called, is home-range oriented, living singly or in pairs. Its range extends from the *terai* forests and Jammu to Mudumalai Sanctuary in Tamil Nadu, though in the past it was reported even in the Palni Hills. It occurs in

even to steep slopes and not raiding agricultural crops even if they are close at hand, the gaur has avoided, as it were, the pitfalls suffered by the wild buffalo, which in the historical past, had a far greater distribution and numbers.

Extending from the Agasthyamalai hills at the southern tip of the Western Ghats to Satara and Kolhapur in Maharashtra and up to the central segments of the Narbada river in Madhya Pradesh, the gaur distribution sweeps eastwards and northwards past the Amarkantak massif where the Narbada and Sone have their sources,
• •

Left, gaur, largest of the world's wild oxen Nagarahole, Karnataka and *above*, only small pockets of pure wild buffalo survive in Assam, Madhya Pradesh and southeast Nepal.

Nilgai Sariska, Rajasthan.

into the Chota Nagpur tracts of Bihar, Orissa and West Bengal and then on to the northeastern regions of the subcontinent.

The animal attains its best proportions in the moist, semi-deciduous and evergreen forests of southern India. The glistening black bulls, bulging muscles rippling under the skin, heavy-horned and with a pronounced dewlap and hump on the withers, white stockinged feet in contrast to the dark pelage of the body, are the prima donnas of the parks and sanctuaries of the South — Nagarahole, Bandipur and Bhadra of Karnataka, Mudumalai and Annamalai of Tamil Nadu, Parambikulam and Periyar of Kerala. Mollem in Goa, Tarboa in Maharashtra, Pench, Kanha, Achanakmar off Satpura in Madhya Pradesh, Belta in Bihar and Simlipal in Orissa are other places where the gaur can be readily seen.

The older bulls are frequently found solitary or in twos. Male dominance is mainly achieved by lateral displays in slow, measured steps wherein the masculine attributes of the bulls, the dorsal ridge, the dewlap and foreshoulders are displayed to best advantage. There is rarely any actual combat.

Also called the Indian Bison, (which is a misnomer as the only two true bisons which survive today are the European and American), the gaur is very susceptible to bovine diseases. Rinderpest and anthrax have decimated their herds in the past in Bandipur, Mudumalai, Periyar and Kanha, in the first two more than once. They have yet to recover their previous numerical strength in these areas.

Till they attain an age of about two years, gaur calves are preyed upon by the tiger, and it is this which prevents the small herd of gaur in Bandhavgarh from increasing in numbers.

Fearless Buffalo: Were it not for the similar appearance of the ubiquitous domestic buffalo, the **Asiatic wild buffalo** (*Bubalus bubalis*) would surely have ranked as one of the most impressive and magnificently built animals in the world today. It is the most powerful and heaviest but yet most proportionate of all the South Asian wild bovines, and in the record specimens it carries the largest horns of any surviving animal in the world today. The females carry even longer though more slender horns than the bulls. A large buffalo bull can scale nearly 2000 lb (over 900 kg).

Seals of the Indus Valley civilization (2500 B.C.) depicting the wild buffalo testify to its then existence in the river basin. In the more recent historical past, the range of the animal extended over the riverine and forest grasslands in the Ganga, Brahmaputra, Narbada and Godavari river systems. Today it is found mainly in the surviving Brahmaputra valley grasslands — Kaziranga, Dibru, Manas. A small herd survives in Kosi Tappu in Nepal. The peninsular Indian wild buffalo population, perhaps the purest genetically, survives in small scattered populations in Udyanti in Raipur district, Bhairamgarh, Indravati and Pamed in Bastar district of Madhya Pradesh, and perhaps a small herd in the Koraput district of Orissa. The total population in the subcontinent would in all probability be less than 2000.

Its preference for alluvial grasslands most coveted by man for agriculture is the main reason for the wild buffalo's loss of habitat. Its fearless, even truculent behavior has also not helped. But what has perhaps been a most vital factor, both direct and insidious, contributing to both the numerical and physical decline of the wild buffalo, is the propensity of the bulls to commandeer domestic buffalo cows for mating. The deprived owners of the livestock take pot-shots at the offending bull if one is around, as it can cause the loss of access to milk and often the loss of the impregnated domestic buffalo cow who cannot safely deliver the oversize calf. Not infrequently, the wild bull prevents the return home of the domestics, which not only means the permanent loss of the livestock to the owner but also the creation of feral buffalo populations which are not of the same proportions and grandeur as their wild sires. This genetic "swamping" is very evident amongst the wild buffalo populations that come in contact with the domestic animals, as in Kaziranga and southern Manas.

Though calves are occasionally killed by tigers, the willingness of the wild buffalo to stand its ground and drive off and even attack a tiger, helps in keeping away all but the largest and most determined tigers. They form a phalanx and face their adversary, the youngsters in between.

The threat display involves a direct frontal approach, the muzzle slightly depressed to show the vast sweep of their massive horns to their best advantage. Snorting and foot-stamping are other manifestations. Horned combats, resulting in injury to one or both participants, though uncommon are not unknown.

The major part of the day is spent in grazing or resting, with a midday dip, an almost unvarying routine, especially in the hot season. The necessity of water in adequate quantity is, therefore, a restrictive factor in the wild buffalo's movements and habitat selections.

In an economy-conscious world where even a living being has to have a price-tag attached to it to be of "value" to a decision-maker, the wild buffalo is genetically one of the most important wild animals in the world today owing to its close affinity with the most important domestic animal in Southern Asia. Yet man has allowed the wild buffalo to become one of the most threatened animals in India, and to be almost wiped out elsewhere.

PRIMATES

Classified in the same Natural Order as man, non-human primates have always excited man's interest. Hindus in the region will hardly ever assault monkeys as they are held to be sacred, and their protection is further strengthened by the Hindu legend that the monkey god Hanuman, with his monkey army, helped the divine prince Rama recapture his bride Sita.

Primates include apes, monkeys, lemurs and tree shrews. They evolved from arboreal ancestors, developing the prehensile hands and feet distinctive to them.

There are two suborders of primates: the more primitive *Prosimii* and the more advanced *Simiae*. *Prosimii* include tree shrews and lorises whose brains are not as highly developed as those of the *Simiae*. More widespread than the *Prosimii*, the *Simiae* include the many types of monkeys and one species of lesser apes found in the Indian subcontinent. They are mainly diurnal and arboreal, though some species spend a considerable amount of time on the ground.

Most primates are essentially vegetarian. Some are exclusively so, while others add animal food, such as insects, crabs, mollusks, birds, birds' eggs and even mammals, to their vegetable diet. A macaque, which can be distinguished from a langur by its sturdy, squat and solid build, has cheek pouches to store food which cannot be consumed immediately. The langur, by contrast, is tall, slim and stately, and has a special pouch in its stomach which serves the same purpose. Apes, tree shrews and lemurs eat whenever food is available.

While most *Simiae* primates are social animals living in troops of up to a hundred individuals and are to be found almost throughout the subcontinent, thriving in tropical conditions, tree shrews and and lorises are found only south of the Ganga and in eastern India. Of the 21 species of primates found in the subcontinent, including Sri Lanka and the Andaman and Nichobar Islands in the Bay of Bengal, there are three types of tree shrew and two species of loris. The former, until recently classified as insectivores, are the smallest of all primates and though in appearance tree shrews resemble squirrels, there is little of the squirrel in their habits.

Shrews: The **Madras tree shrew** (*Anathana ellioti*) is a small, rat-sized, squirrel-like animal which has prehensile hands and feet. Reddish-brown to gray-brown in color, it has a bushy tail and a pale oblique shoulder stripe. Well-distributed south of the Ganga, it lives on trees in tropical rain forests and thorny jungles. It is diurnal and catches insects on the ground, but it also feeds on fruit and often takes to the trees as a means of escape. It is easily tamed and is commonly kept as a pet in southern India.

In the northeast, the **common tree shrew** (*Tupaia glis*) extends its range across Sikkim, Assam and Manipur. Similar to the Madras tree shrew, it has short ears and a bushy tail. Its dorsal parts and tail are brown to reddish-brown, speckled or grizzled. The ventral parts are buff to brown, and there is a pale stripe just in front of the shoulders. Two subspecies are found in India, one in thick rain forest and mountain jungle, the other in bamboo bushes and trees near human

dwellings.

Though expert climbers, common tree shrews do not leap from tree to tree as squirrels do, nor do they jerk their tails or cling head downwards on tree trunks. Instead, they spend a considerable amount of time nosing for food among fallen leaves and in rock crevices. They eat fruit and also small mammals and birds. Found in pairs, they are more sociable than their peninsular cousins, and as many as five tree shrews have been observed together. Of the third species, the **Nicobar tree shrew** (*Tupaia nicobarica*), very little is known. It has a long tail, and its ventral parts are a pale brown, the dorsal part is brownish-black while the head and limbs are brown. Two different subspecies are found, in the Great and the Little Nicobar Islands.

Lorises: Two subspecies of Loris are the only primate species in this part of the world which are nocturnal. The **slender loris** (*Loris tardigradus*) is found in Sri Lanka and southern India, while the **slow loris** (*Nycticebus coucang*) prefers the densest parts of tropical rain forests in eastern India.

The slender loris is a small, thin and lanky creature with long slender limbs. Its body is well-furred, with a dark-gray, reddish-brown back. It has a white muzzle and huge, round eyes enclosed in a black or dark-brown circle. Though it has the same secretive and nocturnal habits as the slow loris, it is not confined to dense jungles and is found both in tropical rain forest and in more open woodland and swampy coastal forest. Usually found singly or in pairs, it sleeps through the day in shady, inaccessible places — in the hollow of a tree or at the leafy extremity of a branch, rolled up in a tight ball, with its head between its legs and grasping its perch with its arms.

The slow loris also sleeps through the day, rolled up in a ball, but during hot weather it stretches out on a branch. Its diet includes shoots, fruit, insects, reptiles and birds, in fact anything it can lay its "hands" on. True to its name, the slow loris is very deliberate in its movements. When hunting insects it never springs, but catches them with a sudden lunge, never letting go of the branch on which it maintains a tenacious grip. Unlike the solitary slender loris, the slow loris is found in small family groups. In appearance it is less lanky, with a brown streak on its crown and dark markings on its pale brown face.

Macaques: Few people, if any, would need an introduction to either the macaque or the langur. While some of the species are commonly seen around temples, bazars, villages and even railway stations, others live in isolated pockets in some of the most inaccessible areas.

Of the three types of monkeys found in the region, the macaques are the largest family, being represented by eight species. Northeast India is the home of some of the rarest macaque species, such as the **stump-tailed macaque** (*Macaca arctoides*), which is found in the hilly forests of Assam, Arunachal Pradesh and Nagaland. Its fur is dark chestnut and shaggy. Its forehead is bald with only crown hairs radiating from the center, short in front, longer at the back and on the sides. Its face is pinkish; its buttocks and genitalia

Preceding pages: monsoon in Nepal terai; and spotted deer in Wilpattu, Sri Lanka. *Left,* the rhesus macaque, common throughout North India and *above,* black-faced langur. *Right,* the rare lion-tailed macaque found in the South Indian hills; *far right,* the golden langur confined to a small pocket on the Assam-Bhutan border.

reddish. As among all other macaques, the sexes are alike, though the male is sometimes heavier and bigger.

The stump-tailed macaque is fairly terrestrial but does spend a lot of time in trees as well. Just before daybreak, troops of up to 30 individuals head for their feeding grounds, and if there

are any *ficus* trees with ripe fruit, they will almost certainly be found there. They rarely stray far from their feeding trees. In the afternoons, they rest or groom themselves, before feeding again and returning to their resting trees. Though extremely noisy while feeding, they have been known to raid village fields in absolute silence. They are relatively unafraid of man. In fact, Naga tribals are said to be afraid of them, for they can be terribly pugnacious when it comes to giving up a field they are feeding on. They use their hands to carry food to their mouth, and after filling their cheek pouches, again use the flat of the hand to press their cheeks to bring food back into the mouth.

The **pig-tailed macaque** (*Macaca nemestrina*) inhabits the same forests as its stump-tailed relative, but it is more arboreal and keeps strictly

to dense evergreen forests. It is one of the largest of the genus, with long legs and an elongated muzzle. Its face is bare, light brown, and its crown hairs are short, radiating from a central whorl and forming a thick cover of erect hairs. The body color varies; the dorsal parts are grayish-olive to russet (with a buff to yellow tinge in places) while the forehead and crown are darker; the ventral parts are mostly grayish while the lower abdomen is slightly reddish. The face and hindquarters are pinkish-brown and the tail is short, dark reddish-brown on top and carried half-erect like a pig's tail.

The pig-tailed macaque is one of the few monkey species found in the subcontinent which faces a threat from human poachers. Its meat is sought after by certain Naga tribes and it is also in great demand in Southeast Asia for "coconut picking" — the monkey is sent up the tall palms to pick the fruit. Shy of man, it abandons the trees and tries to flee from any threat by running on the ground. Because of its wariness, attempts to obtain reliable estimates of its declining population have been unsuccessful.

The **Assamese macaque** (*Macaca assamensis*) gets its name from Assam, but its habitat is not confined to the northeast. Its range starts from as far west as Mussoorie in Uttar Pradesh and moves eastwards to the hill ranges of Assam and the forests of the Sunderbans in the Ganga delta. It is relatively large, with a pendulous well-haired tail, which is anywhere from a third to a half of the head and body length. The face is pale and flesh-colored with four or five deep diagonal wrinkles. The body fur is felted, and the crown hair is as if brushed back. The Assamese macaque, like the pig-tailed variety is also hunted for its meat, but to a lesser extent.

Large troops of this macaque are not uncommon, often seeking strength in numbers, and sometimes large troops gang up to raid crops. They are particularly abundant in the valleys around Darjeeling and a troop can sometimes consist of over a hundred individuals, moving around in the forests like a ghost army. They prefer hilly areas and dense jungles, and by and large prefer to keep their distance from humans; and like most macaques display an amazing indifference to humans unless molested.

The **long-tailed macaque** (*Macaca fascicularis*) is really a Burmese monkey, and but for its existence in the Nicobar Islands, it can hardly be described as an Indian animal.

The Ubiquitous Rhesus: Perhaps the best known macaque in India is the **rhesus macaque** (*Macaca mulatta*) which lives in a variety of habitats, including cities, villages, farms, forests and mountains. It inhabits the semi-desert forests of Rajasthan, the swamps and mangroves of the Sunderbans, and extends across to Burma in the east. It is at home in trees, or on the ground, and equally at ease sitting on a temple roof or a tin shed in a railway depot. Devoid of fear of humans, it often grabs food from unwary pilgrims. The origin of its commensalism is not clear and it is also not known if commensal groups differ from wild populations morphologically.

The rhesus has the usual squat, thickset build of a macaque. The hairs on its crown radiate backwards from the forehead without the neat center parting which marks its relative, the macaque of southern India. Its body is olive-brown, with orange-red fur on its loins and rump which distinguishes it from all other Indian monkeys. Almost throughout its range, the rhesus is free from human molestation, but its capture for scientific research has affected its status.

Rhesus macaques live in highly organized troops, the largest of which are found in the plains where over a hundred individuals coexist under the leadership of a dominant male. In very large troops, smaller subgroups are formed, each under a male, and a clear-cut social order exists within the troop. The relationship between adult males ranges from peaceful and even cooperative to highly antagonistic, while females are quite tolerant of each other. Grooming forms a major part of their daily activities, but it is the relationships of juveniles which is most fascinating. Little play-groups of three to four young individuals display a natural exuberance rarely seen in other animals.

Southern Cousins: Almost as if a line had been drawn across the subcontinent by some unseen

of highly dominant males who collaborate when necessary. In a highly defined social setup, the fluctuations of a male's status depends on various factors. In an instance where a dominant male once broke a canine, he kept his mouth shut as long as he could, but once the secret was out, the other males set upon him and considerably reduced his status.

Further south, in Sri Lanka, the **toque macaque** (*Macaca sinica*) replaces the bonnet macaque. Among the smallest of regional macaques, it has a gray face which is reddish in the case of mature females. The dorsal parts are gray to ocher, brown or red, while the limbs are a lot paler, the ventral parts being almost whitish. The crown hairs form a central whorl or a cap; and the tail, longer than the head and body, has a black tinge. Though there are three subspecies

striking black body. it has a tail almost two-thirds the length of its head and body, with a small tuft at the end which is very pronounced in the case of adult males and from which the macaque gets its common name. It is perhaps the most arboreal of all macaques, normally remaining at the top of the forest canopy. Because of its shy nature, black color, and its habit of living in dense, dimly lit, lonely forests, it is rarely seen. Found in the dense forests of peninsular India, it is most commonly found in the Western Ghats, the Nilgiri, Anaimalai and Cardamom Hills and also in the vicinity of Periyar Lake in Kerala.

Until recently, the lion-tailed macaque was considered to be highly endangered, but the discovery of a large population in the rain forests of Karnataka has tripled the estimate of its numbers. Information on this macaque is still

in India and Sri Lanka. It has a glossy black body and the back of its head is yellowish-brown with a brown crown. Females differ from males slightly in that they have a white patch on the insides of their thighs. It generally inhabits the *sholas* (woods of the plateau, strips of forest surrounded by grassland, usually with a stream running through) of the Western Ghats south of Coorg, and the Nilgiri, Anaimalai, Brahmagiri and Palni Hills. Though essentially arboreal in the Nilgiri, it can often be seen crossing the grassland, from one *shola* to another. Destruction of its habitat has threatened the very existence of the Nilgiri langur. Troops are sometimes quite large, with as many as 30 animals. They travel over a well-worn route, each individual stepping in exactly the same spot as the leader. Though shy of humans, they

hand, the rhesus macaque of northern India is replaced by another pale-faced monkey commonly seen with strolling showmen in southern India. The **bonnet macaque** (*Macaca radiata*) is similar to its cousin, the rhesus, except for the reddish rump and long dark hairs which radiate in all directions from a whorl on its crown. Found near villages and in jungles, it is particularly fond of *ficus* trees, and where there are two or more banyan trees and water, the chances of finding a troop of 20 to 30 animals are quite high.

Found more or less throughout southern India, troops of bonnet macaques living in the jungles are quite shy, but those which are quartered near human settlements lose all fear of man. The troops are controlled by a central core

recognized, all are confined to Sri Lanka, and its range overlaps that of the Hanuman langur. Sometimes the two intermix, but it is always the macaques which dominate and they spend time grooming the larger langurs.

The toque macaque is found in jungles in low, dry areas, and in wet zones from high elevations to the seashore and lower hills. A troop consists of up to two dozen animals, and it is most active during the day, feeding and moving along the tree-tops. The toque, when frightened, will shelter behind foliage and it lives in constant dread of leopards, pythons and even crocodiles.

In the south, there is yet another macaque: the **lion-tailed macaque** (*Macaca silenus*), which can be distinguished from other macaques by its long, gray or brownish mane around its face and its

relatively sparse, but it *is* known to share its habitat with three other primates. While the bonnet macaque avoids a confrontation, there have been reports of ferocious battles being fought with the only other black colored primate — the Nilgiri langur (see below) — with both sides suffering severe casualties. The lion-tailed macaque are very deliberate in their movements, and when crossing from tree to tree, they avoid jumping, but descend to the ground and walk across in single file. A troop usually consists of 10 to 20 individuals, and the females usually outnumber the males.

Langurs: Every morning, at dawn, the rain forests of Periyar Tiger Reserve echo to the deep booming of the **Nilgiri langur** (*Presbytis johnii*), which is among the five langur species recorded

Left, gray capped langur, Sri Lanka and *above*, the capped langur, forest dwellers in northeastern India.

sometimes raid plantations but, by and large, they are fairly elusive.

In Sri Lanka, the **purple-faced langur** (*Presbytis senex*) takes the place of the Nilgiri langur, both of whom share a common geographic distribution with the Hanuman langur. Brownish-black in color, with a lighter crown and nape, its whiskers are almost white, and they sweep backwards to cover the ears. The throat and chin are white and the tip of the tail is a pale brown.

There are four subspecies, all of which are

found in Sri Lanka, and its habitat includes wet forests, as well as parkland and dense montane cloud forests invaded by grassland. It is both arboreal and ground-dwelling, and on broken ground it can be seen walking around on boulders. A forest-dwelling animal, it is fearless when not molested by humans, and it is exclusively vegetarian, feeding on new leaves, flowers and fruit. There is no marked dominance hierarchy with any animal of either sex taking on the role of leader, but the male usually tries to herd his females, and may exercise a peace-keeping function. Troops are small, not exceeding 10 to 15 animals, and sometimes one finds an all-male group.

The range of the **Hanuman langur** (*Presbytis entellus*) stretches north and then east to encompass almost the entire subcontinent. Represented

warning system" against the tiger and the leopard, both of which it hates without reservation. Consequently, it has developed an effective relationship with deer, and chital can often be seen feeding under a tree inhabited by langurs. Both species react to each other's alarm calls, and nine times out of 10, langur and chital alarm calls lead to a tiger or leopard sighting. The langur live in large troops and their diet includes some of the (for many creatures) most poisonous leaves, which are avoided even by insects. They can also be seen sitting on the ground, eating mud from which they get the required salt intake. They are territorial, but rarely does a group fight to defend its ground.

In 1907, reports of a cream-colored langur came in from the east bank of the Sankosh river, near the India-Bhutan border, but it was only in

animal which leaps from tree to tree at the approach of humans. A troop can have as many as 40 animals, and the movements are controlled by a dominant male who moves first, followed by the rest. Juveniles make a shrill, nervous, whistling sound before jumping, but otherwise they move and feed in relative silence.

The range of the **capped langur** (*Presbytis pileatus*) extends further east from Manas, covering northern Assam, Arunachal Pradesh and parts of Bangladesh. A large, colorful monkey, it has a black face and head with sharply contrasting paler cheeks suffused with red. The dorsal color is gray to blackish-gray and the distal half of the tail too is black. The ventral parts are a brownish-yellow or orange, while the insides of the thighs and the hindquarters are tinged with light cobalt-blue, this tinge being more prominent

here cannot be dismissed.

Finally, among the Indian primates are the lesser apes, though represented by only one species, the **Hoolock gibbon** (*Hylobates hoolock*), which is found in the rain forests of Arunachal Pradesh, Assam and parts of Nagaland. When standing erect, it reaches just under three feet. It has small legs on which it runs, sometimes along the boughs of trees, but usually it prefers swinging from branch to branch, using its grotesquely long arms. Adult males are dark brown while adult females are blonde. Young males and females are black with a silvery white band above the eyebrows.

The Hoolock gibbon's habits in the wild are relatively unknown. Each group is usually a family, with each adult male having a single female consort. It feeds on fruit, leaves, young

· ·
***Above*, toque macaque, Sri Lanka and *right*, Hoolock gibbon is the only ape found in India.**

by 16 subspecies, it can be found above the snow line in Kashmir, in Sri Lanka in the south, Rajasthan in the west and right across to Burma in the east. It is a large, black-faced, gray-bodied langur with long limbs and a tail which is longer than its head and body. Indifferent to man if left alone, it will retreat quickly if threatened, but, on the other hand, Hanuman langurs living near temples are known to mob pilgrims, panicking them into parting with their food.

In the wild the Hanuman langur's keen eyesight makes it an effective part of an "early

1953 that the tea planter-naturalist, E.P. Gee, came forward with any real evidence of the **golden langur** (*Presbytis geei*) as it was subsequently named. It has a cream back which looks golden in good light, darker sides and a black face with no sign of any hair. It has a long tail with a tassel at the end. In winter the langur looks a lot more golden than it does in summer when its coat looks almost white or creamish.

The golden langur is a highly arboreal species, descending to the ground only during the early hours of the morning or late in the evening to drink from a river or a stream. It lives in dense, tropical deciduous forests, and is exclusively vegetarian. Its range extends over south-central Bhutan and northwestern Assam. Easily seen on the Bhutan side of the Manas river, it is a shy

in adult males.

Little is known of the habits of the capped langur, but they prefer dry tropical forests and dense evergreen jungles. Only during the dry season do they leave the sanctuary of the trees to drink. They are extremely shy, either taking flight through the trees or sitting absolutely still when approached. Left alone, they are noisy animals, and very often it's the *whoosh* of a branch bending under their weight as they leap, that gives them away.

Yet another species of langur, the **silver leaf monkey** (*Presbytis cristatus*), is found mainly in southern Burma, but may also extend its range into Tripura and Bangladesh. However, no record of it has been made in the subcontinent in recent years, but the possibility of its existence

shoots and birds, and is known to have a special liking for spiders. The Namdapha Tiger Reserve in Arunachal Pradesh is probably one of the best areas in which to look for gibbons. Their loud whooping early in the morning sounds more like a bunch of boisterous schoolboys at an afternoon tea party.

But the gibbon, like many of its order, is also facing a stiff challenge to its survival, as pressure for land and timber mounts. So far, primates in the region have been lucky, living under a religious umbrella, as it were. But, as traditional protection afforded by religious belief in their sacredness wanes, the future, not only of the Hoolock gibbon, the langurs and the macaques, but also that of the lesser primates, will be increasingly threatened.

Stories like "Red Riding Hood" are something we grow out of, but how many of us actually forget them? The little girl, the granny and the wolf . . . it all comes flooding back and in the mind's eye, one can picture the scene in the cottage so easily — the large ears, the fangs and everything else that goes with the "big, bad, wolf"! Not surprisingly then, most women in Bihar even today keep the children home with stories of the wolf, for even the tiger does not command the respect most *Canidae* do.

The Dog Family: In India, the *Canidae* (as the dog family is known) are among the most widely distributed of all beasts of prey. A near relative, the **striped hyena**, is mainly a scavenger by habit, but will on occasion, attack an animal if it can be overcome easily. Unlike the cat family, the paws are tipped with nails which are non-retractile, and this is one of the characteristics which points to a relationship between dogs and bears. To find any further resemblance, one would have to go back to the fossil remains of primitive animal forms which suggest a common ancestral stock. The different modes of life adopted by their forebears led to differences in structure and habits which are now so apparent in the two families. While the progenitors of the wolves, jackals, foxes and dogs became hunters who took their prey by swift and enduring chase, the ancient bears probably lived as they live now — feeding on grasses, roots, herbs, fruits and insects. Yet the bears still retain the ability to kill for food, and a bear will eat meat whenever an opportunity is offered.

The *Canidae* are among the most efficient predators in the world — with the exception of the jackal which lives mainly off carrion — and their physical evolution has built them into perfect killing machines.

A long pointed muzzle with large erect ears, a well-shaped head, deep-chested muscular body and a bushy tail enable them to secure prey by swift and open chase. The feet are equipped with five toes, including the dew-claws, and the toes, resting on deep, well-cushioned pads, are held close together by elastic-rimmed webs. *Canidae* do not rely on their feet for striking at their prey, or even gripping it — their feet are designed solely with one specific purpose — to follow prey over hard ground. Besides the ability to outlast their prey over a large distance for which their lungs are well developed, the main weapon for attack is the powerful set of teeth set in powerful jaws which allows for a tenacity of hold that is their mainstay in attack. With a few exceptions, most dogs have a great array of 42 teeth and a powerful set of cheek muscles gives them a vice-like grip. Interlocking canines and incisors form formidable weapons for seizing or lacerating live prey, and the latter are well adapted for biting, gnawing, or stripping the skin from flesh. Further, their cheek teeth also adapt them to a vegetable diet, for meat eaters as a rule, *Canidae* also live off grass, herbs and fruit.

The dog family is among the most diversely distributed species throughout the world. The animals found in the subcontinent do not differ in essential habits from their cousins in other parts of the globe, the marked difference being only in size and local coloration. Food habits also depend largely on local conditions, as do the number of animals living in a pack. It is a well recorded fact that a pack of wild dogs living in a certain area will sometimes swell, then decline again leaving a more or less constant population. Food relationships within the pack are a complex business, and any undue increase or decline in the number of any one species affects the lives of many others.

A highly developed sense of smell and keen eyesight are two of the most prized assets of the dog family. All are nocturnal, though most kills are made either in the late afternoon or at dusk, leaving people to argue about their nocturnal habits. Within their own packs, they have an advanced communication system; **dholes**, as wild dogs are known in India, communicate with each other by whistling, and the pack will usually set a perfect ambush, meeting with a higher rate of success than some of the better known carnivores. For foxes and other animals which do not live in packs, the prey is usually rodents and small animals. For them, their speed is more a method of escape, though in the case of jackals, wolves and even hyenas, "play dead" is yet another method of escape.

The Dogged Hunter: The dhole, or the **Indian wild dog** (*Cuon alpinus*), is perhaps the most widely distributed of all species. Three races are known to us, a trans-Himalayan race which are paler, the deeper red species of the Himalaya and the tawnier peninsular form. Their range in India starts from Ladakh where they are said to hunt wild sheep and goats. In the lower reaches they inhabit forested areas. They prefer hunting by day, though on rare occasions they will hunt at night also. Like wolves, they too hunt in packs which are usually family groups, the social life originating from a prolonged association between parents and young.

Once on the trail of the unfortunate victim, their prey is followed by scent in silence, though in heavy cover the yaps of the leader indicate the

line of approach. Once the animal is in visual contact, the pack often breaks out into excited whimpering and yapping, panicking the herd ahead to stampede. In the chaos that follows, an individual is guided away from the main body and then brought down ruthlessly. Large packs are known to have taken on animals like the gaur and the buffalo, and records of tigers being killed by dholes also exist. The tiger is not hunted by dholes, a battle usually taking place more out of a chance encounter than anything else.

Until a decade ago, accused of killing more than they could eat, wild dogs were considered vermin and many state governments offered cash incentives to hunters to wipe them out. Shikaris of yesteryear often talked of an absolute "stillness" that would set in in their shooting blocks when dholes appeared. "You might as well

Big and Bad?: The **Indian wolf** (*Canis lupus*), unlike the dhole, is not often seen as its habitat has suffered adversely at the hands of man. Its range extends from Ladakh and Kashmir, into the desert zone and the dry open plains of peninsular India. Found more in the bare and open regions, the wolf has often come into conflict with humans for it is not averse to attacking livestock. In Bihar's Hazaribagh district and in Karnataka, wolves have occasionally taken to man-eating, lifting small children of up to 12 years of age from their homes. It is perhaps interesting to note that in the Hazaribagh Gazetteer published in 1910, the government then offered Rs 50 to anyone killing a man-eating wolf which was twice the amount offered for a man-eating tiger.

Camp Followers: The long-drawn, eerie howling of the **jackal** (*Canis aureus*) at dusk or just before dawn is perhaps more familiar to most people than the animal itself. Three races occur, and it is found throughout India and Sri Lanka. Its closest relative is the wolf, but it is much smaller in build, and lacks the arching brows and elevated forehead which give the wolf a noble look. The Himalayan jackal has a slightly darker coat, but by and large they are pale and tawny with a bit of white and black around the shoulders, ears and legs.

Perhaps the most nocturnal of all *Canidae*, jackals usually come out as dusk creeps across the subcontinent. On a cloudy day, they will sometimes come out earlier, and in very hot weather, they may make a daytime trip to a water hole.

superb bush, with the black of its back continuing to the upper half of its ears, and the white tip to its tail distinguish it from the Indian fox of the plains. Red is the dominant color of its lovely coat though local variations from gray to yellow occur.

Three races are recognized in India; the **hill fox** of the Himalaya which ranges from Ladakh and Kashmir to Sikkim; a northern desert subspecies and the western desert **whitefooted fox** which ranges from Rajasthan to Kutch.

Red foxes are said to pair for life and they occupy the same den year after year. They live in thorn bushes and willows fringing the edges of streams and are sometimes found in cultivated areas.

They occasionally venture out during the day but usually hunt at night, generally alone or at

go home," one would often be told; but of late, dholes have often been observed close to a potential prey-species, both seemingly unconcerned by the other's presence. On the other hand a herd of over 300 chital has been observed to run blindly through a human habitation when wild dogs appeared. Maybe, both the hunter and the hunted know when the former is on the

• •

Left, the much-maligned wolf is now a rare sight. *Above*, an inquisitive desert fox and *right*, a hill fox in Kashmir.

Its size, large skull and teeth distinguish the wolf from the rest of the family. Animals from the plains of India have sandy fawn coats stippled with black. The wolves from Ladakh have blackish coats, and their winter coats are variegated with long, black and white or black and buff underwool.

In the Indian desert they shelter from the heat in burrows dug in the sand dunes, or they remain above ground, lying up in fields or patches of scrub and thorn forest. Their diet depends mainly on local conditions — they will hunt wild goats, sheep and deer, but will also live off rodents during the lean periods. Their shrinking habitat in most parts of the country and the constant conflict with man has reduced their numbers dramatically.

Kalighati watchtower in Rajasthan's Sariska Tiger Reserve is an excellent place to observe these animals, of which very little is known. In jungle terms they are referred to as "camp followers" and tales of the jackal following meekly in the wake of the lord and master of the Indian jungle, the tiger, are common to Indian folklore. Jackals play an important role in clearing carcasses and offal, but they sometimes gang up into a pack and attack deer fawns or antelope in a manner similar to that of dhole. They also feed on fruit and some vegetables, and prefer to live around towns and villages, contributing in a large way to village sanitation.

Wily Elegance: The richly colored fox of the Himalaya, the **red fox** (*Vulpes vulpes*) is one of the most attractive animals. Its long silky fur and

the most with a mate. They prey chiefly on rodents which include squirrels, and they also take a toll of ground birds, like the chukor, partridges and pheasants. In winter, driven by hunger, they will sometimes raid human habitations for food, picking up offal and other tidbits of food.

The **Indian fox** (*Vulpes bengalensis*) is the common fox of the Indian plains, smaller and more slender than the red fox. Its tail has a black tip and its ears are not black as those of the red fox. Its coat too is never as luxuriant, and the general or dominant color is gray. It ranges through the entire country, from the foothills of the Himalaya to Cape Comorin. It will sometimes attack poultry, and feed off rodents and insects, shrubs and berries. It will gobble up emerging termites as they take to the wing, and by its constant destruction of rats and other pests, it is of great value to the farmer. It rarely enters forested areas, preferring the cultivated areas near a canal, using a bund to live in. Its main defense is its speed and nimble turning ability — it will also double back on its own tracks to throw trackers off balance.

Ungainly Scavenger: The build of a hyena and its dog-like appearance would suggest it to be part of the *Canidae*. Its legs and feet are similar to those of a dog but the structure of the skull, the teeth and other points in the anatomy of the animal would place it in the cat family. A sort of a link between the two orders, the hyena at first sight looks like an ungainly dog. A scavenger by nature, it seeks food entirely by smell, its sight and hearing being almost defunct. It too is a

mestic dogs and it often resorts to "playing dead" to get away, for its persecutors lose interest in a seemingly lifeless body. It is famous for its laughing chatter, and though some photographs and notes have been taken of its denning behavior recently, little else is known about these animals. Supposedly common, they are rarely seen mainly because of their nocturnal habits, and they too have been reported to indulge in man-eating, snatching babies occasionally from the doorways of houses.

Big Climbers: If the hyena resembles a dog in its physical appearance, a bear has little of the physical characteristics which make the dogs deadly predators.

It has massive limbs which are more suited for climbing than for running and it uses its huge claws to grasp branches and to dig for roots. It

and it has a V-shaped breast patch. Its range extends from the base of the Himalaya to the forested tracts of Assam, down to Sri Lanka. It prefers areas with cover and rocky outcrops to shelter in, and it usually emerges at dusk to feed through the night.

During the monsoon a sloth relies heavily on an insect diet, and to see it attacking a termite mound with the accompanying sound effects is a sight one can rarely forget. Sloths living around human settlements seem to delight in raiding maize crops and sugarcane. Where date palms are tapped, they climb trees to attack the toddy. The sloth is the common performing bear used by wandering gypsies for roadside shows. Usually quick to run away when threatened, a female with cubs is a dangerous proposition for she gets extremely hostile and savage.

brown bear. A "yeti scalp" in one of the monasteries of Nepal proved to be that of a brown bear. The Tibetan blue bear is also reported from the same area, but this animal is an almost unknown species.

Finally, in the lower reaches of the Himalaya is found the **Himalayan black bear** (*Selenarctos thibetanus*) which is almost jet black in color with the typical V-shaped mark on its breast. Found in Kashmir and in Assam, it favors steep forested slopes and can be found up to 12,000 feet (3600 meters), which is the limit of the snow line, or as low as the *terai* jungles. It is nocturnal, but is surprisingly active by day in Kashmir's Dachigam National Park. It attacks if surprised and many people have been mauled and killed.

Himalayan black bear prefer fruit for a diet and in October, when the oak flowers in

camp follower, but gets to the kill after the vultures and jackals have had their fill, feeding mainly on bones and coarse remains—its powerful jaws being perfectly adapted for bone crushing.

In the subcontinent, the **striped hyena** (*Hyaena hyaena*) extends its range through forested districts, open country and ravines. Often a hyena will enlarge a porcupine burrow where it lies through the day, foraging for food almost exclusively by night. In search of food a hyena will tramp along with its awkward, ambling gait and once it has located a kill, it will stand its ground to hold it against even the rightful owner. No match for the tiger, it is known to have often taken on a panther successfully. It is otherwise a shy animal, avoiding a confrontation with do-

feeds on roots, insects and will feed on carrion if an opportunity presents itself. It has an extremely poor range of vision and its hearing isn't too sharp either. It has a large, thickset head with small eyes and rounded ears and a tail so small it is barely noticed. Even among the bears, each species has different powers of scent and sight, a brown bear being able to pick up the wind-borne smell of humans a mile off while the sloth is notoriously short-scented. Dull in all other senses except the sense of smell, bears are, not surprisingly, usually relaxed and, at first appearance, easygoing.

The **sloth bear** (*Melursus ursinus*) is a shaggy creature with long unkempt hair and squat hind legs, its long muzzle and lower lip giving it an uncouth look. The tip of the muzzle is dirty white

The **brown bear** (*Ursus arctos*) is of a much heavier build and its brown coat distinguishes it from the Himalayan black bear. The bare open meadows above the tree line in the Himalaya is the home of this bear. It hibernates during the cold winter months in caves on the rocky slopes. It spends much of its time looking for insects under rocks and will stalk voles and marmots, which it digs out of their burrows. Shortage of food at these altitudes drives it to eat carrion, and in Zanskar a brown bear was once seen fighting off Tibetan ravens while it fed on an ibex which had died earlier of natural causes.

Brown bears have never been known to attack humans, but it can be disastrous if one of them gets into a sheep pen. Reports of the yeti in the Himalaya have been attributed to sightings of the

· ·
Left, dholes or wild dogs are amongst the most efficient hunters in the wild and *above*, the striped hyena is distributed throughout India.

Dachigam, they are literally all over the place —sometimes a two–three mile walk yields almost a dozen animals. They climb trees with great ease, and have a strange technique of climbing down — carefully making their descent until a few feet are left, then landing with a thump as they seem to lose interest. Sometimes, cubs stay with the mother, which explains small parties of three or four, otherwise these bears are solitary, sleeping in rocky nests and hollows of trees. The black bear found in Assam is marginally smaller, and a good population of these animals still exists.

Bears: It comes as a surprise to many that bears and dogs come from the same ancestral stock. Neither their appearance, nor their habits, show any close affinity. Yet, fossilized remains reveal a close relationship. The explanation for the subsequent differentiation could lie in the fact that dogs became hunters and therefore developed the necessary lines and limbs to help swift movement, whereas bears probably lived, as they do now, on insects, termites, roots, fruits and honey, and therefore developed heavy bodies and strong paws to facilitate digging and climbing of rocks, cliffs and trees.

In general, bears have large heads, unusually small eyes and round ears. Their large bodies and heavy limbs are covered by a shaggy coat. They have very short tails. Their prime sense is that of smell. Their senses of touch, sight and hearing not being well developed, bears can very often be taken by surprise. In such situations their reactions are unpredictable and bears are often known to attack even when approached gently.

Bears lumber along with a shuffling gait and walk miles every day in search of food. When frightened or alarmed, they can gallop at a fast though clumsy pace. All bears are good swimmers. It is interesting to note that their footprints are very similar to those of man.

Bears find much of their food on the ground or just below the surface. Their long, curving claws, longer in the forefeet, are well-adapted for digging. Their mobile, protruding lips are used to suck up termites from their deep galleries. Their padded feet and inward-turned forepaws are suitable for climbing. The belief that bears are vegetarian is mistaken; they eat a varied diet, occasionally including animal flesh. Another popular misconception is that bears kill by hugging their victims. Actually, they usually swat the enemy with a swinging arm blow, like a boxer's "hook," and digging claws deep, they scalp the victim and then disappear as quickly as they can.

Some types of bear hibernate during winter to avoid the cold, but more often it is a means of surviving a period of extreme shortage of food. The heart action is reduced almost to a standstill and all body functions are suspended. No energy is expended and, therefore, no food is required. With the coming of spring, bears emerge from hibernation in good health.

. . . .

Left, **the handsome red panda is distributed throughout the eastern Himalaya and** *right,* **one of the several species of squirrel.**

The **sloth bear** (*Melursus ursinus*) has inhabited the subcontinent from very early times. Bear fossils have been found here. Originally confused with the sloth, scientists have now classified it under a separate genus in view of differences in skull structure and the fact that the two middle incisors are missing in the upper jaw of the sloth bear.

Though widely distributed over India and Sri Lanka, this bear, oddly enough, does not extend east of Assam.

The animal is four–five feet (120–150 cm) in height and weighs an average 250 lb (115 kg).

With its shaggy, dusty-looking black fur, it looks somewhat uncouth. It has a V-shaped patch of white on its chest, which is a distinguishing feature. To add to its untidy appearance, it has a mangy-looking face, round eyes with hairless lids, and a long, dull-gray snout with protruding, pendulous lips. Its bowed forelegs with inward-turned forefeet make it a specially good climber. For no apparent reason, the tall *Terminalia arjuna* is its favorite tree. Claw marks on trunks and branches are proof of this. The long, four-inch (10-cm) ivory-white claws on its forefeet are perfect digging implements. Large and muscular, a sloth bear has great power and vitality packed into its huge body.

The sloth bear is mainly nocturnal, spending most of the night rummaging for food. It can

smell buried food and can be seen digging furiously to get at even one tasty grub. It is very intelligent and remembers the seasons and places where its favorite food is found. Wild fig, jambul, ber, bael, mohwa, amaltas and ebony fruit are all well-liked. Small groups of sloth bear have been seen seemingly drunk on the heady fermented juice of mohwa flowers. It has a very clever way of grabbing honeycombs. In the darkness, it climbs a tree on which honeycombs hang and knocks down a single comb with a firm swipe of the paw, probably realizing that it cannot manage more than one at a time. The bees, confused in the darkness, buzz around the branch or settle on other combs, while the bear happily sucks the honey and eats the grubs in the comb that has fallen to the ground.

Termite-hunting is a bear's major occupation.

the cubs on her back and looks after them till they are two or three years old. Male bears move away from the group and lead a solitary existence.

Sloth bears are hunted for their fur and their gall bladder, which is said to have medicinal properties. They are also captured and trained to perform. It was only early in the 20th Century that man took to hunting the sloth bear. Before that they were to be seen in immense numbers.

The **Himalayan brown bear** (*Ursus arctos*) is seen in different sizes but all are of a heavy build. An average male can measure 5′ 8″ (170 cm) in length. The coat varies from a rich dark-brown in summer, to a tawny, worn-out brown in old animals. Its white-tipped fur sometimes gives it a silvery sheen. It has a heavy underwool during winter. It lives in the cold north temperate zone in

nent V-shaped patch of white or yellow is seen on the breast. Found in Kashmir, the Himalaya and Assam, this bear lives below the tree line, around 12,000 feet (3660 meters). In winter it comes down to 5000 feet (1525 meters). It is a good climber and gets most of its food off fruit trees. Pears, apricots, berries, honey, corn, insects, termites and larvae of beetles, make up its varied diet, but sheep, goats and even larger cattle are attacked and eaten by this nocturnal predator. It attacks and mauls even human beings in self defense.

The mating season is in late autumn. Two cubs are produced near spring. They remain with the mother for a year or two. Bears are sometimes seen with four cubs. These must belong to two successive litters.

Pandas: Although pandas resemble bears in

distinguishing feature.

Found in Nepal, Sikkim and the Eastern Himalaya, the red panda lives at altitudes above 5000 feet (1525 meters). Adept at climbing, it is arboreal and gets a good grip on branches with its well-formed toes and semi-retractable claws. Large molars, with many pointed edges for grinding food, are assets for its almost totally vegetarian diet — roots, grasses, leaves and fallen fruit. On rare occasions it will also eat eggs, grubs and insects as supplements to its normal diet.

A fine sense of smell, far better than its sight and hearing, is its main guide. When excited, a strong odor is ejected by the anal gland. A scent trail is left on trees and other surfaces to enable one panda to find another, an activity most probably linked with the mating season.

Not much is known of the red panda's

Using its powerful paws to tear down the mound, the bear reaches the termites at the bottom. It puffs and blows away the dust and sucks up the termites with great skill. Its overhanging upper lip is pressed back against the nostrils, protecting the animal from inhaling dust. As if designed for the purpose of clearing a passage for suction, there is an empty space at the point where one would expect the two middle teeth of the upper jaw to be. A concave palate facilitates the process.

The sloth bear grunts and squeals loudly while turning over stones in a stream, eating grubs and insects with its blubberous mouth. It grunts very differently when angry.

The sloth bear mates in the hot weather. Two cubs are born in the winter, after a gestation period of seven months. The mother bear carries

the higher reaches of the northwestern and central Himalaya, among the bare peaks above the tree line. It hibernates in winter and in spring lives on new grass shoots, insects, voles and marmots. Since food is scarce in its habitat it also attacks sheep, goats, ponies and livestock.

The brown bear rarely climbs and usually picks its food off the ground and digs in search of tubers and roots. Berries, wild fruit, peaches, apricots, apples, mulberries and walnuts offer a welcome change of diet. The mating season is in summer. Cubs are born in December and remain with the mother for four to five years.

The **Himalayan black bear** (*Selenarctos thibetanus*) is smaller than the brown bear. It has a smooth black coat, black claws and a brown muzzle with a white or buff lower jaw. A promi-

many ways — round heads, heavy bodies, short legs and a bear-like gait, they are classified under the order *Procyonidae*, which includes the racoon, the North-American carnivore.

The **giant panda** (*Ailuropoda melanoleuca*) which occurs in China has not been seen in India. The **smaller panda**, which resembles the giant variety, is found in India. The **red panda** or **catbear** (*Ailurus fulgens*) looks like a toy teddy-bear, with a very long tail. It has a round head, upright pointed ears and a short muzzle. It has a glandular sac near the anus. The soles of its feet are matted and hairy, as in the case of the polar bear. It is rich brown in color, with alternate brown and white rings on its bushy tail. Its face and lower lip are white and a prominent red stripe from the eyes to the nape of the neck is its

• •
Left, skulls of the tiger, mouse and the otter and *above*, Himalayan black bear occasionally feed on carrion.

breeding habits or its period of gestation. Two young are normally seen in spring. The mother, or sometimes both parents, look after the young for a year.

Pigs: Pigs, peccaries (a South America hog-like animal) and hippopotamuses form an order called *Artiodactyla*. In India only two subspecies of pig are now found — the wild boar and the pigmy hog.

Wild Boar (*Sus scrofa cristatus*): Of the six or seven species found earlier on the subcontinent, this is now the only one found in India. It is a large, heavily built animal, the male averaging 36 inches (90 cm) in height and 200 lb (90 kg) in weight, though 38-inch (95-cm) and 500-lb (225-kg) specimens are not uncommon.

The typical feature of a pig is its elongated, suddenly truncated, movable snout, ending in a flat disk-like surface supporting the nostrils. The upper canines grow upwards and outwards. These are dangerous appendages used to great advantage by the boar. The most distinct difference between the Indian boar and its European counterpart is its grayish-black coat which is very sparsely covered with hair. However, it has a fuller crest or mane of black bristles rising from the nape of its neck and running to its hind quarters. When it scents danger, this crest stands up as an impressive erect ridge of angry bristles along the back.

food — roots, tubers, insects, mollusks, offal, carrion, small mammals, and even the remains of a tiger-kill. It is also a determined crop-raider and attacks cultivated areas near the forest edge. In fact, a whole field of peanut could be uprooted by a sounder in a night, the boars digging up the roots with their snouts.

The sharpest sense in a boar is that of smell; its sight and hearing are mediocre. It is noted for its courage and determination, its self-possession, and its daring. It is one of the few animals that can stand up to a tiger. Many cases are known of tigers, despite their agility and strength, being gored to death by a ferocious boar. Bleeding and torn boars are known to have kept up the fight, showing a rare tenacity and a grim determination to survive. During the day the boar is not as self-confident as it is at night. Surprised in broad

A sow bears four to six young in a litter, after a gestation period of four months. Before the birth, she builds a comfortable shelter. With tall grass or bamboo, she lays out a circular pattern with the heavier ends on the outer edge. She then burrows below the material she has laid down thus making a chamber under a protective roof. In the snug room thus formed, she has her young and shelters them.

An abundance of pigs was once found in Indian forests. Pig-sticking and hunting have reduced their numbers. The wild pig is popular prey for those who fancy its protein-rich meat — humans, tigers, leopards, crocodiles and wild dogs attack it. Destruction of its habitat is another factor that has affected its numbers. However, in parts of Madhya Pradesh such as Bandhavgarh, sounders of up to 70 are again

the species. Rediscovered in 1971 in the *dooar* grasslands, it was later reported in southeast Bhutan, parts of Bangladesh and the Kamrup, Goalpara and Darrang districts of northern Assam. Although not seen there for many decades it may still occur in the *terai* forests of Nepal, Uttar Pradesh and Bihar. It can be seen at the Manas sanctuary.

Mongooses: These were originally classified under the civet family. However, since various distinctive features have been observed, they have now been grouped in a family by themselves, the *Herpestidae*. A long body, short limbs, a long, bushy tail, and bright beady eyes are characteristic of the mongoose. Its ears are small and form neat semi-circles close to the head. Its ear is admirably structured and consists of many folds which tightly close the opening of the ear. This is

Above, wild boar feeding on hangul carcass and *right,* long thought to be extinct, the pigmy hog was rediscovered in 1971.

An immense area covering India, Burma, Thailand, Sri Lanka and West Malaysia is the home of the boar. Scanty bush jungles, forests with clearings and grassy areas are its favorite haunts. It always lives in the proximity of water and enjoys wallowing in shallow pools but not in slush like the buffalo. It is a noisy animal and grunts loudly when it fights, and when it sharpens its tusks against tree trunks and other hard surfaces the squeak and clatter can be heard from quite a distance away.

Being omnivorous, the pig eats a variety of

daylight, it prefers to bolt. The boar's high intelligence becomes evident when it moves to new grounds, cautiously following deep *nullas* (watercourses) to avoid detection or camouflaging itself under lone palms or clumps of bushes.

Pigs do not seem to have any fixed breeding cycle. Dunbar Brander has described how in Central India he saw during the spring rut a congregation of about 170 animals that formed a circle in a forest clearing. In the arena were two master boars locked in combat, two others seemed to have just finished. In all there were 11 master-males competing quite obviously for the best sow. A notable feature of the fight was that it seemed a clean contest, governed by rules, and not just a matching of brute strength. The gathering looked on calmly.

being seen.

The **pigmy hog** (*Sus salvanius*), only 10 inches (25 cm) high, is the smallest of all pigs. Short-tailed, with small ears, short snout and upper tusks, it has a coarse, blackish-brown, scanty-haired coat. By and large, its ways are similar to those of a wild boar.

First classified by Hodgson in 1847, it lives in thinly populated savannas as well as areas with tall thatch-grass, rain forests in the tropics, and deep niches within primitive forests. It moves in groups of five to 20. It has nocturnal habits and feeds on roots, bulbs, insects and lizards.

The young appear in April–May. A litter of four is normal.

Human settlements, ruthlessly infringing on the pigmy hog's natural habitat, have endangered

probably a natural protection against the dust that is raised when the mongoose burrows into the earth.

Its strong predatory instincts make the mongoose a good hunter. It preys on hares, rats, mice, snakes, frogs, lizards, crabs and grasshoppers and is partial to birds' eggs. Roots and berries also form part of its varied diet, though it shows a strong preference for meat. Its sharp-edged, blade-like teeth are made for meat-tearing and cutting. The prey is bitten, crushed and then eaten. Sometimes, the mongoose drinks the blood of its victims. It often sucks eggs after piercing a hole in the shell.

Unlike cats, which stealthily surprise their prey, the mongoose attacks openly and directly, pouncing relentlessly on its victim. It follows its quarry by its scent and tracks it down to its burrow and digs it out. Its body seems built for the purpose, with strong forefeet and well-developed digging claws. Though it is a low-slung animal, it gains height for a quick look around by standing on its hind legs.

The mongoose has a reputation as a killer of snakes, including the deadly cobra. It is its agility that enables it to avoid the snake's bite. Also, when excited, its hair bristles and this makes it seem larger than it really is, thus baffling the enemy. Cautiously, the mongoose waits for an opportunity to overpower the snake. In that split second when the snake lowers its head after an attempted strike, the mongoose snaps on to the back of the snake's head and crunches it to death.

When the opportunity offers, a mongoose will kill more than it can consume — out of sheer

The **ruddy mongoose** (*Herpestes smithi*) is about the same size as the common mongoose. It is not seen very often as it lives in forested areas. Its distinguishing feature is the black tip on its tail.

The **stripe-necked mongoose** (*Herpestes vitticollis*) is the largest of the Asiatic mongooses. It is distinguished by a dark-black stripe that runs along its neck from ear to shoulder. Its coat is a rich, gray color highlighted with red tips. It is found in clearings of swampy areas, near running water, or in open scrub country, from where it sometimes enters forests. It has a keen preference for a meat diet and hunts chital fawns, mouse deer, hares, field rats, bandicoots, frogs, fishes and crabs, but it also eats fruit and roots.

The **crab-eating mongoose** (*Herpestes urva*) is almost as long but heavier than the common

long, clawless otter of the East Indies to the eight-foot (2.5-meter) long Brazilian otter. However, all of them have a number of common features. All are largely amphibious; all have five digits on their feet and non-retractable claws. The two otters generally called clawless do in fact have rudimentary claws.

The otter is a beautifully streamlined animal. It has short legs, a thick neck and a long and powerful tail, which is its most striking feature, accounting for almost half its length. The tail is furry like the rest of its body and its main use is in swimming. When otters stand on their hind legs, the tail is used to keep balance.

While otters feed primarily on fish, they kill any prey they can handle and, indeed, range over several miles of land in their quest for food. It has also been observed that certain Indian otters

attributed to the excitement of the hunt. Little is known of their breeding habits. The young are born in conveniently located hideouts, usually beside a stream, with at least one underwater entrance. The mothers care for the young till they are nearly fully grown.

The smooth Indian otter is about the same size as the common otter but has a sleek smooth coat, which varies in color from blackish to sandy-brown. Essentially a plains otter, it has adapted itself to life even in the arid regions of northwestern India. Like other otters, it prefers living next to water, but during the dry season it can adapt itself to living off the jungle. These otters are often trained to act as decoys for capturing river dolphins. They also make engaging pets.

The clawless otter is so called because its claws are very rudimentary and do not project beyond

excitement and bloodthirstiness. Domestic poultry are often their victims, which somewhat strains their relations with humans, but this has to be weighed against the immense good they do by keeping the numbers of rats, mice, snakes, insects and scorpions under control.

The **common mongoose** (*Herpestes edwardsi*) is yellowish-gray in color. It has a grizzled coat and tail, with a white or yellowish-red tip. Common all over India, Nepal and Sri Lanka, it is found on open land and in scrub jungle where it lives in thickets. It is diurnal and can be seen scurrying along even at the hottest time of the day. It breeds thrice a year, three to four young being born after a gestation period of two months. The mother is often seen moving with the young in a family group.

mongoose. It has an untidy, rough coat of a dark-gray color. It occurs in Nepal and Assam and can be seen there near small streams, on the banks of which it hunts for crabs, deftly cracking the shell of its victim by knocking it against a rock. When attacked, it protects itself by squirting out a fetid fluid from its anal glands on its attacker.

Otters, Martens, Weasels and "Badgers": Otters belong to a large family known as *Mustelids* which also includes stoats, weasels, minks, martens and badgers. Otters are found all over the world with the exception of Australia, New Zealand and the polar regions. As can be expected of a group of animals that has such a varied distribution, otters vary considerably in size, ranging from the three-foot (one-meter)

often fish as a cooperative, forming a semicircle to drive fish towards the shallows.

Three species are found in the Indian subcontinent: the **common otter** (*Lutra lutra*), the **smooth Indian otter** (*Lutra perspicillata*), and the **clawless otter** (*Aonyx cinerea*). The common otter, which is distinguished from the other races by its fuller and rougher coat, is found in Kashmir, the Himalayan ranges and Assam. In South India a subspecies is found. Basically a creature of hills, rivers and streams, it has been recorded at altitudes exceeding 12,000 feet (3660 meters). Their upward migration has probably a lot to do with the migration of fish. Hunting mainly at night, they move over land from one stream to another. A characteristic often observed is that they kill more fish than they require. This is

Left, the slender loris is mainly a nocturnal creature and *above*, striped palm squirrels are often seen in cities.

the toe pads. This is the smallest of the Indian species and is dark brown in color (the South Indian subspecies is distinctly darker). It is found in the lower Himalaya extending up to Assam. The South Indian species is confined to Coorg and the Nilgiri ranges. Its habits and ways are similar to those of the other Indian otters, except for its preference for crabs and some other aquatic creatures over fish.

Martens are purely land animals and their feet are adapted for running and climbing trees. They prefer an arboreal existence, hunting their prey in trees. They have long snouts, large ears and a long tail which helps them maintain their balance while leaping from one branch to another. In India, two types are found: the **beech**, or **stone marten** (*Martes foina*) and the **yellow-throated marten** (*Martes flavigula*). The stone marten is found in the alpine and temperate zones of Kashmir and the Himalaya, as far east as Sikkim. They are rarely found below 5000 feet. They inhabit both the forest and the barren areas above the tree line. Martens in the higher regions live primarily on rodents and mouse hares. The jungle dwellers have a more varied diet of birds, honey and fruit.

The yellow-throated marten gets its name from the yellow band that runs down its neck. It is larger than the stone marten and is found in the Himalayan and the Assam ranges. It lives in the

. . . .
Above, the Indian porcupine and *right*, pangolins are found south of the Himalaya and also in Sri Lanka.

plains and hunts in the trees, where its extreme agility makes it a menace to the other inhabitants. It also hunts snakes and rodents on the ground and has been known to attack young deer. The South Indian subspecies, the **Nilgiri marten** (*Martes gwatkinsi*), is confined to the Nilgiri and Coorg ranges.

There are several types of **weasel** in India, the most common being the **Himalayan weasel** (*Mustela sibirica*), of which there are three subspecies. Another Himalayan weasel is the **ermine** (*Mustela erminea*) which is found in Kashmir.

The **pale weasel** is found in the upper reaches of the Himalaya. Besides these, two other types are found in India, the **striped-back weasel** (*Mustela strigidorsa*) and the **yellow-bellied weasel** (*Mustela kathiah*).

Though weasels can climb trees, they usually spend their time on the ground and often chase their prey into underground burrows, where rats and mice live. Their slim bodies are specially adapted for such activities.

True **badgers** are not found in India, though two types akin to it do exist. They are the **ferret badger** and the **hog badger**. The first gets its name from its being a mixture of a ferret and a badger. It has a long protruding snout which it uses for probing for food. It uses its non-retractable claws for digging. It is also known for its ability to climb trees. The Indian race (*Melagale millsi*) is confined to Assam and Nepal, where it is reported to be encouraged by the local population to enter their houses to eat cockroaches and other pests. The hog badger (*Arctonyx collaris*) looks like a bear with its short stumpy legs and long powerful claws. It has a long mobile snout like that of a pig. It ends in a disk on which are the nostrils. It has a blackish-gray coat, pale throat and a dark stripe on the cheek. It is nocturnal and lives in the tropical forests and prefers rocky areas. Its range extends from Northeastern India to Southeast Asia. It is omnivorous. It is seclusive and is rarely seen. When attacked, it discharges a stink from its glands.

The **honey badger** or **ratel** (*Mellivora capensis*) is again bear-like with a squat body, short legs and stumpy tail, sharp teeth, strong claws and stink glands. It is tawny-white above and black on the sides and below. The underpart of the face and tail are also black. Found all over India, from the Himalaya to Cape Comorin, it lives both in deserts and deciduous forests. Ratels live where they can burrow easily. They prey on mammals, birds, poultry, reptiles, insects, and, like bears, even eat fruit and honey. Ratels feed on carrion and are known to dig up graves. They are fearless and even attack man in self-defense. They live in pairs and two young are produced in a litter.

Insectivores: Included under this order is a group of animals with varied life-styles like tree shrews, hedgehogs, moles and ground shrews. Small and active, these animals, with the exception of the tree shrew, are commonly nocturnal. The common features which lead to their being grouped together, other than the fact that they are insectivorous, are their tapering snout which protrudes far beyond the jaw-bone, their short limbs with five toes each, their distinctive gait, and teeth especially suited to insect eating, all the teeth being more or less similar.

The **tree shrew** (*Anathana ellioti*) belongs to the family *Tupaia*, which in Malay means squirrel — a suitable name because, though it has the tapering snout of a shrew, yet it resembles the squirrel in appearance in many ways. Rounded ears, a long tail, feet well-adapted for climbing, naked soles that grip better, long toes and sharp claws are all squirrel-like characteristics. It is a rusty gray-brown on top and its underparts are near white. It is found in the deciduous forests south of the Ganga. In the eastern Himalaya and

Burma, from the plains to 6000 feet (1830 meters), a close relative, the **Malay** or **common tree shrew** (*Tupaia glis*) is found. Although it is arboreal and retreats to the security of trees when attacked, it feeds on the ground, looking for its insect-food under rocks, in cracks and crannies and under heaped leaves. Active and alert, it never leaps from branch to branch like a squirrel, nor does it jerk its tail and move with its head pointing downwards. Not much is known of its breeding habits and it is seen with only one young at a time. A family of tree shrews establishes territorial rights over an area and chases out all intruders.

Hedgehogs: The pig-like flattened snout of this animal gives it its name. Two species are seen in India: the **long-eared hedgehog** (*Hemiechinus auritus collaris*) which has deep blackish-brown fur on its head and underparts and the **pale hedgehog** (*Paraechinus micropus*) which is light-colored and has parted spines on its head.

Hedgehogs are small and can fit into the palm of one's hand. They have an odd-shaped, rounded body, stubby legs with claws used for digging and well-formed eyes and ears. Their back and flanks are covered with closely-set spines. A remarkable facility in hedgehogs is their ability to stretch their loose, spiny skin with a muscular action to cover their head and limbs. Rolled up into spiky balls, hedgehogs manage to protect themselves.

Desert areas and the plains abound in these species. They are nocturnal and at dusk move out of their holes, which are dug under thorny bushes. Insects, worms, rats, mice, birds' eggs and lizards are their food. They cover long distances in search of it.

Moles: Cylindrical bodies, very short necks, strong shoulders, and very large forelegs used for digging, are perfect equipment for these diminutive animals that live mainly underground. Their bodies narrow gradually to a short tail. Moles have minute eyes and their fur is so thick and soft that mud does not stick to it while they are burrowing.

The **Indian short-tailed mole** (*Talpa micrura micrura*) has a very short tail and minute eyes. It is found in the central and eastern Himalaya and in Assam up to heights of 8000 feet (2440 meters). It rummages for insects in black vegetable mold and eats larvae, grubs and earthworms. It lives in burrows under the shelter of trees. Another variety, the **white-tailed mole** (*Talpa micrura leucura*)

seen with the mother, each holding the tail of the one in front, thus forming a chain.

Rodents: More than a thousand species, each found in enormous hordes, are classified under the order *Rodentia*. They are to be found on land, in water and even in the air. Squirrels, marmots, rats, mice and porcupines are all common rodents. They are all small and share an important common feature—their teeth are specially structured and they all eat their food in a similar manner. Otherwise they present a great variety of characteristics.

A rodent's front teeth are deeply rooted and are like sharp chisels — designed for cutting. The four incisors, two each in the upper and lower jaws, are covered with a very special layer of hard, yellow enamel that does not wear out in spite of the heavy use to which they are put. Rodents

color are therefore common. Some rodents like marmots are known to hibernate during the winter, some migrate, while still others remain active even in severe conditions. Their burgeoning numbers are kept in check by predators, parasites, diseases and natural calamities.

Flying Squirrels: These are arboreal and conspicuous. They have a slim build and a long bushy tail. A translucent membrane connects their limbs, forming a parachute. Although known as flying squirrels, they cannot truly fly and can only glide through the air, covering wide gaps. Before alighting, they rise upwards in order to make a smooth landing. When not in flight, the elastic parachute is tucked close to the body and can barely be noticed. Flying squirrels are nocturnal forest animals and roost in tree-holes or build large, leaf nests. They live on fruit, nuts,

north of the Ganga. A maroon-colored squirrel, with a yellow line in the middle, black-tipped tail and reddish underparts, **Hodgson's flying squirrel**, is found in Assam and the eastern Himalaya.

Among the smaller flying squirrels, the **small Travancore flying squirrel** (*Petinomys fuscocapillus*) is the only variety found in the south. The blackish-buff **Kashmir flying squirrel** (*Hylopetes fimbriatus*) lives in the western Himalaya, near the tree line. The **particolored flying squirrel** (*Hylopetes alboniger*), blackish with white underparts occurs in the eastern Himalaya and Assam, together with the **hairy-footed flying squirrel** (*Belomys pearsoni*) recognized by clumps of brown hair near its ears.

Giant Squirrels: These live only on the tops of very tall trees and rarely come to the ground. They leap from one tree to another across gaps

has a longer tail, thick at the end, covered with white hair. It occurs in the Khasi and Naga hills.

Ground Shrews: Pointed snouts reaching far beyond the lower lips, round ears, small eyes, small bodies covered with soft fur, comparatively bare tails, feet adapted for climbing and digging, and two curved front teeth are the distinguishing features of ground shrews.

The **gray musk shrew** (*Suncus murinus*) is common in India. The male has a musk gland on either side of the body and gives out a strong smell of musk, especially during the mating season. It enters human dwellings and is of help to them since it cannot tolerate rats. It also destroys insects.

This shrew breeds before it is fully adult, two or three young being born at a time. They can be

have no canine teeth. At the rear end of the mouth are six pairs of molars with sharp cusps that grind the food into a paste. The gap between the front and rear teeth serves an interesting purpose. The animal's cheeks, that are hairy on the *inner* surface, can be drawn into the gap to form two chambers in the mouth. The inner hair between the two chambers acts as a mesh preventing coarse particles from passing to the rear chamber but letting more finely chewed food pass into it for grinding by the molars. All rodents break up their food by nibbling, scraping and gnawing. It is later ground by strong molars which have transverse grooves.

Easily adaptable, rodents are found all over the world and can survive climatic conditions up to heights of 18,000 feet (5500 meters). Changes in

bark, gum, resin, larvae and buds. Their monotonous call can be heard at night. Their breeding habits are not known. Young squirrels do not have fully developed parachutes.

Of the larger flying squirrels that are about 3½ feet (105 cm) in length, many varieties are found in India. The **Kashmir woolly flying squirrel** (*Eupetaurus cinereus*) is found in northern Kashmir and Sikkim above the tree line and lives on rocks and cliffs. The **common giant flying squirrel** (*Petaurista petaurista*), light brown on top with a yellow-brown tail, and the **large brown flying squirrel** (*P. petaurista philippensis*) are found in peninsular forests, south of the Ganga. The **red flying squirrel** (*P. petaurista albiventer*), rich brown in color, with pinkish-buff underparts, occurs in the western Himalaya,

Left, a long-eared hedgehog and *above,* the black-naped hare.

up to 20 feet (six meters) wide. They are very agile and active and can be seen stretched across high branches. They have loud rattling calls and raise a warning alarm when any alien creature is sighted. They live alone or in pairs and build their nests on very slim branches, safe from predators. When the trees lose their leaves, these nests can be clearly seen. Their breeding habits are not known.

The **Indian giant squirrel** (*Ratufa indica*) is found in both deciduous and evergreen forests. It occurs mainly in peninsular India, south of the

Ganga. The **grizzled giant squirrel** (*Ratufa macroura*) occurs in South India and Sri Lanka. Its back and tail are brownish-gray in color. The **Malayan giant squirrel** (*Ratufa bicolor*) has a dark black-brown coat and is buff underneath. It is found in Nepal, Sikkim, Bhutan, Assam, Burma and Malaysia.

Himalayan Squirrels: The **orange-bellied Himalayan squirrel** (*Dremomys lokriah*) is dark reddish-brown, touched with yellow. The fur on its back is grayish-brown, the longer hairs forming a single yellow ring. The lower parts are orange. This species has a pointed snout and lives in forested areas above 5000 feet (1525 meters). Though arboreal, it finds its food on the ground, a favorite being fallen fruit.

The **hoary-bellied Himalayan squirrel** (*Callosciurus pygerythrus*) is gray with a reddish belly,

palmarum) has three stripes on its back and occurs commonly in the damp forests of western and eastern India and also in the south. Unlike the five-striped squirrel, it is an animal of the forest, where its shrill call can be heard repeatedly.

The **dusky-striped squirrel** (*Funambulus sublineatus*) has a speckled greenish-gray coat and four longitudinal stripes on its back. It is small and shy and is found in the dense forests of South India. The **Himalayan-striped squirrel** (*Callosciurus maclellandi*) is small and has a grayish-brown coat with black, brown and buff lines. It is found in Assam and Burma around heights of 5000 feet (1525 meters).

Marmots: Marmots belong to the squirrel family. They dig underground burrows and live in them. Stoutly built, they have short tails and

Indian gerbil (*Tatera indica*) is reddish-brown in color, with pale streaks on either side of the tail. It is found all over the peninsula. The **Indian desert gerbil** (*Meriones hurrianae*) is smaller, sandy-yellow colored and occurs in the desert and semi-desert areas of northwest and central India.

Gerbils live on the plains near cultivated fields and eat grain, roots, leaves and grass. The desert variety eat seeds, tubers and nuts. They appear in large numbers and are crop-pests. As many as 19 young are born after a gestation period of a month.

Voles: These, the *Microtinae*, form yet another division in the order *Rodentia*. They are somewhat different from rats in appearance with their short muzzles, round heads, small ears, short tails, and rounded bodies designed for burrowing. Their teeth have special features. The

cylindrical bodies, mole-like heads, small eyes, short limbs and short tails are their distinguishing features. Digging with their teeth, they live in burrows in open grassy ground. They feed on grass, roots and leaves. When attacked they expose their teeth in anger and bite fiercely. The **bay bamboo rat** (*Cannomys badius*) is a small chestnut-brown rat. It occurs in the lower Himalaya in Nepal, Sikkim, Bhutan and Assam. The **hoary bamboo rat** (*Rhizomys pruinosus*) has a flecked, grizzled, dark-brown coat. It is found in Assam, China and Southeast Asia. Hill tribes eat its meat. There is no information regarding its breeding habits.

The Indian Porcupine: Very different from the other families of *Rodentia*, porcupines belong to the family of *Hystricidae*. Hair modified to form long spines is their distinguishing feature. They

· · · · · · · · · · · mongooses · · · · · · · · · · · ·
Above, ruddy mongooses are found in forested areas and ***right***, common mongoose.

the longer hairs forming two light rings. It lives in dense forests in Nepal, Sikkim, Bhutan and Assam. It makes a grass nest high up in the trees and raids orange groves.

Striped Squirrels: The **five-striped palm squirrel** (*Funambulus pennanti*) is a small species with three dark longitudinal stripes on its back and two pale ones on the flanks. It is found all over the subcontinent, south of the Himalaya, and often lives around human habitations. It is active and scampers up and down trees all the time.

The **three-striped palm squirrel** (*Funambulus*

very small ears. The **Himalayan Marmot** (*Marmota bobak*) has a pale, tawny color. Its face and the end of its tail are dark brown. The **long-tailed marmot** (*Marmota caudata*) is of a handsome rich, reddish-brown color with a black back and very long tail.

Marmots are found in the Himalaya, in Nepal, Sikkim, Kashmir, Ladakh and Garhwal at an altitude of 14,000 feet (4300 meters). They live on roots, leaves, grass and seeds. They are often seen sitting on their haunches, calling out with a loud whistling scream. The young are born in spring and are three to four in number.

Gerbils: Gerbils belong to the rat family. They can be identified by their tails, which end in tassels. Their unusually long hind feet seem to prompt them to leap from place to place. The

grinders are flat with triangular cuts on the surface, making them specially good for crushing coarse grass and roots. They live in the higher areas of the Himalaya in Kashmir and Ladakh. **Royle's vole** (*Alticola roylei*) is common at a height of 10,000 feet (3000 meters). It lives in rocky areas which abound in coarse grass. It is reddish-brown in color, with pale sides and underparts and a dark tail. It has protruding ears. The **Sikkim vole** (*Pitymys sikimensis*) is dark brown and occurs at heights around 12,000 feet (3700 meters). Old tree stumps and roots are its favorite haunts. It is a forest animal and makes a grass nest.

Bamboo Rats: These form a separate family of rodents, the *Rhizomyidae*. They look like moles but have rodent-like projecting incisors. Their

live in rocky areas, open land, forests, tall grass or near cultivation. Nocturnal in their habits, their sense of smell is very good. They are very intelligent and cannot easily be trapped or poisoned. Vegetables, grass and roots form their chief food, and they can destroy gardens by burrowing. To balance their diet with a regular intake of calcium, they scrape and gnaw bones and horns. This is proved by the pieces of bone strewn around the entrances of their burrows.

Six to twelve-inch (15-30 cm) bristles grow from the neck and shoulders of the porcupine. Its back is closely covered with long, backward-slanting quills, ringed with black and white. There is an inner layer of shorter quills. However, the strong, short, white quills at the back are its most dangerous weapons. The hollow white quills near the tail produce the warning rattling sounds.

When attacked or irritated they puff themselves up by erecting their spines, they fume and grunt and rattle their hollow back-quills. It is mistakenly believed that porcupines shoot their quills. In fact, they back into their adversaries and suddenly lunge forward, leaving their enemies looking like pin-cushions. These quills enter the bodies of the animals attacked, and sometimes fatally damage the organs of even large animals like tigers and leopards.

The Indian porcupine (*Hystrix indica*) is found all over India from the Himalaya to Cape Comorin and in Sri Lanka. In the hill ranges of South India, the color varies to a rich reddish-brown and there the animal is known as the **red porcupine**. **Hodgson's porcupine** (*Hystrix hodgsoni*) which occurs in Assam and Bengal at

tongue is linked to the stomach and is controlled by muscles attached to the pelvis. With quick movements, the tongue protrudes and is suddenly drawn back, covered with insects. Rhythmic movements of the throat sieve the debris, acting as a filter.

The pangolin's body is designed to meet specific needs and the legs are perfectly built for digging. They are curved; the forefeet are longer and have blunt claws. The pangolin lives in deep burrows under the ground.

A strong sense of smell guides the animal. Its sight and hearing are poor. Its prehensile tail helps to make the pangolin a good climber. The strong tail is also used in self defense. When moving, the back is arched and the tail held above the ground. Often, the animal stands on its hind feet to get a better view of the surroundings.

shape of the skull is also different. Hares have long ears, long hind legs and are born in burrows, with closed eyes and almost naked skin. Both hares and rabbits have short tails. Mouse hares are small and have no tails. They have rounded ears and short front legs.

There are three important varieties of Indian hare. The **black-naped hare** (*Lepus nigricollis nigricollis*) is a large, heavy variety, with a dark, blackish-brown patch on the back of its neck, up to the shoulder. The upper part of its tail is also black. It is found in most parts of the peninsula.

In the **rufous-tailed hare** (*Lepus nigricollis ruficaudatus*) the nape-patch is gray, while the body and tail are a rich reddish-brown. Black patches are found on the back and face. The underparts are white. This variety occurs from the south of the Himalaya to the river Godavari.

It is reddish-brown in color and has a band on the upper neck. It has a shining coat of short, straight hair. It is found right across the Himalaya between 11,000 and 14,000 feet (3350 and 4300 meters). In the eastern Himalaya it is found at lower levels. It is commonly seen in rocky areas above the tree line, among coarse grass or under trees. It lives in a burrow. Both timid and inquisitive, its behavior is interesting. It races across the ground playing hide and seek with any intruder. Not much is known of its breeding habits or whether it hibernates.

The true rabbit does not exist in India. The nearest to it is the **Assam rabbit** or the **hispid hare** (*Caprolagus hispidus*), which is the same size as a hare but has a shorter, dark-brown tail. It has a coarse fur of dark-brown bristles which becomes paler below. The outer side of the ears is brown,

heights of 5000 feet (1525 meters) has a very small crest. Another variety, the **brush-tailed porcupine** (*Atherurus macrourus*), is said to dwell in lower Bengal, Assam and further east up to Malaysia. It has a long tail with a tuft of bristles and is rather rare.

Pangolin: This scaly anteater is a quaint old-world animal, a survivor from past ages. A series of strong overlapping, brownish-gray scales, a form of modified hair, cover the upper part and sides of the body and the long tail. This covering is said to be bullet-proof. The underparts are covered with coarse bristle-like hair.

Living on an exclusive diet of ants and termites, the pangolin has no teeth. However, its tongue is glutinous, attracting ants that stick on to it. It is long and can protrude 10 inches. Its

When attacked, the animal rolls itself into a tight ball showing great muscular power and is almost impregnable. The only sound it emits is a strong hiss, when alarmed or disturbed. Usually one young is produced at a time and the baby is carried by the mother on her back and tail.

Two species are found in India: the **Chinese pangolin** (*Manis pentadactyla*) which occurs in the northeast, and the **Indian pangolin** (*Manis crassicaudata*) found in peninsular India. It is hunted for its flesh and for its scales which are said to have medicinal and magical powers.

Hares and Mouse Hares: Hares and rabbits of the family *Leporidae*, and mouse hares of the *Ochotonidae* are distinguished from rodents by the fact that they have four incisors in the upper jaw, unlike the rodents which have only two. The

The **desert hare** (*Lepus nigricollis dayanus*) is sandy-yellow in color and has no nape-patch. The upper part of its tail is a blackish-brown. It is found around the desert in Sind (Pakistan), Punjab, Rajasthan and Kutch.

Hares live in bush, jungle and near cultivated land on the outskirts of villages. They are nocturnal and can be seen singly scampering across roads and fields at night. Grass and vegetable matter are their main diet. One or two young are produced during the colder months. Leopards, jackals, wild dogs, mongooses, owls and crested hawks prey on them. Men hunt them for their meat and fur.

The **Himalayan mouse hare** (*Ochotona roylei*) looks like a guinea pig. It is small and has a round head, round ears, short muzzle and no tail.

Left, common palm civet and *above,* smooth Indian otters.

the eyes small, the hind legs short and stout, the claws long and teeth large. Bark and roots are its main food. Seen in the *terai, dooars* and Himalayan foothills, it is very elusive and therefore very little is known about it.

Bats: There is no mammal that can fly in the real sense of the term except the family of bats, *Chiroptera*. Their flight is sustained, unlike that of the so-called flying squirrel which really only leaps and glides. The oldest bats, found in the form of fossils, must also have had this ability to fly as they have proper wings.

Bats can be divided into two distinct categories: the larger, fruit-eating bats (*Megachiroptera*) and the insectivorous bats (*Microchiroptera*), which are generally smaller.

The very name, *chiroptera*, derived from Greek, means hand-wing. Bat's wings are attached to their forearms. From the wings, flying membranes extend to the feet and spread between the legs, enclosing the tail. An additional flying membrane joins the neck to the forearms. Thus, an unbroken, complete parachute is formed. Bats have strong hearts and lungs. Powerful flying muscles make them strong fliers. The tail which curves towards the belly acts as a brake.

Fruit bats have excellent grinding teeth. The molars are oblong and have smooth crowns divided by a deep long groove. The food is ground to a

pulp and the juice goes directly into the gullet through these grooves. Fruit bats feed in the early evening and have good eyesight.

Insectivorous bats have teeth which serve a different purpose. They have molars with sharp, pointed cusps in the crown, forming a W shape. These are perfect for holding and piercing. Vampire bats are known to drink blood. They have front teeth designed for piercing. Insectivorous bats feed at night and manage to fly with the help of a highly developed echo-apparatus, similar to a sonar system. They have very strong voice-boxes and muscles and can produce shrill signals at a rate of 50 pulses per second. When these

· ·

Left, short-nosed fruit bat and *above,* flying-fox eating wild figs.

sound vibrations strike an object, they are reflected back and picked up by the bat. This helps bats to avoid colliding with objects.

In cold weather, bats hibernate.

The **flying fox** (*Pteropus giganteus*) is the largest Indian bat. Its wings spread across four feet (120 cm). It has a reddish-brown head with a black snout and black wings. Its neck, shoulders, chin and flanks are varied hues of brown. It is seen all over the subcontinent except in arid areas like West Rajasthan and the higher reaches of the hills. Flying foxes roost together on trees in noisy groups and fly to far-off fruit orchards in search of fruit. They breed once a year, after a gestation period of five months.

The **fulvous fruit-bat** (*Rousettus leschenaulti*) is medium sized and light-brown in color. It has a strong smell of fermented fruit juice. Common in the Indian peninsula, large colonies roost in caves and in ruins and fly out looking for fruit at dusk. They breed twice a year. The young are carried by the mother for two months.

The **short-nosed fruit-bat** (*Cynopterus sphinx*) is large and brown and is recognized by its divergent nostrils and white-margined ears. Found in peninsular India, it roosts among palm leaves and aerial roots of the banyan and eats fruit and sips honey from flowers. Its breeding habits are not exactly known, although young are seen carried by their mother in September.

The medium-sized sandy-gray, **bearded sheath-tailed bat** (*Taphozous melanopogon*) has a beard which is drenched during the rainy season with a thick fluid produced by the chin glands. Colonies of over 4000 are found in ruins and cave temples, clinging to walls. They fly out before dusk and feed on insects. Found in peninsular India, the young are born in April–May and separated from the mother permanently after a month.

Another species, the **Indian false vampire** (*Megaderma lyra*) is dark gray in color. The nose-leaf seems truncated. Groups of around 30 live together in wells or caves and feed on rats, small birds, geckos and frogs. The young are born in April and are carried by the mother till almost full-grown.

The **great eastern horseshoe bat** (*Rhinolophus luctus*) has long, woolly, curly fur that is jet black with ashy-gray tips. It has large ears and a horseshoe-shaped nose-leaf covering the upper lip and cut in the middle. Found in the Himalaya, Western Ghats and Sri Lanka, it occurs in pairs, but is seldom seen. Little is known of its breeding habits.

The **Indian pipistrelle** (*Pipistrellus coromandra*) is small in size, dark above and pale below, with dense fur between the eyes. A fast flier, it is busy all through the night. It lives in the eaves of houses and enters them while looking for insects. Its breeding habits are not known. Two young are seen in May.

REPTILES

Reptiles are a well-represented and diverse group of animals in this region, with over 400 species of snakes, lizards, turtles and crocodilians in India alone. Contrary to popular belief, it is not only in forested areas that one comes across reptiles; most of the larger, rodent-eating snakes and lizards are prevalent in open, cultivated areas, which have an abundance of rats and fresh-water. In fact this is probably the only animal group that has benefited somewhat from the large-scale conversion of forestland to farmland over the last 50 years. Thus, driving along country roads bordered by fields, one often sees a

Snakes: There are 238 species of snakes in India, ranging from the giant **reticulated python** (*Python reticulatus*) which grows to 30 feet (10 meters), to the tiny **worm snake** (*Typhlina bramina*) which achieves just over four inches (10 cm), and is often mistaken for a worm. Snakes inhabit a wide range of environments, from paddy fields and open sandy areas to thick rain-forests, mangrove swamps, mountains up to 15,000 feet (4500 meters), and even the open sea. Their food varies considerably, depending on the size of the snake and prey availability. Frogs and rodents are perhaps the most generally acceptable

Right from the egg stage through to adult-hood, most snakes have a variety of natural enemies. Many have startling defense stances, the most well known of which is the dramatic hood display of the cobra, which inflates its body and expands its rib cage to spread a "hood" to intimidate enemies. Others exhale breath force-fully, and "hiss." The **saw-scaled viper** (*Echis carinatus*) produces this sound by rubbing its rough scales together.

Venomous Snakes: Although there are more than 50 species of venomous snakes in this region, the majority, for various reasons, pose no threat to man. The king cobra, for example, lives in dense evergreen forests which people do not usually venture into; nor is the king cobra given to unprovoked attacks as is commonly believed. The 20 species of sea snakes that inhabit the

color from cream to black; generally, it is brown. The hood may not have the typical speacle or monocle marking. **Russel's vipers** are heavy-bodied snakes with narrow necks, triangular heads and a regular chain-like pattern on the back. The scales are very rough and the overall color is yellowish and brown. **Kraits** are blue-black and shiny with transverse thin white cross bands, which may be very faint or even absent. The saw-scaled viper is the smallest of the Big Four, growing to just a foot in South India; it is brownish with white markings and has the triangular head typical of the vipers. In some areas, this viper is amazingly abundant, such as in Ratnagiri District in Maharashtra.

Harmless Snakes: There are several species of non-venomous "garden snakes" common throughout the region. The large **rat snake** is

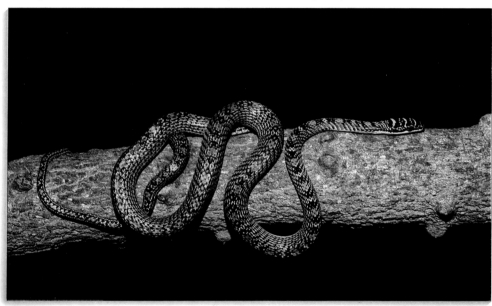

monitor lizard (*Varanus bengalensis*) running across the road, or a large rat snake (*Ptyas mucosus*) hunting along a bund between fields.

Reptiles play a significant role in Hindu religion and mythology and several of the major deities are associated with snakes. But while people worship snakes, they also fear them, and snakes are usually killed on sight; even the harmless species are not spared, as all snakes are generally considered venomous.

Consumer exploitation has been high in this animal group. Before it was banned in 1976, the skin trade tanned 10 million snake skins a year, and several species such as the **rock python** (*Python molurus*) became locally extinct in many areas. The illegal skin market nevertheless continues to flourish.

items for the open-country species, but there are interesting exceptions. The **king cobra** (*Ophiophagus hannah*), the largest venomous snake in the world, which grows to 16 feet (five meters) in India, are "ophiophagus"; that is, they eat only snakes, mostly the ubiquitous rat snake. Sea snakes eat fish, and small burrowers like the fascinating group of shield-tails or uropeltids eat insect larvae and worms.

Some snakes lay eggs; others have living young. Several species of egg layers such as pythons, cobras (*Naja naja*) and water snakes have been found to stay with the eggs until hatching. The king cobra is the only snake in the world which builds a nest: the female, incredibly, scrapes leaves and humus into an 18-inch high mound in which she lays her eggs.

coastal waters are timid, shy animals which won't bite unless restrained or injured, and the same is true of the banded krait. Other species such as the pit viper usually have only a mild venom which is adequate to kill small prey like frogs and lizards, but which causes only pain and swelling in larger animals like adult humans.

The Big Four to watch out for are the cobra, krait (*Bungarus caeruleus*), Russel's viper (*Vipera russelli*) and the saw-scaled viper. Together, they cause 10,000 snakebite deaths every year in India alone. It is important to learn to recognize these four, and to remember that antivenom serum, available at large hospitals, is the only cure for their bite. Each of these snakes is fairly easily distinguishable, though it is easy to confuse them with other harmless species. The **cobra** varies in

Preceding pages, **the elusive gharial.** *Left,* **the harmless and beautiful golden tree or flying snake, common in Sri Lanka but rarely seen in India and** *above,* **Tucktoo gecko, common in northeastern India.**

often mistaken for a cobra, but has a more pointed head, large eyes and of course does not spread a hood. The bright green **vine snake** (*Ahaetulla nasuta*) with its pointed head and elliptical eye pupils is the target of many derogatory myths. In Tamil Nadu it is known as the *kunn kuthi pambu,* eye-pecking snake. The **bronze-back tree snake** (*Dendrelaphis tristis*) is very fast, thin and chocolate-brown with a light-bronze stripe down its back. It, too, is widely feared and stories abound about its evil characteristics. Other groups of harmless snakes include the **kukri snakes** (*Oligodon*), **wolf snakes** (*Lycodon*), **trinkets** (*Elaphe*), **racers**, **cat snakes** (*Boiga*) and freshwater snakes. There are several interesting burrowers, like the stubby **sand boas** (*Eryx*), the **worm snake** and the **shield-tail**.

The most productive places to see the common species of snakes are in agricultural areas and bordering bushes and thickets. Just before sundown is a good time, since this is when cobras, rat snakes and others hunt for rats and frogs. But the excellent camouflage of these reptiles plus the heavy hunting pressure for skins, which has made them wary and timid, makes it difficult to spot them. As opposed to temperate areas where snakes are often diurnal and live in accessible places, here most species tend to be nocturnal and live in secure rat holes, termite mounds and

particular snake. One exception seems to be the Keoladeo Ghana (Bharatpur) Bird Sanctuary where in the winter months one can almost always see big rock pythons basking on low branches or in front of the burrows they live in. The tourist's first encounter with a snake in India is usually through the snake charmer, who travels around the country with his sick, de-fanged cobras and makes them "dance" to his flute. In truth, snakes hear practically no air-borne sounds and the cobra's swaying dance is a defensive movement with which the snake warily watches the flute and the "charmer," potential enemies of which it is terrified.

The Irula Cooperative is a venom-production center where tourists can see the Big Four of venomous snakes and the extraction of venom. It is run by the Irula hunter-gatherer tribals.

women step up to propitiate them with flowers, ghee and *kum kum* powder. In West Bengal, the Jhampan festival, which takes place in July–August is conducted by *Jhampanias*, priests who are the gurus of snake charmers. They arrive at the ceremony in colorfully decorated carriages (*jhampans*) with baskets containing king cobras, cobras, vipers, kraits, rat snakes and other species. Snake charming, folk songs and other festivities take place.

Lizards: There are over 150 species of lizards in the subcontinent. The majority are forest dwellers and difficult to sight. The most commonly seen are a few species of **geckos** (*Hemidactylus*) which quickly colonize houses, darting about on the ceiling in the evening after cockroaches, mosquitoes and other prey. In spite of this free pest-control service, geckos are unpopular

with a bright blue throat fan. It is capable of great bursts of speed, sometimes streaking along on its hind legs like the South American basilisk. **Skinks,** the smooth, crestless lizards, often mistaken for snakes, are another widely distributed group, and range in length from three to 12 inches (eight to 30 cm). The young of several of these skinks have brilliant, almost electric tails, usually bright blue or orange.

There is one species of **chameleon** (*Chameleo zeylanicus*) found throughout India and Sri Lanka, but its capacity for camouflage makes it almost impossible to spot. Their large, independently moving eyes help them to avoid enemies and find their insect prey. The long, flexible tongue, almost a foot long, is shot out with amazing speed to catch a passing butterfly or termite.

∙ ∙
Above, mugger or marsh crocodile and *right*, sea turtles hatching.

other cool refuges.

In some parts of the region there are specialized groups of people who hunt snakes (traditionally for the skin trade) and they are the best guides. The Irulas of Tamil Nadu are probably the best snake hunters in the world and the Irula Cooperative in Madras can be contacted for a day's snake hunt around Madras. From a faint, barely visible scrape on the ground, an Irula can tell the species and size of the snake, which way it went and how long ago.

Places of Interest: Unlike mammals, there are few places where one can be sure of seeing a

Members catch and supply the Big Four snakes to the Cooperative, where they are kept for three weeks and the venom extracted thrice. The snakes are then released back into the wild. There are snakes on display at the Madras Snake Park, Calcutta Snake Park, Poona Serpentarium and Sundervan in Ahmedabad.

There are several festivals and ceremonies associated with snakes. The most dramatic is the August *nag panchmi* harvest festival at Battis Shirala near Sangli, Maharashtra. Wild cobras are caught by the local farmers and laborers and worshiped for the few days of the festival. Then they are released into the fields, unharmed. In the evenings during the festival, one can see large numbers of cobras lined up, hoods spread, in front of the temporary snake charmers, as

animals overall; people mistakenly believe they are poisonous, and that a gecko falling into food can cause fatal poisoning.

The social behavior of geckos is fascinating, with a very definite pecking order and ferocious territorialism between males. Their main predators are "house snakes" like the wolf snake and cat snake as well as false vampire bats.

Another widely distributed group of lizards is the *agamids*, and of these the **garden lizard** (*Calotes versicolor*), unfortunately called the bloodsucker, is the most common. The male in breeding color is an impressive creature, with his handsome, sharp crest, orange head and colorful dewlap or throat flap, which is expanded during territorial displays. The **Sita's lizard** (*Sitana ponticeriana*) is a four-inch long colorful agamid

The largest, most conspicuous lizards of this region are the *varanids* or **monitors** of which there are four species. The **water monitor** (*Varanus salvator*) grows to over six feet (two meters) and is the most colorful, with black and yellow markings. Where unmolested they get very tame; on the outskirts of Colombo, they can be seen scavenging around rubbish dumps or hanging about markets in expectation of scraps. In India they are found in the Andaman and Nicobar Islands, the Sunderbans delta in West Bengal and at Bhitar Kanika in Orissa, the only places which still have mangrove forests. The **Bengal monitor**, a uniform or speckled brown, is a three-foot long lizard common throughout India, Sri Lanka and Nepal which frequents open cultivated areas as well as wooded and forested tracts. The **yellow monitor** (*Varanus flavescens*) is a brightly marked monitor, smaller than the Bengal monitor and with a stubby head. It is found only in parts of the north such as the states of Bihar, Uttar Pradesh and West Bengal. A similar looking lizard, the **desert** or **Agra monitor** (*Varanus griseus*) is confined to the northwest, notably the Rajasthan desert.

Lizards of this region are unique in many ways. Over 75 species of Indian lizards are endemic, that is they are found in very limited geographical ranges, many in evergreen forests such as those of the Western Ghats. Of these several are known only from a few museum specimens and the natural history of most is largely unstudied. One of the most dramatic looking of the endemic lizards is the dragon-like creature, *Lyriocephalus*, of the Sinharaja forest in southern Sri Lanka,

(*Geochelone elegans*) conspicuous by its black and yellow markings. Its typical habitat is open scrub forest in the dry southeast and northwestern parts of the country. Large numbers are killed in the south for the shell, which is made into souvenirs for the tourist trade.

Of the five species of marine turtles in this region, four nest on Indian beaches and during the two-month nesting season it is possible to witness the whole egg-laying sequence, since once the female begins her task of procreation she is oblivious to the close presence of humans. In Tamil Nadu, the **olive ridley** (*Lepidochelys olivacea*) nests from November to February and the World Wildlife Fund office in Madras conducts regular "turtle walks" at night to see this phenomenon and to collect nests for safe incubation; otherwise they usually end up at the local

with its strange knob on the head and startling colors. Another, *Cophotes*, is one of the viviparous lizards in the region.

Turtles and Tortoises: Generally, turtles live, feed and breed mostly in water, and tortoises mainly on land; but, as is often the case, there are notable exceptions. There are 26 species of freshwater turtles and tortoises in India, and five species of marine turtles, which feed in coastal waters and lay their eggs on suitable beaches. Of the freshwater turtles, the most abundant are the **flap-shell turtle** (*Lissemys punctata*) and the **black pond turtle** (*Melanochelys trijuga*), both of which are widely eaten. In West Bengal especially, thousands are slaughtered every week, in spite of protective legislation. Among the tortoises, the most widespread is the **star tortoise**

market. But the real turtle nesting extravaganza takes place in February–March at the Gahirmatha beach in Bhitar Kanika Sanctuary, Orissa, where over 200,000 ridleys come to nest in the space of three or four nights.

Places of Interest: The Crocodile Bank just outside Madras has a freshwater turtle breeding program and several species can be seen there. Turtles are kept and fed, in some cases ritualistically, at several shrines in India such as at Dakor, 35 miles (56 km) from Ahmedabad (Gujarat). At the right time of year, walking

. . . .

Above, tree frogs ensuring the continuance of their species. *Right,* demoiselle cranes, Gujarat; *far right,* monitor lizard.

along known nesting beaches at night can be a very rewarding experience. In Sri Lanka, the giant **leatherback turtles** (*Dermochelys coriacea*), which grow to six feet, nest on the southern coast and the Wildlife and Nature Protection Society of Sri Lanka has a yearly hatchery where eggs are buried and the young released into the sea on hatching. At Kosgoda in Sri Lanka, four species of sea turtle nest most of the year. One of them is the **loggerhead** (*Caretta caretta*) which has not been seen on Indian beaches.

Crocodilians: Perhaps the most unique of the world's crocodilians, the long-snouted, fish-eating **gharial** (*Gavialis gangeticus*), is found in India and Nepal and inhabits the large, fast-flowing rivers (Ganga, Mahanadi, Brahmaputra and their tributaries). By the mid-1970s, the gharial had been rendered almost extinct due to heavy

has earned an unenviable reputation because some of the big ones occasionally take cattle, goats or even a human to vary its diet; there are areas along rivers in Sri Lanka where villagers construct safe, fenced-in bathing areas to protect themselves from the whims of the "salty." In India, "salties" are found in the Andaman and Nicobar Islands, Bhitar Kanika in Orissa and the Sunderbans in West Bengal. Mugger are extremely adaptable and live in any freshwater (sometimes even brackish water) habitats, from large reservoirs to small streams. During extreme dry months or drought they make deep tunnels or even trek miles overland looking for water. Mugger were once common throughout India but, again because of hunting pressure, are now confined to a few protected reservoirs and rivers. Mugger breed well in captivity and the Govern-

hunting pressure for its valuable skin and from loss of habitat due to the damming of rivers. But thanks to timely conservation efforts — wild-egg collection and captive rearing — there are now over 2000 gharial in captivity and over 1200 have been released into the wild. Gharial are very unusual-looking creatures with big bulging eyes, long narrow jaws studded with razor sharp teeth and the big pot-like growth at the end of the snout which the adult male sports. They feed almost exclusively on fish.

The other two species of crocodiles in this region are the **mugger** or **marsh crocodile** (*Crocodylus palustris*) and the **saltwater crocodile** (*Crocodylus porosus*). Both are found in India and Sri Lanka; the mugger, like the gharial, is found in Nepal as well. The saltwater crocodile

ment Crocodile Project has over 5000.

Places of Interest: The three Indian species, plus others such as **Siamese crocodiles** and **African dwarf crocodiles**, can be seen at the Madras Crocodile Bank which has over 2000 crocodilians including crocs from Africa, Thailand and North and South America. In the wild, gharial can be seen at the Chitwan National Park in Nepal, and the Corbett National Park in Uttar Pradesh; saltwater crocodile at Bhitar Kanika, Orissa; and mugger at Hiran Lake, Gir Sanctuary (Gujarat), and Ranthambhore National Park (Rajasthan), where one or two can often be seen basking on the banks. At Panama Wewa near Arugam Bay in Sri Lanka, wild mugger are very approachable and can be seen by the score basking, feeding and socializing."

BIRDS, RESIDENT AND MIGRANT

The distribution of birds over the globe is a fascinating subject, and the reason why some species are so widespread and others so restricted is largely a matter of speculation. The changing physical pattern of the world over geological periods has much to do with the presence or absence of birds in various parts of the world. A striking example of discontinuous distribution, as a result of geological changes, is provided by the existence of laughing thrushes and spider hunters in northeastern India in the Himalaya, and then again, after a gap of 2000 miles, in the Western Ghats in southwest India. It is presumed that at one time there was a continuous Satpura range of mountains joining these two areas and these species then were presumably linked. With the disappearance of the mountains under geological forces acting through the Deccan Plateau only a relict population of these species remain in two distant parts of the country.

But ornithologists wonder how some land birds manage to colonize areas across the oceans, far away from their original home, like some on Christan Da Cunha 2000 miles away from land, while some, which have proliferated all over the United States, have been unable to reach even the West Indies. The same is the case with Sri Lanka. Though most Indian species have no difficulty in crossing the short sea barrier (even poor fliers and essentially land birds like the paradise flycatcher going over), it is a curious fact that no vulture has crossed the negligible sea barrier and, consequently, there are none beyond the southern tip of India. Only one or two **scavenger vultures** (*Neophron percnopterus*) have been seen in Sri Lanka, and the fact that these birds are strong fliers, seen everywhere in South India, makes their absence across Palk Strait inexplicable.

Sri Lanka has approximately 397 species and subspecies and 358 forms are almost identical with those of India. Largely for geological reasons there are several endemic species of birds found only in the southernmost hilly areas of the island. Among these are the **green-billed coucal, Ceylon blue magpie, yellow-fronted barbet** and **Legge's flowerpecker**. It is also noteworthy that a special race of the **paradise flycatcher** (*Tchitrea paradisi*) has evolved in island isolation in Sri Lanka. Unlike the Indian form this bird has no white phase.

At the other end of India, Nepal, an exceptionally beautiful country, has a splendid assortment of colorful birds, some like the **Himalayan snow-cock** (*Tetraogallus himalayensis*) and many birds of prey are found even above the tree line. In fact an **eastern steppe eagle** (*Aquila nipalensis*)

was found on the South Col of Everest. From its jagged peaks in the north with arctic conditions, to moist lowland forests in the south, there are as many as 800 species of birds as compared to the 1200 of India. Many species are of course common to both countries, and because of its geographical position the birds of Nepal have strong affinities with those of the palaearctic region. But it has only one truly endemic species, the **spiny babbler** (*Turdoides nipalensis*) as against the 10 in India.

As a result of the drastic changes in India's environment in the course of the last five decades

— particularly as a result of the cutting down of forests and extending the range of grasslands and agricultural areas, there has been a corresponding change in the pattern of the avifauna throughout the country. Woodpeckers, for example, have been drastically reduced and seed-eating birds, finches and larks, have multiplied.

Zoogeographically speaking, the world is divided into the Palaearctic, Nearctic, Neotropical, Ethiopian, Oriental and Australian regions. India's avifauna has strong links with the African as well as with the birds of the Indo-Chinese region. Only a few have palaearctic affinities. But there are several species which are endemic to India, i.e. they are not found anywhere else in the world, and a few of these might be mentioned. The **chir pheasant** (*Catreus*

wallichii), larger than a village hen and "reminiscent of an English hen pheasant," is found in West Himalayan conifer and deciduous forests; the **pinkheaded duck** (*Rhodonessa caryophyllacea*), a rare species even in the last century, was last seen in Bihar in 1935 and is probably extinct. Another bird which is feared to have become extinct is the **mountain quail** (*Ophrysia superciliosa*), last recorded in Naini Tal in UP in 1876. But specially after the rediscovery of Jerdons Courser, an expedition to find the quail has been planned by the Bombay Natural History Society. They intend to comb the area where it was last seen along the foothills of Mussoorie in the Himalaya. This bird is reputed to be a close sitter, refusing to fly until virtually stepped upon. Therefore a dog squad will be taken along to flush it from the

• •

Tragopan, one of the several beautiful Himalayan pheasants.

undergrowth, if indeed it survives. The outcome of the expedition is keenly awaited.

The **white-winged wood duck** (*Cairina scutulata*), a resident of the swamp forests of Assam, though not endemic, is on the danger list because of habitat destruction. Sir Peter Scott has bred these birds in captivity in Slimbridge in the United Kingdom and some have recently been reintroduced in Assam.

Not all endemic species in India are rare or extinct. The **Indian robin** (*Saxicoloides fulicata*) for example, slightly larger than a sparrow, a black bird with white on the shoulder, and a rusty

red patch under the tail is found "in dry open lightly wooded country" throughout India. The **rufousbellied babbler** (*Dumetia hyperythra*) and the **blackheaded babbler** (*Rhopocichla atriceps*) are also common birds, the range of the former extending from the Himalaya to South India and the latter to the evergreen biotops of the Western Ghats.

Speaking about rare and extinct species, one of the most exciting events of the century was the rediscovery of **Jerdons Courser** (*Cursorius bitorquatus*) on Jan. 14, 1986, in Cuddapah in Andhra Pradesh. An attractive bird about the size of a partridge but with longer legs, pinkish-brown with two white bands across the breast. This courser whose nearest relations are in far-away Africa, was last seen in 1900, and had eluded the keenest observers because it appears to be nocturnal in its habits and was only rediscovered at night in the glare of a motor vehicle's headlights. A sanctuary is now being established by the Andhra Pradesh Government in the area where some birds of this species still exist.

Ecologically, India is a rich country, with few vacant niches where exotic species can get a foothold. The **Java sparrow** (*Padda orizivora*) is perhaps the only foreign species which has acquired a breeding status in India; but the fact that it is not spreading significantly is fortunate because the problems caused by exotics — their displacement of the local avifauna for example — are well known.

Out of the 8650 species in the world India has as many as 1200, and so on a land surface of only 4 percent, it has 16 percent of the total number on the earth. If subspecies are included there are 2061 forms in all, and out of these 1750 are residents and the rest are migrants. If vagrants and pelagic species like shearwaters, petrels and boobies are included, the total may go up to 2346. Ornithologists have classified birds into 27 Orders and 155 Families and India's status in ornithological terms can be judged from the fact that it has representatives from 20 Orders and 77 Families.

Easy Access: In spite of urbanization there are places very near India's busy cities which have a wealth of birds. Any visitor to Bombay with an interest in birds will find Borivali National Park, on the outskirts of the city, very rewarding, particularly during the migratory season from September to April. In a small stretch of country between the hills and the lake, he might well see a wide spectrum of both forest-dwelling as well as aquatic species — **racket-tailed drongos, tree pies, jungle owlets, minivets, ioras, golden orioles, magpie robins**, three species of **bulbuls** and of **sunbirds, hornbills, woodpeckers** and the dazzling **peacock**, India's national bird. With luck, even the gorgeous **paradise flycatcher**. On

the damp meadows encircling the lakes, there will be **bee-eaters**, **kingfishers**, **drongos**, **mynas**, **pipits** and **larks**, while **swallows** and **swifts** hunt in the sky. In the water there can be **gulls** and **duck** of many species, with **plovers**, **egrets**, **herons** and maybe even an **osprey** plunging into the water to catch fish with its talons. Altogether, the Borivali National Park is a splendid place to see a multitude of species living cheek by jowl, yet in their separate micro-habitats.

An even more glamorous place than the Borivali National Park is the world-famous Keoladeo Ghana (Bharatpur) National Park, just 30 miles (50 km) from Agra. It is one example of man's tampering with the natural ecosystem, resulting in a spectacular increase in its birdlife. It is the artificially maintained water levels within this comparatively small (11 sq mile/29 sq km) park that sustains its wealth of birdlife. Bharatpur is considered to be unique in the total number of bird species as well as the quantity of birdlife which it harbors. It has an impressive assortment of land and arboreal birds, but the grand spectacle is provided by the aquatic species. For example there are four species of cormorants, eight species of egrets, three ibises, 17 species of duck and geese, and two species of crane, of which one, the **Siberian crane** (*Grus leucogeranus*) is one of the rarest species in the world, and Bharatpur is its only known wintering ground in India.

Protection: As in most countries, in India too, there is both national and international protection for birds. Under the Wildlife Protection Act of 1972 no birds except certain specified vermin like crows can be trapped and killed without a permit from the appropriate wildlife authority. Permits are granted only for game birds which are not endangered. But a most timely measure to check commercial exploitation by poachers is CITES, the Convention on International Trade in Endangered Species of Flora and Fauna, which came into force in 1975. This Convention has three schedules, and in Schedule I are listed those species which are totally protected. Some of the rarer protected bird species in India include the chir pheasant to which we have already referred, the **Himalayan monal** (*Lophophorus impejanus*), **Sclater's monal** (*Lophophorus sclateri*); **Blyth's** and **western tragopan**, the Siberian and the **black-necked crane**; the **great Indian** and **Houbara bustard**, the **Bengal florican**, and the **Nicobar pigeon**. With the stopping of imports by Western countries and the consequent ending of the high prices fetched by the sale of these birds, the main incentive for poaching is removed.

. . . .

Left, whiskered terns, Bharatpur, Rajasthan and *right,* the diminutive common kingfisher.

In an agricultural country birds play a very important role in the cross-pollination of flowers, the dispersal of seeds, and keeping insect pests under control. In his Azad Memorial Lecture, Dr Salim Ali said "over 50,000 species of insects have been described from the Indian subcontinent, doubtless with many more still to come. Many of them such as locusts, beetles, moths, caterpillars and termites are extremely harmful pests of agriculture and forestry upon which our national economy leans heavily." He went on to say that a single pair of **Colorado beetles** (*Leptinotarsa decemlineata*) "would without checks — in which birds play an important part — increase to 60 million in a year."

It is not realized what a significant role birds of prey play in keeping down rodent population. An

owl, for example, is reputed to kill as many rats as 30 cats, and rodents destroy a substantial portion of India's food-grain production. Another way in which birds add to the health of the ecosystem is through guano, the droppings of fish-eating water birds which is considered to be the finest nitrogenous fertilizer in the world. The famous Guano Islands off the coast of Peru are a major economic asset of that country. At least in one water-bird sanctuary in India, Vedanthangal near Madras, the agriculturists surrounding the sanctuary area protect the birds because they recognize the value of guano as a fertilizer with matchless properties.

While, on the one hand, a conservation consciousness is growing in the country, and birds are not being wantonly destroyed, the increasing use of pesticides in agriculture and for public health, has led to the death of birds, particularly birds of prey, which are on top of the food chain. Grain-eating birds eat insects killed or contaminated with synthetic poisons. The toxic preparations are ingested into their systems and when they in turn are devoured by predatory birds, the predators either die or lay sterile eggs. It is to be hoped that biological control methods will soon replace the organo-chlorine and organo-phosphorus compounds which do such widespread damage to the environment. Bird watchers in India lament that the skies are virtually empty. The king vulture is hardly ever seen, and even birds like the white-eyed buzzard, which was so common in the past are now rarities.

Birds are reputed to be good indicators of the health of our environment because their fast

BIRDS OF THE SUBCONTINENT — A SAMPLING

For the purpose of this guide it has seemed appropriate to list the birds not in taxonomical order, but according to the frequency with which they are likely to be encountered. For reasons of space the description has had to be limited to size, main coloring (omitted for the commonest species) and the most noticeable characteristics.

House Crow (*Corvus splendens*): In spite of the fact that this is the commonest bird in every locality which has a sizable human population, little is known about its life history. The nesting season, during which they make loose ungainly nests from all available material, is from April to June.

smaller cousin, even invading highly populated areas, functioning side by side with the house crow. Although not as quick and bright as the house crow, it is physically stronger, and is responsible for destroying a large number of our smaller birds. The jungle crow is also a victim of the koel's "parasitism" during the nesting season.

House Sparrow (*Passer domesticus*) (6"/2.3 cm): The busy twittering flocks of house sparrow are at home in the most congested localities. Indeed, the sparrow is a true commensal of man and breeds away from human environments only in exceptional circumstances.

Pariah Kite (*Milvus migrans*) (24"/9.4 cm): The commonest bird of prey in Indian skies. Despite its unflattering name ("pariah" means scavenger), it is a rather beautiful bird. With the general look of an eagle, it is reddish brown all

(9"/3.5 cm) is perhaps the most characteristic of the birds of the subcontinent. It is thoroughly at home among humans. One size smaller than a dove, the common myna has a dark brown back with bright yellow legs and beak as well as a bare yellow patch on the face, and white patches on the wings, which show up conspicuously in flight. It does not depend on the leavings of man, because it is omnivorous and eats fruit, earthworms and insects. The nesting season is long-drawn (April-August). Mynas enjoy argument, and quite often small flocks can be seen screaming, fluttering and attacking one another on the ground. No casualties result.

Brahminy or **Blackheaded Myna** (*Sturnus pagodaram*): A rather dressy creature; slightly smaller than the common myna, its glossy black crown contributes to its handsome looks. It is

metabolism gives us an advance warning of environmental hazards to come. Humans must protect them even if only to protect themselves — for the early warning system they provide.

The notes on birds that follow (pp. 144-52) cover only a small and inevitably arbitrary sampling, but they attempt to include those species which are most common over the greater part of the region and are, therefore, most likely to be seen by the visitor. The keener naturalist can add many more birds to his list by visiting bird sanctuaries such as the Keoladeo Ghana in Bharatpur (Rajasthan), Vedanthangal (Tamil Nadu) and Nal Sarovar (Gujarat) for the winter migrants, and any of the many wildlife sanctuaries for resident species.

Koel (*Eudynamys scolopacea*): The male is all black, about the same size but slimmer than the crow. The color of the male and the crimson eyes make identification easy. The female is brown, profusely spotted and barred with white. The male's loud, monotonous calls of *kuo kuo kuo* are a feature of the Indian summer, and are supposed to herald the monsoon. The female has a metallic clicking call which carries a long way.

The koel is the only bird which seems to out-maneuver the crow. The female manages to lay its egg in the crow's nest and the young koel often pushes the fledgling crows overboard.

Jungle Crow (*Corvus macrorhynchos*): This bird is heavier than the house crow and is black all over, without a gray patch on the neck. It has recently begun to encroach on the territory of its

over, and a good identification mark is its forked tail. In spite of its apparently leisurely flying habits, it can swoop swiftly and accurately in crowded city streets, and make off with some item in a dustbin or a sandwich in a child's hand. It perches and nests on high trees. Like many birds of prey it nests after the monsoon.

Brahminy Kite (*Haliastur indus*): Can be distinguished from the pariah kite by its white head and underparts and rounded not forked tail. Both are likely to operate in the same areas, but the brahminy kite has a preference for picking rubbish off water surfaces, while the pariah is more terrestrial.

Mynas (Family *Sturnidae*): This family is widely distributed on the subcontinent and Sri Lanka. The **common myna** (*Acridotheris tristis*)

• •
Left, great cormorants resting in their nest, Gal Oya, Sri Lanka and *above*, black-necked stork on the sea coast.

omnivorous, not averse to human society, and builds even inside human dwellings.

Pied Myna (*Sturnus contra*): In north and northeastern India this is the dominant member of the Sturnidae Family, found almost everywhere within the human environment.

Bank Myna (*Acridotheris ginginianus*): Common in north and northeastern India, this myna has a bare red patch around the eye. It is at home among people, and "saunters along confidently on [railway] platforms, in and out of passengers' feet." It nests in tunnels excavated along embankments and large groups build together in colonies.

There are two migrants in the Sturnidae Family, the **Rosy Pastor** (*Sturnus roseus*) and the **Starling** (*Sturnus vulgaris*). The rosy pastor renders enormous service by devouring locusts and keeping their numbers under control in their breeding grounds in Central Asia.

Hill Myna (*Gracula religiosa*): Well-known for its talking and mimicking skills, this bird is trapped in large numbers for export, and is a valuable foreign-exchange earner. It is found mainly in the Himalayan foothills and in the Western Ghats.

Bulbuls (Family *Pycnonotidae*): The 120 species now placed in this Family are found only in the old world, 19 in India, nine in Nepal and about six in Sri Lanka. Bulbuls are sober-colored

• •
Above, barn owls common through South Asia *and right,* the long-eared owl is a winter visitor to northern India.

but elegant birds. Most are olive green, yellow or brown, while one species is black.

Red Vented Bulbul (*Pycnonotus cafer*): This, the commonest of the bulbuls, is very characteristically Indian. Bigger than a sparrow, slim and elegant, with a longish tail, it is mainly brown with a prominent black crest and a red patch under the tail. It is common throughout India, and can adapt itself to busy cities, although being arboreal it is less visible than the sparrow and myna. A liquid call from within a leafy shrub or tree is likely to be the first indication of its

presence. This extremely pleasant call has resulted in its being known as "the Indian Nightingale" (there are no nightingales in India). The quiet beauty of its voice and looks, and its trusting disposition, have given it a special place in Urdu poetry.

Redwhiskered Bulbul (*Pycnonotus jocosus*): Equally common, with its black recumbent crest and crimson cheek-patch, in addition to the red vent, this is a very attractive species.

Whitecheeked Bulbul (*Pycnonotus leucogenys*): Though modestly wearing only a sulfur-yellow patch at the root of the tail, this bulbul has the liveliness of the Family. It is distributed south of the Himalaya down to Bombay, and eastwards up to Central India.

Purplerumped Sunbird (*Nectarinia zeylonica*): Because of its general looks and habit of "hovering" in front of a flower, this is sometimes mistakenly called a hummingbird (there are no hummingbirds in India). Two sizes smaller than a sparrow, with a stumpy tail and a long thin curved beak, the male glistens in crimson, green and purple and its pale-yellow front is just the foil required to set off its brilliant upper plumage. Male and female are a devoted couple, always together, and are usually present wherever there are large bright flowers. They breed throughout the year, nesting in the most exposed situations, but by a wonderful feat of camouflage, the nest is often mistaken for rubbish by friend and foe alike.

Purple Sunbird (*Nectarinia asiatica*): This is really purple only during its breeding season. In fact, at other times, the male assumes the sober light-yellow and brown appearance of the female. Nesting is mainly between March and May. The species is more widely distributed than the purple-rumped, and can be found throughout the country. Even in this sparkling group the **Yellow-backed Sunbird** (*Aethopyga siparaja*), with its distinctive yellow rump, is outstanding, and makes an arresting sight in evergreen forests.

Drongos (Family *Dicruridae*): These are solitary, insectivorous, and arboreal birds, mostly black and with a long forked tail. Of the 20 species in the east, nine are found in India. The commonest is the **Black Drongo** (*Dicrurus adsimilis*), a slim, elegant all-black bird, easily recognizable by its two long forked tail feathers. A white dot at the base of the bill is the hallmark of this species. Although smaller than a myna, the drongo is a tough character, and can often be seen chasing away crows from its territory. On the other hand, it does not harm the nests or eggs of smaller birds, and several species find safety in building nests close to a drongo's. It is this watchdog activity which has earned it the Hindi name of *Kotwal* (policeman).

Parakeets (Family *Psittacidae*): There are no parrots in India, and what the visitor may be tempted to call a parrot will turn out to be, in fact, a parakeet. The shape is that of a parrot and the basic color is parrot-green; and over this the male **Rose-ringed Parakeet** (*Psittacula krameri*) has a dark pink stripe around its neck.

The rose-ringed parakeet makes itself conspicuous when noisy flocks streak across the sky to settle on a tree with ripening fruit. The early mornings and evenings are their working time, and owners of fruit trees have to continuously look for new ways of keeping them away.

Uninhibited in whatever they do, the parakeets have a prolonged and ridiculous courtship display in which the beak plays an important role. There are some handsome birds in this family. In Northern India the **Alexandrine** or **Large Indian Parakeet** (*Psittacula supatria*) which is as large as a pigeon, can be identified by the maroon patch on the shoulder. The **Blossom-headed parakeet** (*Psittacula cyanocephala*), apart from its red head, also has maroon shoulder patches, but prefers the countryside to the city.

Crimson-breasted Barbet or **Coppersmith** (*Megalaima haemacephala*): A bird which is heard by everybody, but seen by few. Its loud repetitive tapping sound has been called "the most monotonous sound of the Indian countryside." If you do manage to follow the sound to its originator, you will see a dumpy bright-green bird (bigger than a sparrow) with a bright-red chest, yellow throat and heavy whiskers. It is widely distributed in India and is equally at home in an uninhabited forest and busy city.

Large Green Barbet (*Megalaima zeylanica*): Another barbet more often heard than seen. It is larger than the myna—grass-green overall with a brown head. The colors merge completely with the foliage, and to add to the problems of the bird watcher its *kutroo, kutroo, kutroo* calls have a ventriloquistic quality, leaving one wondering from which direction the sound comes.

Tailor Bird (*Orthotomus sutorius*): This bird is so trusting that it even nests in bungalow verandahs. Two sizes smaller than a sparrow, it is olive-green with a chestnut cap and a long thin upright tail. Its *towit-towit-towit* calls go on for minutes on end. The Hindi name *durzee*, also pays tribute to its skill as a tailor. It sews itself a tidy little nest by stitching together, with twigs, the leaves of suitable plants and providing a professional inner lining.

Ashy Wren Warbler (*Prinia socialis*): Frequenting small shrubs, this cousin of the tailor

bird is about the same size and shape. It is dark gray above and creamy below, with a loose dangling tail. The nest, which it constructs in low bushes, is a poor imitation of the tailor bird's. Like the latter, it calls vigorously for long periods from the tops of small trees.

Indian Wren Warbler (*Prinia subflava*): A close cousin of the Ashy Wren Warbler, but one which is restricted to drier habitats, it is more gregarious. Its nest is usually slung between weed stems, not too far from the ground.

Cattle Egret (*Bubulcus ibis*): An all-white heron with a yellow bill and black legs. The yellow bill, in contrast to the black bills of its cousins, is an easy identification mark. In the breeding season, during the rains, it acquires an orange-buff plumage on the head, neck and back.

The birds often stand around grazing animals to snap up insects raised by their feet.

Little Egret (*Egretta garzetta*): This bird has a black bill and legs and yellow feet. It was hunted in the old days for its ornamental, pure white feathers, which appear in the breeding season, and which were once in great demand for gracing women's hats.

Pond Heron or **Paddy Bird** (*Ardeola grayii*): A little smaller than the cattle egret, this is a very widely dispersed species, found wherever there is water, whether fresh or brackish — on the coast or around the meanest pond. It has phenomenal patience and will wait frozen for long periods in the hope that a frog, fish or crab will blunder within striking distance of its powerful bill. When at rest, it is all brown, but in flight the white wings and rump show up prominently. Like all herons,

it is unmusical, capable only of a harsh croak when communication is necessary.

Night Heron (*Nycticorax nycticorax*): The heron which city dwellers are likely to come across; little larger than the pond heron, gray black above and white below. They are gregarious and often roost in colonies, departing after sunset into their favorite marsh for feeding. During this flight their loud *kwaark kwaark* is invariably heard.

Flycatchers (Family *Muscicapidae*): Literally catchers of flies, they can twist and turn with incredible dexterity while chasing their prey. Of the 378 known species, India has 38. Many of these reside in the Himalaya and the Western Ghats, but some are at home in the plains.

Paradise Flycatcher (*Terpsiphone paradisi*):

Undoubtedly the most gorgeous, it is about the size of a bulbul, silvery white with a glistening black crest and long pliant tail feathers. The female is chocolate-brown and lacks the ribbon-like tail, but is most engaging nonetheless.

White Spotted Fantail Flycatcher (*Rhipidura albicollis*): Another lovely creature—smoky-brown, about the size of a sparrow, with a distinctive white eyebrow and white-spotted front. It will waltz about on a branch with its fan-like tail spread out.

Tickell's Blue Flycatcher (*Muscicapa tickelliae*): Is mainly blue with a pale-orange breast. Sparrow-sized, like all members of the family, it is hardly ever at rest, and it has a pleasant jingling song which is usually the first sign of its presence.

Water Birds: There are some water birds which are generally found together, whether along the

coast or in and around an inland water body. While some fly back and forth, plunging into the water when prey is sighted, others walk in the squelch within close reach of their food. Each species has its own specialized food.

Gullbilled tern (*Gelochelidon nilotica*): Easy to identify because of its silver-white feathers and, in contrast to other terns, by its black bill and legs.

Brown-headed Gull (*Larus brunnicephalus*) and the **Black-headed Gull** (*Larus ridibundus*): The commonest of the gulls in India, seen usually in large congregations. In flight the former can be identified by a white circle on its black primary feathers.

Common Sandpiper (*Tringa hypoleucos*): Lives up to its name by being invariably present wherever there is a little stretch of water. It is

brown above and white below and a streak of white extending upwards through the shoulder reveals its identity.

Spotted Sandpiper (*Tringa glareola*): Shows up the spots on its back when it is lit up by the slanting rays of the sun in the morning or evening. The lack of the white intrusion on the brown shoulder is a useful clue for differentiating it from the commoner bird.

Green Shank (*Tringa nebularia*) and **Red Shank** (*Tringa totanus*): Both are large sandpipers, about the size of a partridge, but with long legs. Green shanks often give themselves away by their rather melodious *tew tew* calls, and they seem to have strong social bonds.

Blackwinged Stilt (*Himantopus himantopus*): Always stand out in waterside congregations, conspicuous by their long red legs. They have weak

flight, in which the legs trail behind the tail, but they are competent swimmers.

Little Ringed Plover (*Charadrius dubius*): In a gathering of water birds it is easy to spot this plover. It is about the size of a quail, with yellow legs and a black band around the neck. Like many other plovers, it employs the "broken-wing technique" to protect its nest from predators. It will pretend to have broken its wing, trailing it on the ground, and thus induces the pursuer to follow hopefully. Then it flies off suddenly when the predator, man or beast, is some distance from the nest. The nest is merely a scrape in the ground, and the bird relies on the obliterative coloring of the eggs, and of its own body, for camouflage.

Golden Plover (*Pluvialis dominica*) and **Gray**

Plover (*Pluvialis squatarola*): Two attractive water birds, about the size of a partridge, which migrate to India. The former species, brown above, decorated with gold, favors moist pasture land while the gray plovers without the gold coloring are usually found along the coast. They take a few swift steps, stop erect for a moment, dip down quickly, pick up a morsel, and move along again.

Bird watchers are sometimes treated to an exhibition of a flock of small birds turning and twisting in flight in perfect unison, and are left wondering whether there is a leader directing operations. They are likely to be **Little Stints** (*Calidris minutus*), migrants for the winter. They are smaller than quails, gray-brown above, white below, and appear to be incredibly active.

Doves and **Pigeons** (Family *Columbidae*):

These two names are to a certain extent interchangeable. The characteristic quality of these birds is that they can drink like horses by immersing their bills in the water and sucking it up. Most birds have to raise their heads so that the water can trickle down from the bills.

Blue Rock Pigeon (*Columba livia*): Of the 20 species of pigeon in the subcontinent, this is the most common. Although there are wild populations, they are also partial to the most congested localities, and are disliked for the mess they make in godowns, warehouses and other storage areas.

Their throaty cooing and the bullying courtship display of the male, which the female tries to escape, is a familiar sight.

Green Pigeon (*Treron phoenicoptera*): These are found in the hills and in wooded areas. They are modestly but attractively colored, in shades of green, purple and yellow. Because of their tasty flesh, built on a diet of fruit and berries, they are much sought after by sportsmen.

There are nine species of doves in India, of which four are fairly common, and their English names give a hint about their general appearance. All of them are a little larger than the myna.

Collared Dove (*Streptopelia decaocto*): This has a prominent black hind collar on its soft brown neck, and is found in the drier portions of India.

Spotted Dove (*Streptopelia chinensis*): This is

rounded wings and are poor fliers, but they have strong beaks and legs and spend much of their time turning over fallen leaves looking for worms and insects. They "babble" a great deal and hence their name. There are about 45 species of babblers in India.

Jungle Babbler (*Turdoides striatus*): Smaller than the myna; a gray-brown bird with a yellow bill and legs and an untidy look about it. Known as the "Seven Sisters" because they move around in groups of about that number, they have strong family attachments and the young are sometimes fed not just by the parents, but also by members of the community. They are found in well-treed gardens and wooded areas where there is a reasonable quantity of leaf litter.

Common Babbler (*Turdoides caudatus*): Similarly colored as the jungle variety, but a

gregarious than the spotted species.

Whitebreasted Kingfisher (*Halcyon smyrnensis*): Perhaps the most widely distributed, it is easily visible because of its penchant for sitting and calling from exposed locations. It is smaller than a pigeon, but its electric-blue wings, thick red beak, and white front-catch the eye. Even a small patch of water, like a garden pool, may offer it a meal. Indeed, it is not dependent on water for its food and manages to survive in the driest of places on a varied diet.

Common Kingfisher (*Alcedo athis*): Of bulbul size, with a white throat, orange breast, black bill and cobalt-blue wings and head, this is a well-distributed species in the old world. Since it is dependent on fish and aquatic insects, it is found by the coast, along river banks, estuaries and around inland lakes and marshes. It nests be-

Black-headed Oriole (*Oriolus xanthornus*): Lives only in well-wooded areas, and is therefore not as common as the golden. It is distinguished by its black head and throat. A harsh nasal *waak* usually reveals its presence.

Common Iora (*Aegithina tiphia*): Like many arboreal birds, likely to be heard before it is seen. Smaller than a sparrow, it is usually well camouflaged, for during the non-breeding season it is clothed in shades of mustard green. In the breeding season, however, the rich yellow and black coloring of the male catches the eye, particularly when it performs its courtship display by flying up and fluttering down in a manner obviously designed to display its brilliant colors. It has several beautiful calls, one of which spans a full octave.

Wagtails (Family *Motacillidae*): All species of

Above, red-wattled lapwings and *right,* the white-bellied sea eagle is seen along the coast of India and Sri Lanka.

the most widely distributed and can be identified by the white spots against a dark background on the back and sides of the neck. It is a curious fact that in its *kruk kru kroo kroo* calls, the final *kroo* is never repeated more than six times. Usually the effort ends with the third or fourth utterance.

Little Brown Dove (*Streptopelia senegalensis*): Like the collared dove, a bird of the drier regions.

Babblers (Family *Muscicapidae*): This is an old-world group of insect-eaters. They have short

slightly smaller bird which prefers drier areas.

Spotted Babbler (*Pellorneum ruficeps*): Among the many species of babblers inhabiting forested areas, this one needs to be mentioned for its exceptionally beautiful voice. It is about the size of a bulbul, with a white breast prominently spotted with brown. A group of birds calling together from the edges of an evergreen or deciduous jungle provides a joyful and melodious outpouring which is seldom excelled even in the bird world. Less attractive is the monotonous call of solitary birds rendered as *"he'll beat you,"* repeated endlessly.

Quaker Babbler (*Alcippe poioicephala*): Somewhat similar in appearance to the spotted babbler and found in the same locality, this one also has a pretty voice. It is largely arboreal and more

tween March and June in tunnels excavated in embankments.

Pied Kingfisher (*Ceryle rudis*): A rather arresting bird, specially while it is hunting. It is black and white, larger than the myna. It flutters over water in a vertical position and plunges bill first to land on its prey.

Orioles (Family *Oriolidae*) — **Golden Oriole** (*Oriolus oriolus*): In a competition to select the handsomest bird in India, this bird would certainly be short-listed. It is larger than a myna, golden yellow all over, with black wings and a pink bill. The black streak through the eye seems to say that no detail of its make-up has been overlooked and then its glorious long-drawn whistle compels the watcher to try and locate it. Orioles are completely arboreal.

wagtail share certain mannerisms—the tail wagging, the short spurts of running, and undulating flight.

Large Pied Wagtail (*Motacilla maderaspatensis*): The only resident species of wagtail; about the size of a bulbul. During the breeding season (March to September), the male produces a pleasant song.

Gray Wagtail (*Motacilla caspica*): In India breeds only in the Himalaya, and is the commonest of all migrants. As ringing data show, it has a remarkable tendency to return to the same spot year after year during its migrations.

White Wagtail (*Motacilla alba*): Has a black head and a white "face." Breeds in Kashmir and spreads out widely over the subcontinent in winter, sometimes reaching Sri Lanka.

Munias (Weaver Birds) (Family *Ploceidae*): Smaller than sparrows, munias are not true weavers as their untidy globular nests reveal. Of the seven species in India, the **Spotted Munia** (*Lonchura punctulata*), the **White-throated** (*L. malabarica*) and the **White-backed** (*L. Striata*) are the commonest. The English names give an indication of the color patterns of these birds which are mainly brown and white. A rather elegant species, popular as a cage bird, is the **Red Munia** or **Avadavat** (*Estrilda Amandava*). Munias are very sociable birds, and unless pre-occupied with feeding or preening, they stay closely huddled together. The stiff-legged court-ship dance of the males, consisting of a leap upwards, returning to the same spot each time, is a comic but entertaining performance. Munias are caught in their thousands to be sold abroad as pets.

Roller or **Blue Jay** (*Coracias benghalensis*): This pigeon-sized bird with a startling dark-blue plumage, brings the only touch of brilliant color to bare brown fields in the dry season. It is usually perched on electric wires adjoining agricultural lands, and from this vantage point it swoops down on insects, frogs or lizards on the ground.

Redwattled Lapwing (*Vanellus Indicus*): This is a ground bird in the sense that it feeds and nests on the ground, but it is energetic in the air and often seen in rapid wheeling flight, calling stridently all the while. It is about the size of a partridge, but with long legs and its well-known call sounds like the plaintive question, "*Oh . . . . did he do it?*" and leaves no doubt about its identity. The redwattled lapwing has a crimson wattle by the side of the eye while the **yellow wattled lapwing** (*Vanellus malabaricus*), a bird of drier regions, has a yellow lappet in the same place.

Magpie Robin (*Copsychus saularis*): A black and white version of the christmas card robin. Avoiding both city and jungle life, it patronizes gardens and groves. During the breeding season, just before the rains, it becomes both audible and visible, for its coat takes on a smart sheen, and it positions itself on a pillar, or top of a tree and sings loudly and unselfconsciously. It is said to be the most beautiful songster in the country. But in this respect its close cousin, the **Shama** (*Copsychus malabaricus*), a denizen of forests, has an even more melodious and attractive song. The shama has a chestnut belly and a long drooping black and white tail.

The magpie robin is a good example of a songster which sings to establish territorial rights over its breeding area. Rival males are driven off by aggressive singing and posturing. In the event that a male is unable to establish its sway over a territory, it refuses to raise a family and leads a bachelor existence.

Birds of Prey: There are about 60 species of birds of prey in India, 12 in the Family *Falconidae* and 48 in *Acciptridae*. The pariah kite and the brahminy kite have already been mentioned.

Shikra (*Accipiter badius*): Found everywhere, in open country, as well as in city gardens. It is the size of a pigeon, gray above and white below, closely cross-barred with brown. It flies with rapid wing beats and is among the most expert of hunters.

Harriers: In open country, during the migratory season in winter, harriers are an exciting feature of the environment. The **Pale Harrier** (*Circus macrourus*) is a little smaller than the pariah kite, ashy-gray with a black tip to its long pointed wings. In the words of one writer, it knows how to overcome the laws of gravitation as it sails close to the ground. A close cousin is the **Marsh Harrier** (*Circus aeruginosus*) of which the adult male is reddish-brown and the female and young are like a slender pariah kite with rounded tail and buff cap.

Blackwinged Kite (*Elanus caeruleus*): A bird with a specialized hunting style. About the size of a jungle crow, it hovers in the air to take aim at a morsel on the ground and then parachutes down with wings held up at an angle to land on its prey. It is distributed patchily throughout the region.

Kestrel (*Falco tinnunculus*): This is another bird of prey which hovers competently. A migrant from the Himalaya and beyond, though there is one resident race in distant South India. Pigeon-sized, it is brick-red above, with a gray head.

Red Headed Merlin (*Falco chicouera*): Has a gray back and a red head. Pairs hunt in concert, leaving the quarry little chance to escape their talons.

Vultures: Though classified with birds of prey, vultures are not hunters of live prey. They live on the carcasses of dead animals, offal, and some, like the **Scavenger Vulture** (*Neophron percnopterus*) even on human waste. **The White-backed Vulture** (*Gyps bengalensis*) and the **Long-billed Vulture** (*Gyps indica*) are the commonest. The **King Vulture** (*Sarcogyps calvus*) is about as large as a peacock, minus the tail, and its high status amongst vultures can be seen from the respect it receives from the other species when the birds are gorging themselves on the flesh of an animal. Vultures and kites have become unpopular because they cause aircraft crashes, but overall they render a tremendous service through their highly efficient scavenging operations.

. . . .

Far left, immature open-billed storks. *Left,* the rare black-necked crane is confined to the Tibetan plateau and a few Himalayan valleys.

A Sanskrit proverb holds that "A hundred divine epochs would not suffice to describe all the marvels of the Himalaya" — so long to describe, how much longer to understand. Modern scientific study of Himalayan ecology has but touched a tiny tip of the knowledge to be learnt. But even that tip inexorably leads to the grimmest conclusions. Man's onslaught has rendered the Himalaya amongst the most endangered environments in the world. In the subcontinent, the Himalaya rank as the region most in need of conservation, both because of the deterioration in environment and in view of our relative ignorance of the biology and ecology of high-altitude communities. Slowly, this begins to change but the task is immense. The Himalaya contain more endangered species of mammal than any other area of India and are remarkable in possessing almost one third of the world's mammalian species that could be called true mountain animals. M.K. Ranjitsinh has noted that "the outlook for wildlife in most parts of the Himalaya is grim, in some places even desperate," and G.B. Schaller warned that just as we are becoming more aware of the splendor of past and present wildlife of the Himalaya we are denying it a future. He describes mountains without wildlife as "stones of silence," an evocative and thought-provoking phrase.

Rich Variety: What would we be losing? The youngest, largest and highest chain of mountains in the world, the Himalayan range must lay claim to being one of the most fascinating and spectacular natural wonders of our earth. To speak of the Himalaya may give a false impression of biological homogeneity when in fact it covers a wide and varied mosaic of different biotypes — east-west, north-south and altitudinally. Geologically divided into the three regions of trans-Himalaya, middle Himalaya, and outer Himalaya and Siwaliks, the vegetation ranges from lush subtropical forests of the foothills to the bitterly cold high-altitude deserts of Ladakh and the Tibetan plateau. Thrown up 60–70 million years ago with activity still continuing, the Himalaya have acted both as a bridge and a barrier. The asymmetrical collision of the continental plates resulted in an inflow of oriental fauna through the northeast before the Afro-Mediterranean elements which followed through the northwest. The present flora and fauna species of the east and west regions reflect this —the former showing a close relationship with the western-Chinese pattern and the latter having Euro-Mediterranean affinities. Besides these, many species have evolved from the previously

present Central Asian or palaearctic fauna and given rise to high endemism with strong generic links to Tibet and Central Asia.

Elusive Cat: No animal better epitomizes the character and concerns of the mountain environment than the **snow leopard** (*Panthera uncia*), that beautiful and elusive cat of the high altitudes of Central Asia. A survivor of the icy rigors of the Pleistocene era, its range is immense, covering the entire Himalaya between altitudes as low as 6000 feet (1850 meters) in winter to 18,000 feet (5550 meters) in summer. Being a shy inhabitant of remote habitats, it has seldom been seen by any

- -
Above, the Himalayan tahr ranges from Pakistan to Arunachal Pradesh and *right*, Himalayan tahr; Sagarmatha National Park, Nepal.

but those humans sharing its mountainous home. Only recently have some facts emerged about the ecology of this high-altitude predator.

Somewhat smaller than the leopard (*Panthera pardus*), but with a relatively longer tail, the snow leopard has a thick and beautiful spotted coat of soft gray, paling to pure white on the underside. This has certainly contributed to its rarity, for although strictly protected, many still fall to poachers' bullets and traps, for in the world of fashion there remain those ignorant and rich enough to make taking such risks worthwhile. The snow leopard uses large areas in order to

obtain enough sustenance. In winter months, it sometimes ventures near villages to lift domestic livestock, but its main prey are the wild sheep and goats that share with it these stark and snowy wastes.

Mountain Sheep: The Himalaya contain more species of sheep than any other mountain range. Pride of place must go to the **Marco Polo sheep** (*Ovis ammon polii*), whose ratio of horn-length to body-weight exceeds that of any animal in the world. These horns form open graceful spirals with the tips arcing up, out and then down again. A northern subspecies of the **argali** (*Ovis ammon*), Marco Polo sheep may still be fairly common in the Russian Pamirs and Wakhan corridor of Afghanistan, but within the subcontinent it is a rare animal existing only in northern Hunza where its magnificent head has

long attracted hunters. In its spartan, near-desert landscape home, particularly severe winters also take their toll of this grand creature.

Another race of the argali is the **nayan** or **great Tibetan sheep** (*Ovis ammon hodgsoni*). This is the largest of all wild sheep. Long in the leg and graceful, it inhabits the trans-Himalaya plateau, an area of desolate plains and low undulating hills, experiencing extreme temperatures, from scorching summers to freezing winters. Nayan are migratory, wandering wherever food and water

• •
Above, **chukor are often seen in small coveys on bare, arid hillsides in the western Himalaya.** *Right,* **the kiang or Tibetan wild ass is restricted in India to a small area of Ladakh.**

may be found, and are natural prey of the **Tibetan wolf** which is the chief predator of the trans-Himalayan uplands and plateaus.

The **urial** or **shapu** (*Ovis orientalis*) is the smallest of the wild sheep and is distributed through the western Himalaya where several different races are distinguished. While horn shapes and colors differ, the adult rams all wear a great ruff growing from either side of the chin and extending down the throat. Adapted to differing environments, from the barren stony ranges of Sind and Baluchistan to steep grass hillslopes in Ladakh, this progenitor of domestic sheep has also attracted hunters' bullets and many populations have been decimated to rarity.

Another Himalayan mammal, originally classified as a sheep, is the **bharal** (*Pseudois nayaur*). Its physical characteristics are so intermediate between sheep and goats that taxonomists have had trouble classifying it. Expressing thoughts on their evolution in his book, *Mountain Monarchs*, G.B. Schaller writes that "in general the behavioural evidence confirms the morphological evidence that bharal are basically goats. Many of the sheep-like traits of the bharal can be ascribed to convergent evolution, the results of the species having settled in a habitat which is usually occupied by sheep." For bharal, like sheep, graze on open slopes, whereas goats prefer more precipitous cliff habitats. It is an animal of the Himalaya and trans-Himalaya zones and is still common in some places as far apart as Eastern Ladakh and Bhutan.

Mountain Goats: The Himalaya house three species of true goat — the **ibex** (*Capra ibex*),

occupying the highest altitudes; with the **markhor** (*Capra falconeri*) and **wild goat** (*Capra hircus*), inhabiting cliffs generally below 12,000 feet (3700 meters). The ibex, found in the Himalaya west of the Satluj gorge, leads a tenuous existence in spite of its adaptability, as the balance between death and malnutrition in its austere habitat is delicate indeed. The spectacular markhor found in the Pir Panjal range and west to the Hindu Kush and Karakoram, lacks the underwool of the ibex and prefers to remain below the snow line. The markhor's horns are uniquely spiraling whereas the wild goat has scimitar horns similar to those of the ibex.

The **Himalayan tahr** (*Hemitragus jemlahicus*), differs from true goats in having short curved horns rather than long sweeping ones. This tahr is found throughout the Himalaya from the Pir

Panjal to Sikkim and Bhutan in several vegetation zones between 8000 feet and 15,000 feet (2500-4500 meters) though rarely going far above the tree line. A beautiful and robust creature, the male Himalayan tahr has a conspicuous coppery brown ruff and mantle of flowing hair draping from the neck and shoulders to its knees and from its back and rump to its flanks and thighs.

Serow (*Capricornis sumatraensis*) and **goral** (*Nemorhaedus goral*), two of a group known as goat-antelopes, are also found in both western and eastern areas. The third member of this group, the **takin** (*Budorcas taxicolor*), a large heavily-built relative of the musk-ox, is found only in restricted numbers in the eastern Himalaya. Recently the Royal Government of Bhutan declared it the national animal and set up

special reserves for its protection. Gregarious by nature, the takin partakes of long seasonal migrations and is at home in general as well as rhododendron forest. The movements of **serow** and **goral** in their selected habitats are very restricted. The serow, solitary and reclusive by nature, occupies small cliffs and thickly forested ravines, whereas the goral prefers grassy slopes with broken ground, usually at lower altitudes in the southern Himalaya.

Ruminants: Evolutionally, the earliest known ruminants are the antelope and gazelle group of the family *Bovidae*. In the Himalaya they are represented by the **Tibetan antelope** or **chiru** (*Pantholops hodgsoni*), and the **Tibetan gazelle** (*Procapra picticaudata*). The chiru is another creature of the high Tibetan plateau and may also be found seasonally in northern and eastern Ladakh. With a special breathing system and the finest underwool to protect it from the extreme cold, the chiru is well adapted for the high altitude desert areas that constitute its home. Tibetan gazelle have all but disappeared in Ladakh though they may be found in Pakistan and Bhutan as well as in the Tibetan plateau.

Other animals which occasionally cross the main Himalayan divide in small numbers from the trans-Himalayan ranges are the **wild yak** (*Bos grunniens*) and **kiang**, the Tibetan wild ass (*Equus hemionus kiang*). The yak is the largest animal of the mountains; massively built and heavily coated, it inhabits the coldest, wildest and most desolate areas and is one of the highest-dwelling animals in the world. The kiang, whose close relative runs in the Rann of Kutch in Gujarat, is another creature of the Tibetan plateau and plains of northern Ladakh.

Of the other ungulates of the Himalayan region the **sambar** and **barking deer**, though found at high altitudes in the southern Himalaya, are not truly mountain species. However, two species of **red deer** are endemic to the area and both are highly endangered. Indeed, the status of the **shou** — so-called **Sikkim stag** (*cervus elaphus wallichi*) though it was never found in Sikkim — is so uncertain that it may well already be extinct. The position of the **hangul** or **Kashmir stag** (*Cervus elaphus hanglu*), is a little better with a population of around 500 living protected in the Dachigam National Park in Kashmir.

In contrast to the restricted ranges of these red deer, the **musk deer** (*Moschus moschiferus*) may be found over a wide area of central and northeastern Asia. In spite of this, their status is hardly less endangered for the male carries the musk pod which, commanding exorbitant prices, has made the musk deer the chief target of every poacher in the Himalaya. Though protected by most stringent laws, unscrupulous perfume manufacturers still encourage the decimation of this delightful creature. Threatened thus throughout its range, the best chances for viewing it are within preserved areas such as the Kedarnath Musk Deer Sanctuary in Uttar Pradesh and the Sagarmatha National Park in Nepal.

Bears: The ungulates described here constitute the largest group of mammals in the Himalaya and many are the main prey species of the larger predators. Though the snow leopard may be the most spectacular of these, the largest carnivore of the mountain species is the **brown bear** (*Ursus arctos isabellinus*). Once abundant in the Himalaya, in some parts of its range the brown bear is now even more seriously threatened than the snow leopard. As an inhabitant of the less-vegetation-rich higher altitudes, the brown bear is more of a predator than its lower-living relative, the **Himalayan black bear** (*Selenarctos*

thibetanus), whose ratio of fruit to flesh is higher. But the black bear is also omnivorous and a great meat lover, eagerly scavenging carcasses as well as occasionally bringing down sick or young prey of its own. The black bear has the largest range of all the Himalayan mammals, extending over the full mountain range and into Southeast Asia. Safer from human attack than most of the large Himalayan species, it nevertheless comes into conflict with people due to its propensity for crop raiding. Being especially fond of maize, many injuries and deaths on both sides occur during the harvesting season. A third member of the bear family to be listed amongst Himalayan fauna is the **Tibetan blue bear**, but it is so rare that almost nothing is known of it.

Wild Dogs and Cats: Distant evolutionary re-

latives of the bear family are the dogs. The most conspicuous representative in the Himalaya is the **wolf** (*Canis lupus*). Feeding on hares and marmots as well as the larger goats and sheep, the wolf is an animal of the western region and may be found in Ladakh, where it is still relatively common. Another member of this family is the **wild dog** (*Cuon alpinus*), which can be found in the Himalaya and trans-Himalaya, but its rarity in the more accessible areas makes its status uncertain and little information concerning it is available. Of this family, the **hill fox** (*Vulpes vulpes montana*) is the most widespread and common in many habitats. But fox pelts also command a good price and it is not ignored by the ubiquitous poacher.

Several members of the cat family may be included in the Himalayan fauna in that their

The monal or Impeyan pheasant is the national bird of Nepal, where it is also known as the *danphe* (bird of nine colors).

ranges, including those of the tiger and leopard, extend deep into the Himalaya and at high altitudes. Of the lesser cats, some like the **jungle cat** are recognized as having a separate Himalayan race. However, there are two, other than the snow leopard, which are specifically mountain species—the **lynx** (*Felis lynx isabellina*), and **Pallas's cat** (*Felis manul*). The latter is a Central-Asian species and though found in Ladakh, is rare and apparently restricted to the lower Indus valley there. The lynx, which occurs in the upper Indus valley, Gilgit, Ladakh and

Tibet, is a race of the lynx of northern Europe and Asia. Similarly rare, both Pallas's cat and the lynx are threatened by trapping and shooting.

Smaller Species: Besides these larger animals, there is a diversity of smaller species—hares, mouse hares, bats, weasels, martens and more—with varying degrees of rarity, range and reports. It is impossible to describe all here, but mention must be made of the two races of marmot, the **Himalayan marmot** (*Marmota bobak*), and the **long-tailed marmot** (*Marmota caudata*), both endearing and common creatures of the higher Himalaya. The **red panda**, a small animal which extends east from the Nepal Himalaya, is another well-known lesser mammal of the range. Colorful and cute, it is largely arboreal and nocturnal so is seldom seen in the wild.

Birds: The avifauna of the Himalaya similarly present a fascinating and varied range of species, mainly a conglomerate of palaearctic and Indo-Chinese elements, the former predominating in the western section and the latter richly represented in the eastern areas. Several bird families are endemic to the Himalaya including **broadbills, honeyguides, finfoots** and **parrotbills.** The **chir pheasant** and **mountain quail** are endemic and some 14 other palaearctic species including the **Himalayan pied woodpecker, blackthroated jay** and beautiful **nuthatch,** are considered by Ripley to give strong evidence of relict forms.

Innumerable and diverse, the colorful species of birds that colonize the Himalayan region defy precising and the several volumes covering various regions should be consulted by interested visitors. Yet some species must be mentioned. The **Himalayan pheasants** include such spectacular and gloriously plumed members as the resplendent **crimson tragopan** and the **monal** with its glistening rainbow plumage. The **blood pheasant,** so called for the blotches of crimson that streak its feathers, is distributed only in the eastern Himalaya and graphically exemplifies the Chinese influence in the avifauna there. Most common and abundant is the generally lower-altitude **kaleej pheasant,** of which five or six races are recognized. The dapper, gray, black and chestnut **koklas pheasant** is found more or less on the entire length of the Himalayan system. The **eared pheasant** and **peacock pheasant** should perhaps be mentioned amongst the Himalayan *phasianidae*, though their distribution only touches on the far northeastern section. Others in this family are the **partridges** and snow cocks, the **Himalayan snow cock** and the **Tibetan snow cock.**

If for no other reason than their impressive size, two birds of prey of this region draw a mention. The **golden eagle,** a powerful hunter, 3½ feet (one meter) from beak to tail, is capable even of taking large mammals such as musk deer

fawns and the newborn young of mountain sheep; the **lammergeier** or **bearded vulture** is best known for its habit of dropping bones from a height to splinter them on the rocks below, thus releasing the marrow and creating bone fragments on which it feeds.

Migration: The Himalaya are important in the context of Indian bird migration. Of the 2100-odd species and subspecies of birds that comprise the subcontinent's avifauna, nearly 300 are winter visitors from the palaearctic region north of the Himalayan barrier. One of the most endangered migratory birds of the subcontinent, which nests around the high-altitude lakes of Eastern Ladakh, is the **blacknecked crane.** Hardly half a dozen pairs are known to breed there, though recently its extremely low known world population figure was increased by the discovery of a colony in China. Many of the geese and ducks to be seen in the north Indian wetlands in winter return to these high-altitude lakes for nesting between May and October. Apart from the host of long-distance trans-Himalaya migrants and those that descend to lower levels and the northern plains in winter, there are also species which partake of local seasonal migration within the Himalaya itself. One delightful though not too common example is the crimson-winged **wall creeper,** fascinating with its distinctly butterfly-like flight.

Until recently it was thought that the mountains formed an insuperable barrier so that migrating birds had to take circuitous routes following the courses of river valleys. However in 1981 it was established by Salim Ali, doyen of Indian ornithologists, that even small birds of starling size are able to withstand the cold and rarefied atmospheres at heights of 20,000–22,000 feet (6000–6700 meters) and some of the larger ducks, geese, eagles etc. have been observed at heights calculated to be even greater than this.

Forests: The below-tree line areas of the western region hold forests with close resemblances to European elements and have a greater representation of conifers. Among them the aptly named deodar, *tree of the gods*, must rank as the most magnificent. Its massive height and girth make it much prized for its timber uses and some of the finest stands have fallen to the axe. The colorful flowering of rhododendrons in their masses is an unforgettable Himalayan experience. The deep crimsons, reds, pinks and creamy yellows of the blooms have no better setting than their natural environment and backdrop of snowy peaks. The majority of the 80 varieties are found in the eastern Himalaya which is also very rich in orchids, presenting a profusion of delicate shapes and colors. This eastern zone is at a lower altitude and has higher precipitation with a higher snow line, thus adding to its distinctive botanical identity.

A desert environment is one where two basic needs of life — water and shelter, are at a premium and, therefore, it is not a biome in which any lifeform is likely to have originated. The story of life here is one of the heroic struggle of the survivors who adopted a strategy to withstand the harsh physical conditions — extreme paucity or total absence of free water, inhibitive high temperatures reaching over 130° F (55° C), and desiccation augmented by hot winds. At the other extreme, low temperatures, below zero, accentuated by bitter cold Himalayan winds are another challenging factor in certain deserts. Since the desert landforms of the world are far more recent (about 7 million years old) than the rain forests, the adaptations are often not in physical form but in behavioral pattern — an example of marvelous ecological adjustment rather than evolution.

The strenuous life activities of desert wildlife are concerned mainly with getting water, conserving this important resource, avoiding overheating, getting enough food, and avoiding and escaping from enemies while exposed in the coverless landscape.

The Great Indian Desert, also known as the Thar Desert, is situated between 22° and 32° north latitude in the states of Rajasthan and Gujarat, and lies across India's western frontier with Pakistan. It extends over 270,200 sq miles (700,000 sq km). Landforms such as shifting sand dunes, fixed sand dunes, interdunal lands, rocky outcrops, flat pavements and salt flats of ephemeral lakes are some of the habitat types of the Thar. These are inhabited by a rich variety of plant and animal life.

Base of Life: The Thar Desert is distinct in vegetative biomass, specially the sewan grass which covers extensive areas called *pali*. Typical shrubs are phog (*Calligonum pollinoides*) growing on sand dunes, khair (*Capparis decidua*), a leafless shrub growing to a middle-size tree, aak (*Calotropis procera*) and thor (*Euphorbia caduca*), representing the juicy shrubs. Jal (*Salvadora procera*), khejra (*Prosopis sinreria*) and rohira (*Tecoma undulata*) are the main trees scattered very thinly over the desert. There are no cacti and there is no carpet of flowers of annuals. But khair, rohira and aak, when in flower in March, add color to the landscape and are the center of activity for insects and birds.

• •

Left, wild asses in the Rann of Kutch, Gujarat and *right,* conservation measures have helped the great Indian bustard make a comeback.

Most of the major insect orders are found in the Thar Desert. There are 17 species of termites. The colorful members are the **butterflies** of the group *Lepidoptera*. The **dung beetle** (*Coleoptera ordes*) which rolls dung balls larger than itself, has an advanced form of a "copter" mechanism. Its flight wings, neatly placed under a hard cover, slide out as if under electronic automation for take off. The hot sandy areas are ideal for swarms of **locusts** and **grasshoppers**, many of which are brightly colored. The **velvet mite** which has disappeared from many areas due to chemical sprays, is still to be seen in the desert. Moisture is

the governing factor of all insect activity and insects spring to life with the first monsoon shower. They constitute an important source of protein for insectivorous birds and reptiles and even mammals, and being 60–85 percent water, a source of water too. They are thus an important ecological link as first-stage consumers and act as producers for the second-stage consumers—reptiles and birds.

Reptiles: Forty-three reptile species inhabit the Indian desert today. The **spiny-tail lizard** (*Uromastix hardwickei*) lives in underground colonies in flat calcareous interdunal areas and *kankar* (limestone) pans. Its L-shaped burrow is six–eight inches (15–20 cm) deep. Its design helps in withstanding sudden changes of weather conditions. The burrow is held exclusively by the owner. With a few drops of rain falling, one can observe the process of closing the hole. With moisture in the air, the calcareous nature of the soil helps to seal the opening. The excavated earth heaped around the hole acts as a check-dam against sheet run-off of the rain water.

Though a snake called **pivana** (breath sucker) has been identified as the **Sind krait** (*Bungarus caevuleus*), myths about the breath-sucking power of the viper continue to circulate all over the desert. It is the snake of the desert's core area.

The deadly **saw-scaled viper** (*Echis caenatus*), another poisonous snake, does not leave a serpentine mark on the sand. Its almost parallel lines created by its looping movement, leave no clue of its direction of movement. The color of the Russel's viper (*Vipera russelli*) matches that of the sand so well that only by scanning the ground

is rich in both species and in population — numbers sometimes swelling to 2000-4000 birds at a single spot. No niche of the Thar is devoid of birds. Even in the face of challenging terrain, temperature and repeated deadly droughts, many species of birds have decided to be resident here.

Outstanding among the birds is the **great Indian bustard** (*Chriotis nigricaps*). It weighs 18-30 lb (eight-14 kg) and stands 16" (40 cm) high on strong legs designed for walking. This tall, heavy bird can be seen walking with confidence and grace in the desert. It holds its head at an angle; its body feathers form a pattern of black bars and dots; its head looks like a crown; its snow-white neck makes it conspicuous in the landscape. While changing its feeding grounds or to escape danger, the bird reluctantly takes to wing. The bustard feeds on a varied diet—

a sudden twitter in the sky and one spots the flight of a distant pair. A few more definite and louder twitters are heard in the same direction. These are the **Indian sandgrouse** (*Pterocles exustus*) flying for their morning drink. At a water hole they wheel and turn to land, first at some distance from the free water and later directly on the water hole. Soon they crowd in hundreds for the day's sip and take off, to return the next day — the same place, the same time. They live in small flocks of 10-15. They are distinguished by the male's chestnut band on his chest, spots on the body and a tapering long pintail. Similar is the watering behavior of **painted** and **spotted sandgrouse**. They feed on grass and grains and pick up grit to grind the grain between their powerful gizzard muscles.

The **gray partridge** (*Francolinus pondicerinus*)

Insectivorous birds like the **bee-eater** (*Merops superciliosus*), **blue tailed bee-eater** (*Merops philippinus*), **common bee-eater** (*Merops orientalis*), **Indian roller** (*Coracias bengalensis*), **larks**, **shrikes**, **orioles**, **drongos**, **babblers**, **flycatchers** and **warblers** enrich the avifauna. Among bulbuls, the **white-cheeked bulbul** (*Pycnonotus leucogenys*) is commonly seen on khair bushes.

Sparrows, including the **house-sparrow** (*Passer domesticus indicus*) and **Spanish sparrow** (*Passer hispaniolensis*) fly in gliding movements and congregate on khair bushes near water holes in incredible numbers. They are in constant motion, diving into the leafless bush every time a predatory bird makes a swoop. **Whitethroated munia** (*Lonchura malabarica*) gather in small flocks and perch on dry bushes.

inch by inch can one discover the serpentine spring, ready to uncoil and attack.

Desert monitors (*Varanus griseus* and *Varanus bengalensis*) are miniature dragons with dinosaurian looks. They raid nests, and feed on rodents and insects. The **toad agama** or **horned toad**, curiously named since it is no toad and has no horn, is actually a lizard. The blue, green, yellow, crimson, red and black spots in contrast to its sand-colored body, make it colorful. It screws itself into loose sand, to "swim" under it to escape predators. The **sandfish** (*Ophiomorus tridactylus*) is another lizard which swims under sand. The color-changing **chameleons** are commonly seen on the bushes and trees looking for insects.

Wings of the Desert: The avifauna of the desert

cereals, grasshoppers, locusts, dung beetles, lizards, snakes, berries and small, sparrow-size birds. It lives in family flocks of four-six but at times over 40 birds assemble on a feeding or breeding ground. A polygamous male every now and then inflates its neck air-sac and fluffs its feathers to display its size to court females.

Overhunting, since it provided substantial meat, trampling of its eggs (generally one, sometimes two and rarely four) by cattle, and loss and disturbance in its habitat, had not long ago reduced its numbers to near extinction. Thanks to public awareness and conservation efforts, including establishment of the Desert National Park, the bustard population has recovered and is now placed at over 1000 in the desert alone.

The morning silence of the desert is broken by

is known for its morning call and its elegant walk. It is the only species of the Francolinus genus that dares to live in the harsh desert. Its secret is its comparatively low dependence on drinking water. It lives in family coveys of eight-10 birds but separates in pairs for breeding in spring.

The **bush quail** (*Perdicula asiatica*) and the **common quail** (*Coturnix coturnix*) only inhabit the favorable fringes of the desert; they do not reach the core. The **peafowl** (*Pavo cristatus*) and **roseringed parakeet** (*Psittacula krameri*) live only close to human settlements where water is available and can hardly be called desert birds in the true sense. **Ring doves** (*Streptopelia decaocto*) are common and congregate at watering places in hundreds. Spotted doves and red turtle doves are seldom seen.

Left, beautiful gray partridges and *above*, elegant male chinkaras.

Winter Visitors: The desert even attracts many visitors! Its rich food supply, clear, stormless weather, warm, sunny days and clear comfortable nights, attract birds of the temperate region. Hundreds of thousands of **common crane** (*Grus grus*) and **demoiselle crane** (*Anthropoides virgo*) pass through the desert during October on their to and fro winter migration. The cranes live in grassy depressions and along salt flats like Tal Chhapar, Kanodia Tal, the flood flanks of the Luni river and shallow drying lakes and open agricultural fields in the Saurashtra region of

Gujarat. The graceful **greater flamingo** (*Phoenicopterus roseus*) and the colorful **lesser flamingo** (*Phoenicopterus minor*) visit the shallow saline lakes all over the desert, including Sultanpur near Delhi. Their assemblies of over a thousand birds are seen in several places. In May and June, at Nal Sarovar (Gujarat) over 100,000 of these birds congregate. They probably assemble every summer to locate sites for their nesting somewhere in the Greater Rann of Kutch.

The saline ponds in the process of drying, if they happen to hold enough water till winter, attract **rosy** and **gray pelicans** (*Pelecanus onocrotalus* and *P. philippensis philippensis*) and migratory waterfowl—**barheaded geese** (*Anser indicus*), **whistling teal** (*Dendrocygna javanica*), **ruddy shelduck** (*Tadorna ferruginea*), **pintail** (*Anas acuta*), **shoveler** (*Anas crecca*), **coot**

melodious note. Migration of **rosy pastors** (*Sturnus roseus*) and **starlings** (*Sturnus vulgaris*) in swarms across the desert is seen once in October and on their return flight in February–March.

The **houbara** (*Chlamydolis undulata macqueenii*) hit world headlines in the late 1960s when some oil-rich Arabs managed to persuade the Indian Government to permit them to hunt the birds with falcons. This "sport" created a problem since the size of the bag became a status symbol with the sheiks. The hunts played havoc with the population of this lesser bustard. In 1978, as a result of countrywide protest, this sport was ended once and for all.

The **sandgrouse**, identified by its black lower-half belly and wing tips, is a gregarious bird. Large flocks of them visit water holes for a

mostly fawns and fawn-colored females and a few jet black, dominant, co-dominant, and light-colored, recessive bucks. The does are hornless, whereas the bucks have a pair of spiraled horns ending in a rapier-sharp tip which lends the buck a masculine magnificence.

Ferocious combats of territorial blackbuck are common. Rival bucks are chased away and the 20–30 doe harem is regrouped with an impressive display of speed and determination. They are short-grassland animals. They are water-dependent, and, therefore, do not venture into the waterless region of the desert. However, even highly brackish water is acceptable to them.

The buck was once the dominant mammal of the desert region but, as a result of merciless persecution over 50 years, it is now confined only to certain pockets. It is estimated that there

The gazelle is the only species of the Indian antelope of which the female have horns, vestigial though they be. The horns of males are over nine inches (23 cm) long and are pointed at the tip, well adapted for a fight to the finish. The chinkara buck is able to stand up to desert predators, including large eagles and foxes.

Normally, one fawn (rarely two) is dropped after eight months of gestation. The most vulnerable period in the life of the gazelle is the period of parturition. But nature's scheme of protection by camouflage, and literally getting a fawn up on its legs in four–six hours, helps the newborn infant to follow its mother to safety. But its principal survival strategy is to manage in situations of total absence of free water. It manages even where rain is a rare and chance occurrence and year after year may pass without

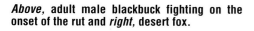

Above, **adult male blackbuck fighting on the onset of the rut and** *right,* **desert fox.**

(*Fulica atra*), and waders including **curlew**, **sandpiper** (*Calidris testaceus*) and **snipe** (*Capella sops*).

A significant recent event in Indian ornithology was the establishment of the fact that the **desert courser** (*Cursorius coromandelicus*) nests in the Indian desert. This bird is cream-colored and arrives in November to feed on termites and insects. The **Kashmir roller** (*Coracias garrulus*) arrives by October and stays till March. In contrast, **orioles** (*Oriolus oriolus*) visit the desert in hot summer and delight one with their

morning drink. They come in hundreds and thousands, without a single twitter. All one hears is the soft, whistling wing beats of the flying birds wheeling, landing and taking off.

The large **pintail sandgrouse** flies into the area in large flocks during winter, but not as large as reported by Alan Octavian Hume in the late 19th Century as "tens of thousands — like a thin cloud — darkening the air."

Antelope Territory: The core of the desert ecosystem is the prime habitat of the true antelope, the **blackbuck** (*Antilope cervicapra*). It inhabits the open plains, short grasslands and saline depressions called *chappar* or *rann*. It depends for its survival on its keen sight and high speed (40 miles / 60 km per hour) with occasional leaps. It lives in large herds of 40 to 60 animals,

are 15,000 in Jodhpur District in areas which have been notified for strict protection, but the most impressive of them are to be seen in the Velavadar National Park in Gujarat where more than 2500 of them live in a short-grassland area of less than 14 sq miles (36 sq km).

Striding across clumps of grass, the **gazelle**, or **chinkara** as it is also called, stops only on the crest of a sand dune. One wonders why this animal, having pointed hooves unsuited to walking on loose sand, has chosen to live in the desert. In fact, sand dunes form less than 10 percent of the Great Indian Desert, the other 90 percent of landforms include craggy rocks, pavements, and compacted salt-lake bottoms, interdunal areas, and fixed dunes, for which the gazelle is well equipped to fly over at high speed.

even a trace of water vapour in the atmosphere. The gazelle is able to survive in these conditions because it has an inbuilt adaptive system to produce metabolic water in the physiological process of digestion. Its kidney chemistry is such that it can excrete highly concentrated urine, thus helping the body to economize on water.

The gazelle is well distributed throughout the desert. There are some pockets where it is much less wary than elsewhere because it has received protection from the desert's human inhabitants, specially the Bishnois, and even the meat-eating Muslims.

The third member of the antelope group (not the family) is the **nilgai** (*Boselaphus tragocamelus*), the largest antelope of India. Ecologically, the animal's heavy demand on forage is not in the interest of the meager forage resources of the desert and, therefore, its water-dependence has discouraged its distribution in the heartland of the Thar. It is actually the female that is called *nilgai* (blue cow) and the male, blue bull, though they have no resemblance to or relationship with the sacred cow. The bull is strong, with spiky horns totally out of proportion to its body size; they are more like spurs at the wrong place. However, they are effective and efficient in ripping open a rival male during courtship quarrels. The fights between bulls are highly ritualized, starting with an arching of bodies, straining of necks, holding tails erect like flags, and looking slyly at each other from the corner of their eyes. They move in closing circles, finally falling on their knees, trying to get at each other's vulnerable points. The victim is chased out of the victor's territory enclosing the cows in estrus. Though the right of exclusive mating is fully demonstrated by the leader, recessive males sneak in to cover the cows while the dominant male is busy chasing away his rivals. After eight months of gestation, around September, when grasses and cover are sufficient, one fawn (occasionally two) is dropped. The increasing number of nilgai in certain areas, in the absence of a predator, is becoming a problem.

The pale-chestnut-colored **wild ass** (*Asinus hemionus khur*) of the desert is a fascinating creature — for its survival capacity, if for nothing else. Its body cells are capable of withstanding dehydration and also have the capacity of holding reserves of water when it is available — a perfect adaptive strategy in the harsh environment of the desert. The wild ass, an animal of the open sandy desert, is now confined to the Little Rann of Kutch. Its withdrawal from the sandy tracts to the *bet* (islands) in the Rann is recent. These "islands" within the temporary marshes provide a protected habitat to this endangered population, and hence its withdrawal there. Unfortunately, even from these *bets* the cattle of the Maldharis are edging the wild ass out. They now live mostly in *Prosopis juliflora* bushes, a modified habitat, on the fringes of the Rann. The bushes provide good cover and their dry pods a sugar-rich diet. Normally, the ass feeds on grasses, salt-tolerant bushes and even dry leaves of aak (*Calotropis procera*). Like the antelope, this species relies on its keen sight and speed for its safety. It is capable of running at 40 miles (60 km) an hour. The wild ass lives in herds of 30 to 40 members (sometimes as large as 100) under the leadership of a stallion who guides the direction of movement. Their current population is estimated to be somewhat over 1000 animals, all in the Little Rann.

Underground Dwellers: The **desert gerbil** (*Meriones hurranae*) has adapted itself to living in extreme climates with temperatures of over 120° F (50°C) in summer and freezing nights in winter, when the temperature falls below zero. The hot winds, call *loo*, enhance desiccation, and cold winds from the Himalaya increase the chill at night. The gerbil's strategy for desert living is to burrow in the ground, where its living chambers are cooler by 40 percent and more humid by 45 percent than at the surface in summer and warmer by 70° F (20°C) in winter. It is active in the late evening, when the temperature is comfortable. It changes its feeding timetable in winter by becoming totally diurnal. Dr. Ishwari Prakash and his team have experimented on the desert gerbil, feeding their sample on 100 percent dehydrated food for 21 months, without any adverse effect on the rodent's health. The secret of living without water, for months and even years, is its metabolic chemistry which, during the process of digestion, produces water.

The gerbil lives in colonies, sometimes in open fixed dunes, but mostly under khair or zizyphus bushes. The burrows are interconnected and have many escape routes. It feeds on grass seeds, fallen fruits and even stems. It also eats insects. Its long bushy tail is its rudder to balance and guide its direction while taking long leaps. The rich population, 800 burrows per hectare, provide sufficient food as well as water (since 65 percent of its body is water) to its predators.

Other common rodents of the desert are the **desert hare** (*Lepus nigricollis dayanus*) and the **hedgehog** (*Hemiechinus auritus*). The hare is a fast runner and depends on its camouflage coloration when an enemy approaches. The hedgehog is purely nocturnal and rolls itself into a spiny unappetizing ball. The hare is purely vegetarian and the hedgehog an insectivorous rodent. Both live in burrows. The **common hare** (*Lepus nigricollis*), with gray or black nape needs proximity to water. It is distributed on the fringes of the desert. The **crested porcupine** (*Hystrix indica*) occurs in the hilly terrain of Jalore and Siwana. It is totally nocturnal.

Predators: The main predator of the desert is the **Indian wolf** (*Canis lupus*). Once widely distributed over the desert, preferring hilly and broken country, after massive destruction of the antelope, the wolf was forced to take to preying on sheep and goats and it soon became the shepherd's nightmare. It was therefore singled out for destruction, to be killed by any means, including smoking mothers and their pups to death in burrows. This very nearly dropped the final curtain for the species in the desert. It is now reduced to a dangerously low number, extremely limited in its distribution.

The Indian wolf preys not by chase but by surprise attack and, therefore, does not need the company of other wolves. It lives in pairs or family packs and sometimes organizes co-operative hunting.

The **jackal** (*Canis aureus*), widely believed to be strictly a scavenger, is also an effective predator, specially when helpless does are parturient and the fawns are too weak to stand. It is absent in the core area of the desert owing to its need for water.

The **common fox** (*Vulpes bengalensis*) and the **desert fox** (*Vulpes vulpes*) are both widely but thinly distributed throughout the desert region. The common fox, distinguished by the black tip on its tail, is aggressive. It attacks gazelle and kills fawns and even grown females. The desert fox preys only on rodents, gerbils, desert hare, birds, and reptiles like the spiny-tail lizard. A fox hole, specially when it has pups in it, is often located under the same bushes as those of the gerbils and in the midst of hundreds of their burrows. Why predator and prey live in such deadly proximity is

An Indian sandgrouse family.

still unexplained. The fox hunts during the cooler hours of the day to avoid over-consumption of water which it obtains only from its prey.

There are also the predators of the air. The **blackwinged kite** (*Elanus caeruleus*), **crested honey-buzzard** (*Pernis ptilorhynchus*), **shikra** (*Accipiter badius*), **tawny eagle** (*Aquila rapax*) and **laggar falcon** (*Falco biarmicus jugger*), stay all the year round and nest in the desert. The owls and nightjars take over at night. The **short-eared owl** (*Asio flammeus*) and **spotted owlet** (*Athena brama*) are common. But the majority of the avian predators arrive almost with the influx of the prey birds. They include the **goshawk** (*Accipiter gentilis*), **sparrowhawk** (*Accipiter nisus*), **long-legged buzzard** (*Butea rufinus*), **desert buzzard** (*Butea vulpinus*), **Bonelli's hawk-eagle** (*Hieraetus fasciatus*), **steppe–eagle** (*Aquila nipalensis*), **greater spotted eagle** (*Aquila clanga*), **lesser spotted eagle** (*Aquila pomarina*), **Lanner falcon** (*Falco biarmicus cherrug*), **peregrine falcon** (*Falco peregrinus*), **oriental hobby** (*Falco severus*) and **kestrel** (*Falco tinnunculus*).

The Thar is overcrowded with cattle, and hundreds of them die every day, leaving enough for the vultures to scavenge. The common among them are the **whiteback** (*Gyps bengalensis*), **longbilled** (*Gyps indicus*) and **Egyptian vulture** (*Beophron percnopterus*). The **king vulture** (*Torgos calvus*) is present in small numbers, mostly in pairs. The vultures cope with the arid climate and high temperature by shifting vertically. After an early morning meal, they soar at 3000-4000 feet (910-1210 meters) in the cool air and descend only in the evening to roost.

The wide faunal spectrum of the Indian desert — insect to antelope and wolf — and its unique life-style, represent a finely balanced biological pyramid. But in the present context of "development plans," and the dream of "making the desert bloom," the Indian desert is in danger. It is already the most crowded desert of the world. The additional water, more cattle and more men being introduced in large numbers, will increase congestion and destroy its essential nature. Much has already been destroyed by excessive cattle grazing, reckless killing of wild animals, removal of the natural vegetation for fuel and even depletion of its underground water.

This landform with its impressive and inspiring philosophy of living on a bare minimum—a lesson in ecological humility, deserves to be understood better. The Great Indian Desert, colorful and living with its natural wildlife, needs a better deal since it is India's only gene pool of drought-resistant species. It needs greater care in handling than other ecosystems, since it is one of the most fragile. An attempt to salvage a tiny dot 1160 sq miles (3000 sq km) out of 270,200 sq miles (700,000 sq km) of natural desert, was made by establishing a Desert National Park 28 miles (45 km) west of Jaisalmer, to preserve a sample of the discipline of the desert. Despite its initial encouraging start, specially the steps taken to rebuild populations of vanishing species like the desert fox and the great Indian bustard, and preserving the spectacle of the landing sand-grouse and flocks of houbara, there has subsequently been some slackening of effort. Renewed and intensified action, including an expansion of the area of the park, is urgently called for if the initial progress is to be consolidated (indeed, if it is not to be lost).

Is anybody listening?

In February 1976, India declared an Exclusive Economic Zone along its extensive coastline and now has jurisdiction over 2 million square kilometers of sea area.

A rich and varied marine life is present in the Indian seas which is also characterized by a diversity of habitats — the barrier reefs and atolls of the Lakshadweep Islands, the fringing reefs of the Andaman-Nicobar Islands, the Gulf of Mannar and the Gulf of Kutch, the mangrove and coastal lagoons, lakes, backwaters, estuaries and mudflats, and the rocky and sandy shores, harboring myriads of animal and plant species.

Human Impact: Man's greatest impact on marine life is in the coastal waters and estuaries. Using diverse types of fishing craft and gear, India alone fishes about 1.6 million tonnes of marine fish annually, with sardines, mackerel, Bombay-duck and prawns forming the major catches. **Thirutai** or **gray mullet** (*Mugil cephalus*), **kanumbu** (*Mugil macrolepis*), **Indian salmon** (*Polynemus indicus*) and **bhekti** (*Lates calcarifer*) in the hauls are not uncommon.

Marine penaeid prawns breed in the sea and the larvae of some species such as the **tiger prawn** (*Penaeus monodon*) and the **white prawn** (*P. indicus*) emigrate to the Cochin backwaters and with the tidal waters are allowed to enter the paddy fields through sluices, where they are netted every few days as the water is allowed to ebb with the tide.

Visit to Kovalam: Kovalam, the picturesque palm-fringed beach, 10 miles (16 km) south of Trivandrum, is also a place where you find abundant marine life, the most desired being the **spiny lobster** (*Panulirus hormarus*) and the **brown mussel** (*Perna indicus*).

In Lakshadweep: Ten of the islands of the Lakshadweep archipelago are inhabited. The lagoons in these islands are relatively shallow and the largest is in Minicoy. Luxuriant growth of branching and massive corals such as species of *Acropora*, *Montipora*, *Pocillopora* and *Porites*, along with associated fish and invertebrates occur in the reefs. The one item most sought after in the lagoons is bait fish, some 60 or so species used for attracting the **skipjack** and young **yellowfin tuna**. The reefs also support spiny lobsters and a good many species of fish. A few miles to the north of Kavaratti Island lies Pitti Island which is one among the very few rookeries for sea birds in India. Both the **sooty tern** and the **noddy tern**

. . . .
Mangrove swamps surprisingly harbor a wide range of fascinating life.

breed on this tiny island about 7½ acres (three hectares) in area. A number of other species of sea birds also congregate here.

The **green turtle** (*Chelonia mydas*) is known to nest at Suhuli Parr, Pitti Island and Minicoy Island. It is at this southernmost island in the Lakshadweep that *mas* — a cured smoked and dried product which is a must with every meal for the islanders — is made from the tuna meat. The once ornate sail fishing boats of Minicoy known as *odams* are now almost a thing of the past, having been replaced by mechanized boats fitted with a bait well for carrying live bait fish for rod and line fishing for tuna.

Mannar: Krusadai Island in the Gulf of Mannar is an important center for students of marine biology from all over the country. The island now comes within the delineated area of the National Marine Park in the Gulf of Mannar, covering a chain of 21 islands from Rameswaram to Tuticorin. The park has been established with a view to conserving the fringing coral reef and sea grass ecosystems from further human interference and giving adequate protection to the **dugong** or **sea cow** (*Dugong dugon*), **sea turtles** and other vulnerable and endangered species, including the unique **enteropneustan** or **acorn worm** (*Ptycodera flava*) occurring in Krusadai.

South of this, off Tuticorin, are the pearl banks or *parrs* and conch beds. Prior to the mid-1960s, a number of pearl fisheries were conducted from time to time in the Gulf of Mannar, the pearl oyster being *Pinctada fucata*. A falling number of oysters in the *parrs* has resulted in the failure of this fishery during the last 20 years.

The **conch** (*Xancus pyrum*) is also known as the sacred conch on account of its use in religious ceremonies. Skin diving is done for collecting conch in depths up to 65 feet (20 meters) from November to mid-May in the Gulf of Mannar and June to October in Palk Bay with the search always on for the rare **sinistral shell** (*Valampuri chanku*) which is considered priceless.

Seaweeds: The Mandapam–Rameswaram coasts are rich in seaweeds but the natural beds are being rapidly depleted to meet industrial demands. A number of *Agrophytes* (species of *Gracelaria*, *Gelidiella* and *Hypnea*), and *Alignophytes* (species of *Sargassum* and *Turbinaria*) occur in the area. It is a common sight to see a few hundred men, women and children collecting seaweeds from the intertidal and shallow areas in and around this chain of islands for supplying to the seaweed processing industries in the hinterland and other parts of the country.

Dugong and Whale: The **dugong** is the most

endangered of India's marine animals. The residual population of this herbivore in the Gulf of Mannar and Palk Bay is very vulnerable. Excessive and unregulated fishing with mechanized boats and canoes resulting in incidental capture, injuries due to boat hits and various methods of illegal take have drastically depleted the population. At the turn of the century they were so abundant in the area that there used to be regular organized herding and spear fishing for them. They are closely associated with the sea grass ecosystem in the shallow sub-littoral and intertidal areas where beds of *Halophila ovalis*, *Zostera sp.* and *Cymodacea spp.* occur. It is today a rare event to see a dugong in the foraging grounds or in the open water around the islands. They move individually or in small groups, with the calf riding on the cow while submerged.

Every three or four minutes they come up to the surface to breathe, normally in a horizontal position, but when curious about a floating object or an approaching boat, or when there is wave action, they break the surface more vertically. The uprooted floating sea grass sticking to the dugong's head probably gave rise to the legends about mermaids.

Not far from here, in the Sri Lankan waters off Trincomalee is where the **blue whale** (*Balaenoptera musculus*) has recently been observed to calve. The stranding of **baleen whales** (*B. musculus, B. borealis*) and young and adult **sperm whales** (*Physeter macrocephalus*) in the Gulf, Palk Bay and along the Madras coast indicate the proximity of the breeding grounds of these species.

Turtles: The world's largest aggregation or arribada of sea turtles takes place along the Gahirmata coast of Orissa where, in January or early Febuary, over 300,000 **olive ridley** (*Lepidochelys olivaceus*) females emerge for nesting along a six-mile (10-km) stretch of the beach within five to seven days. Access to this nesting beach which forms the eastern fringe of Bitarkanya Sanctuary is difficult. A second arribada of the same magnitude takes place at Gahirmata in March or early April. The hatchlings, in millions, emerge after an incubation period of about 45 to 58 days, depending on the time of the arribada and the prevalent temperatures. A recent significant discovery is that turtle eggs developing above a pivotal temperature all turn out to be females and those below, males.

A headstarting program of olive ridley can be seen at Kovalam (earlier Covalong) 22 miles (35 km) south of Madras (not to be confused with the place of the same name in Kerala) where due to heavy egg predation by man and wild animals, freshly laid clutches of eggs of the olive ridley are transplanted in hatcheries and the hatchlings released on the same beach.

All five species of sea turtles are on the endangered list. Several stretches of the beaches along the mainland coast and Andaman-Nicobar and Lakshadweep have been identified as nesting sites

. . . .

Above, the mudskipper, an amphibious fish, is found amongst mangrove swamps. *Right,* winter morning on a North Indian river; *far right,* a Neptune crab.

of the **green turtle** (*Chelonia mydas*), the **hawksbill** (*Erethmochelys imbricata*), the **leathery turtle** (*Demochelys coreacea*) and the olive ridley, with very little known about the **loggerhead** (*Caretta caretta*).

Plankton Blooms and Noxious Animals: A major feature along the west coast of India is the very large scale blooms of the nitrogen-fixing blue-green algae (*Trichodesmium erythreum*) from February to May. No deleterious effects are noticed. On the other hand, "red tides" caused by the dinoflagellate (*Notiluca miliaris*) results in fish mortality. Still more dangerous are blooms of *Hornellia marina*, another highly toxic dino-flagellate which are seen at the onset of the monsoon along the Kerala coast, causing mortality of fish, crustaceans and other invertebrates.

In treading in the lagoons of the Lakshadweep

namely the passive **whale shark** (*Rhineodon typus*), growing to a length of 40 feet (12 meters) or so is a visitor to the Indian coastal waters and, to date, the largest number of captures of this giant shark has been along the Gujarat coast where it is harpooned or caught in gill nets for its liver oil, the carcass being discarded.

Game Fish: Sport fishing possibilities in the sea are great, especially as excellent game fish such as **tuna, seerfish, wahoo, marlin, swordfish, sailfish, barracuda, dolphinfish, rainbow runner, telang queenfish, pelagic shark** and many others are available. There are areas along the west coast of India (Ratnagiri, Goa, Karwar, Cochin), the Gulf of Mannar (Tuticorin, Mandapam), the Lakshadweep sea and the Andaman and Nicobar Islands where these can be taken in rod and tackle. They are now obtained in surface trolling from

one has to be careful not to step on the spines of the well-camouflaged **stone fish** or to handle the beautiful **scorpion fish**, the spines of which are venomous and injury from which could be excruciatingly painful.

Among the coelenterates, the sting of the nematocysts of *Physalia physalis*, commonly known as the **Portuguese Man-o'-War** ·could even be fatal. *Physalia* occurs along the east coast with the commencement of the northeast monsoon. *Porpita porpita* and *Vellela vellela*, two chondrophorans which immobilize prey organisms with their stinging cells, are closely associated as commensals with young fish. Among corals, the sting from the polyps of *Millipora* is said to be very painful.

The Whale Shark: The largest of all fishes,

sailboats, mechanized boats and catamarans.

Mangrove: The estimates are that there are nearly a million acres (405,000 hectares) of mangrove forests along India's coasts, the most important being the Sunderbans in West Bengal. While large areas have already been denuded of mangrove for conversion to agricultural land, human settlement, industries, salt production and other uses, an awareness has grown concerning the need for conservation and management of this resource. Mangrove waters get greatly enriched with nutrients and act as an important nursery for many species of marine animals which later return to the sea for maturing and breeding. Some, like the much sought after **Indian shad** (*Hilsa ilisha*) in West Bengal, enter the estuaries for breeding in freshwater.

PARKS AND SANCTUARIES

The concept of the unity of all life, and its roots in and dependence on the environment, is an ancient one in South Asia. *All* life is deemed sacred, each creature has its place and function in nature's mosaic. This view lay at the root of the advocacy of compassion for all living creatures and *ahimsa* (non-violence) preached by the Buddha and Mahavira.

It was as early as in the 3rd-Century B.C. that Emperor Ashoka issued his edicts, which included injunctions concerning human behavior towards animals, and set up sanctuaries for wild animals. This designation of areas as protected is perhaps the first such governmental decree on record anywhere. But even before this, in Vedic literature of a thousand years earlier, there is mention of sacred groves in which all life was protected. The Buddha himself preached his first sermon in a Deer Park near Sarnath, a place some miles away from Varanasi.

With the passage of the centuries, much of the strength of this tradition was, in practice, lost, though the precepts were never wholly forgotten. In more recent years, it was, paradoxically, the hunters, the *shikaris* of the subcontinent, who played a major role in the preservation of forests and wildlife. It was essentially for sport that the Mughal emperors declared large tracts of forest as reserves. Both prior to and during British rule, other princes did the same in territories they controlled, the "Native States" that were permitted to survive under British control and protection. Many enlightened British administrators in India who started as *shikaris* turned into pioneer conservationists and earnest naturalists, as did many Indian *shikaris*.

The years of World War II and those that immediately followed brought devastation, at an ever increasing rate, to the region's forests and wildlife. To the insistent clang of alarm bells and pressure from public opinion, led by informed and active conservationists, generally sympathetic (though, in this behalf, not always effective) governments have established national parks and sanctuaries all over the region (India alone now has 55 National Parks and 247 Sanctuaries). Thanks to these, many species that would otherwise have disappeared by the end of this century have been assured a future and a number are thriving again in parks and sanctuaries in which habitats favorable to them have been preserved and even, in some cases, extended by reclamation.

It is a selection of these parks and sanctuaries and what can be seen in them that is presented in the pages that follow. The variety is fascinatingly rich and the settings are among the most beautiful to be seen anywhere. In view of shared characteristics, Indian and Nepali sites have been grouped together, while Sri Lankan sites have been placed in a separate section owing to certain special features to be seen there.

What the visitor will find most heartening is that these parks and sanctuaries have been set up and are being extended in countries where pressures of human population growth are being most severely felt, where only by conscious self-restraint and self-denial can the temptation to plunder nature's unguarded treasures for immediate and urgent need, be resisted. Serious lapses, unfortunately, still occur, but it is being increasingly realized that shortsightedness in such matters would, in the not too distant future, bring disaster to both man and beast.

Preceding pages: the extremely rare and elusive snow leopard; and Sagarmatha National Park. *Left*, returning the compliment.

DACHIGAM NATIONAL PARK

The entry point into this wildlife reserve, one of India's most scenically beautiful, is only 14 miles (22 km) from Srinagar. First protected in 1910, this mountainous area forms almost half of the Dal Lake's catchment area and its importance in supplying Srinagar with pure drinking water was recognized by the then Maharaja of Jammu and Kashmir who initiated steps for the preservation of this environment. Maintaining the well-wooded and grassy slopes of this catchment area ensures a minimum of erosion and that the waters that feed the city are almost as clear and clean as in the Marsar Lake from which they flow. The area was also protected as a hunting preserve by the Maharaja. It was declared a sanctuary after India became independent and was upgraded to National Park status in 1981. Between 1910 and 1934, 10 villages were relocated outside the boundaries of the reserve, hence the name *dachi-gam,* a word which translates "10 villages."

Within its two sectors, Lower and Upper Dachigam, spread over 55 sq miles (140 sq km), it incorporates a variety of vegetational types — riverain forest, grassland, broad-leaved woodland, coniferous forest, bare rock faces and alpine pastures and scrub — spanning heights ranging from 5500 to 14,000 feet (1700 – 4300 meters) above sea level. Two ridges rise steeply on either side of the park, forming a natural boundary encircling an area of great topographic variety — deep gullies and wooded slopes, huge rocky outcrops and sloping grasslands. On the northern ridge rises the Mahadev peak (13,011 feet/3966 meters). The interlocking valleys continue into Upper Dachigam where, amidst 14,000-foot (4300-meter) ridges, nestles Marsar Lake, from which flows the Dagwan river. The park's only road, part metaled, part jeep track, runs six miles (10 km) through the Numbal Beat of Lower Dachigam, along the main valley of the tumbling clear trout waters of the Dagwan river.

Home of the Hangul: The Dachigam area has been protected to preserve its unique Himalayan range of flora and fauna. Paramount among the latter is the **hangul** or **Kashmir stag** (*Cervus elaphus hanglu*), one of the most endangered species of red deer in the world. Dachigam is now the only place in the world with a viable hangul population. Though its decline was mainly the result of poaching, its home also suffered from other harmful forces: the presence of a large number of grazers bringing thousands of sheep, buffaloes and goats to feed on the lush high pastures of Upper Dachigam. The area was overgrazed and erosion was becoming apparent. Fanning this was the thinning of the birch and pine forests of these upper areas by the grazers who used the trees for building their summer homes and, in the lower areas, destruction of the forest by local inhabitants encroaching on the park for fuel and timber. To make matters worse, a Government sheep farm took a four-sq-mile (10½-sq-km) chunk out of the park's prime hangul habitat, adding to the upper area's summer grazing pressures, and endangering the south-facing grassland slopes of Lower Dachigam through intensive sheep grazing.

These are continuing problems for the Wildlife Department even today. But in the last decade they have been greatly reduced so that the hangul population has increased — a Government census in 1983 enumerated at least 500 individuals against an estimated 300 in 1954. The sheep farm is now separated by a fence and the grazers, though not totally removed either (yet), have been greatly reduced in number. More effective patrolling keeps poachers at bay and removers of forest produce to a minimum. Both the environment and the number of animals have thus greatly improved and with a permit available from the Chief Wildlife Warden in Srinagar, a visitor may enjoy the many splendors that the park has to offer.

A comprehensive appreciation of this undulating environment *must* include exploration on foot along the tracks and animal paths that run along the valley floors and traverse the slopes and ridges. Every season in Dachigam has its characteristic beauty and interest; the flora present marked variations throughout the year and much of the fauna partake of local migration and also include several hibernating species.

Winter Visitors: In winter, Upper Dachigam is inaccessible and even Lower Dachigam sees the temperature drop to as low as 14°F (–10°C) and between late November and early February may be shrouded in a thick blanket of snow. But it can present a stunning sight — a black and white scene of immense beauty and a stillness that accentuates the few forest sounds. High-altitude bird species move to the lower valleys for winter feeding on the remaining seeds and berries, even those to be found in

Gray langurs.

the old droppings of other creatures. Flocks of **cinnamon sparrows** appear and the **black and yellow grosbeak** presents a startling splash of color against the white backdrop. Its clear call rings through the air, mingling with the chattering of the **black bulbuls**, a vociferous species in winter abundance. Even the **monal pheasant**, the male splendidly multicolored, may be seen at this time in the lower valleys. Winter with its lack of camouflaging foliage is one of the best times to view hangul. They congregate in large mixed herds in the shelter of the lower valleys where the park authorities have established mineral licks. In the harshest winter months, additional feeding is also put out and groups of 60 or more may be seen gathered there.

At this time too, one is likely to meet with large troops of **Himalayan gray langur**, an impressive long-coated subspecies of the black-faced gray langur (*Presbytis entellus*), to be found over much of the subcontinent. Its winter diet consists largely of tree bark; its favorite trees, such as the poplar, being easily identified by the several dead branches that have become ring-barked from their gnawings.

The main predator in the park is the **leopard** (*Panthera pardus*). Though these are few in number and only rarely seen, winter is the time one is most likely to come across the carcass of a hangul that has succumbed to this carnivore, and from which many scavengers will also feed — **jackal, hill fox, yellow-throated marten** and **wild boar**. (Boar are not indigenous to the area, having been introduced from the Jammu region by a maharaja for hunting purposes. Unsuited to the harsh winter climate, they are, it seems, dying out.) The **Himalayan griffon** and the **lammergeier** or **bearded vulture** are also lured by carcasses and the attractive **long-tailed blue magpie** will generally be found feeding also.

In the efforts necessary for successful foraging, winter is a time when one may meet with those smaller mammals, mainly nocturnal, that are otherwise extremely shy — **jungle cat, leopard cat, otter, Himalayan weasel**, may reward the silent and patient observer.

Spring and Summer: By March the serene, harsh beauties of winter have given way to the richness of spring. As the leaves begin to sprout, the Himalayan langurs are quick to take advantage of the new source of food. Messy feeders, they drop many half-eaten twigs and branches to the forest floor. Hangul will frequently be found associating with these monkeys, waiting eagerly beneath their tree to feed on these dropped morsels.

Now another large mammal for which Dachigam is justly famous makes its appearance — the **Himalayan black bear** (*Selenarctos thibetanus*). Having spent the winter hibernating in rocky shelters, it emerges hungry from its foodless sleep. Being omnivorous, it too will take advantage of a leopard kill, and in these first weeks many overturned stones lie along Dachigam's paths as testament to the bears' search for ants and other insects and grubs. As the trees come into leaf, the bears move into their branches which will provide the bulk of their diet for the rest of the year.

In spring the lower forest blossoms into a profusion of delicate hues. Wild cherry, pear, plum, peach, apple and apricot bloom white and pink amid the varying fresh greens of the new leaves. The main valley contains principally broad-leaved genera; oaks, elms, willows, poplars will be found there, while the side valleys, locally called *nars*, become thick with the creamy flowers of the *Parrotiopsis jacquemontiana*, a shrub of the witch-hazel family, which is interspersed with trees of walnut and Indian horse-chestnut. The hill slopes turn green and the valleys dark under the thick canopy of developing leaves. The fruits begin to appear, much to the bears' delight.

Spring sees an appreciable change in bird-life too. The prominent winter species have disappeared to higher altitudes and others appear to feed on the new vegetation and begin their breeding cycles. The beautiful **golden oriole** suspends its cradle from a high branch. The **minivets** flash scarlet and yellow as they move in noisy feeding parties with the **tits, warblers** and **finches**. Tree holes often house **pygmy owlets** and **woodpeckers**, most conspicuous amongst which is the **Himalayan pied woodpecker**, a smart black and white bird with red vent and, in the male, matching red cap. Among the lower-level shrubs and grasses hop the **babblers, buntings** and **laughing thrushes**, the **streaked laughing thrush** being one of the most commonly seen birds of Lower Dachigam.

The lower forests now lose the langurs as they move with spring to higher valleys. The male hangul are on their way up too, dropping their antlers and beginning the new growths encased in "velvet." The females remain longer and give birth to their calves in the long grass of the lower slopes in May and June. The young are spotted and well-camouflaged for their early days when

Hangul.

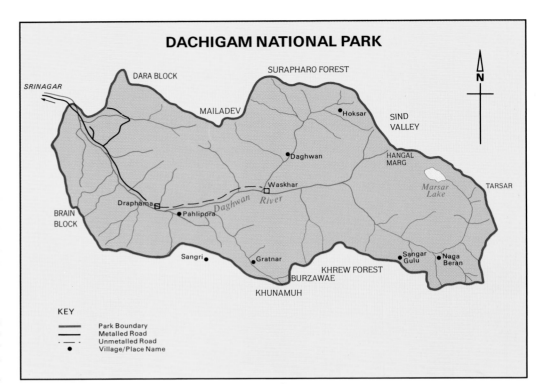

the hinds leave them hidden and alone, returning only periodically to feed them. This is the time the black bear turns predator — they can be seen crisscrossing the steep slopes in their search for the defenseless newborns. But after the first couple of weeks the main danger is over, since the calves can now outrun any would-be predatory bear. The calves then stay with their mothers, moving upwards to the high pastures of the park once the snows have receded.

The Upper Reaches: Winter remains late at these altitudes and comes early, but during the few summer months Upper Dachigam presents truly glorious views — vast rolling meadows, splashing clear streams, waterfalls, silver birch stands, deep azure skies and high snow-dotted ridges combine in delightful harmony. Comparable to the famous Valley of Flowers in the Garhwal in Uttar Pradesh, the green summer grass of these highland meadows is all but eclipsed by the immense array of alpine flowers dispersed in it—crimsons, golds and purples are the ground carpet's dominant colors while more detailed patterns are picked out in blues, reds, orange and other more subtle hues. The delicately colored

blue poppy is here and a number of medicinal plants like *Saussurea sp.*, as well as other representatives of the rarer Himalayan flora, are to be found.

The change in elevation occasions a new variety of birds—the **red-browed finch** is an attractive one to look for in the birch forests. Higher still, above the tree line, **redstarts, wagtails** and the **Himalayan rubythroat** can be seen hopping among the rocks edging Marsar Lake. Alpine accentors are here and the **wall creeper** with its characteristic butterfly-like flight.

The park's higher altitudes still harbor a few **Himalayan brown bear** (*Ursus arctos isabellinus*), endangered and rare throughout its range.

The brown bear is an inhabitant of the rolling uplands; ecologically separated from the forest-dwelling black bear, in Dachigam their ranges overlap. However the brown bear's exact status is uncertain and few sightings occur. By contrast, the other hibernating mammal of these upper reaches, the **long-tailed marmot** (*Marmota caudata*), is both visible and very audible. These endearing rodents of the squirrel family have their burrows on the treeless grassy slopes and their high-pitched whistling screams echo against the ridge walls. Feeding and scurrying among the many boulders at the stream's edge, if disturbed by the call of a soaring chough or sight of an intruding human, they stop to perch up on their haunches, thus enhancing their field of vision.

Traditionally, Upper Dachigam provided important grazing for the hangul and large-scale summer migrations there were recorded. However, Dr Fred Kurt who studied the hangul in Dachigam for several years found almost no evidence of their presence in Upper Dachigam and had to conclude that "human interference led to considerable loss of the former range and that the present range is restricted to Lower Dachigam." Besides this effect on the hangul the presence of the Banjaris, Bukarwals and Gujjars, with their herds of livestock, had a seriously deleterious effect on the environment.

In spite of Dr Schaller's warning, the number of livestock head increased in the 1970s to an estimated 10,000. In 1977 this caused such pollution in the Dagwan river that the waters could no longer be collected. In the following year, the number of grazers was drastically reduced and grazing restricted to a limited number of valleys in Upper Dachigam. This is presently the situation and the result has been a return of the

hangul to some of their summer haunts. In ungrazed, closed valleys, they may again be seen in this beautiful setting.

Summer passes quickly in these high valleys and by late August the first frost and flurries of snow appear to herald winter's return. Hibernating animals feed up quickly before their long winter sleep, while other fauna move once again to the protection of the lower altitudes.

Autumn Sightings: Autumn in Lower Dachigam presents another blaze of color as the leaves change shades to reds, golds, yellows and various hues of orange. The different species are easily distinguishable then in their varied tones with the majestic chinar towering above the others and last to retain a stately burnt-orange beauty before the bareness of winter. October is the main rutting month for the hangul and the lower valleys reverberate with the deep roaring calls of the stags. With full-grown antlers now clean of "velvet," the stags look their impressive best. A full-grown male will carry a head of 10 or 12 points, though occasionally more may be counted. The bears are feasting on walnuts and acorns, laying on fat to tide them through the coming winter. Soon the monkeys and grosbeaks will again be in evidence—a sure indication that the circle of seasons has again turned fully to winter.

Being so close to Srinagar, the state's capital city and a popular tourist destination, Dachigam, unlike the majority of the subcontinent's parks and sanctuaries, also lends itself admirably to those with only a day or two to spare. Even such a brief visit is highly recommended, but aim for early morning or late afternoon as this is when the animals are most active and visible. A stroll along the flat paths of the **Numbal Beat** of Lower Dachigam, accompanied by one of the Wildlife Department staff, will be as rewarding for viewing wildlife as any of the more strenuous routes. Those with more time and energy may like to explore some of the lower *nars*; **Drognar** and **Munyu**, side by side, leading north from the jeep track, may be particularly rewarding in the late spring as these are favorite calving areas of the hangul and therefore may afford a view of the heavily spotted young. The rare **serow** can be seen here.

Upper Dachigam is for those who enjoy trekking and camping equipment is essential for such a journey, although within the park some shelters are available in the **Sangargulu Valley** of Upper Dachigam and at **Gretnar**, several thousand feet lower, where the **koklas pheasant** resides.

Dagwan river.

Yellow-billed blue magpie.

CORBETT NATIONAL PARK

Just short of 300 km northeast of Delhi, cradled in the foothills of the Himalaya lies the **Corbett National Park**. It is India's first national park and also one of her finest.

This park has quite a history. Long ago, on the banks of the river Ramganga, there lived a flourishing community. Today, some evidence of their culture is found in fragments of terra-cotta and the remains of their temples along the river. This community lived by clearing some of the forest in the *duns* (valleys) and had to fight a constant battle to keep their farmlands free from the invading jungle.

The First in a Series: The 40 years following the arrival of the British in this area in 1820 were disastrous. Trees were felled mercilessly for timber and these virgin forests were devastated. It was a Major Ramsay who took the first real systematic measures which, in years to follow, were to restore the forests to their former health. Cattle stations were removed, cultivation was stopped, a fire-fighting force was established and, most important, the removal of

Below, a jungle stream and *right*, elephants bathing in the Ramganga river.

timber without a license was totally prohibited. Then, in 1907, the possibility of creating a game sanctuary in this area was first mooted, but was rejected outright. Two forest officers, E.R. Stevens and his successor, E.A. Smythies, were to take up this cause again. However, it was only later, when Smythies was conservator that he consulted Major Jim Corbett who knew this area well, regarding the possible boundaries for a proposed national park.

During the 1930s, tiger shooting was in vogue and many a viceroy, governor-general and other dignitary visited this area — the famous *terai* and *bhabar* tracts of the then United Provinces — to bag their tigers from elephant-back and high *machans* in elaborate *tamashas* (entertainments): tiger shoots. However, it was through the efforts of other hunters, the true conservationists, who abhorred this form of sport and massacre, that Sir Malcolm Hailey, then Governor of the United Provinces, keenly accepted the recommendation that an area of 99.07 sq miles (256.59 sq km) be set aside for the park. Thus, on Aug. 8, 1936, the Hailey National Park, India's first, was established.

Tribute to an Enlightened Hunter: In 1952, a few years after India attained independence, the park's name was changed to Ramganga National Park, after the life-giving Ramganga river that flows through almost the whole length of it. In 1957, it was renamed once more, Corbett National Park, in honor and memory of the late Jim Corbett, the legendary, hunter-naturalist turned author and photographer who had helped in demarcating the park's boundaries and setting it up. It was in this area that he had shot the dreaded "maneaters," the notorious Kanda Maneater being one of them. His books on these thrilling, true-life adventures, *The Maneaters of Kumaon* and *The Man-eating Leopard of Rudraprayag*, are perennial best-sellers, well-known all over the world.

The man who had influenced Jim Corbett most to hang up his guns and take to the camera was a forest officer, F. W. Champion, the pioneer of wildlife photography in India. His masterpieces, *With a Camera in Tiger-land* and *The Jungle in Sunlight and Shadow*, were photographed and written in these very same jungles.

In the late 1960s and the early 1970s, the world was hit by the awareness that the Indian tiger (*Panthera tigris tigris*) was on the brink of extinction and that of an estimated 40,000 at the turn of the century, less than 2000 survived in the wild. A far-

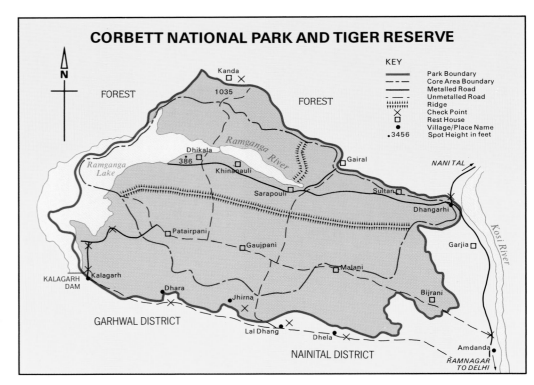

CORBETT NATIONAL PARK AND TIGER RESERVE

reaching project was envisaged. Its philosophy was that, if the tiger and its habitat were totally protected in tiger reserves, then other species of fauna and flora too would flourish as nature would maintain her own balance. Thus, with the help of the World Wildlife Fund, Project Tiger was launched at Dhikala in the Corbett National Park on Apr. 1, 1973. This National Park was one of the first tiger reserves along with seven others in the country; today, there are 15 such reserves. The tiger census for 1984 reveals that there are now 4005 tigers in India.

Topography: The Corbett National Park or just "Corbett" as it is also popularly known is situated in the hilly districts of Pauri Garhwal and Nainital of the northern state of Uttar Pradesh. It lies between latitude 29° 13′ North and 29° 35′ North and longitude 78° 33′ East and 78° 46′ East. The park comprises an area of 201 sq miles, (520.6 sq km). Of this, an area of 123.5 sq miles (320 sq km) is the core — the *sanctum sanctorum*, where no kind of disturbance is permitted. There is a move to expand the park by another 425 sq miles (1100 sq km). However, at the time of writing, only an area of 116 sq miles (300 sq km) is to be added immediately to the northern area of the park. This expansion is keenly sought after by conservationists as it will link the park with other forests through corridors. This is important to help the overflow of animals to level out, prevent inbreeding and ensure that viable gene pools are maintained.

The area in the Himalayan foothills in which the park is situated is known as the South Patlidun. In elevation the park ranges between 1312 feet (400 meters) at its lowest to 3970 feet (1210 meters) at its highest. Corbett is, in fact, a large valley with its long axis from east to west. Through this valley run three thickly forested ridge systems roughly parallel to one another and in the same direction. Small offshoots of these ridges run north to south and the valleys formed in between are known as *sots*. The ridge to the north forms the boundary of the park in that direction and Kanda, the highest point, with its magnificent panoramic view of the park is here.

Between the northern ridge and the median ridge which is the longest is the Ramganga river, which enters the park from the northeast, flows through the park into the reservoir and makes its exit at Kalagarh towards the southwest. The southern ridge is a bit lower and this area of the park is drier

and is notable for its more deciduous type of vegetation and its own rugged charm.

A topographic change of significance that took place in the park was the inundation of 16 sq miles (42 sq km) of prime habitat when almost a tenth of the park's area was lost to the waters of a multipurpose hydel dam at Kalagarh. This is the largest earthern dam in Asia and lies at the southwestern fringe of Corbett. The construction of the dam certainly was not in the best interest of the park. Conservationists had feared that the changes that would come with such a dam would bring about adverse effects but the changes by and large have been absorbed by the remarkable resilience of nature.

The waters first started to fill up in 1974. In 1976, when they had inundated a greater part of the reservoir, the elephant migration routes linking the park with the western and northwestern reserved forests were cut off. Not for long though. Those great, accomplished surveyors of gradients and trailblazers soon established other routes. There was a shift of animals from the affected areas to higher ground. There will also be changes that are less apparent at this stage and though some research has been done, much more is needed and is planned to study these changes in detail. The lake, besides just its scenic charm, has added to the park in a few ways. A large number of species of water birds, both migrants and others, have begun to frequent its waters, though mainly in winter. Crocodiles — both the long-snouted, fish-eating **gharial** (*Gavialis gangeticus*) and the **mugger** (*Crocodylus palustris*) have found new homes here and their numbers have increased. They can often be seen sunning themselves on the sand banks.

For anglers too the lake is a paradise. Sporting fish such as the **mahseer** (*Barbus tor*) and **malee** (*Wallago attu*), abound in the lake and in the river. The mahseer is a well-known fighting fish. Fishing with rod and line is allowed if a permit is first obtained. Fishing in the river, however, offers greater pleasure as well as good exercise to the sportsman who is called upon to pit his skill to outwit the mighty mahseer. The lake offers better fishing perhaps, but lacks the thrill and sport of the river.

Flora and Climate: Vegetation in the park is confined chiefly to the bhabar tract type of the Siwalik hills; different kinds of vegetation are found all along the varied topography, which comprises hilly and riverain areas, temporary marshy depressions,

Great horned owl.

plateaus and ravines. The park is known for its almost pure sal (*Shorea robusta*) stands in the lower hilly ridges and flat valleys. Some associates of sal here are haldu (*Adira cordifolia*), rohini (*Mallotus philippinensis*), and karipak (*Murraya konigi*).

The riverain area is clothed in shisham (*Dalbergia sissoo*), khair (*Acacia catechu*) and others. In early summer it's an unforgettable sight to witness the soothing green of the shisham islands in new leaf.

On the higher ridges we find bakli (*Anogeissus latifolia*) which enriches the hues of the park with its reddish leaves and pale bark. The chir (*Pinus roxburghii*), anauri (*Legestroemia paruiflora*), and gurail (*Bauhinia racemosa*) are some others that find root-holds at these contours, along with bamboos. The common shrub is *Clerodendrum viscasum* and a weed which is causing some concern is the lantana.

The *chaurs*, the savannah grasslands, are covered with a variety of grasses like *Themeda arundinacea*, *Vetiveria zizanioides* and *Thysanulena maxima*.

A hundred and ten species of trees, 51 species of shrubs and over 33 species of bamboo and grass are found here.

There are three distinct seasons in Corbett: *Cold* — November to February; *Hot*

The park has a healthy tiger population.

— March to June; *Rainy* (Monsoons) — July to October. In winter the nights are cold at an average of 41° F (5° C), with frost and some fog which lasts till late morning, but the sun is pleasant and the day temperature averages 77° F (25° C). In the hot season, June is the hottest month, with day temperatures going up to an unbearable 112° F (44° C) but the nights are pleasant with an average temperature of 70° F (21° C). In the monsoon season, from June to October, the park remains closed to tourists. There is very heavy rain, between 60 inches and 112 inches (1500 mm and 2800 mm). The roads are washed away by the heavy downpours and when the sun does shine the jungle steams with humidity. The animals move to the hilly areas of Corbett at this time for the cool breeze and to avoid the **daans**, a blood-sucking fly, which plagues them in the lowlands. Surely, these few months are times of a well deserved rest from the attentions of man for the denizens of the jungle.

Rich Variety: Over 50 mammal, 580 bird and 25 reptile species have been listed in Corbett. The insect life in itself is astounding and though not much work has been done in this respect even the layman will be amazed at its abundance, mainly after the

monsoon.

Corbett is well-known and a haven for its **tigers**. There is plentiful prey — four kinds of deer, wild boar and other lesser animals — for them to live on. With a bit of luck, it's possible to see a tiger on the road as you enter the park and motor down to Dhikala. Pug marks are seen in abundance on the roadsides, paths and animal trails. It's by tracing these pug marks, which bear individual characteristics, that the estimated population, which has shown a marked increase from 40 in 1972 to 90 tigers in 1984, is known.

Leopards (*Panthera pardus*) are found in the hilly areas of the park. They do sometimes venture into the lower jungles but at much risk to themselves from tigers. There have been many cases of leopards being killed and eaten by tigers. The leopard is, however, a great survivor and can sustain itself on even small birds and rodents.

The lesser cats such as the **leopard cat** (*Felis bengalensis horsfieldi*), the **jungle cat** (*Felis chaus*), the rare **fishing cat** (*Felis viverina*) and some others are found here, but being nocturnal are rarely seen.

The **sloth bear** (*Melursus ursinus*) is found in the Bijrani–Malani areas of the park. It can be seen on the roadsides in the

early morning or late evening, busily demolishing termite mounds for the grubs, or in the mahwa (*Madhura indica*) trees, relishing the sweet sticky flowers, which ferment in the hot season and are intoxicating.

The **Himalayan black bear** (*Selenarctos thibetanus*) is seen in the higher hills towards Kanda but only rarely and that too in the cold winters.

The **dhole** (*Cuon alpinus*), the wild dog, is also rare and seen in the southern areas of Corbett towards Bijrani. The **jackal** (*Canis aureus*) is commonly seen around all the campus areas. During the fawning season, jackals are most active and can be seen killing and carrying off newly dropped chital fawns.

The **yellow-throated marten** (*Martes flavicula flavicula*), the **Himalayan palm civet** (*Paguma larvata grayi*), the **Indian gray mongoose** (*Herpestes dwardsi*), the **common otter** (*Lutra lutra monticola*) and the **blacknaped hare** (*Lepus nigricollis ruficaudatus*) are some of the smaller resident mammals. The **porcupine** (*Hystrix indica*) can also be seen at night near the garbage dumps of the campus at Dhikala.

Elephants (*Elephas maximus*) are one of the main attractions of Corbett. The whole jungle belongs to them. It is possible to see a

Game-viewing from elephant back.

herd or even a lone tusker crossing the road. Corbett's elephants by and large are well behaved, but one must always remember that, "Elephants have the right of way." The park's elephant population varies from about 200 to 300 and more in summer, when the sub-herds amalgamate and form large herds.

Of the four species of deer that are found here are the **chital** (*Axis axis*), the well-known **spotted deer** and considered one of the most beautiful in the world. This is one of the chief prey animals of the carnivora. A smaller cousin of the chital, the **para** (*Axis porcinus*) is found in the more open grassland and riverain areas. The **sambar** (*Cervus unicolor*) is the largest Asiatic deer and is sought after by the larger adult tigers of the park. The **kakkar** (*Muntiacus muntjak*), also called the **barking deer**, is the smallest of the four. Nervous and shy, it warns the jungle's denizens of danger with its hoarse, dog-like bark.

The goat-antelopes are represented by the **ghoral** (*Nemorhaedus goral*) in Corbett. Ghorals can be spotted on a drive up the hilly road to Kanda.

Wild boar (*Sus scrofa*) are found in the forests as well as in the grasslands, sometimes seen in sounders of 10 to 30 pigs. Even the tigers respect the large male boars. In encounters sometimes, tigers are known to have been killed by a large male wild boar.

The **langur** (*Presbytis entellus*) and the **rhesus** (*Macaca mulatta*) are well distributed throughout the park and also warn the jungle with their alarm calls, when they see either tiger or leopard from their tree-top perches.

Avian Attractions: Corbett has many attractions for the bird watcher also. Over 580 species of birds are found here. Most of the water birds are migrants and arrive in winter. Some of these are the **greylag** and the **barheaded goose**, **ducks** of many kinds, and **great crested grebe**, **snipe**, **sandpiper**, **plover**, **gull** and **wagtail**. Some of the residents are **darters**, **cormorants**, **egrets**, **herons**, the **blacknecked stork** and the **spur-winged lapwing**. The commonly seen raptors in Corbett are the **osprey**, **crested serpent eagle**, **blackwinged kite**, **shikra**, **Pallas's fishing eagle**, **grayheaded fishing eagle**, **spotted eagle** and **harrier**.

Some of the other birds found in the forests are **minivets**, **shrikes**, **babblers**, **doves**, **drongos**, **cuckoos**, **parakeets**, **barbets**, 17 kinds of **woodpecker**, **thrushes**, **peafowl**, **kalij pheasants** and **red junglefowl** — the ancestor of all domestic fowl. The rare **chir pheasant** is found in the higher hills near Kanda. The vultures commonly found are the **Indian white-backed**, **Himalayan longbilled** and the **king** or **black vulture**. On elephant rides, the mahouts keep a wary eye open for the circling vultures as they help pinpoint a carnivora's kill.

The nocturnal birds are the **nightjars**, **thick-knees**, **owls** and **owlets** and, by the river, the **great stone plover** and **stone curlew** hunt at night.

Reptiles: The Ramganga is the home of the descendants of the prehistoric reptiles, the gharial and the mugger. The gharial is the rare fish-eating, long-nosed crocodile, only just saved from extinction in the park through captive breeding and release to augment the few survivors there. A few species of **turtles** and **tortoises** are also found in and around the lake.

The **Indian python**, **viper**, **cobra**, **krait** and **king cobra**, the largest of poisonous snakes, also inhabit Corbett, as do **monitors** and other lesser lizards.

Facilities: The park is open from November 15 to June 15. The best time to visit it depends on one's priorities of interests. For wildlife photography, the best months are April to June.

There are many Forest Rest Houses in Corbett which can be reserved in advance. These are situated in picturesque areas of the park. For the more adventurous and serious-minded wildlifers, photographers, anglers, and those who just want to be in the jungle, these undisturbed locations are invaluable. In most of these rest houses, the basics are provided but one has to carry one's own food and it's always wise to take a sleeping bag along too. It is also advantageous to have one's own vehicle here. At some of these locations, elephants for wildlife viewing are stationed. Walking in some areas is permitted, but only when accompanied by a guide.

The **Dhikala Complex**, which at the moment draws most of the visitors, caters in full to all the needs of various budgets.

Dhikala is a very picturesque location indeed, and the areas around it, including the famous **Dhikala Chaur**, abound in wildlife. Elephant rides for wildlife viewing in the mornings and evenings can be booked here. This form of transport for wildlife viewing is the best as the visibility is excellent and a silent and close approach to wild animals is possible. It is also possible to view wildlife from one's car with a guide. A motor vehicle certainly causes less disturbance to the animals than man on foot.

Early morning on the Ramganga.

Python swallowing a chital.

DUDHWA NATIONAL PARK

Dudhwa National Park, which emerged from a struggle against a welter of vested interests, is even now threatened by a surge of ever-increasing demographic pressure. A viable pattern of coexistence between humans and other forms of life is urgently required if the latter are not to be overwhelmed.

The North Kheri Forest Division, as the area in which the park is located was previously called, has the finest quality sal (*Shorea robusta*) in India; the Forest Department, in its eagerness to exploit this commercially, opposed the establishment of the park, oblivious of their simultaneous responsibility of protecting India's wildlife. "Sportsmen" too were reluctant to surrender the right to kill the so-called game animals that lived there in substantial numbers. The surrounding population protested that they would be denied building materials for their homes and grazing areas for their cattle.

Thanks to the avid and virtually single-handed lobbying by the present writer and the firm conviction of a conservation-minded prime minister, the late Mrs Indira Gandhi, the division was declared a wildlife sanctuary in 1965 and a National Park in 1977, despite opposition and objections.

Barasingha Country: Dudhwa National Park, covering 190 sq miles (490 sq km) of grassland and woodland, consists, as mentioned earlier, mainly of sal forest. The Neora river and the bed of the Soheli which is dry before the confluence run along the southern edge, between which and the sal forest to the north lie the grasslands that are the **barasingha's** or **swamp deer's** preferred habitat, about 40 sq miles (100 sq km) of which have been preserved in the park. The rest have been taken over by cultivation.

By far the largest numbers of barasingha, for which the park is best known, occur in the Sathiana and Kakraha blocks, in the southwest and southeast sectors respectively, which together comprise some 17–18 sq miles (4500 hectares). Sathiana is the wetter area, much of it being inundated for at least short periods during the monsoon season. Grasses are generally tall and coarse, sometimes forming dense thickets that are difficult to penetrate even by elephant. Several swampy depressions, which contain water for all or most of the year, cross the land from north to south, and numerous jamun trees (*Syzygium cuminii*) attest to the wetness of the habitat; the high-water mark on trees close to the Neora river may be up to six feet (two meters) and in some years more. The western end of Sathiana is better drained than the east; the grasses appear to be shorter, and there are large stands of *Imperata cylindrica*, but the various-aged plantings of sisam trees (*Dalbergia sissoo*) obscure the animals. Other timbers of specialized utility are semal (*Bombax ceiba*), khair (*Acacia catechu*), sirsa (*Albizzin procera*), haldu (*Adira cordifolia*) and tun (*Toora cedrela*).

Tigers and Leopards: The **tiger**, originally the glamorous objective of every sport killer's rifle sight, and now the cynosure of every wildlife tourist's questing eye, exists in fair number in the park. Unfortunately, there is hardly any buffer zone, and the forested area is surrounded by agricultural crops, mainly sugarcane, which has replaced the tall grasses which tigers used to inhabit in earlier years. With the decimation of their prey species by firearms, the tigers have come into conflict with the adjoining human population.

Dudhwa is celebrated for the successful hand-rearing by the writer of a tiger cub, Tara, from virtual domestication to free, self-sustained life in the wild. After 20 months of hand-rearing, Tara was launched into the jungle. May 5, 1986, was her 10th birthday.

Leopards are few in Dudhwa, as is usually the case in habitats suited to tigers, where competition from the senior predator depresses their population, in spite of the fact that the prey overlap between the two species is limited.

Since Dudhwa provides the optimum habitat for barasingha or swamp deer (*Cervus duvauceli duvauceli*) the remnants of the once prolific deer species is crowded into the wetlands of the park, which has the distinction of having the largest population of this threatened species in the subcontinent. **Mirchia Jheel** once infamous for its battues of the barasingha, where it was common for as many as 30–40 stags to be gunned down in a morning's "sport," is now under cultivation as are other previous habitat areas. Herds of 200 and over may, however, still be seen in the southern grasslands, their presence rendered more spectacular by the propensity for segregation of the antlered males.

Return of the Rhino: An exciting innovation is the attempted reintroduction into Dudhwa of the great **Indian one-horned**

Swamp deer.

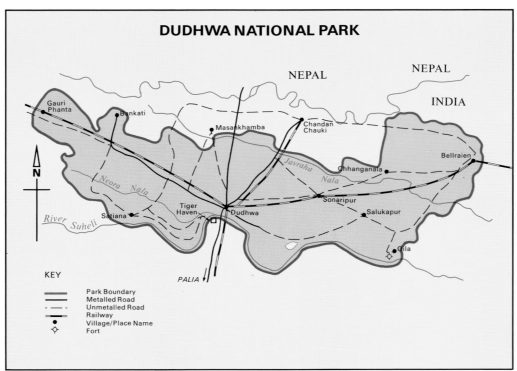

DUDHWA NATIONAL PARK

NEPAL

NEPAL

INDIA

Gauri Phanta

Bankati

Masankhamba

Chandan Chauki

Bellraien

Javraha Nala

Chhanganala

Neora Nala

Sonaripur

Salukapur

Tiger Haven

Satiana

Dudhwa

River Suheli

Gila

PALIA

KEY

— Park Boundary
— Metalled Road
- · - Unmetalled Road
— Railway
● Village/Place Name
✧ Fort

rhinoceros, made possible as a gift to conservation by the late Indira Gandhi. Two males and five females have been translocated from Assam and Nepal, and are thriving. An increase in their numbers with such a small initial population may well be restrained by tiger predation on their young, and severely threatened by the entirely spurious and vicious trade in its remains by humans. The introduction of a further number of colonizers is therefore necessary.

Wild elephant, previously only seasonal visitors, were driven, during the 1960s and 70s, by massive habitat destruction in Nepal, to cross over to Dudhwa, and a herd of over 30 animals spent nearly 10 years in the park. As wide-ranging animals they have since returned to Nepal, to remnants of their habitat still surviving in Sukla Phanta and Bardia Wildlife Reserves across the border. Further visits would be welcome, especially as the magnificent herd bull is by computation more than 11 feet (four meters) tall at the shoulder.

Other animals seen in Dudhwa in fair to dwindling numbers are **sloth bears, ratels, civets, jackals, fishing cats, jungle cats** and **leopard cats**. Among the deer, in addition to the barasingha, are the **sambar**, the **chital** (considered the handsomest deer in the

world), the **hog deer** and the **barking deer**. Also **wild pigs** and the **blue-bull**, our largest antelope.

In winter, basking on the sandy banks of the Soheli-Neora river, running along the southern boundary of the park, the **snub-nosed crocodile** or **mugger** may be seen. **Otters** are fairly common, as also **pythons** and **monitor lizards**.

Avian Variety: Birdlife is prolific, and one ornithologist has said that Dudhwa could establish its claim to fame even merely on account of its owls and storks. Among the night birds of prey are the **great Indian horned owl**, the **forest eagle owl**, the **brown fish owl**, the **tawny fish owl**, the **dusky horned owl**, and the **brown wood owl**. The collared **scops owl** and the **jungle owlet** are among the more vociferous of the lesser varieties. Apart from the **sarus crane**, there are **black-necked storks, white-necked storks, black storks, painted storks, white storks, open-billed storks** and **adjutant storks**. Raptors are of infinite variety, and occasionally species of **hawks** and **eagles** appear which tax the talent of the most gifted of ornithologists. Six **vultures**, including the **cinerious**, are present at times. Among the bustards, the great Indian bustard has disappeared, while the **Bengal**

and the **likh florican** overlap, in greatly diminished numbers. The **swamp partridge** has a transitional habitat, with the black and the gray partridges occupying higher grasslands and sandy soils. Among the colorful birds are varieties of **woodpeckers, orioles, pittas, kingfishers, minivets, flycatchers** and **sunbirds**; also **hornbills, bulbuls, prinias, chats** and **warblers**, whose innumerable species were obviously enumerated by a birdman with a sardonic twist of humor.

Migratory birds are plentiful, especially **waterfowl**, and as Dudhwa is close to the Himalayan foothills, various species stop over in the course of their migration to the plains in winter. However, national as well as international pressures are becoming manifest. The white ibis has vanished, and the ethereal trumpeting of the fighting demoiselle cranes is heard no more.

Dudhwa National Park is one of India's most exciting and vigorous wildlife reserves, but also, at the same time, one of the most vulnerable. Looking into the crystal bowl of the future, two alternatives are discernible. A restricted world of wild nature cordoned off from the exploitation of humans, or an uncontained human population explosion gathering for a Gadarene rush into a polluted ocean.

NEW HOMES FOR THE RHINOCEROS

Five hundred years ago the Indian one-horned rhinoceros had a much wider distribution than at present and included much of the Indo-Gangetic plain, Assam, Bengal, Burma and Thailand. By the early 1980s it was restricted to a few pockets. With over 70 percent of the world's population restricted to a single park (Kaziranga), it was long felt necessary to reduce the possibility of disaster to the species through disease or flood by establishing new populations.

The primary needs of the rhino are a well-watered habitat with plenty of food and permanent water holes. One of the few areas of suitable habitat within the rhino's previous range was Dudhwa. The rhino was present in the area until the latter half of the 19th Century. Other possible sites are Champaran in Bihar, Intanki in Nagaland and Lalighabri Sanctuary in Arunachal Pradesh.

The article alongside reports the translocation already achieved in Dudhwa National Park and stresses the need for increasing the number of transferees if the population is to be viable.

Jungle butterflies.

Tiger Haven on the edge of Dudhwa National Park.

ROYAL CHITWAN NATIONAL PARK

One possible meaning of *Chitwan* is "Heart of the Jungle" and it could not be more aptly described. With its tropical creeper-clad forests, great meandering rivers, lush seas of tall elephant grass, and the magnificent backdrop of the Himalaya in the distance, Chitwan is a most romantic jungle. And for its 370 sq miles (960 sq km), it has a richness and variety of wildlife matched by few other parks.

Until the 1950s, a virulent form of malaria prevalent in the region kept Chitwan relatively free of human settlement. Between 1846 and 1950, when Nepal was ruled by the Rana prime ministers, Chitwan was a hunting reserve, exclusively for the ruling classes. It was jealously guarded, if only to preserve it for more hunting. During that period, Chitwan was the venue of many a grand hunt to which the royalty of Europe and India, and the top brass of the British Raj, were often invited. These hunts were lavish operations with several hundred elephants and beaters being employed to round up and drive big game towards the shooters.

Massive Slaughter: However, several years were often allowed to lapse between such massive hunts; they were not always held in the same area, and the habitat was left relatively intact, so the hunted species recovered their losses fairly rapidly. In the last hunt of 1938–9, in which the then Viceroy of India, Lord Linlithgow, also took part, a record bag of 120 tiger, 38 rhino, 27 leopard and 15 bear was taken. That so much big game was still there to shoot in spite of two previous hunts in the same decade indicates what an incredible wildlife haven Chitwan must have been.

In 1950 the Ranas fell from power and the new government opened up Chitwan for settlement. A malaria eradication program was launched in 1954 to attract settlers from the overpopulated hills and by 1960 Chitwan was declared free of malaria. The human population rose from 36,000 in 1950 to 100,000 in 1960 and extensive forest areas were cleared for cultivation. Poaching was rampant, both for the pot and for money, with the rhino being the main target since its horn fetched a handsome price.

When in 1962 a rhino sanctuary was declared south of the Rapti river the **barasingha** (*Cervus duvauceli*) and the **wild buffalo** (*Bubalus bubalis*) had already be-come extinct. And despite the efforts of the 130-strong armed guards, called Gainda Gasti or Rhino Patrol, poaching continued and by the 1960s only about 100 rhinos remained, down from 800–2000 in 1950.

Chitwan was finally gazetted as Nepal's first national park in 1973 and a few years later a contingent of the Royal Nepalese Army was called in to combat poaching. Ever since, poaching of rhino within the park has been almost unheard of, although some does take place outside its limits.

The park headquarters are at **Kasara Durbar** where an old hunting lodge houses the offices and a small museum. Near Kasara is the **Gharial Project** and at **Sauraha** a visitors center, which provides information on the park. The network of roads in Chitwan is not very extensive but adequate for safaris by four-wheel drive vehicles. It is managed and administered by the National Parks and Wildlife Conservation Department.

Topography: Along the length of Nepal, in the middle, runs the Mahabharat Range; viewed from the plains, it is a blue mass of mountains. To its south, and almost parallel to and hugging it, runs a lower range of broken hills called the Siwalik. At times, such as in Chitwan, the two ranges separate and enclose huge flat valleys known as *doons*.

The park straddles the Siwalik range, the highest point in it being about 2000 feet (600 meters). Although much of it is hilly, a portion of it lies on the floodplain of three large rivers, the Reu, the Rapti and the Narayani, at an elevation of about 465 feet (140 meters).

Much of the park is bounded by these rivers and their tributaries. Both the Rapti and its tributary, the Reu, are low during the dry months (December to April) and are fordable for four-wheel drive vehicles at a few places. But during the monsoon, after a heavy downpour, flash floods turn them into raging torrents and hundreds of trees may be washed downriver. During such times even the pluckiest of elephants will refuse to cross them. These two rivers meet about half a mile (one km) east of where they link with the huge Narayani river, which has its origins high up in the Tibetan plateau. It meanders through the flat valley floor and forms a series of large gravel islands, known as *bandarjhula*, from Sigraulighat to Amaltarighat. The Narayani eventually cuts a narrow gorge in the Siwalik and becomes the Gandak in India before joining the holy Ganga — the Ganges.

Climate: Chitwan has a monsoonal climate with high humidity most of the year. In March and April the air is relatively dry. Apart from the cool months of December to February, the weather is generally hot during the day, particularly from May to September. Mid-June heralds the coming of the monsoon, which is the most dramatic time of year, with heavy showers and occasional floods. After the monsoon the jungle is lush and green and the sky crystal clear, with the snow-covered Himalaya 50–60 miles (80–100 km) away, clearly visible, especially in the evening. During the winter months a thick mist descends on the forest around 10 p.m. and persists into the late morning. The humidity reaches its peak in the early hours of the morning and the dew dripping from the trees onto the forest litter below makes a sound loud enough to convince newcomers to Chitwan that it is raining outside.

Two Types of Forest: The vegetation of Chitwan is tropical moist deciduous and two main types of forest may be recognized; the sal forest and the floodplain forest. On high ground and in the hills, where drainage is good and flooding does not occur, is the sal forest, so called after the dominant tree, sal (*Shorea robusta*). This forest covers roughly three-fourths of the park area and attains a height of 130 feet (40 meters) or more at the base of the hills but becomes stunted higher up. A common associate of sal is saj (*Terminalia tomentosa*), another large tree, easily recognized by its gray bark that resembles the skin of a crocodile. The kusum tree (*Schleichera trijuga*) bursts into a riot of red when the new leaves sprout in February–March, later turning to green, and the large-leaved tantari (*Dillenia pentagyna*), a medium-size tree, bears clusters of bright yellow flowers in the late spring. Other components of the sal forest are the sturdy karam or haldu (*Adina cordifolia*) and the middling-size sandan (*Ougenia dalbergoides*).

Giant vines and creepers, such as debre lahara (*Spatholobus parviflorus*) and bhorla (*Bauhinia vahlii*) twine upwards, using the larger trees for support. Sometimes a branch or a whole tree may collapse under their weight. The trees and their limbs also harbor several species of orchid and other epiphytes. On the very high ridges of the Siwalik grow sallo or chir pine (*Pinus roxburghii*).

On the floodplain, which is prone to waterlogging and flooding during the monsoon, patches of grassland and riverine forest occur. Dense stands of elephant grass, often 20 feet (six meters) high, are composed of *Saccharum spp.*, *Phragmites karka*, *Themeda villosa*, *Arundo donax* and *Arundinella nepalensis*. Some grasses are shorter, usually under seven feet (two meters) tall, such as *Imperata cylindrica* and *Bothriocloa intermedia*, and are commonly found in old village sites, although taller species are gradually displacing the short grasses. In Chitwan, most grasses flower between August and November, different species at different times — and there are many species! The change of color of the grass canopies from white to purple to yellow and various shades of pastel is a memorable sight.

Interspersed in the grassland are trees such as shisham (*Dalbergia sissoo*), khair (*Acacia catechu*) and simal (*Bombax ceiba*), especially on mid-river gravel islands and on the sandbanks of the Reu, Rapti and Narayani rivers. Both shisham and khair average about 45 feet (14 meters) in height but the simal is the largest tree in the park. Its flowers attract a variety of birds in the spring and during the course of a day dozens of species may be spotted in a single tree.

Mature riverine forests are often dense with a great variety of shrubs and other trees. In moist places, such as the **Itcharni Tappu** and other areas near **Sauraha,** there are thick patches of bhellar (*Trewia nudiflora*). The dark crooked skeletons of dhak (*Butea monosperma*) suddenly burst into flower in February and are aptly called "Flame of the Forest."

The beautiful white flowers of bhanti (*Clerodendron viscosum*), seen in March and April, have a lovely fragrance and attract numerous colorful butterflies and bees. Also in moist spots, several kinds of strangler figs (*Ficus spp.*) may be seen draped over their hosts, at varying stages of takeover. Foxtail orchids decorate some trees with their purple blossom in April, and the magnificent orange flowers of sungawa (*Dendrobium densiflorum*) in June–July.

Fire, an Ecological Factor: Apart from rainfall and flood, an important factor in the ecology of Chitwan is fire. Each year some 50,000 to 100,000 villagers enter the park for two weeks, some time in December and January, to collect thatch grass and reeds, both vital building materials for their houses. Having reaped their harvest, they set fire to the grassland and the fire spreads into the hills. Burning is intermittent and continues until the end of April or the beginning of May, when the pre-monsoon showers put an end to it. These fires have been an annual event, perhaps for hundreds

ROYAL CHITWAN NATIONAL PARK

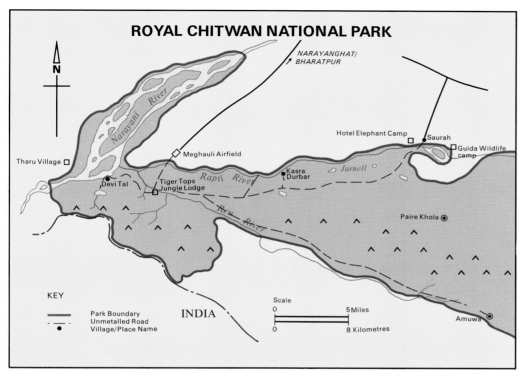

KEY

— Park Boundary
-·- Unmetalled Road
• Village/Place Name

INDIA

Scale
0 — 5 Miles
0 — 8 Kilometres

of years, and this must surely affect the composition of the forest. Perhaps it explains the predominance of fire-tolerant species, such as sal and simal, and also why tall coarse grasses are gradually replacing the short grass from old village sites.

Burning effectively "opens up" the grassland and the forest and the leaf-fall of spring improves visibility even further, so wildlife sightings at this time of the year are particularly good. Regrowth of grass is fast and herbivores concentrate on the once burnt grassland to graze on the succulent new grasses, and chital herds a hundred strong may sometimes be seen.

In and Around the "Tals": The floodplain is crisscrossed by numerous seasonal water channels and dotted with marsh, swamp and lakes. Only a handful of lakes are of any size; **Tamar Tal** and **Lame Tal** near Kasara Durbar, and **Dhakre Tal**, **Lame Tal** and **Devi Tal** near Tiger Tops. The last is the largest and most spectacular of all.

These lakes are the rhino's favorite haunts and also support a number of water birds, fish, turtle and **marsh mugger** (*Crocodylus palustris*). The mugger may grow to over 10 feet (three meters) long and with its blunt nose and huge jaws lined with dirty yellow teeth is sinister looking, the wavy outline of its mouth giving the impression of a nasty smile. The mugger will eat anything that it can overpower and kill, from birds and amphibians to deer, wild boar and even python. They prefer enclosed waters but are also found in rivers.

The **gharial** (*Gavialis gangeticus*), on the other hand, lives only in rivers and feeds largely on fish. Easily recognized by its slender snout, it is larger than the mugger and may reach 16 feet (five meters) in length. The Narayani, with about 40 adults, has the largest single concentration of wild gharial anywhere. Several young gharial, artificially hatched and hand reared at the **Gharial Project** near Kasara Durbar, have been released in batches since 1980 and many have survived. The gharial is, however, very wary of man and will slither into the river even when as far as 150 feet (46 meters) away. But look for their tell-tale eyes and nostrils gleaming over the surface of the water. The best time of year to see crocodiles is winter (October to February) when they come out of the water and bask in the sun, often all day long.

Another peculiar aquatic predator in the Narayani river is the rare **Gangetic dolphin** (*Platanista gangetica*). About seven feet (two meters) long when adult, this spindle-shaped animal feeds on crustaceans and fish on the riverbed and breaks the surface every minute or so to breathe. Its hissing sound is unmistakable and it may be seen at the Narayani-Rapti confluence from July to September and at Amaltarighat for most of the year, except when the water is low from January to April. The **smooth-coated otter** (*Lutra perspicillata*) is another common aquatic predator and to watch a family playing outside its den is an endearing sight.

Indian pythons (*Python molurus*) are common near large bodies of water and these heavy reptiles, which may reach 16–20 feet (five–six meters) in length, sometimes waylay deer which come to drink. An adult python can swallow a full-grown **hog deer** (*Axis porcinus*), weighing 45 lb (20 kg) and then go without food for months.

Birds — Resident and Migratory: Chitwan is a bird-watcher's paradise. It is not unusual to spot a hundred species in a single day, depending of course on the time of year. Over 440 species of birds have been recorded, of which a little under half are year-round residents. These include the beautiful **Indian peafowl** (*Pavo cristatus*) common in the floodplain, **openbill stork** (*Anastomus oscitans*) near marsh and lakes, small **pied kingfisher** (*Ceryle rudis*) over

Left, sal forest. *Below*, strangler fig.

open rivers, and three-toed **goldenbacked woodpecker** (*Dinopium shorii*) in the sal forest. The **blackheaded oriole** (*Oriolus xanthornus*) fills the forest with song, and the loud honking of the **giant hornbill** (*Buceros bicornis*) may be heard.

Of the many winter visitors, such as ducks, geese, waders and leafwarblers, the **brahminy duck** (*Tadorna ferruginia*) is the most conspicuous, not only because of its numbers but also its colors and call. Another distinguished winter visitor is the huge **blacknecked stork** (*Xenorhynchus asiaticus*), a rare bird seen on open river banks. By comparison, the summer visitors are much fewer but include such colorful birds as the **paradise flycatcher** (*Terpsiphone paradisi*) and the **golden oriole** (*Oriolus oriolus*) which arrive in February – March, and the **Indian pitta** (*Pitta brachyura*) and **green-breasted pitta** (*Pitta sordida*) in April–May.

Among the rarities of Chitwan's birds are the **grayheaded fishing eagle** (*Ichthyophaga ichthyaetus*), seen near swamps and lakes; the **great slaty woodpecker** (*Mulleripicus pulverulentus*) near the forested hill streams; and the **yellow bittern** (*Ixobrychus sinensis*) in tall marsh grass. In late spring the rare **Bengal florican** (*Eupodotis bengalensis*)

males may be seen in the grassland, displaying to their mates, their white wings in sharp contrast to their black bodies.

The best months for bird-watching are February and March, when the winter visitors are still around, the summer visitors have started to arrive, and the breeding birds become very vocal and conspicuous. Also, the visibility is at its best because of burning and leaf-fall, and the trees are in blossom, which attracts the birds.

Spotting the Mammals: In terms of seeing wildlife, the floodplain belt is the best as it harbors a larger concentration of animals than the sal forest. Chitwan's estimated 400 **rhinos** (*Rhinoceros unicornis*) are found almost wholly in the grassland and riverine forest. Chitwan is one of the two last strongholds for this endangered rhino (Kaziranga in Assam being the other), and it harbors a quarter of the world's total.

In the Siwalik hills is the **gaur** (*Bos gaurus*), the most magnificent among hoofed animals. During the spring the gaur descend to the grassland in search of new shoots after the fires and the forests around Devi Tal, Tamar Tal, **Dumaria** and **Khagendramalli** are particularly good spots for seeing them in February–April.

Of the four species of deer found in

Chitwan, the **hog deer** (*Axis porcinus*) is restricted almost exclusively to the grassland, and the **chital** (*Axis axis*) to the lowland parts as it avoids sloping ground and hilly terrain. The **sambar** (*Cervus unicolor*) and the **barking deer** (*Muntiacus muntjak*) are found throughout the park.

Also common throughout the park, but mainly in the floodplain, is the **wild boar** (*Sus scrofa*) which often lives in large groups of 20, even 30 or more, animals, although six – 10 is the average. The wild boar and the four kinds of deer all form important prey species for the **tiger** (*Panthera tigris*) and the **leopard** (*Panthera pardus*).

Monkeys also feature strongly on the leopard's menu and two species occur in the park. The handsome **gray langur** (*Presbytis entellus*) with long limbs and tail and a black face, lives mainly in the sal forest in troops of 10–20 individuals. Langurs are not particularly shy and will allow a fairly close approach, but not the Chitwan **rhesus macaque** (*Macaca mulatta*). Unlike their counterparts found near railway platforms and temples which show complete contempt for man, the rhesus of Chitwan is extremely shy.

The Rare Ones and the Great Cats: Although Chitwan has over 50 species of mammals,

they are often not easily seen because of their nocturnal and secretive habits. Rare mammals in Chitwan include the **wild dog** (*Cuon alpinus*), the **serow** (*Capricornis sumatraensis*), the **hyena** (*Hyaena hyaena*), the **spotted linsang** (*Prionodon pardicolor*) and the **ratel** (*Mellivora capensis*).

The two large predators in the park are the tiger and the leopard. They do not mix well — the tiger may attack and even kill the leopard. The tiger controls the prime habitat with the leopard often moving out to the edge of the park. However, the two can live side by side. Because of Chitwan's closed environment, encounters between the two are reduced somewhat. Poor visibility aids the leopard and by altering his schedule and becoming more diurnal he may share the same area as the tiger. Moreover, competition between the two is further reduced by the tiger's preference for larger prey species than those of the leopard. Chitwan has a fair number of leopards but they are not often seen. It is estimated that about 40 breeding adult tigers exist in the park, which makes a total of up to 100, including cubs, subadults and transients. You may sometimes see a tiger, a pair, or exceptionally a family of female and cubs, but despite such good numbers tiger sightings are not common.

Chitwan leopards are rarely seen in the open.

Tiger Tops Lodge, Chitwan.

114

ROYAL BARDIA WILDLIFE RESERVE

About 250 miles (400 km) to the west of Khatmandu, in far western Nepal, lies the **Royal Bardia Wildlife Reserve**, also known as **Karnali** because of the great river of that name that drains the region. Initially set aside as a royal hunting preserve during the Rana regime (1846–1950), it was declared a wildlife reserve in 1976 with an area of 134 sq miles (348 sq km), increased in 1985 to 374 sq miles (968 sq km).

The reserve is bounded to the west by the Karnali river and its distributary, the Girwa, and to the east by a section of the Nepalgunj-Birendranagar highway. A large part of the reserve is hill country as it drapes the southern flanks of the Churia or Siwalik hills, the outermost range of the Himalaya. The crestlines of the Churia form its northern boundary.

From the base of the Churia the ground slopes gradually southward for about five miles (eight km), and this highly porous ground is called the *bhabhar*. Thereafter, it flattens out as far as the eye can see. This is part of the Gangetic plain, and the strip between the Bhabhar and the Indian border is known as the *terai*. The southern edge of the reserve is mainly *bhabhar*, with a small piece of *terai* at the southwest.

Flora and Fauna: Bardia, with its stately sal (*Shorea robusta*) trees, its tall termite mounds, its patches of grassland, locally known as *phantas*, is very reminiscent of Dudhwa in Uttar Pradesh. The forests are tropical dry deciduous. Since a great part of the park is high ground with good drainage, it is dominated by the sal, a hardwood tree. The sal associates with many other trees, notably saj or asna (*Terminalia tomentosa*), and on the highest ridges of the hills, with chir pine (*Pinus roxburghii*). The sal forest and its shaded ravines are the home of **sambar, barking deer, porcupine, sloth bear** and **kaleej**.

On the lower ground is a mosaic of grassland and riverine forest with the simal trees (*Bombax ceiba*) standing above all others. The simal when old are gigantic in size and develop huge buttresses at their base for extra support and their large red, sometimes orange, flowers are a memorable sight in the early spring. The *phantas* are old village sites where a small herd of **barasingha** (*Cervus duvauceli*) and **blackbuck** (*Antilope cervicapra*) may still be seen.

The waters of the Karnali emerge from the narrow gorge at Chisapani, fan out over a gentle slope and eventually slow down to a sluggish pace on the plains. A couple of miles downriver of the gorge it branches out into two main channels or distributaries — Karnali to the west and Girwa to the east — which enclose large and small islands of sand and gravel. Here shisham (*Dalbergia sissoo*), khair (*Acacia catechu*) and simal flourish (such an assortment of trees is common on all riverine sites). These islands are the favorite haunts of the ungainly **nilgai**, the subcontinent's largest antelope.

But much of the park is drained by another smaller river, the **Babai**, which courses down the Siwalik range and collects spring and rain water from its numerous seasonal and perennial tributaries. The Karnali–Girwa and the Babai attract a large number of migratory waterfowl.

Wildlife Viewing: The best place for this is the old reserve area between the Karnali–Girwa and the Babai rivers, especially along the former, and the adjoining *phantas* such as **Baghora** and **Lamkoili**.

At present, only one private facility for tourists exists in Bardia. A couple of miles to the south of Chisapani (west) on the east bank of the Karnali–Girwa, is the **Karnali Tented Camp** which runs landrover, raft

Far left, **Karnali river** and *left*, **termite mound**.

and walking safaris. It also runs fishing expeditions for the mighty **mahseer**.

You need four–five nights to fully appreciate the jungle and its sights in Bardia. A trip there is a mixture of wildlife, culture and adventure. All, even any one, of the following day-trips will confirm this.

Rafting Down the Girwa: Start by rubber raft from Karnali Camp around 9 a.m. and float down the Girwa river. A couple of hours later, stop at a strand downriver for lunch. While food is being cooked, you may watch birds, study tracks on the riverbank or just relax in the sun. After lunch, resume your journey and raft down to **Manu Tappu Ghat**. On this river trip you will see many species of birds — **duck**, **heron**, **gull**, **tern**, **kingfisher**, **cormorant** and **osprey**; and perhaps also **rhesus monkey** (*Macaca mulatta*), **langur** (*Presbytis entellus*), nilgai (*Boselephus tragocamelus*) and **otter** (*Lutra perspicillata*). If you are lucky, you may even glimpse the **Gangetic dolphin** as it surfaces for air; Manu Tappu is a particularly good place for this. On your drive back to camp, via the *phantas*, you will add more animals to your spotting list, such as **chital** and **wild boar**.

Trek Out and Float Back: Take an early morning walk up to Chisapani gorge,

birding as you go. Cross the river by ferry or by raft, then follow the old trading route that runs along the west bank of the Karnali. The road has been cut out of stone into a steep hillside and is well worn by centuries of use by traders and their pack animals. You will meet traders from Dailekh and Achham to the north, heading for Chisapani with their produce and then returning home with salt, kerosene and other goods. These are hardy men and women, with even hardier beasts of burden, mainly goat and sheep, each laden with 25 lb (55 kg) load on its back. The hillside is forested and during the mid-morning, bird-watching conditions are excellent.

After about 2½ hours of walking, you descend to the riverbank for lunch just short of the small village of **Kachalipur**. Rafting back through the gorge, you will be struck by the peculiar rock formations along the banks which provide excellent hideouts for otters, and good vantage points for **crocodiles** to bask in the sun.

Gray and crimson **wall creepers** (*Tichodroma muraria*), common winter birds in the gorge, fly about on the vertical cliffs, and here and there white droppings of cormorant and darter decorate the black rock. As you come out of the gorge, a spectacular

Below, chital hind; *right*, elephants crossing the Manas river.

view of the floodplains opens up in front of you.

Drive and Walk: Drive southeast (with packed lunch), for about eight miles (13 km) and near **Amreni** turn northwards towards the base of the hills. The forest here becomes dense and dark, giant creepers drape the sal trees and the "tentacles" of the strangler figs literally squeeze the life out of their hosts. You may see evidence of the passage of **wild elephant**—droppings, tracks, uprooted trees, and trees stripped of their bark. Carry on to **Danawa Tal guard post** and trek into the hills for a couple of hours. On the stream beds look for the tracks of the animals that have passed here — **tiger**, **leopard**, **monkey**, **porcupine**, **civet** and others.

Stop by a pool for a picnic lunch and then drive back to the base of the hills and take the road to the Babai river. **Peafowl** and **red jungle fowl** are common here and you may also see **gharial** or **mugger crocodiles**. On your return drive, visit the *phantas* again. Towards late afternoon, the jungle comes alive with the activity of its denizens and you may spot blackbuck, barasingha and wild boar, not to mention the abundant chital.

Spotter's Luck: But what you see, and how much, depends on chance, and in any of these three outings you could well see tiger, leopard, sloth bear and wild elephant. If the **rhinos** introduced here in early 1986 flourish, they are then likely to become Bardia's star attraction. Predators of Bardia also include **hyena**, **wild dog**, **jackal**, the large and the small **Indian civet**, **mongoose**, **python**, mugger and gharial. The tall grass also harbors some **hispid hare**, believed, until recently, to have become extinct. Over 350 species of birds have been recorded.

The tourist season here is from November through May; for the rest of the year the reserve is inaccessible because of the monsoon floods. The weather is generally warm, but gets cold in the early morning and evening in December and January. During these two months, each year, local villagers are allowed to enter the park for a couple of weeks to collect thatch grass and reed to use as building materials for their houses. Having collected their harvest, the villagers set fire to the grassland and forest, and much of the undergrowth is burnt to ashes. But regrowth is quick and numerous herbivores congregate on the now open *phantas* to feed on the new succulent grasses. Thus the best wildlife sightings in Bardia are between January and April when the vegetation is "open" and visibility better than at other times.

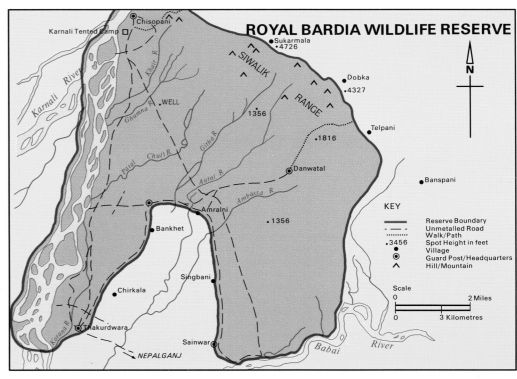

ROYAL BARDIA WILDLIFE RESERVE

KEY

——	Reserve Boundary
- - -	Unmetalled Road
··········	Walk/Path
.3456	Spot Height in feet
●	Village
◉	Guard Post/Headquarters
∧	Hill/Mountain

Scale
0 ——— 2 Miles
0 ——— 3 Kilometres

KAZIRANGA NATIONAL PARK

No two places could be more diverse in their physical appearance and character, yet the twin sanctuaries of Assam which would form a perfect triangle with Guwahati are together completely representative of the Indian northeast. While Kaziranga is flat country with elephant grass and shallow swamps interspersed with large patches of semi-evergreen forest, Manas lies at the foot of the Bhutan hills and through it flows the Manas river which spills into the plains, splitting into two streams, the Beki and the Hakua. On either side of the Manas river, plentiful wildlife and magnificent scenery combine to form one of the world's best and most picturesque wildlife reserves.

Like Manas, Kaziranga too lies on the banks of a river — the mighty Brahmaputra. The name, literally translated, means "son of Brahma" who, according to Hindu mythology, is the creator of the universe, but the massive river could just as easily have been named after Shiva, the destroyer. Each year, with the onset of the monsoon, it overspills its banks and the surrounding areas are ravaged ruthlessly. In Kaziranga, the river forces people and the wildlife to take shelter on whatever high ground they can find, and, according to a local estimate, it washes away almost a thousand hog deer each year. But, when the river withdraws, leaving *bheels* (swamps) with a shallow spread of water, Kaziranga comes into its own, offering the visitor some of the best views of the **Indian one-horned rhinoceros** and **wild buffalo**.

Kaziranga: The monsoon and the Brahmaputra leave Kaziranga with a comparatively short season — January to May. Approachable from either Guwahati or Jorhat, it is sandwiched by the highway to the south and the river to its north. The reserve sprawls over 165 sq miles (430 sq km) of grassland and impenetrable vegetative luxuriance comprising close-tangled and thorny rattan cane, elephant grass and tall trees of the evergreen forests. Until 1908, Kaziranga was a sportman's and poacher's paradise, but the rapidly declining population of rhino forced the authorities, in 1926, to constitute it a reserve forest, closed to shooting. Some estimates put the then rhino population at about a dozen and the subsequent revival of this massive and powerful animal, reminiscent of prehistoric ages, has been one of the more notable feats of faunal conservation. In 1940, Kaziranga was officially declared a wildlife sanctuary.

Along the main highway, at **Baguri** and **Kohora**, lodges have been built by the forest and the tourism departments, and at **Mihimukh**, which is two miles (three km) from the lodge at Kohora, riding elephants can be hired to enter the sanctuary.

In almost all wildlife reserves in India, the visitor needs to give himself a few days to have a reasonable chance of seeing wildlife at close quarters. Kaziranga, however, is the exception where one can hope to see most of the mammals for which it is known in a single day. During the day, especially in the morning, Kaziranga has a thin ground mist which blurs the distant horizon and which creates a very special atmosphere in the area — covering its creatures with a ghostly haze; undoubtedly, Kaziranga is one of the few unspoilt valleys of the Brahmaputra.

In the 1930s, Kaziranga was virtually a closed book and the sanctuary was opened to tourists only around 1938. The rhino, the main attraction in the park, was then unused to humans and would quite blindly (they are notoriously shortsighted and charge whatever they perceive as a challenge) take on any intruder. Fortunately, at the last minute they tended to veer off, leaving almost everything in the area badly shaken but rarely hurt. The rhino is now a lot more used to humans, and though a mother with a calf may demonstrate in front of a riding elephant, they often let people get amazingly close to them.

The only natural enemy of the rhino is the **tiger** of which there is a sizable population in the park. The tall grass and the patches of forest provide excellent cover for the big cats which are therefore rarely seen. Sometimes a tiger will attack and kill a rhino calf despite the mother's aggressive vigilance, but the rhino suffers more at the hand of man. Its horn, believed to be an aphrodisiac by the ancient Indians and highly sought after by Chinese medicinemen, is a lucrative target for poachers who usually operate from the Darrang district across the Brahmaputra river and sometimes from the Mikir hills where the animals retreat during the floods. The rhino, being a creature of set habits, follows well-worn trails and even defecates at the same spot each day. Taking advantage of its regular habits, a pit large enough to accommodate its body is dug by the poachers in its usual path and then covered with leaves and grass. The unwary animal falls into the pit where it is killed and its horn hacked off with a *dao*. Other parts of the body also command sale value. As both

Swamp deer.

Rhinoceros and cattle egrets.

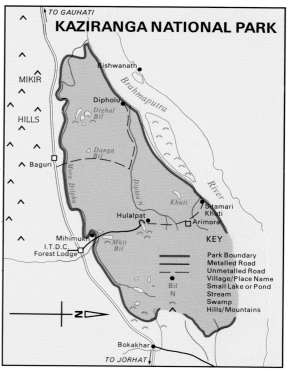

KAZIRANGA NATIONAL PARK

KEY

Park Boundary
Metalled Road
Unmetalled Road
Village/Place Name
Small Lake or Pond
Stream
Swamp
Hills/Mountains

sexes carry the horn, the threat is doubly compounded.

The wild buffalo herds in Kaziranga, like the rhino, have also got relatively used to humans and can be approached on elephant-back with little danger. By and large, buffalo herds are shy of humans, and mothers canter off with their woolly calves if threatened. However, solitary bulls are often bad tempered and quick to charge with or without any provocation. If a good elephant holds its ground, the bull will usually pull up short, a picture of wild defiance. These bulls often stay in the vicinity of herds, and sometimes mate with domestic buffalo cows as well. The Kaziranga buffalo have over the years suffered from domestic genes invading the wild stock, and unlike the wild buffalo of Manas, the animals are thought to be feral in most cases.

The presence of buffalo and rhino make walking in the sanctuary a difficult proposition. A third species ensures that visitors enter only riding elephants or in vehicles. Herds of up to 200 **wild elephants** can be seen migrating from the Mikir hills to the *bheels* and, like the buffalo, it is again the solitary bull elephant which is prone to create trouble. The large number of un-tusked males (*makhnas*) in the northeast often causes confusion, for what is taken to be a large female turns out to be a male. A riding elephant, on occasion, can wander into a herd of wild elephants; on the other hand, a wild elephant will even caress a trained one with its trunk, oblivious of the dreaded human cargo on its back.

As one starts from Mihimukh where nearly 20 elephants are stabled (owing to patrol duties and pregnancies, only four or five are usually available to tourists and it is advisable to reserve a day in advance), the Himalaya, which are more than a hundred miles to the north, can be seen on some days. Small herds of **barasingha** (swamp deer) and the odd **wild boar** are usually among the first animals seen. A subspecies of the barasingha of Kanha and of the other variety found in the *terai* of Uttar Pradesh, these deer of Assam have slightly splayed hooves and are found on high ground in the proximity of water. When the stags are regenerating their antlers, it is not uncommon to find herds in an all-male group.

The **chital** does not extend beyond the Brahmaputra, its eastern range in India being Manas, but there are plenty of **para**, as hog deer are referred to in this region. Mixed herds, of both sexes, are often scattered around the various *bheels*, and

these small deer are among the main prey species of the tiger in Kaziranga. Solitary hog deer are often seen.

Among the other animals found in Kaziranga, the wild boar is fairly common. Some **gaur** (the word *gaur* in Assamese refers to the rhino, while the gaur is called a bison) are also found here, but they are scarce and rarely seen. **Leopard cats** and **otters** are not uncommon, while the odd **leopard** may be chanced upon. A wide variety of snakes, including the **rock python** are also found while the prehistoric-looking **monitor lizard** is relatively easily seen.

Birds: Grasslands are often excellent raptor country, and Kaziranga is no exception. — the **crested serpent eagle** is common, **Pallas's fishing eagle** and the **gray-headed fishing eagle** are frequently seen. Dawn is welcomed by the loud calling of the **swamp partridge** which shatters the misty silence of the morning while **red jungle fowl** tentatively step on to a jeep track before taking off at a mad run in front of a jeep. The **Bengal florican** and a variety of water fowl, of which the **bar-headed goose** and the **whistling teal** are the most frequently seen, are among the other birds found in the sanctuary. A large number of **pelicans** nest close to Mihimukh on a large semul tree and the clumps of forest are alive with the screeching of the **rose-breasted parakeet** and an assortment of birds common to the northeast. As one would expect, the swamps are home for a diverse avifauna of the shallow watersides. **Black-necked adjutant** and **open-billed stork**, **egret** and **heron** of all shapes and sizes and other waders can be found around the *bheels* which are clogged with water hyacinth. When this once exotic plant first appeared in Kaziranga, no animal would condescend to feed on it except the wild boar which ate the roots during the dry season. Now buffaloes as well as elephants browse on it, though somewhat reluctantly.

Firmly entrenched on the Indian tourist map, Kaziranga has its own peculiar problems. Poaching continues to be a major threat to the rhino population, with over 35 animals being killed each year at an average. A disproportionate increase in human populations along the highway and the sanctuary has created socio-economic problems which are not easy to tackle and Assam is only just recovering from the after-effects of political turmoil. On the other hand, air travel and regular transport links have made the area a lot more hospitable and the northeast is no longer as inaccessible an area as it used to be, even in the recent past.

Capped langur.

MANAS TIGER RESERVE

Manas: This sanctuary, in contrast to Kaziranga, is far removed from the National Highway and the mainstream of human life passes it by. Barpeta Road, the railhead which also serves as the sanctuary's headquarters, is almost three hours by road or rail from Guwahati.

Manas has a much longer season than Kaziranga, the only wet period being from mid-May to September, but the best period to visit the area is either in November or February. Unlike the open swamps and grasslands of Kaziranga, where the visitor may see a large number of animals, wildlife viewing in Manas is never regular—or easy. But when one is confronted by an animal, it is usually at close quarters and, invariably, exciting and dramatic.

Few places can hold a visitor in its grip the way Manas can. Over 1000 sq miles (2600 sq km) in area, the Manas river at Mothanguri forms the boundary between India and Bhutan, and one of the great attractions of the park is the **golden langur** which inhabit the tall flowering trees next to the Royal Hunting Lodge where the King of Bhutan retreats once a year or so.

The topography of the reserve is dramatically diverse; the river spilling out of the foothills; the lower sandy stretches where islands of trees stand like sentinels over herds of **wild buffalo**, with **fishing eagles** and **ospreys** searching the fast flowing streams for fish. There are the great forests of mixed deciduous vegetation which shut the light off at ground level, and finally small glades of grassland where elephant herds leave their calling card by uprooting every invading sapling that tries to encroach into the glades.

In terms of diversity in animal life, Manas again stands alone. There are twenty species of birds and animals here which are listed under Schedule I (highly endangered) in the *IUCN Red Data Book*, and of these species, some like the **hispid hare** and the **pigmy hog** are today found only here. Both these remarkable animals have been reduced to a rarity, so much so that their extinction was once thought to be just a matter of time. The situation today is less desperate.

As one drives into Manas from Barpeta Road, leaving the long semul-lined drive and the Bansbari tea estate behind, the gravel road snakes through open grassland which is said to be prime country for the

hispid hare, which is also known as the Assamese rabbit. During late evenings, just as dusk gives way to darkness, the beam from a vehicle's headlights sometimes spotlights the scurrying figure of this elusive and rare animal.

Mothanguri is the ideal, and perhaps the only place to stay in. Situated on a rise overlooking the Manas river, there could be few places so endearing to a naturalist. From the balcony of the rest house, one overlooks Bhutan while on the Indian side the forests are tinged with pink, especially in February when the semul trees are explosions of color. The Project Tiger people have a number of riding elephants which provide the ideal means to move about and give the visitor the best approach to wildlife, but the saddles or *howdahs* are quite different from the broad seats of North and South India. Here, one needs to straddle the animal or sit sideways on the saddle, a painful exercise at the best of times. Red ants, notorious for a rather painful sting, also seem to have been designed by nature to drop onto you from their leaf nests in trees, and there is little one can do other than watch out for them.

While the golden langur are usually approachable on foot from the boat landing on the Bhutan side, the colorful **capped langur** is only approachable from elephant back. Extremely shy, these primates usually move away, but if one were to watch them quietly for half an hour, they seem to forget your presence and go about their business of eating and grooming with the nonchalance so typical of the langur family. The **Assamese macaque** is rarely seen in the forests, but they inhabit the islands downstream and move in large troupes from place to place. The **slow loris** and the **Hoolock gibbon** also extend into Manas, but sightings are rare.

Most of the animals found in Kaziranga are also found in Manas. **Rhino** is not as plentiful, but a reasonable population exists, but here these animals are extremely shy and make off at the slightest disturbance, using the heavy undergrowth to their advantage. Two of the main attractions, however, are the **water buffalo** and the **elephant**. The ideal way to observe buffalo is to hire a boat at Mothanguri and spend the better part of the day drifting downstream before being picked up by motorized transport some 22 miles (35 km) away. The herds come to the river during the day to cool off and they stare curiously at the drifting boat, their sweeping and majestic horns thrown back in graceful arcs. The lone bull, always game for

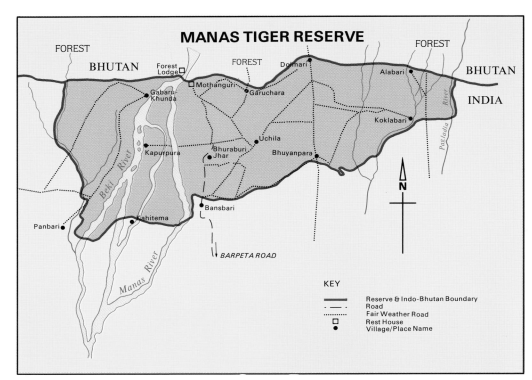

Wild buffalo are restricted to a few pockets in northeast India.

a fight, will toss his head as only a bull can and sometimes he will follow along the side, presenting a sight which is rarely forgotten. On elephant-back too, one sometimes succeeds in surprising a herd in the water, which then struggles to the bank through the mist and the water.

Locating elephants in the thick forest is never an easy task, but once a herd is found the riding elephant often manages to get into the herd. To be surrounded by a herd of trumpeting wild elephants can leave one weak around the knees, and to be charged by a lone bull is by no means an uncommon occurrence here. Fortunately, the trained elephants are adept at making a quick getaway, but the image of a charging tusker with its ears fanned out is a memory that can never fade.

A lot more elusive and shy is the **Indian bison**, or **gaur**, which stands taller than a buffalo at the shoulder. Sometimes, one can see a large herd in the grassy glades, but at the slightest sound or movement, they thunder off into the cover of the forest. Another method of looking for gaur is to drive along the foothills, on jungle tracks which are hemmed in by tall grass on either side. The area is full of **hog deer** and sometimes a **tiger** can be seen plodding along the tracks, looking for a chance to kill. This stretch is good for the other big cats too. When fires are lit to burn the grass, a **clouded leopard** may emerge from behind a smoldering tree trunk where he had been feeding off insects which are forced out by the smoke. Manas provides an ideal habitat for the **sloth bear**, yet another species inseparably linked with Manas, and they too can usually be seen at dawn or at dusk. In fact, the sloth is often seen when the light is too poor for photography. Picked up by a spotlight, it will scuttle away but sometimes curiosity gets the better of him, and the animal will come close to the jeep, staring at it with myopic eyes.

Manas is the eastern range of **chital**, and the Field Director of the park, Deb Roy, who is himself yet another institution in Manas, fears that the small surviving population is hardly breeding for reasons which are not known. The **muntjac**, or **barking deer**, **hog deer**, **sambar** and, in places, **swamp deer**, represent the deer family in fairly good numbers. The sambar is perhaps the most widely distributed of all Indian deer and though only one species is recognized, there are changes in color and the average size of antlers from one region to another. If one were to sweep across the top half of India from west to east, the Rajasthan sambar is a dull brown, which changes to a slightly deeper shade of red as you approach Bihar, which also has some of the best stags. The reddish tinge gets even more pronounced as we move further east. Another notable thing in Manas is the raw patch sambar develop on their throat — it looks quite a bit like a sore. This interesting phenomenon is common to all the large deer in eastern India.

For insects, butterflies and reptiles, the northeast is prime country and the blaze of color at ground level in the jungle holds one in breathless wonder. In the canopy above, winged stars steal the show; **scarlet minivets** flash their orange and yellow towards the watching heavens; a **bee-eater** clicks its beak as it grabs a bee; **magpie robins** and **bulbuls** fill the air with their constant chatter. But the main attraction is the **giant hornbill** which *whooshes* its way from tree to tree. Two subspecies of the giant are found here along with the **pied** and the **gray** varieties, sharing more or less the same habitat. **Red jungle fowl** and **kaleej pheasants** scratch for their food from under the fallen leaves, while the great river offers ornithologists its own brand of avifauna with **mergansers** and **brahminy ducks**, **egrets**, **pelicans** and **herons**, **eagles**, **falcons** and **harriers**.

Manas undoubtedly is a very special place.

Far left, hornbills and *left*, ground orchids.

KEOLADEO GHANA NATIONAL PARK (BHARATPUR)

Only 110 miles (176 km) from Delhi and 31 miles (50 km) west of Agra and the Taj Mahal, Keoladeo Ghana is a wonder of the natural world no less worth seeing than the marble tomb of Shah Jahan's queen. Over 350 species of birds find a refuge in the 11 sq miles (29 sq km) of shallow lakes and woodland which make up the park. A third of them are migrants many of whom winter in Bharatpur before returning to their breeding grounds as far away as Siberia and Central Asia. Some 120 species nest in the park and the heronry at Keoladeo Ghana is said to be one of the finest in the world. The park is open throughout the year although most visitors choose to come between the months of October and March when wintering wildfowl assemble in their thousands.

History: While many of India's parks have been developed from the hunting preserves of princely India, Keoladeo Ghana is perhaps the only one where the habitat has been *created* by a maharaja. The park, a mile or so from Bharatpur town, still commonly known as "Bharatpur" rather than by its official name, is the handiwork of the royal family of Bharatpur. The maharaja developed the area in the late 19th Century. Until then it was no different from the arid scrub woodland of the surrounding countryside except that it formed a slight depression which collected rainwater during the monsoon and attracted wildfowl for the period before it dried up. The maharaja recognized the area's potential and augmented the water supply by diverting water from a nearby irrigation canal. He also constructed small dams, dykes and shooting butts to turn the area into the finest wildfowl hunting preserve in north India. In a few years the new ecosystem so flourished that it was able to support thousands of water birds.

The maharaja celebrated his success in style, with extravagant shooting parties for the dignitaries of British and princely India. Their exploits are recorded to this day on a sandstone inscription in the park.

Perhaps surprisingly, the birds survived these depradations and still came to Bharatpur in huge numbers. In 1956 the hunting preserve became a sanctuary, but the VIP shoots continued until 1964 and the maharaja himself retained his personal shooting rights until 1972.

The end of the shooting parties did not mean the end of Bharatpur's problems. The viceroys and maharajas were replaced by unruly tourists with transistor radios and hundreds of domestic cattle and buffaloes belonging to local villagers. In order to control these problems Bharatpur was upgraded to a national park in 1981 and renamed Keoladeo Ghana. Keoladeo is the name of the ancient Hindu temple devoted to the god Shiva which stands in the center of the park. "Ghana" means dense, referring to the thick forest which used to cover the area.

Geography and Habitat: Keoladeo Ghana lies 1214 feet (370 meters) above sea level and, besides the wetland for which it is famous, contains various other habitats from woodland, scrub and pasture to denuded saline patches. The lakes are fed entirely by rain and river water brought by canal from the Gambhir and Banganga rivers. In the monsoon some four square miles (11 sq km) of the park can be inundated. One waterway, the Ghana Canal, bisects the park, running northeast to northwest.

One main metaled road runs through the center of the park from the northern entrance, through the main wetland area on

Far left, sarus cranes pair for life; *left*, egrets in flight.

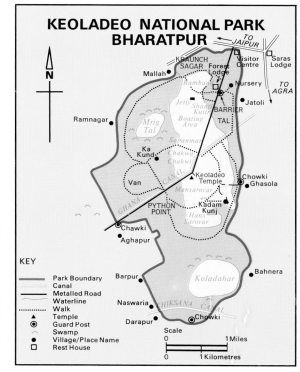

KEOLADEO NATIONAL PARK BHARATPUR

KEY

— Park Boundary
— Canal
— Metalled Road
— Waterline
---- Walk
▲ Temple
◉ Guard Post
⌒ Swamp
● Village/Place Name
□ Rest House

Scale
0 ——— 1 Miles
0 ——— 1 Kilometres

the eastern side of the park, where it follows the course of the Ghana Canal. At intervals along the road raised paths lined with babul trees (*Acacia nilotica*) lead off into the wetland. Babuls are the dominant tree in the park and these paths and undergrowth along them provide excellent blinds for bird-watching. There are many good paths in the park and several trails, beginning and ending at various points on the road, are recommended to visitors.

Bharatpur forms part of the vast Indo-Gangetic plain and its climate is therefore hot in summer (max 116°F/47°C, min. 95°F/35°C), humid in the monsoon (July–September) and comparatively cool in the winter (max 95°F/35°C, min 41°F /5°C), becoming quite chilly at night. Average annual rainfall is 26 inches (66 cm).

Flora: Keoladeo Ghana contains a bewildering variety of flora representing 64 families, 181 genera and 227 subspecies. Besides the babul, other native species of tree include ber, kalam, khajur and khejri. Dozens of species of grasses and reeds abound, providing rich grazing for birds and mammals alike. The wetland habitat of the park has been described by the naturalist, Anne Bastille, as "a living soup of frogs, toads, water snakes, snails, leeches, turtles, pondweeds, carp, water hyacinth, catfish, water beetles, duckweed, lilies, protozoans, wild celery and plankton." Even this description is by no means a comprehensive list of ingredients. Among the fish are **rohu** (*Labeo rohita*), **bata** (*Labeo bata*), **calbasu** (*Labeo calbasu*), **catla** (*Catla catla*), **mrigal** (*Cirrhina mrigal*) and **sarana** (*Barbus sarana*). Some grow to a good size and a 33 lb. (15 kg) sarana has been caught in the park. Predatory fishes include **murrel** (*Ophocephalus strictus*) and **freshwater shark** (*Wallago attu*).

Visiting the Park: Although many people visit Bharatpur for the day, it is recommended to stay at least one night in one of the hotels which provide simple accommodation within or just outside the park. This gives the visitor the chance to see Keoladeo Ghana at its best — in the early morning and evening. Entry tickets to the park are available at its main entrance. One can drive motor vehicles from the entrance as far as the **Forest Lodge** and the offices of the warden located in **Shanti Kutir**, formerly a hunting lodge of the maharaja. However, from there on, the only vehicles allowed are bicycles and cycle rickshaws. Both are available on hire from the Forest Lodge and the "rickshaw wallahs" take a

genuine interest in the birdlife and have been trained to recognize the different species. Boats are also available to take groups of visitors on a circular tour of the wetland starting from the jetty near Shanti Kutir, and a boat trip shortly after dawn is perhaps the most enchanting introduction to the park.

At the start of the peak tourist season in October the heronries are still occupied, although breeding begins shortly after the onset of the monsoon. Thousands of birds nest together in mixed heronries, dominated by different species in different parts of the sanctuary. Some of the most spectacular heronries are situated near the road and can be approached by the raised paths running off it. The crowded and noisy colonies are constructed in babul trees which stand half-submerged in water. As many as eight or nine species of birds may nest in one tree. **Painted storks, white ibis, openbills, spoonbills, egrets, herons, cormorants** and **shags** are in abundance, while thousands of **moorhens** and **jacanas** breed in the floating vegetation on the water surface. The amount of food necessary to support the heronries is enormous. It's been estimated that 2,000 painted storks breeding in an area of no more than a square mile (2.5 sq km) require four–six tons of food each day to support themselves and their nestlings. In the 30 to 40 days they breed they consume at least 1200 tons of food — and this is only one section of the population of one species breeding in the park. The painted storks, like many other birds in Bharatpur during the monsoon, are local migrants which come to the park between July and October to breed.

In October birds from further afield gradually begin to arrive. Among the ducks, geese and waders that come to Keoladeo Ghana are **gadwal, wigeon, shovelers, garganey, marbled, common** and **falcated teal,** and the **red-crested, common** and **white-eyed pochard.** Unmistakable as they fly overhead are the musical **whistling teal. Greylag** and **bar-headed geese** also appear in large numbers and waders include various species of **plover, sandpiper** and **snipe.** Two species of **pelican,** the **rosy** and **dalmatian,** join the resident **gray pelican.**

In recent years the Bombay Natural History Society has been ringing birds at Keoladeo Ghana. Common teal, garganey and wigeon have been recovered in the USSR as far as 2858 miles (4600 km) away. A shoveler was found in Samarkand, and ruff and reeve as far as 3635 miles (5850 km)

Bharatpur during monsoon.

Painted stork.

124

away in Yakutian in the USSR. The ringing operation has also provided evidence which has helped to prove that Keoladeo Ghana is a staging post for many migrants who build up their reserves of fat in the park before departing for their final destinations in places such as South India.

Besides the waterfowl, there are many terrestrial migrant species. **Warblers**, **pipits**, **wagtails** and **buntings** are also winter visitors. But of all the migrants the most sought after is the **Siberian crane**.

There are only two wintering places left for the western race of this extremely rare species. One is in Feredunkenar in Iran and the other is Keoladeo Ghana. The journey to Bharatpur takes them 3977 miles (6400 km) from their breeding grounds in Siberia. They arrive in December and stay until early March. These impressive, pure-white birds, with their black primaries and crimson bills and facial patches, are one of four types of crane in the sanctuary. The **demoiselle** and **common cranes** too are visitors, the **sarus** being the only resident. Unlike other Indian cranes, the Siberian crane is entirely vegetarian. It feeds on underground aquatic roots and tubers in loose flocks of five or six. Some birds, however, remain in their breeding pairs and establish their own territories.

They see off intruders with a spectacular display, throwing their heads backwards and forwards, accompanied by loud cries. These pairs often have one chick with them on arrival whose immature brown and white plumage changes to pure white and black during the winter. The inability of these cranes to produce more than one chick is one reason given for their scarcity.

Although Siberian cranes had been known to visit India for centuries (Ustad Mansur, a court artist of the Emperor Jahangir, made a detailed painting of the crane in the 17th century), it has never been a common species.

Many species at Bharatpur are specialist feeders like the Siberian crane. It is this which allows so many birds to flourish in such a small area. Each helps itself to one ingredient of the wetland soup. Flamingos sieve the water for plankton, spoonbills rake the mud with their lower mandibles for mollusks, tadpoles and weed, while egrets and herons spear their prey, and geese and brahminy ducks graze at the water's edge.

An indication of the strength of the food chain in the sanctuary is the number of birds of prey, migratory and resident, which it contains. At least 32 species of birds of prey and seven species of owl have been observed.

Among notable migrants are the **steppe eagle**, **pale** and **marsh harriers**, **osprey** and **peregrine falcon**. Resident Indian species are no less striking. These include the **tawny eagle**, **ring-tailed fishing eagle**, **crested serpent eagle**, and **Brahminy** and **black-winged kites**. Four species of vulture can be seen, notably the less common **king** or **black vulture**.

The migrants leave for their breeding grounds around March, when many of the small, terrestrial birds in the park are preparing to nest. Even without the migrants, there are many birds still to be seen and, although the spectacle of the winter season is missing, the visitor has the pleasure of having the park more or less to himself. Egrets, herons, cormorants, storks, plump purple **moorhens** and elegant pheasant-tailed jacanas are all residents. **Pied kingfishers** hover dramatically overhead before plunging into the water after their prey and **darters** perch like cormorants, hanging their wings out to dry. In the hot weather, before the monsoon breaks, **red-wattled lapwing** and **stone curlew** hatch their eggs in well-camouflaged nests on the ground, and pairs of sarus cranes, seen in India as symbols of fidelity, perform their courtship dances. Terrestrial birds too are in abundance. At the onset of the monsoon, **weaver birds** begin to construct their elaborate pendulous nests from date palms and other trees.

Mammals and Pythons: The most easily sighted of the mammals at Keoladeo Ghana (besides the lively little ground squirrels) are the sounders of **wild boar** which root around the jungle near the Forest Lodge and in thickets. **Sambar** and **nilgai** can be seen near or in the shallow waters of the wetland, although **chital** or spotted deer are restricted to the park's dry areas towards the south and west. There is also a small population of **blackbuck**. Rhesus macaques and langurs are present but not encouraged by the authorities. The common **mongoose** can often be seen running across the road or in the undergrowth at its edges, and smooth **otters** are another attractive and entertaining animal to look out for on the lakes. Three types of wild cat, the **jungle**, **leopard** and **fishing cat**, are present as are the **Indian** and common **palm civets**. **Jackals** can be very vocal at night and striped **hyenas**, **foxes**, **porcupine**, **hare** and a variety of smaller mammals have also been seen.

A bonus to visitors fond of reptiles are the large **rock pythons** which can be seen sunning themselves, especially at **Python Point** beyond the Keoladeo Temple.

Spoonbills.

Egrets and painted storks.

RANTHAMBORE NATIONAL PARK

The great virgin jungles of Central India were an awesome gift of nature which have been vandalized and largely destroyed over the years. What survives is but a small portion of its northwestern extremity.

This region, with its relics, is a historically important reminder of the misty past. The fort of Ranthambore was the center of a Hindu Kingdom which was invested by Allaudin Khilji's army in 1301 A.D. He later defeated its king, Raja Hamir, and the Rajput women are reputed to have committed the terrible ritual of *sati* in the fort. However, the area soon slipped back into the hands of the Rajputs and again became a powerful kingdom. The Mughal Emperor, Akbar, invested it in 1569, the year after he took the fort at Chittor, and conquered it in 40 days of warfare. The event was important enough to be commemorated with five magnificent miniature paintings by the emperor's renowned artists, Miskina, Paras, Khem Karan, Mukund, Shankar and Lal, in the imperial copy of Abul Fazl's *Akbar Nama*,

Jogi Mahal.

the official chronicle of Akbar's reign.

The Kachchwaha rulers of the principality of Amer (later known as the Jaipur state) received the fort from the Mughals and it remained with them till 1949 when Jaipur state was merged into Rajasthan. The forests around the fort, then known by the name of the nearby township of Sawai Madhopur, were the private hunting grounds of the Maharajas of Jaipur. Among the most famous of their hunting parties was one organized for Queen Elizabeth II and the Duke of Edinburgh in 1961. It was thanks to the desire to preserve game for sport that the forest and its inhabitants first received protection and thus survived long enough to be rescued by Project Tiger.

In 1972, it was estimated that there were 1827 tigers in India, of which Rajasthan had 74 and the number of tigers estimated in the Ranthambore Sanctuary's 60 sq miles (155 sq km) was 14. That year saw the launching of Project Tiger and this sanctuary, named after the fort, became one of the eight sanctuaries and national parks of the new project. Over the years, the sanctuary has become a national park with a core area of 158 sq miles (410 sq km) with a tiger population of 40 according to the 1986 census. In 1984, an additional area of 40 sq miles (104 sq km) of adjoining forest was designated the Sawai Man Singh Sanctuary, after the late Maharaja of Jaipur.

Friendly Tigers: Ranthambore is famous for its **tigers** and justly so. Over the last decade, as a result of strict preservation, tigers have become more and more active during the day, thus giving the lie to the earlier belief that they are nocturnal animals. More than in any other park or sanctuary in India, tigers are now encountered here in broad daylight. They have lost all fear of humans and are quite unperturbed by their presence.

Besides hunting in broad daylight as well as at night, some other unique aspects of tiger behavior have been observed and photographed. Once, for instance, a magnificent large male hunted openly from the thickets on the edge of the lakes and ran down its sambar prey in the water. A tigress too indulged in similar behavior. There have been instances when a tiger and a crocodile from the lake have confronted each other. On one memorable occasion a tiger battled with a crocodile over a sambar carcass and finally took possession of it in broad daylight, after a long fight.

It was generally believed that tigers are solitary creatures and only the mothers take care of their cubs so long as these are unable to care for themselves, and tigresses with cubs were seen only rarely. Here too their behavior seems to have undergone a change. In 1986, two tiger families, one with two cubs and another with three, have been extremely trusting of human presence in jeeps and have been observed for long stretches of time in jungle clearings in broad daylight, even when the cubs were but a few weeks old. The family with three cubs includes a large male which seems to have chosen to live with the cubs without being aggressive. In fact, this male is also seen with another tigress in the same Bakaula nala region from time to time.

Because of such tiger activities, Ranthambore is probably the best park in which to photograph them. In recent times it has become a center of attraction for wildlife photographers from all over the world. Sighting a tiger can never be a sure shot, but here one comes as close to it as is possible.

Other Predators: This park also has a large population of **panthers** which are the second largest predators of this forest. The prey species of tigers and panthers overlap, and because of possible conflicts between them, the latter are found more often on the periphery of the park. **Kachida valley** accounts for the highest number of sightings of these cats. They do not appear to be as fearlessly diurnal as tigers have become and therefore their sightings are not as frequent.

Another interesting feature of the park is the visibility of **marsh crocodiles** in and around the lakes. Over the years, their number has increased and these reptiles, eight to 10 feet (2½–three meters) in length, are not uncommon. They are easily seen in the water or basking on the shores of the lakes. Often they are seen crossing from one lake to another. Interestingly, they eat dead sambar on land and try to drag the carcass into the water, even during daylight hours.

Other predators in Ranthambore are **hyenas**, **jackals** and **jungle cats**. **Caracal** too have been recorded. The last sighting of wild dogs was way back in 1954; it is not known why they have disappeared from these forests completely.

Ranthambore has **sloth bears** which one may encounter while driving through the park. **Lakarda** and **Anantpura** are the areas where they are seen most often.

Sambar are seen everywhere and in large herds around the lakes. They are in hard horn and at their best during the rutting period in the winter months, though their antlers tend to be smaller than those of their counterparts in Central India. Sambar are known to wallow in and like water, but here they can be observed in water for hours, eating and swimming in the lakes. Actually, one would expect such behavior from barasingha rather than sambar.

Chital are extremely common throughout the park and they come to water in their hundreds particularly in the warmer months. **Nilgai** too are found all over the park with the greatest concentration around the lakes; they roam in smaller herds than those of sambar and chital.

Sounders of **wild boar** can be seen around the lakes with an occasional **chinkara** (Indian gazelle) also coming along. Among others, **Indian hare** and **mongoose** are most visible on the edge of the water. **Monitor lizards** are common though shy; they are usually quick to notice vehicle movement and, by the time one notices them, they are scampering off to their burrows.

Though this park is famous for its animals, it is rich in birdlife as well. **Bonelli's eagle, crested serpent eagle, great Indian horned owl, gray partridge, painted partridge, sandgrouse, quail, spur fowl, common pea fowl, tree pie, paradise flycatcher, pheasant-tailed jacana, painted stork, black stork, white-necked stork,**

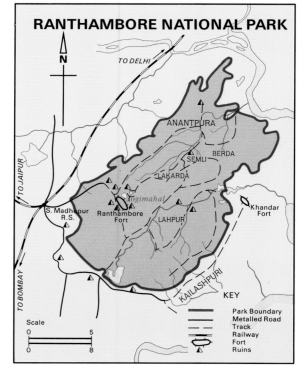

RANTHAMBORE NATIONAL PARK

N

TO DELHI

TO JAIPUR

ANANTPURA

SEMLI
BERDA
LAKARDA

Jogimahal

S. Madhopur
R.S.

Ranthambore
Fort

LAHPUR

Khandar
Fort

TO BOMBAY

KAILASHPURI

KEY

Scale

0 — 5

0 — 8

Park Boundary
Metalled Road
Track
Railway
Fort
Ruins

spoonbill and **green pigeon** are among the resident birds of the park. In addition, during the winter months, the park receives migrant visitors, primarily a variety of **ducks**.

These forests are around the Aravalli and the Vindhya ranges, each of which has distinctive geological features. The forest is of typically dry deciduous type with dhok being the most prominent tree. Ronj, ber, salai, occasional mango groves, palm trees, banyan and pipal trees give it a character all its own.

Photographer's Dream: The entry point to the National Park from Sawai Madhopur town takes the visitor to the foot of the Ranthambore fort and the forest rest house **Jogi Mahal**. India's second-largest banyan tree rules supreme here with its visiting langur troupe. In front of the forest rest house is **Padam Talao** (tank) which takes its name from the water lilies in it. At the far end is the **Raj Bagh Talao** followed by **Milak Talao** which dries up in summer. These lakes attract considerable concentrations of ungulates which in turn attract tigers. On several occasions they have been seen from the edge of the lake and Jogi Mahal itself, hunting or resting in the water. Drives around these lakes are a wildlife photographer's dream. From Jogi Mahal one can take pleasant drives to **Nal Ghati** and **Lahpur** through the enchanting **Dhok Avenue**, to **Bakaula** and **Anantpur** via **Lakarda**, or to **Kachida valley** and **Anantpura**. These are the most frequented routes visitors take and both morning and evening outings are rewarding as animals are active at that time. A jeep is a must as the forest roads make it rather tough going at places.

The park is studded with remnants of its historic past. Old defensive walls, wells, mosques and other structures bear mute testimony of kingdoms and battles long forgotten. Overgrown with pipal trees, they blend with their natural surroundings, thus lending to it an incomparable charm. **Raj Bagh**, a quadrangle with *baradaris* (sitting areas) between Padam Talao and Raj Bagh Talao, is a mixture of architectural styles with ruins of fountain systems and apartments. Tigers have often been seen roaming about freely in these ruins and some visitors have been lucky enough to be able to photograph them in these unlikely surroundings. The whole forest is dominated by the massive battlements of Ranthambore fort — worth visiting even for its own sake.

Left, **park headquarters and *below*, an evening jeep ride.**

127

SARISKA
TIGER RESERVE

In the Aravalli range which cuts across Rajasthan, a few pockets of forest still survive. Sariska is one such. It was part of the erstwhile princely state of Alwar whose late Maharaja, Jai Singh, was a keen shikari and his favorite hunting ground was Sariska, which received strict protection under his rule. In 1955 this forest was declared a sanctuary and it became a tiger reserve under Project Tiger in 1979. An area of 308 sq miles (800 sq km) is the project area with a core of 185 sq miles (480 sq km).

This region has always been good **tiger** country, and though the forest is much smaller now than it used to be, it remains a haven for them. At the last count in 1985, a population of 35 was reported. Unlike in Ranthambhore National Park, these tigers have not become diurnal. In fact, tiger sightings during daylight hours are uncommon but it appears that they are increasing as human interference decreases.

Panther, **jungle cat**, **jackal** and **hyena** are among the other carnivores of the forest. At the last census of 1985, three **caracal** were reported; to come across one on a drive would be a very rare event indeed. Sariska forest had not had any record of **wild dog** till three of them began to be sighted fairly regularly since the beginning of 1986. The fact that wild dogs have not been reported from adjacent areas only deepens the mystery of their sudden arrival. What effect their predation will have on the ungulates, has yet to be seen.

The **Siliserh Lake** is on the edge of the tiger reserve, just off the road between Sariska and Alwar. This road has considerable traffic and one is not likely to see many animals when driving on it though it runs through the sanctuary. But the lake itself has **crocodiles** which can be seen basking on the banks, particularly in winter. There is also a small place on a hill by the lake which is now a hotel.

Among the prey population are the **sambar**, **chital**, **nilgai**, **wild boar**, **hare** and numerous **porcupine**. Over the last 10 years or more the prey population has become very visible and their numbers appear to be on the increase.

Wildlife observation here is best done by driving into the forest in the morning or evening. Sariska is the starting point. While there are many roads and tracks, the most

frequented is the surfaced road to **Kalighati**, **Salopka** and **Pandhupole**. One may expect to come across a variety of animals on these drives. Owing to perennial water shortage, the forest department has provided artificial water holes by the roadside which attract the animals.

Animal behavior at a water hole is fascinating to watch and this reserve offers unique opportunities for this. At Kalighati there is a hide at ground level and one at an elevation. There is another at Salopka. Apart from being comfortable, these hides have been carefully located so as to provide maximum sightings and photographic opportunities. Hides should be occupied by early afternoon, well before sunset, as a variety of animals come along to drink at that time. The concentration of ungulates is heavy, particularly in summer. If one is lucky, a tiger, a panther or a wild dog may put in an appearance, though the cats are likely to show up only after dark, and cautiously.

The park is rich in birdlife too. Common **pea fowl** abound, and **gray partridge**, **quail**, **sand grouse**, **tree pie**, **white-breasted kingfisher**, **golden-backed woodpecker**, **crested serpent eagle** and **great Indian horned owl** are among the many species found here. While sitting in the hides at Kalighati and Salopka, one can observe some of the birds at close quarters when they come to drink.

The forest is of a typical dry deciduous type with dhok, khair, tendu, ber, surwal and goria among the flora of the forest. It is lush and green in the monsoon months but in the summer months it is completely dry.

In the Sariska region there are many places of historical interest. The **Neelkanth temples** (6th–13th Century) situated about 20 miles (32 km) from Sariska are in ruins though one of them, of Lord Shiva, is still in worship. The **Kankwari fort** was used by Emperor Aurangzeb to confine his brother Dara Shikoh whom he defeated and later killed to gain the throne of Hindustan.

The late Maharaja Jai Singhji of Alwar built a massive **palace complex** at Sariska in 1902 within a large area of forest. The complex includes the main palace, nobles' quarters, staff quarters, stables and garages, a "French" pavilion and a swimming pool, all of which are now in varying degrees of disrepair. The main palace is now a hotel.

The best time to visit this forest is from November to March. In April, May and June, it is easy to observe the animals as they must come to drink at the water holes, but these months are extremely hot.

The handsome nilgai.

Sambar at water hole.

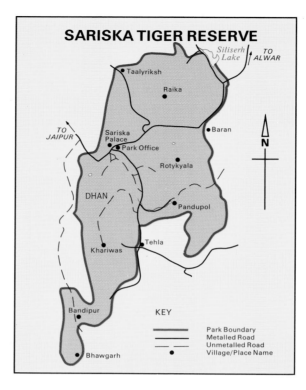

SARISKA TIGER RESERVE

Siliserh Lake
TO ALWAR
Taalyriksh
Raika
TO JAIPUR
Baran
N
Sariska Palace
Park Office
Rotykyala
DHAN
Pandupol
Tehla
Khariwas
Bandipur
KEY
Bhawgarh
Park Boundary
Metalled Road
Unmetalled Road
Village/Place Name

GIR NATIONAL PARK AND SANCTUARY

The lion has always occupied a unique position in India. More than 2000 years ago Emperor Ashoka chose to inscribe some of his edicts on the famous lion capital of Sarnath which is today the emblem of the Republic of India. This magnificent animal once roamed all over North India up to Bihar, but in the last one hundred years it has been wiped out elsewhere and today, the only surviving population of lions outside the continent of Africa is found in the Gir forest. Always considered royal game by rulers in India from time immemorial, lions were protected. But modernization and the disappearance of their habitat have left them with only the Gir, their last habitat and their last refuge.

Home of the Asiatic Lion: In the southwest of the Saurashtra peninsula of Gujarat state, an area of 545 sq miles (1412 sq km) of forest and grassland survives amid increasing pressure of human and cattle population. The forest area itself has shrunk by half since the turn of the century and what remains is the Gir Sanctuary with a core area of 116 sq miles (300 sq km) which has been declared a National Park. It is no longer connected to even the Girnar mountain where, until recently, lions were often reported on the outskirts of Junagadh city. Sasan, with a forest rest house, is the headquarters of the sanctuary.

The Gir is a mixed deciduous type of forest with teak, ber, flame of the forest, jamun, a variety of acacia particularly babul and an occasional banyan tree. It is a hilly tract with many rivers and offers to the visitor long pleasant drives of quiet beauty.

At the turn of the 19th – 20th Century there was a disastrous famine which lives in local memory as the "*chappanio kal*." The lion's prey population fell drastically and lions took to man-eating and their numbers declined drastically. It is believed that they were on the verge of extinction in 1913, with only about 20 animals left.

However, the Nawab of Junagadh, in whose domain most of the Gir forest fell, protected them vigorously and since independence in 1947 protection has continued, and lion hunting has been totally banned since the mid-1950s. As the Gir was the only home of the Asiatic lion, there was an urgent need to establish their status. Consequently, the first systematic census of large mammals in India was conducted in the Gir in 1950 by the late M.A. Wynter-Blyth and the late R.S. Dharmakumarsinhji, both naturalists of outstanding ability. This set the trend for such censuses elsewhere in India, particularly those of tigers. According to the 1985 census, there are 239 lions in the Gir forest as against 205 in 1979.

The best way to observe lions is, of course, in their natural surroundings at dawn and dusk, when these predators are on the move. This can be done from a car as, owing to the protection given to them, they are not shy of motor vehicles. Nevertheless, one cannot be certain about seeing them on all occasions. The Forest Department arranges lion shows every Sunday which become a *mela* of scores of people watching lions attracted by a buffalo. It is proposed that the Forest Department should discontinue the lion shows and instead set up a 'safari park" in a fenced-off area of about 1000 acres (400 hectares) of the forest where seeing lions would be more certain.

The **Asiatic lion** is slightly smaller than its African cousin and its mane is smaller too. Nonetheless, a large male lion of the Gir is indeed a sight to behold. A former Nawab, Sir Mahabat Khanji of Junagadh, ordered a series of Gir lion postage stamps for his state way back in 1929, thus making the Asiatic

Far left, **His Majesty and** *left*, **monitor lizard.**

lion the first wild animal to figure philatelically in India.

There have been two attempts in the past at translocating lions both of which failed in the long run. The Gujarat State Government now proposes to establish a second home for lions in the Barda hills near Porbandar. It is proposed to set aside a 70-sq-mile (180-sq-km) area for the purpose. The success of this enterprise will depend on the availability of prey animals and sufficient area for the lion population to take root undisturbed. It was the obvious lack of these conditions which saw the end of the lions in this area some 80 years ago. Today the Barda hills area is no longer connected to the Gir as was the case then.

The Gir, therefore, remains the sole haven of the Asiatic lion, which, above all, is its unique attraction.

The Hunters and the Hunted: The Gir has always also had a large population of **panthers** and they are more visible here than in other Indian forests. At the last count in 1985 there were 201 panthers as against 161 in 1979. If one is lucky, they can be encountered while driving through the forest.

According to the 1985 census, **sambar** number 772, **chital** 10,446, **nilgai** 2081, **four-horned antelope** 1063, **chinkara** (Indian gazelle) 311, **wild boar** 2212 and **langur** 6912. These are the prey population for the big cats, along with domestic cattle. Over the earlier census of 1979, chital, the most prolific breeders of the lot, have increased by only 2000 with a base population of approximately 8000. The numbers of sambar, four-horned antelope and langur have been virtually stable, whereas nilgai, wild boar and chinkara have actually registered a marginal decline.

Among the other carnivores are the **wild cat**, the **jackal** and the **hyena**, the population of which has increased to 192 in 1985 from 84 in 1979. The census is perhaps reasonably accurate as far as lions are concerned because of their noisy and gregarious habits but, for some of the other species, the accuracy of the figures is debatable.

The sloth bear is conspicuous by its absence from the Gir. Pythons and many species of snakes have been recorded. The Gir is an excellent area for seeing **marsh crocodiles** in its rivers but partieularly in the lake of Kamaleshwar dam. There is a **crocodile breeding farm** at **Sasan**. It is from this farm that these reptiles are taken to restock the lakes and rivers of Gujarat.

The forest is remarkably rich in birdlife too. **Paradise flycatcher, black-headed cuckoo shrike, gray drongo, pied woodpecker, coppersmith, Indian roller, crested swift, fish owl, black vulture, shaheen falcon, Bonelli's eagle, crested serpent eagle, painted sandgrouse, rock bush quail, gray partridge, white-necked stork**, are among the many species of birds found here.

Wildlife viewing in the Gir is best done by driving around the forest. The best drives from Sasan are to **Baval Chowk** and **Kankai**, to **Chodavdi** and **Tulsishyam**, and to **Kamaleshwar dam**. The roads are manageable by a sturdy car, but a jeep is definitely advisable. The best time for viewing is at sunrise and sunset as the animals are most active at these times.

Lions and Man: The Gir is steeped in history and folklore. It has temples of great antiquity like **Kankai Mata** and **Tulsishyam**, a place of pilgrimage with hot springs. The forest is famous for its cattle herders, the Maldharis, whose buffaloes form a substantial part of the lions' food. These herdsmen live in small thorn-fenced settlements called *nes*, which are well worth visiting. Extremely hospitable by nature, the Maldharis are herders whose life has changed but little over the years and their folklore and traditions are a unique record of coexistence of human beings with lions.

A major problem of the sanctuary continues to be the human population and their cattle herds, despite certain steps being taken to meet this situation. For example, a rubble wall around the sanctuary prevents some herdsmen and their cattle from entering the sanctuary, but sizable human and cattle populations remain within it. The cattle population within the sanctuary is estimated at 20,000, and these compete for food and territory with the wild ungulates. Because of such disturbances, one does not in the Gir see sambar, chital, nilgai, etc. in such numbers and concentrations as one does in better protected sanctuaries and national parks. Actually, cattle form a very substantial part of a lion's diet today, and, in seeming paradox, unless the Maldharis and their cattle are progressively removed, the Gir's natural prey population cannot increase; in fact it will continue to remain under constant threat of epidemics and a sudden drastic reduction in numbers.

The sanctuary usually remains closed from June to October and the best time to visit the forest is between December and March. The summer temperature can be as high as 104° F (40° C) while in winter it can be as low as 43° F (6° C).

Right, a chital herd; *far right,* Gir landscape.

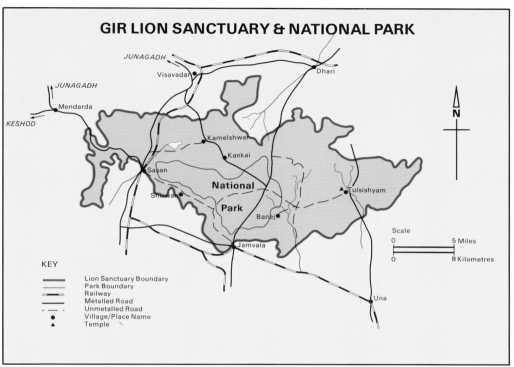

GIR LION SANCTUARY & NATIONAL PARK

KESHOD

JUNAGADH

JUNAGADH

Visavadar

Dhari

Mendarda

Kamelshwar

Kankai

Sasan

National

Park

Shirwan

Tulsishyam

Banej

Jamvala

Una

N

Scale

0   5 Miles

0   8 Kilometres

KEY

Lion Sanctuary Boundary
Park Boundary
Railway
Metalled Road
Unmetalled Road
●   Village/Place Name
▲   Temple

KANHA NATIONAL PARK

Kanha in Madhya Pradesh (five hours driving from Jabalpur, six from Nagpur) has sometimes been called the N'Gorongoro of India. The simile is apt, albeit Kanha is far greener and its cordon of hills far more densely wooded. Unlike Tanzania's N'Gorongoro, the Kanha valley is not a volcanic crater, though the enclosing hills are a consequence of geologically ancient volcanic activity. The horseshoe-shaped Kanha valley, which accounts for nearly a third and the oldest part of the Kanha National Park, is bound by two distant spurs emanating from the main Mekal ridge, forming its southern rim. The spurs, in their gently tapering traverse, nearly close in the north leaving but a narrow opening for the meandering Sulkum or Surpan river, the valley's main drainage. Herds of the Kanha miscellany, the axis deer (chital), the swamp deer (barasingha), the blackbuck (hiran), the wild pig and occasionally the gaur, throng the central parkland of the valley, providing the basis for the comparison with N'Gorongoro. With its confiding herds and relatively tolerant predators, Kanha offers an almost unrivaled scope to a keen photographer of Indian wildlife.

The forests of the Banjar valley and the Halon valley, respectively forming Kanha's western and eastern halves, had, even at the turn of the century, been long famous for their deer and tiger. Expectedly, therefore, they were reserved as the exclusive hunting grounds for the most privileged, the British Viceroy, as early as 1910. The ups and downs in the ensuing decades gave an interesting conservation history to Kanha which celebrated its golden jubilee in 1983. It all started with an area of some 96 sq miles (250 sq km) in the Kanha valley being gazetted as a sanctuary in 1933. This was followed by 116 sq miles (300 sq km) of the Halon valley around Supkhar also being declared a sanctuary in 1935. However, because of extensive deer damage to tree saplings in the forests and crops in nearby villages, the Supkhar sanctuary was denotified within a few years. Both these areas at that time still harbored teeming populations of the Central Indian **barasingha** (*Cervus duvauceli branderi*). This majestic cousin of the nominate **swamp deer** (*Cervus duvauceli duvauceli*) of the sub-Himalayan flood-plains had adapted itself to the hard-ground grasslands and until the turn of the century dominated the Central Indian highlands.

Mounting pressures on the wilderness notwithstanding, Kanha valley survived as a sanctuary into the 1950s. Excessive stock-grazing had, however, jeopardized the bara-singha's grassland habitat and its numbers had greatly declined. Yet a few thousand still found a home in Kanha valley's central *maidans* — meadows with sporadic groves of trees. Then in the early 1950s, a blessing in cruel disguise, as it were, a privileged hunter was allowed to shoot 30 tigers in and around the sanctuary. The furore that followed led to a special legislation and the Kanha valley was declared a 96-sq-mile national park in 1955. Since then, the gains have been steady. In 1962, the park was expanded to 123 sq miles (318 sq km). In 1970, the area south of the Mekal ridge and down to the river Banjar was added raising it to 172 sq miles (446 sq km). Finally, Project Tiger paved the way for the integration of the eastern Halon valley into the park system, initially on a sanctuary status in 1974 and as a full national park since 1976. This gives Kanha National Park its present area of 363 sq miles (940 sq km) which is further buffered by an additional area of 388 sq miles (1005 sq km). The total conservation unit encompasses 750 sq miles (1945 sq km) and is called Kanha Tiger Reserve under Project Tiger.

Rich Habitat: Kanha's topography and geology combine variously to give it its rich habitat diversity. The range of elevation is from 1480 to 2950 feet (450-900 meters) above mean sea level. The bauxite-capped hills sport extensive plateaus, locally called *dadar*, which carry extensive grasslands with only sparse tree growth. Folds at their fringes, where bauxite yields to basalt, have perennial springs. This combination is an ideal habitat for **gaur** (*Bos gauras*), the largest of the world's cattle, **sambar** (*Cervus unicolor*), the largest of the Indian deer, and **chousingha** (*Tetraceros quadricornis*), the only four-horned antelope in the world. **Nilgai antelope (bluebull)** are common here and **sloth bear** are frequent visitors. You may see a **pied** or a **marsh harrier** (*Circus melanoleucus* or *C. aeruginosus*) hovering in the air and swooping on to a cluster of bush quail (*Perdicula asiatica*). The rims of the plateaus have steep rocky slopes and often, escarpments. The latter provide a rare stance for breathtaking views of the valleys below and the hills beyond. Many of these plateaus are large enough for runways and indeed Bamhnidadar, 2780 feet (850 meters) above sea level, on the southeastern rim of the Kanha valley had one operative until 1976. A late afternoon visit to Bamhnidadar to see some of these animals is a must. Watching from here the changing hues of the verdant Banjar valley below, against the backdrop of a gradual, glorious sunset, is an enthralling experience indeed.

The drive down from these plateaus is through exquisite wild country. Huge trees of bija (*Pterocarpus marsupium*), haldu (*Adina cardifolia*) and dhaora (*Anogeissus latifolia*), along with a host of other large and small trees comprise the thick forests on the slopes. Garlands of massive mahul (*Bauhinia vahlaii*) climbers span the spaces between trees. Dense bamboo (*Dendrocalamus strictus*) thickets occupy the understory. Much of these mixed forests have escaped any form of exploitation and are a picture of raw wilderness. Sighting the **red jungle fowl**, the **painted spurfowl**, a shy **barking deer** (*Muntiacus muntjak*) pausing at the roadside glade and some gaur and sambar, is common. What may distinguish such a drive is a **leopard** hurtling down a tree or one simply walking along the road. Water is generally scarce on the slopes during the dry season. But in the upper reaches of the major *nullahs* where they flow through gorges carved in basaltic rock, the flow is perennial. There are also some seepage springs scattered amid the slopes. These water holes are the focal points for numerous animals and birds, large and small. In the lower slopes the forest cover changes, often abruptly, from mixed deciduous to lush green sal (*Shorea robusta*), with or without bamboo.

The valleys with rich alluvium carry a mixed interspersion of stately, near pure, stands of sal and extensive meadows. It is this characteristic parkland appearance of the valleys that typifies the Kanha landscape. The large grassy clearings are a consequence of old, abandoned cultivation, although many have recently come up as a result of a massive village relocation operation under Project Tiger. This important operation was undertaken with great success in order to meet the twin objective of preventing wild animal damage to the crops and cattle of the interior settlements in the park and to release wildlife habitat from human occupation and disturbance in this prime conservation area. Significantly, the operation was smooth and with full involvement of the affected people who were provided adequate and viable alternatives in

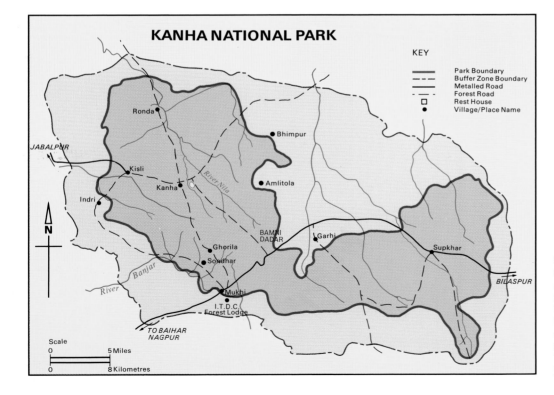

KANHA NATIONAL PARK

KEY

Park Boundary
Buffer Zone Boundary
Metalled Road
Forest Road
Rest House
Village/Place Name

Ronda

Bhimpur

JABALPUR

Kisli

Amlitola

Kanha

Indri

River Nila

BAMNI DADAR

Garhi

Ghorila

Supkhar

Sondhar

BILASPUR

River Banjar

Mukhi

I.T.D.C. Forest Lodge

TO BAIHAR NAGPUR

N

Scale

0 5 Miles

0 8 Kilometres

the form of agricultural land and new organized housing at sites of their choice outside the park. This has been hailed as a major management success of the Kanha National Park in conservation circles, the world over.

Kanha's Jewel: The swamp deer or barasingha is the jewel of Kanha and its rescue from the brink of extinction, the crowning glory of its conservation achievements. The enlargement of grassland habitat through village relocation has been the main basis of this breakthrough. Barasingha feed almost exclusively on grasses and tall grass meadows are essential to the security of their fawns from minor and major predators from August – September, when they are dropped, to late November. By this time, the fawns are strong enough to keep pace with the herds and are well initiated into the art of security through herding. Cultivation of the valley grasslands had appropriated the bulk of the grassland habitat while excessive stock grazing did not allow grasses to grow tall enough in the remainder. In consequence, the rate of success at raising young steadily declined and in Kanha valley itself the barasingha number fell from nearly 3000 in the early 1950s to just 66 in 1970. This was the last surviving population of this subspecies in the world. Fortunately, as a result of measures taken, including village relocation, their population continues to show a steady increase and in 1986 had crossed the 500 mark.

With its multitined beams of antlers bent forward and adorned by crowns of grass tufts, the proud carriage of a dominant barasingha stag, silhouetted in profile through mist against sunbeams breaking through stately sal trees on an early winter morning, can be an all-quenching feast to the eyes of a nature lover. Peak winter, December – January, is the barasingha's rutting season and large congregations are seen in the Kanha and Sonph meadows. It is difficult to paint a picture in words of the impressive display of the big breeding stags, the rivalry among them leading to serious fights amid clouds of kicked-up dust, the almost unconcerned females grazing away, the youngsters looking askance, the chase by the victor, the run for life by the vanquished and the finale in the form of the majestic re-entry of the victor into the herd after a thorough wallow in mud. All this, while stag bellows echo from all directions.

Blackbuck is not an animal of the moist deciduous forests of the hills or the sal forests of the valleys. Yet the central Kanha meadows carry a small number of blackbuck. It entered Kanha valley from the plains outside, probably with the extension of cultivation along the Sulkum river. Now that the cultivation is gone and the overgrazed short grass meadows are changing over to taller grasses, the blackbuck is facing adversity. Its numbers, near 80 in 1972, had dropped to under 10 in 1986. Jackals, normally scavengers but opportunistic predators, have accentuated the jeopardy. When, following strict protection and intensive conservation measures of the 1970s, all wild animal populations showed a rapid increase, including the most populous chital, the jackal took to hunting the rich crop of chital fawns in the meadows by forming small packs. This opportunistic hunting was extended to blackbuck fawns in the central Kanha meadows from where, unlike chital, they had nowhere else to go. However, in a 69-acre (28-hectare) tiger-leopard-proof enclosure — raised originally for the barasingha — just south of Kanha, their number during the same period has gone up from about five to well over 30.

Shravantal is an ancient, small earthbund tank in the central Kanha meadows. This is an important watering source in the area. It even attracts a fair number of water-

(Anticlockwise) Above left, chital herd at a typical Kanha meadow; swamp deer; jackal.

fowl in winter — mainly the **lesser whitling teal**, but also to be seen are some **common teal, pintail, cotton teal** and an occasional **shoveler**.

Sighting Animals: Kanha has a distinct monsoonal climate. Over 90 percent of its annual precipitation of 64 inches (160 cm) arrives between late June and late September. The park remains closed from July 1 to October 31, but an early downpour, washing away portions of fair weather roads may enforce an earlier closure (though seldom before June 20). November is mildly cold while December - January are the coldest and given to severe frost, late night temperatures in valleys dipping to 29°F (-2°C). February - March is pleasant spring time. April starts warming up while May - June is the hottest period. Premonsoon showers in late June kill the heat and herald massive deer congregations in the *maidans*, which quickly shed their brown-yellow and don the rich green of the new flush of grasses. This coincides with the second peak of the chital rutting season. Their rut starts in late March and stretches well into July, the first peak being from mid-April to mid-May. The valleys reverberate with loud, sharp and long-drawn bugling of stags. The *maidans* are dotted with dominant stags displaying to

Flame of the forest.

and courting females and fighting rivals for them.

Vehicular excursions and elephant rides in the park are permitted only by daylight. The best time is in early mornings and late afternoons.

Kanha animals are confiding and a little care in approach can yield prolonged pleasure observing interesting animal behavior within a species and interaction among different species. As soon as a group of animals is sighted the vehicle should slow down, and stop at a distance where the animals take note but do not run away. Soon they resettle, whereafter advances may be made gradually. With patience a vehicle can be positioned between groups of animals on both sides of the road. Vehicles are not allowed to leave the road. Nor is walking allowed while on excursions.

The best chances of seeing gaur are at **Bamhnidadar** in the late afternoons or in the early mornings in the **Bishanpura-Sondhar-Ghorella** area in the Mukki range. All these areas are good for sighting **wild dog** (*Cuon alpinus*), or **dhole** (locally called **sonha kutta**) too. The dhole may also be often seen in Kanha and Sonph *maidans*. Observing **langurs** — the species here is *Presbytis entellus* — is absorbing in itself, but their interaction with other herbivores is even more interesting. Langurs are often locally referred to as the chital's herdsmen because seeing a herd of chital under a tree being foraged by langurs is a common sight. Chital and, sometimes, also **wild boar** (*Sus scrofa*) follow the foraging langurs and greedily feed on the leftovers of fruits and leaves generously thrown to the ground by the latter. The association is further advantageous to the deer and the boar because langurs, from their high stance on trees can see or detect a predator from suspicious movements much earlier than they can and raise the alarm in good time. Langurs are quite serious in such observations and seldom sound a false alarm.

Birds: Kanha's birdlife is rich, the tally of species being close to 300. Mornings are full of rich bird calls. **Peafowl**, sometimes dancing peacocks during March to June, are seen all over. The **Indian roller**, **racket-tailed drongo, red** and **yellow wattled lapwing, green bee-eater**, different **doves** (5 species), **gray hornbill, tree pie, myna, munia, bushchat, warbler, flycatcher, babbler** and **woodpecker** are commonly seen. **Black-headed** and **golden oriole, paradise flycatcher, pied Malabar hornbill, Indian pitta, Indian stone curlew, common gray** and **painted partridge** and **green pigeon** are

often seen on drives and elephant rides. **Black ibis, white-necked** and **lesser adjutant storks, white-breasted** and **pied kingfisher**, different **egrets** and occasionally **cormorants** are seen around water bodies or streams near Kanha, Sonph, Kisli and Mukki. The main birds of prey, often seen swooping down on and catching or feeding on small mammals, snakes and birds, are the **crested serpent eagle, crested honey buzzard, white-eyed buzzard, blackwinged kite, shikra, laggar** and **shaheen falcon, kestrel** and a number of owls and owlets including the **barn owl, brown fish owl** and the **nightjar**. Often **whitebacked** and **scavenger vultures** and occasionally **black** and **longbilled vultures** can be seen scavenging on tiger, leopard and wild-dog kills. For bird watchers staying at Mukki, a trek along the Banjar river and for those at Kisli, going round the Kisli and Kanha campuses can prove highly rewarding. Penetrating into woodland on foot even around the campus is neither advisable nor permitted for reasons of safety.

Tiger Land: The raw beauty of the Kanha wilderness is satisfying because a comparison of the condition of the forests outside with that of those inside is a strong pointer to "conservation in action" in the Park. Kanha's diverse miscellany of mammal and birdlife is without many parallels, because so much is seen so well in so short a time. Yet Kanha is better known as the best place in the world to see **tigers**.

Sighting tigers on drives here is not uncommon, but seeing and photographing tigers from elephant back, sometimes after a thrilling systematic track, is a memorable experience. Elephants usually go out very early in the morning for tiger tracking from Kisli, Kanha or Mukki. An elephant accommodates up to 4 persons besides the *mahout* — the elephant driver and the friend, philosopher and guide of the visitor. Starting the track, he would readily say in Hindi, "Eyes, ears and nose open and mouth shut." This is sound advice and should be heeded in the interest of success in tracking.

With all their senses on the alert, the *mahout* and his elephant take the visitors to a flattish *nullah* bed or to a grassy glade amid stately sal trees. Pug marks, drag of a kill, the various vocalizations of the predator, the crowing and shuttling of the crows, the alarm calls of the langur and deer are signs that could lead to a rendezvous with the secretive tiger. The evaluation of these signs enables the *mahout* to decide the right course. Usually two to four elephants move together up to this stage and then,

after a short conference among the *mahouts*, each takes an agreed given direction — either down or up a *nullah* bank or rustling through the forest, where at the level of the *howda* (seating platform on the elephant's back), the branches of trees and bamboo culms tend to come together. In an air charged with expectation the *mahout* will signal the riders to help bend or push the branches away to clear the passage at their level. A mouse deer might dart through the elephant's legs and the *mahout* would curse under his breath. His senses keyed to the observation and silent analysis of the signs, at times he might attempt an explanation by gestures. The urgency of the moment commanding, he might, however, move on without waiting to ascertain whether he was understood. A mile or two having thus been covered, the visitors would by then have got into the knack of rocking their body in unison with the elephant's, for maximum comfort. Then, with birds merrily chirping away, the *mahout* will suddenly stop in his tracks and peer through the canopy of bamboo, ban-rahar (*Flamingia sop*) or sindur (*Mallotus philippinensis*) bushes lower down. He will adjust the elephant's position for a better view and point out what he had seen — the remains of a kill or the unmistakable stripes. Having made sure of a predator's presence in the area, he will avoid disturbing it by keeping elephant movements to the minimum. He will whistle a signal to the other elephants who, if around, will carefully approach the area. While awaiting their arrival the *mahout* will nudge his elephant now and then. Too much movement might scare away the tiger and total lack of it might allow him to slip away. The strategy is to take advantage of the cat's urge to laze as the day advances. With the arrival of the other elephants, the game of outflanking the tiger, hide and seek, begins and finally the tiger gets reconciled to the elephants' presence — a bit of a nuisance, but harmless. Sometimes a tiger is sighted within two or three hours, and at others in less than an hour. On some days tigers are sighted at more than one area, on some at none.

But, the game of tracking is thrilling and affords a real feel of the dynamic wilderness, something happening or expected to happen all the time. Many a time a **leopard** is seen, though unlike the tiger, not for a prolonged view. Other rare sightings may include a **monitor lizard**, or a **porcupine** or a **python**. Of course a host of birds and often gaur, sambar and muntjac are seen too. Once the tiger settles down, it can be viewed for several hours.

BANDHAVGARH NATIONAL PARK

Bandhavgarh is a new national park with a very long history. Set among the Vindhya hills of Madhya Pradesh with an area of 168 sq miles (437 sq km), it contains a wide variety of habitats and a high density of game, including a large number of tigers.

Geography, Flora and Climate: When originally formed in 1968, Bandhavgarh was a comparatively small park of only 40 sq miles (105 sq km), but in mid-1986 it was extended to include two large areas of forest adjoining it on the northern and southern sides. These extension areas consist mainly of sal forest. In the north a series of ridges, intercut by perennial streams, runs parallel to the main Umaria road which runs through the park. To the south, gently undulating forest is interspersed with grazing areas, formerly agricultural land.

Currently the central area of the park — the original 40 sq miles — remains the principal viewing area. There are 32 hills in this part of the park, which has a large natural fort at its center. The fort's cliffs are 2625 feet (800 meters) high, 1000 feet (300 meters) above the surrounding countryside. Over half the area is covered by sal forest although on the upper slopes it is replaced by mixed forest of sali, saj, dhobin and saja. Towards the north there are large stretches of bamboo and grassland. Most of the bamboo flowered in 1985 and the old clumps died, leaving the ground covered with new bamboo growth. Many streams run through the valleys but only three are perennial. One of them, the Charanganga, has its source at the fort.

Winter temperatures (November–mid-February) vary from almost freezing at night to around 68 °F (20 °C) in the daytime. Summer nights are also cooler than the daytime temperature which rises to 104 °F (40 °C). The park is closed during the breeding season, which coincides with the monsoon (July–October). Rainfall in the park averages 50 inches (120 cm) per year.

History: Bandhavgarh has been a center of human activity and settlement for over 2000 years. Legend has it that Rama, hero of the Hindu epic, the Ramayana, stopped at Bandhavgarh on his way back to his homeland after defeating the demon king Ravana of Lanka. Two monkey architects, who had engineered a bridge between the isle of Lanka and the mainland, are said to have built Bandhavgarh's fort. Later Rama handed it over to his brother Lakshmana who became known as *bandhavdhish*, "the lord of the fort" — a title still used by the present "lord of the fort," the former Maharaja of Rewa. Lakshmana is the particular god of the fort and is regularly worshiped in a temple there.

The oldest signs of habitation in the park are the caves dug into the sandstone to the north of the fort. Several contain Brahmi inscriptions dating from the 1st century B.C. From that time onwards Bandhavgarh was ruled by a succession of dynasties including the Chandela kings of Bundelkhand who built the famous temples at Khajuraho. The Baghel kings, the direct ancestors of the present royal family of Rewa, established their dynasty at Bandhavgarh in the 12th Century. It remained their capital till 1617 when the center of court life moved to Rewa, 75 miles (120 km) to the north. Without royal patronage Bandhavgarh became more and more deserted until forest overran the area and it became a royal hunting reserve. This helped to preserve the forest and its wildlife, although the maharajas made full use of their rights. Each set out to kill the auspicious number of 109 tigers.

At independence Bandhavgarh remained the private property of the maharaja until he gave it to the state for the formation of a national park in 1968. After the park was created poaching was brought under control and the number of animals rose dramatically. Small dams and water holes were built to solve the problem of water shortage. Grazing by local cattle was stopped and a village within the park boundaries was relocated. The tigers in particular prospered and the 1986 extension provided much needed forest to accommodate them.

Within the Park: Bandhavgarh is justifiably famous for its tigers, but it has a wide range of other game. The undergrowth is not as dense as in some northern *terai* forests, but the best time to see the park's inhabitants is still the summer months when water becomes more scarce and the undergrowth dies back.

The most effective way to search for **tigers** is on elephant back. Government elephants belonging to the Forest Department and equipped with walkie-talkies can be boarded from a point near the **Forest Rest House**, not far from the park entrance. It's advisable to book your elephant in advance and to wear plenty of warm clothing if going for an early morning ride in winter. The mahouts are kept well-informed of the whereabouts of the nearest tigers but will generally only

Small creatures are also fascinating.

go for comparatively short trips into the jungle on the north side of the main viewing area. However, there are many tigers in the park and elephants are able to take you up steep, rocky hillsides and down marshy riverbeds which are impassable to vehicles.

There are several good-weather roads in the park. Jeeps are definitely recommended over other vehicles and can be hired from the **White Tiger Lodge** or the **Bandhavgarh Jungle Camp**. It's also advisable to take a guide. The Bandhavgarh Jungle Camp provides an excellent service of good, English-speaking guides, who are also available from the White Tiger Lodge. A forest guard must accompany all visitors into the park. Entry into the park is allowed only during daylight hours. For both elephant and jeep rides the hours immediately after dawn and before sunset are best.

Chinkara, still rather shy, can be sighted on the grassland areas of the park, particularly on formerly cultivated land in the southern extension area, on the edges of the main viewing area. Also to be seen in the grasslands are **nilgai**, **chausingha** and sounders of **wild boar**, as well as the occasional **jackal** or **fox**. In March and April **gaur**, or Indian bison, move down from the higher hills to the southeast of the park and make their way through the southern extension area to the central meadows of the park to graze. The need for water and good grazing draws them to the park and they return to the southeastern hills at the onset of the monsoon.

Muntjac and **sambar** prefer denser vegetation. The main prey animal, however, for the tigers and the park's rarely sighted leopards are the **chital**, which now number a few thousand.

There are two types of monkey common in the park — the **rhesus macaque** and the **black-faced langur**. Drives can also reveal **jungle cats**, **hyenas**, **porcupines**, **ratels** and a variety of other mammals. At least one small pack of wild dogs inhabits the central area of the park.

As the park is relatively new, there is still a good chance of adding birds to the checklist of some 150 species already compiled. Bandhavgarh attracts many migratory birds in the winter months, including birds of prey like the **steppe eagle** and a variety of wildfowl. However, as it has limited water surfaces it cannot compete with parks with large areas of wetland. While you aren't allowed to go into the park on foot, the park headquarters and the Jungle Camp offer excellent opportunities to watch the smaller birds. Attracted by

flowering and fruiting trees, some very attractive and less common birds can be seen — for example the **blue-bearded bee eater**, the **white-bellied drongo**, **Tickell's blue flycatcher**, the **white-browed fantail**, both the **gold-fronted** and **Jerdon's leafbirds**, **minivets** and **woodshrikes**. Any large fruiting tree generally reveals a population of **green pigeons** and some of the noisiest residents — **blossom-headed parakeets. Gray** and, less often, the magnificent black and white **Malabar hornbills**, fly across. On roads through the sal forests it's worth looking out for the large **racket-tailed drongo** and the dipping plumes of the **paradise flycatcher**.

The Fort: The fort still belongs to the Maharaja of Rewa and permission is required to visit it. However permission is available locally and no trip to Bandhavgarh can really be complete without making the effort to climb up to the fort.

There are two ways up on to the plateau, a jeeptrack and a footpath — both steep. It is far easier to see the fort by jeep but much more rewarding to make the journey on foot. There is a convenient place to park vehicles on the southern side of the fort in the lush jungle which surrounds its base. This point is known as **Shesh Saya**, named after a unique 35-foot (11-meter) long statue of a reclining Vishnu carved around the 10th Century, from whose feet the Charanganga is said to flow. A rectangular pool of springwater lies just beneath the statue and the path to the main gate of the fort, the **Karn Pol**, leads off to the left of the pool. On the other side of this imposing gateway lie 560 acres (227 hectares) of grassland, over which are scattered turtle-filled tanks and the many remains of the human inhabitants of the fort — from ancient statues to the barracks occupied by Rewa's troops up to independence. At a brisk pace the walk from the Shesh Saya to the southern side of the fort need only take an hour, but if you stop to see the statues and temples on the way it can easily take much longer. As you follow the path southwards, the most remarkable sights are the 10th-Century rock images of the incarnations of Vishnu. A statue of Narasimha (half-man half-lion) towers almost 22 feet (seven meters) above the grass. There is a carving of Barah Bhagwan (the boar incarnation), and a small temple enshrining a large image of Vishnu in his fish *avatar*. The tortoise incarnation stands unenclosed and flanked by later carvings of Ganesh, the elephant god, and other deities. The charm of this walk lies in discovering

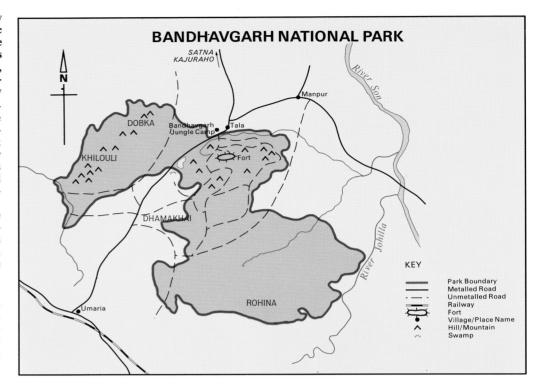

BANDHAVGARH NATIONAL PARK

KEY

Park Boundary
Metalled Road
Unmetalled Road
Railway
Fort
Village/Place Name
Hill/Mountain
Swamp

these monuments in the jungle, unspoilt and unexploited. Some of the statues lie off the main path and so it is best to take a guide. Apart from the *avatars*, well worth seeing are three small temples of around the 12th Century. These temples are deserted but the fort is still used as a place of worship. Kabir Das, the celebrated 16th-Century saint, once lived and preached here.

The natural ramparts of the fort give breathtaking views of the surrounding countryside. **Vultures** wheel around the precipice which also attracts **blue rock thrushes** and **crag martins**. The fort has a small population of **blackbuck**, which have been reintroduced and to some extent protected from tigers in the park below by repairs to the masonry walls at the edges of the fort.

Thus Bandhavgarh offers excellent game and bird viewing and a historical interest which most other parks lack. It is a comfortable drive from Khajuraho and so visitors can enjoy both the temples of the one and the wildlife of the other in one trip. And for those who enjoy train travel Bandhavgarh has two railway stations within reach — **Umaria** and **Satna** — and jeeps which can collect visitors from the station and deposit them on elephant back before breakfast.

Left, green bee-eater; *right*, langur.

NAGARAHOLE AND BANDIPUR NATIONAL PARKS

Tall trees, swaying bamboos and grassy expanses. Calls of mynas and drongos that pierce the gentle murmur of forest streams. A herd of gaur in the morning sun, with massive horned heads and pale green eyes that stare back at you. A blazing afternoon. A pack of wild dogs corners a chital stag in a forest pool. An elephant herd frolicks in water as the setting sun bathes it in gold. As night falls, the haunting cry of a peacock retiring to the top of a tall, leafless tree. A sambar calls in alarm. A tiger is on the move, leaving his tracks on a dusty trail. This is typical South Indian jungle. Most of it is gone forever. Yet in the vast forests of the Mysore plateau in Karnataka state that stretch between the towering Western Ghats and Nilgiri mountains, the experience comes alive even now.

Administered separately, Nagarahole (pronounced *Naagara-holay*) and Bandipur are but two faces of a single spectacular ecological continuum that also includes Mudumalai and Wynad wildlife sanctuaries in the neighboring states. The 333-sq-mile (865-sq-km) **Bandipur National Park** lies south of the Kabini river which meanders through the jungle, while **Nagarahole** (247 sq mile/640 sq km, including proposed expansion) is to its north. The old royal capital city of Mysore is the gateway to both parks.

Due to their geographic proximity the two parks share many features. The balmy climate is common to both. So are most of the plant and animal species. Yet, there are differences too.

The Bandipur that the tourist sees is an open, grassy woodland. The jungles of Nagarahole are taller and denser. Bandipur has superb scenery of mountains, gorges and undisturbed forests. Nagarahole has an astonishing abundance of wildlife. Together, these two parks cover more than 580 sq miles (1500 sq km). About a third of this area has been demarcated as the "Wilderness Zone" in which all disturbances, including tourism and forestry, are prohibited. The facilities for wildlife tourism have been developed in the three "tourism zones." Two of these, called **Nagarahole** and **Karapura** are in Nagarahole National Park while the third is in Bandipur. Two more tourism zones, at Begur in Bandipur and Moorkal in Nagarahole are being planned.

Climate and Landscape: Three seasons are usually recognized. The wet season or monsoon lasts from June to September. The cool season that follows lasts up to January. The hot season or summer extends from February to May. However, seasonal variations of temperature are quite moderate, ranging between 59°F (15°C) at the coldest to about 82°F (28°C) at the hottest. Annual rainfall is lowest at the eastern edge of Bandipur — 32 inches (80 cm). It increases gradually as you proceed in a northwesterly direction, reaching about 60 inches (150 cm) at the western edge of Nagarahole. The landscape is generally one of gentle slopes and shallow valleys at an average altitude of 2300 feet (700 meters). A few peaks are higher, Gopalaswamy Betta (4770 feet/1454 meters) in Bandipur Park being the highest.

Kabini, a tributary of the mighty Cauvery, is the largest river draining this tract. Other important rivers are the Moyar and Mulehole (both in Bandipur), the Lakshmana Teertha and Nagarahole—the last name meaning "Cobra River." An irrigation dam was built across the Kabini in 1974, creating the picturesque lake that separates the two parks.

Two basic types of tropical, mixed deciduous forests clothe the region. Of these, the moist deciduous type, usually occurring in localities getting a rainfall higher than 48 inches (120 cm), is found in the northern and western parts of Nagarahole Park as well as on the western fringes of Bandipur. The dry deciduous type covers the southeastern part of Nagarahole and most of Bandipur. Interestingly, unlike the temperate zone forests, these tropical deciduous forests are leafless in summer rather than in winter. The period of leaf fall, essentially an ecological adaptation to cope with water stress, is relatively shorter in the moist type when compared to the dry.

The moist deciduous forests are tall and dense. The tree canopy is usually two-storied. The upper canopy, about 98 feet (30 meters) tall, is dominated by valuable timber trees such as mathi (*Terminalia tomentosa*), nandi (*Lagerstroemia lanceolata*), honne (*Pterocarpus marsupium*) and tadasalu (*Grewia tilaefolia*). These jungles are reputed as the home of the two most expensive timbers — dark, shiny rosewood (*Dalbergia latifolia*) and the rich, grainy teak (*Tectona grandis*). The lower forest canopy has the prolific fruit yielders — nelli (*Phy-*

llanthus emblica), kooli (*Gonclina arborea*), kadu tega (*Dillenia pentagyna*) and the *Randia S* — all of which attract a host of animals and birds. Bende (*Kydia calycina*), whose bark is a great favorite with elephants, is ubiquitous.

Lower down, the shrub layer is usually very dense and varied in composition. However, in recent decades runaway exotic shrubs like *lantana* and *lupatorium* have established dominance, aggressively invading openings created by logging. In the moist deciduous forests grass growth is not very profuse where the trees and shrubs are dense. But in cleared openings a variety of grasses grow.

A unique feature of these moist deciduous forests, particularly in Nagarahole, are the open grassy swamps locally called *hadlus*. Here the soil is clayey, perennially moist, and supports a luxuriant growth of green grass all the year round. These are ideal spots to watch large concentrations of ungulates, particularly gaur.

The dry deciduous forest type is strikingly different. The canopy is lower, trees are more widely spaced and their trunks are usually stunted and crooked. Many species of the moist type are present but their relative dominance varies. Dindalu (*Anogeissus latifolia*) is usually the commonest tree. Kakke (*Cassia fistula*), "Flame of the Forest" (*Butea monosperma*) and bamboo (*Dendrocalamus strictus*) are all commoners. The second canopy is barely discernible. There are open grassland patches and the entire habitat has a woodland savannah-like appearance. In summer forage and water scarcity pose serious problems to the herbivores.

An even more harsh environment is found around the Moyar Gorge at the easternmost edge of Bandipur. In this region of lowest rainfall, dry deciduous forest gives way to an even poorer, stunted scrub type. The soil is rocky and barren and the vegetation dominated by thorny plants.

Elephants and Others: The Nagarahole-Bandipur forests are perhaps one of the best remaining habitats of the **Asian elephant** (*Elephas maximus*) in the world. Over a thousand of these mighty beasts are estimated to range over this tract. A striking ecological feature of these elephant populations is their seasonal migration. In the wet season when water and forage are plentiful everywhere, the elephants are evenly distributed. This is the best time to see huge herds of them in the open forests of Bandipur. As the cool season ends and summer sets in,

water and forage availability becomes restricted. Elephants congregate around specific localities like the banks of Mule-hole river, Nagarahole Tourism Zone, and, above all, the banks of the Kabini.

Setting out on a jeep ride from Karapura you can reach a place called **Mastigudi** on the banks of the Kabini around sunset to witness a scene reminiscent of Africa rather than Asia. A breathtaking panoramic sweep of a mile-long stretch of the river is dotted with elephants — over a hundred of them. If you are lucky you might even see a herd swimming across, the adults carefully chaperoning the "little" babies. During the 19th Century, G. P. Sanderson developed the *khedda* (stockade) method of capturing elephants at this site. Though the medieval barbarity of the *khedda* is mercifully a thing of the past in this conservation-conscious age, we get a glimpse of it when the waters of the Kabini recede and the remnants of the old stockade are revealed.

Gaur (*Bos gaurus*), largest of the wild bovids, are another attraction in these parks. Though they are still recovering from a population crash caused by rinderpest disease in 1968, gaur are a common sight at Nagarahole and Karapura, though not in Bandipur yet. Herds of 20–30 animals or, sometimes, massive solitary bulls, can be seen placidly grazing as you pass by in a jeep.

Four species of deer inhabit these forests. The largest of them is the **sambar** (*Cervus unicolor*), a shy creature preferring thick cover and becoming active late in the evening. One usually tends to underestimate their abundance in any area. The usual sighting is of two or three animals, normally a mother with her young. During the wet season, occasionally, large temporary associations of 10–20 sambar are seen. Very large stags with fine antlers are also seen in Bandipur.

The commonest deer in both parks is the **chital** or **axis deer** (*Axis axis*). These handsome spotted deer are so numerous around the park headquarters at Nagarahole and Bandipur that one tends to ignore them after a while. They are also the least shy species, congregating around the tourist rest houses at night, perhaps to avoid predators. Being partial to open grassy areas, chital are most often seen in the cleared "view-lines" bordering the "game roads." Human intrusions, such as opening up dense forests, clearing view-lines and creating water holes, have all obviously benefited chital which tend to be less numerous

in the denser more "natural" forests.

Muntjac (*Muntiacus muntjak*) are small goat-sized, reddish-fawn-colored deer with a surprisingly loud bark that carries long distances in the stillness of the night, warning everyone about predators on the prowl. So the muntjac is also known as the **barking deer**. This alert little sentinel of the forest prefers the edge of dense cover venturing out only to graze or eat fallen over-ripe fruit. Usually, one gets only a fleeting glimpse of muntjac dashing for cover. But on the Nagaraja Game Road in Nagarahole muntjacs have become accustomed to tourists and can be seen at close quarters.

Chevrotain or **mouse deer** (*Tragulus meminna*) are tiny, rabbit-sized, evolutionarily primitive kind of deer. Though they appear to be reasonably common, going by the evidence of their tracks, they are rarely seen by tourists because of their entirely nocturnal habits.

The **four-horned antelope** (*Tetracerus quadricornis*) is perhaps the most interesting ungulate in these parks. About the size of the muntjac, but with longer legs, it has a duller brownish coat. The male four-horned antelope has two spiky horns in the usual place and two extra rudimentary knobs set a little forward, giving the species the unique

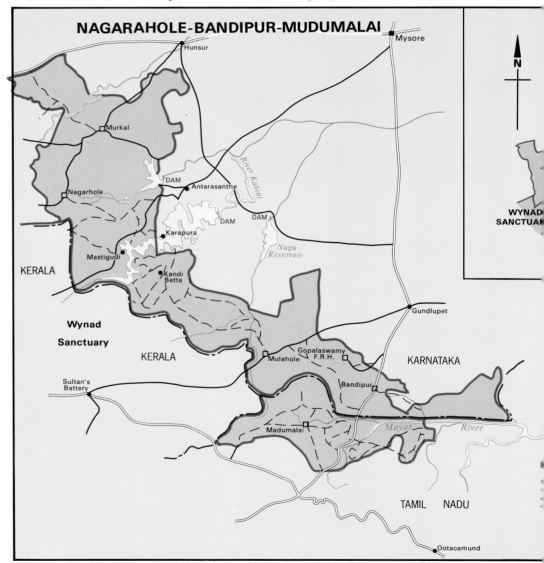

NAGARAHOLE-BANDIPUR-MUDUMALAI

…AHOLE N.P.

BANDIPUR
TIGER RESERVE

MUDUMALAI

Park Boundary
State Boundary
Metalled Road
Unmetalled Road
Town
Village/Place Name

distinction of being the only four-horned animal in the world. It is a thinly distributed species which prefers open, dry, hilly terrain and is uncommon everywhere. Very little is known about its ecology but it is not found in the denser moist forest of Nagarahole. Unfortunately, most park staff who accompany the tourists do not distinguish it from the muntjac though it is seen often on the Russel Fireline Road of the Karapura and Moyar area of Bandipur.

Wild pig (*Sus scrofa*) and **blacknaped hare** (*Lepus nigricollis*) are two other common herbivores. The **Indian porcupine**

Living up in the tree canopy are two kinds of monkeys. The **Hanuman langur** (*Presbytis entellus*) is a longtailed leaf-eating species, extremely common in both parks. The **bonnet macaque** (*Macaca radiata*) is a versatile feeder common around human settlements but rare in the deep jungle.

The Hunters: Among carnivores the least predatory animal is the **sloth bear** (*Melursus ursinus*). It feeds mainly on termites, vegetable matter, honey and, occasionally, carrion. This short-sighted creature is sometimes preyed upon by the other large carnivores! Though bears are seen in all the

tection, dense concentrations of large ungulate prey and dense cover, ideal for the stalking predator, have all combined to create what is perhaps the finest tiger habitat in South India. Heavy predation on gaur, including large solitary bulls, by the tiger is a special feature of Nagarahole. Yet you must remember that even here seeing a tiger in daylight is not as easy as it is in some North Indian parks. Strict avoidance of artificial baiting and the consequent lack of acclimatization to tourism is perhaps one of the reasons why an encounter with a tiger is a chancy event in Nagarahole. Tiger sightings are even more difficult in Karapura and

are seen fairly often by tourists. Bandipur is the best place to see them, followed by Nagarahole and Karapura. The **striped hyena** (*Hyaena hyaena*), another large carnivore, is found very rarely in the scrub forests of eastern Bandipur. Reported to be more a scavenger than a hunter, it is generally not seen by tourists.

A host of smaller carnivores are also present. The diminutive **jackal** (*Canis aureus*) is the only other canid, apart from the dhole. There are three species of lesser cats: the **jungle cat** (*Felis chaus*), the **leopard cat** (*Felis bengalensis*) and the rare **rusty spotted cat** (*Felis rubiginosa*) — all are

(*Hystrix indica*) and **pangolin** (*Manis crassicaudata*) are two other species not commonly seen because they are nocturnal. The former is a rodent with a catholic diet that includes the antlers that deer shed annually. The latter relies on an exclusive diet of ants and termites. Other mammals worth mentioning are the handsome red **giant squirrel** (*Ratufa indica*), large brown **flying squirrel** (*Petaurista petaurista*), **giant fruit bat** (*Pteropus giganteus*), and the secretive **slender loris** (*Loris tardigradus*). Except the giant squirrel, these are all nocturnal and usually heard rather than seen.

areas, the best place to sight them is the Karapura Tourism Zone. If lucky you may see a mother sloth bear taking her cubs piggy-back — an amusing sight.

With such a large and diverse assemblage of prey species, the Nagarahole-Bandipur forests naturally harbor many predators. **Tiger** (*Panthera tigris*), **leopard** (*Panthera pardus*), and the **Asiatic wild dog** (*Cuon alpinus*) also called **dhole**, all coexist in these parks.

Though Bandipur is one among the nine originally constituted Project Tiger Reserves, interestingly it is Nagarahole that is the stronghold of the tiger. Intensive pro-

quite extraordinary events in Bandipur.

However, if you are interested in the leopard, Karapura is undoubtedly the place to go. The forest there supports a high density of the leopard's favorite prey — the langur monkey. Leopards can be usually seen at fairly close range during an evening jeep drive, unless you are very noisy.

The wild dog is a reddish, spaniel-sized, pack-hunting canid. Unlike tigers and leopards which stalk their prey in dense cover, wild dogs course after their prey, which is usually chital or sambar. Because wild dogs hunt mainly during the day and prefer open areas suitable for coursing they

nocturnal; two species of civets, the perfume-yielding **small Indian civet** (*Viverricula indica*) and the arboreal **palm civet** (*Paradoxurus hermaphroditus*), which are also nocturnal; four species of mongooses, the **common** (*Herpestes edwardsi*), the **stripe-necked** (*Herpestes vitticollis*), the **brown** (*Herpestes fuscus*) and the **ruddy** (*Herpestes smithii*) — are found in the tract but identifying them in the field takes some practice. The common **otter** (*Lutra lutra*) is the only mustalid recorded in both parks. Groups of otters can sometimes be seen in the Kabini reservoir.

Birds: The Nagarahole-Bandipur region is

Left to right: yellow wasp; colony of bees.

rich territory for bird watchers. An incomplete checklist of birds exceeds two hundred entries. The backwaters of the Kabini sustain huge gatherings of **cormorants**, **teals**, **ducks**, **herons** and **waders**. The abundance of fish there, including the large **masheer** (*Tor tor*), attracts a number of **ospreys** (*Pandion haliaetus*) and **gray-headed fishing eagles** (*Icthyophaga ichthyaetus*). Among other birds of prey, the **crested hawk eagle** (*Spizaetus cirrhatus*), **serpent eagle** (*Spilornis cheela*) and **honey buzzard** (*Pernis ptilorhyneus*) are all common. The **shaheen falcon** (*Falco peregrinus*), **hobby** (*Falco subbuteo*) and the spectacular **king vulture** (*Sarcogyps calvus*) are some rarer birds of prey seen in the area.

Among game birds, **peafowl** (*Pavo cristatus*), **gray jungle fowl** (*Gallus sonneratti*) and the quarrelsome **red spurfowl** (*Galloperdix spadicea*) are usually seen in the forest while the **gray partridge** (*Francolinus pondicerianus*) prefers the scrub on the fringes.

The other colorful or uncommon birds seen in these forests are: **Malabar trogon** (*Harpactes faciatus*), **blue-bearded bee eater** (*Nyctyornis athertoni*), **Malabar pied hornbill** (*Anthracoceros coronatus*), **great black woodpecker** (*Dryocopus javensis*), **Alexandrine parakeet** (*Psittacula eupatria*), **lesser coucal** (*Centropus toulou*), **Indian pitta** (*Pitta brachyura*), **scarlet minivet** (*Pricrocotus flammeus*), **fairy blue bird** (*Irena pullea*), **scimitar babbler** (*Promatorhinus horsfieldii*), **paradise flycatcher** (*Tersiphone paradisi*), **Malabar whistling thrush** (*Myiophonous horsfieldii*), **green imperial pigeon** (*Ducula aenea*) and **yellow-legged green pigeon** (*Treron phoenicoptera*). The **racket tailed drongo** (*Dicrurus paradiseus*) and **hill myna** (*Gracula religiosa*) are the noisy birds of the day while the **owls** and **nightjars** are heard at night.

Unfortunately, the tourist cannot wander around on foot in the forests to watch birds. Considering the dangers of encounters with elephants, the park authorities have wisely forbidden such explorations. So the bird-watching is generally confined to the vicinity of rest houses and to the jungle safaris on vehicles. The early morning coracle ride from Karapura provides absolutely fantastic opportunities for bird-watching.

Reptiles: Coracle rides on the Kabini may occasionally yield sightings of **marsh crocodile** (*Crocodilus palustrus*) also. The other large reptile, the **monitor lizard** (*Varanus bengalensis*) is sometimes seen in

Below, leopard disturbed on kill and right, the egret was once hunted for their plumes used to decorate turbans and ladies' hats—hence the term aigrette.

140

the forests. Several species of snakes including **rock python** (*Python molurus*), **cobra** (*Naja naja*), **rat snake** (*Ptyas mucosus*), **wolf snake** (*Lycodon aulicus*), **vine snake** (*Anaetulla nastus*), **common krait** (*Bungarus caeruleus*), **Russel's viper** (*Vipera russelli*), **green keelback** (*Macrophisthadon plumbicolor*) and **bamboo pit viper** (*Trimeresurus gramineus*) are also found.

The reptilean and amphibian fauna of the region include a variety of turtles and frogs also. To complete the picture there is a tremendous abundance and diversity of insect life, including many colorful butterfly species.

Getting the Most out of Your Trip: Of the three choices that are available (Bandipur, Karapura and Nagarahole) to you to sample the splendors of the wildlife of the region, it is preferable to choose one or two if you have only limited time at your disposal. Two to three days are needed to derive full benefit from a visit to any *one* of the three. If your visit coincides with the peak of the monsoon, Bandipur is the best choice because of its better accessibility and wildlife viewing possibilities. In June and July Nagarahole and, to a lesser extent, Karapura become rain-soaked and the roads often become so muddy that you may find yourself confined to your rest house.

The forests are lush and green in the wet season. The skies are bright blue and the weather sunny and cool between October and January. But the animals are widely dispersed and, because of the dense undergrowth, are harder to view, particularly in Nagarahole and Karapura. During the dry season, animal sightings are excellent in Nagarahole and Karapura, but generally poor in Bandipur. However, the forests are leafless and bone dry in this season.

It is important to plan your trip well in advance because accommodation is very limited in these parks and at least a month's advance reservation is advisable. It is better to avoid weekend visits to Bandipur or Nagarahole because the heavy influx of tourists, many of them merely misguided picnickers, detracts from quality of the experience for the keen wildlifer. Accommodation is hardest to get in Nagarahole, followed by Bandipur and Karapura in that order. The first two cater to the needs of a large number of domestic tourists and are priced accordingly.

On the other hand, Karapura, though more expensive, is fully geared to meet the needs of a more exclusive clientele. The **Kabini River Lodge** there, with its vast wooded compound, splendid lakeside scenery and gracious old-world air is well organized and uncrowded when compared to the rest houses in Nagarahole or Bandipur. Reservations are also easier to make because of its connections with the network of private travel operators. In Bandipur and Nagarahole reasonably priced Indian food is available at a couple of hours' notice. At Karapura there is usually an excellent Indian or Western menu to choose from. There is also a well-stocked bar, unlike the other two places where you will have to carry your own liquor. The quality of rooms and service is also far superior at the Kabini Lodge. If you have booked your accommodation at Nagarahole, you very rarely run the risk of a last-minute cancellation because of a visiting VIP.

Bandipur is about 50 miles (80 km) from Mysore city and is on the excellent highway that goes on to Ooty. It is well connected by buses to both places. There are only one or two buses a day that run between Mysore and Nagarahole, covering the distance in about three hours. Karapura is the most difficult to reach on such public transport. Though a few buses running between Mysore and Manandawadi in Kerala pass through it after a painful three to four hour journey from Mysore, a one-mile walk to the Kabini Lodge awaits you. For a visitor short on time a two-hour taxi ride from Mysore is the most convenient way to reach any one of these three places. Even though Bandipur and Karapura can be reached at any time of the day, you will have to enter Nagarahole before six in the evening because the route is closed to all traffic at night. In any case, it is better to reach early rather than risk encountering an elephant roadblock late in the evening.

In all three places, tourists are taken into the forest to see wildlife in jeeps or vans between 6 and 9 a.m. and between 4 and 6 p.m. These trips are on specially laid-out dirt roads called "game roads" which usually pass close to grazing areas, salt licks and water holes. The undergrowth is cleared to a distance of about 32 yards (30 meters) on either side to improve visibility and to attract herbivores to the sprouting grass. Usually an excellent view of most common species can be had at a range of 15 to 20 yards (14–18 meters) particularly if total silence is observed by all the passengers in the vehicle. The experienced drivers of these vehicles generally keep at a safe distance from elephants. A Park Guard accompanies the visitors and is reasonably good at spotting large animals. As a rule he is quite useless at identifying birds and smaller mammals. The trained naturalists of the Kabini Lodge who accompany tourists in Karapura are far better in this respect. You are strictly prohibited from getting down from the vehicle. The jungle ride usually lasts about an hour and a half and payment is on the basis of distance traveled.

Short jungle rides on elephant back are available only in Bandipur. Though you see very little wildlife this way you get a good feel of the jungle. Kabini Lodge offers facilities of coracle rides on the river. (A coracle is a round-country boat made of bamboo and buffalo hide.) Special permission from the park authorities is needed for the use of watchtowers in the forests.

Apart from wildlife viewing which keeps you busy in the mornings and evenings, there is very little to do by way of recreational or educational activity in either Bandipur or Nagarahole. In Karapura you can go boating on the lake or even fish outside the National Park limits. Usually, a wildlife movie is screened following dinner around a campfire on the lakeside.

Special Attractions: In Bandipur, a spot called **Rolling Rocks,** where you get a superb panoramic view of the Moyar Gorge ("Mysore Ditch"!) is well worth a visit. An hour's drive in your own transport during the non-wildlife viewing hours will take you to **Gopalaswamy Betta** from where a wonderful vista of the entire region stretches before you. There is also an interesting temple on the hill. In Karapura a visit to the old *khedda* site at Mastigudi and to the Government elephant resting camp at **Balle** which is nearby are not to be missed. Those who are keen on photography should carry at least a 200 mm telephoto lens. Because of the low light levels under the forest canopy, a big aperture setting and fast film (200–400 ASA) will give you more photographic opportunities.

You can profitably combine your trip to Bandipur-Nagarahole forests with visits to the **Ranganathittu Bird Sanctuary** and other interesting tourist spots near Mysore city. About eight miles (13 km) from Mysore is the battle-scarred town of **Shrirangapattana**, once Tipu Sultan's capital. It was here that the Tiger of Mysore, as Tipu was called, fought and died. **A gaur.**

MUDUMALAI, "ANCIENT HILL RANGE"

Right, startled chital. Far right (above), Mudumalai in the dry months and below, a tiger alarmed by the camera.

The large area originally known as Wynad on the northeastern slopes of the Nilgiri mountains now holds three parks in three states. The Wynad sanctuary in Kerala to the west; Bandipur Tiger Reserve in Karnataka to the north; and Mudumalai in Tamil Nadu to the South.

The word *mudumalai* has the same meaning — "the ancient hill range" — in each of the languages of these three states.

The Moyar river flows north through the park and then turns east to form the northern boundary of Mudumalai, separating it from Bandipur. The park is split by the Mysore–Ootacamund highway running north–south and following the left bank of the Moyar river. Despite being only 116 sq miles (300 sq km) in area, Mudumalai has a great variety of attractive habitats.

Although the north–south highway inevitably causes some disturbance, the game viewing can be excellent. The first-time visitor is advised to seek local guidance.

Birdlife: The birdlife is rich and extensive. The variety includes the beautiful **Malabar trogon**, the **Malabar gray hornbill** and the **Malabar great black woodpecker** with its magnificent crimson crest contrasted by its black body. The leading avian predator in the drier and more open forest areas of Mudumalai, where it is fairly common, is undoubtedly the **crested hawk-eagle**. The **crested serpent eagle** is also found. Although rarely seen, many owls can be found in the different forest types. The **common scops owl** and the **little scops owl** are more often heard while the **tiny-eared owl** uses its brown marking to merge with the trees.

During the summer, many of the resident song birds such as **barbets**, **mynas**, **parakeets** and **cuckoos** fill the forest with their calls.

Elephants, Predators and Prey: While the Moyar river forms a political and administrative division, the herds of elephant, gaur and other animals move freely between Bandipur, Mudumalai and the neighboring forests. The great feline predators are only rarely seen although the **tiger** is present throughout the sanctuary. **Leopards** are most often seen in the Kargudi area. The other important predator in the area is the **wild dog** or **dhole** (*Cuon alpinus*).

In 1968 an epidemic of rinderpest reduced the great herds of **gaur** to a few scattered groups in the outlying forest. As in Bandipur, these small groups are now returning to their old grazing haunts. Although the large herds of over 80 which used to be found at Theppakkadu are regrettably no longer seen, smaller composite herds are regrouping with two or more master bulls leading their respective groups.

The **elephant** population seen in various herds throughout Mudumalai is made up of animals migrating through the area on a seasonal basis looking for fresh fodder. Many of the old migratory trails along the Western Ghats are now cultivated hillsides and valleys. Those routes through Nagarahole, Bandipur and Mudumalai reserves continue south and west into the remnants of the great forest areas of Kerala.

The two most common species in the sanctuary are the **chital** or **spotted deer** and the **sambar**. Both have definite local variations. The chital are usually seen in small groups throughout the sanctuary except in Benne in the southwest. In the southeast, however, near the well-watered open grasslands of the Masinagudi area, larger herds are found. At Viewpoint near Masinagudi herds of over a hundred are often seen.

Sambar are found throughout the park, but except for those in the Avarahalla-Manradiar area, they are quite small. In the Avarahalla area, however, the stags have a very distinct local identity, being much darker than usual but with smaller antlers.

Another deer seen here is the solitary **barking deer** or **muntjac** which lives in the same forest habitat as the chital. An unusual sight, but more often seen here than elsewhere in India, is the tiny **mouse deer** or **Indian chevrotain** (*Tragulus meminna*), usually camouflaged with its light-cream mottled pattern on its brown coat.

Of the other mammals, the **wild boar** is the one most often seen, especially along the streams, on the banks of pools or crossing a culvert. In the clearings near Theppakkadu in the north and at Kargudi at the center, both **bonnet macaques** and **common langurs** are found. Occasional sightings of the **giant squirrel** are made, although they are more often only heard. **Flying squirrels,** being nocturnal, are rarely observed.

The only reptile regularly seen is the **monitor lizard**, especially along the road to Mayar powerhouse in the northeast corner.

As in most of the region, the best period for game-viewing is the summer months (March–June).

PICTURESQUE PERIYAR

The Periyar Wildlife Sanctuary, now one of the 16 Project Tiger Reserves in India, is an interesting example of how development need not be incompatible with the requirements of wildlife. A hundred years ago, a British engineer, Colonel J. Pennycuick, conceived a design to dam the Periyar river, which runs through some of the most spectacular forests of the Western Ghats in Kerala state in South India. The dam was constructed in 1895 and the adjoining forests protected by the Maharaja of Travancore. Today the 300-sq-mile (777-sq-km) sanctuary is a Tiger Reserve. The actual reservoir is 21 sq miles (55 sq km) and it meant that the best valley forests were submerged and lost. The black stumps still to be seen jutting out of the water, which are an eerie and wonderful sight in the early winter mornings as the mist rises, are the only remains of the richly vegetated valley. But the dam also made some compensations. Periyar has become one of the most picturesque wildlife sanctuaries in the world and is enjoyed by over 150,000 tourists every year. For the animals, the reservoir and surrounding forests provide protection and a perennial water supply.

The best time to visit Periyar is between October and April, thus missing the southwest monsoon period. In March and April, when water gets low and the grass dries out, animals have to spend more time near the lake and elephants are especially dependent on the lake during this period. This is the time of year when they can often be seen bathing and swimming, both to cool off as well as to get from one feeding area to the next. The grass is also short during this time of year and animal visibility thus increased.

Apart from the hotels, **Aranya Nivas** and **Periyar House** in the tourist complex area and the **Lake Palace** at Eddapaliyam, there are several rest houses which may be booked in advance and which are in prime wildlife areas and are very reasonably priced.

Since boat travel is the only means of transport within the sanctuary (cars can go only up to the tourist center), large areas can be covered in a short time and a three- or four-day stay is satisfactory, with boat rides in the morning and evening and animal/bird watching on the lake shores in between. Sitting on the steps at Eddapaliyam, the visitor can regularly watch **gaur**, **elephant** and **wild pig** on the opposite bank.

However, for the more deeply interested visitor or naturalist who has the time and inclination, a longer stay is certainly worthwhile: Periyar is a truly spectacular sanctuary. Although walking into the sanctuary on one's own is discouraged by the Forest Department, it is possible to go on treks with tribal guides and there are watchtowers overlooking pools which can be used. It must be remembered, however, that the animals feel most comfortable and allow the closest approach by boat.

The only flat areas of Periyar are the marshy grasslands at the ends of the fingers of the lake. The typical habitat is rolling or steep hills. The actual area covered by forest is sometimes surprisingly little, with big areas of grassland between patches of forest. But this is the hallmark of a dynamic ecosystem, that which provides dense forest cover (for shade and browse in the hot months) and, adjacent to it, rich grasslands for the big herbivores.

The forests of Periyar can be divided into four broad categories. The open grasslands, studded with fire-resistant vegetation, harbor many species of grasses such as elephant grass. These are the common dining hall of all the herbivores, from the gaur and elephant to the small wild boar and barking deer. Then we have the most deciduous forest type dominated by trees like *Terminalia* and teak (*Tectona grandis*) which lose their leaves seasonally.

The semi-evergreen forest occurs along wet stream areas and is often adjacent to the tropical evergreen forests. And lastly, the climax forests: the *sholas* or tropical evergreen jungle which occurs in the valleys and where one can see trees 100 to 130 feet (30 to 40 meters) high. The dense tree-canopy allows only a limited stream of sunlight through and in the moist, dark corridors, ferns, orchids and airplants abound. Also to be found here is the small but efficient parasite, the leech. Leeches live on blood and prey mostly on warm-blooded animals that periodically pass through their territory. But there are obviously not enough game animals to go around, as visitors may find to their dismay, and a juicy human limb is always welcome.

There is probably no sanctuary in the world where elephant behavior can be watched in such absolute comfort and safety. It was here that the writer and her colleagues first appreciated the great repertoire of elephant sounds, some which are startlingly human. The total elephant population is about 800 and one can approach to within 20 yards (20 meters) of

In Periyar, elephants are best viewed from boats.

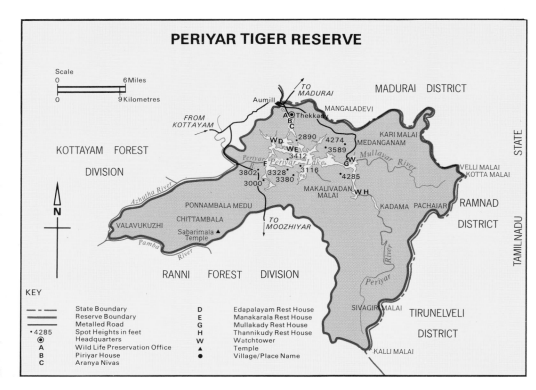

PERIYAR TIGER RESERVE

placid groups feeding, bathing and swimming. Often, after a swim, elephants indulge in their own brand of mudslinging; trunkfuls of dust are sprayed on their backs, an activity which may decrease parasite infestation and protect them from the sun. But whatever the reason, it is a spectacular sight.

Unlike their African cousins, female Indian elephants have no tusks. In fact not all bulls have tusks either. Tuskless males are called *maknas*. A male tusker is of course a magnificent animal, but it may be that the *maknas* are the lucky ones, because sustained poaching for ivory has wiped out most of the big tuskers in South Indian jungles. The high stakes involved make poachers increasingly daring and bold, and forest officials have an almost insurmountable problem on their hands. The ivory criminals have in recent years started hanging live wires to electrocute elephants. Also, tuskers are singled out and crippled by a shot in the knee; the helpless animal is then closely approached and killed. It is equally tragic when a wounded elephant manages to get away from its killers. People report that tuskers with a crippled leg use their tusk as a crutch for support.

Poaching and human encroachment are the biggest problems that the 150-strong Forest Department staff have to contend with. Kerala has the highest human density figures in India and Periyar is an island surrounded by human habitation. Cattle grazing has become a serious problem. Cattle within the park disturb the wildlife, stop effective grass growth and compete with the herbivores for food. But their presence in the reserve can have much more serious consequences. In 1974-1975, the dreaded rinderpest disease which fatally affects bovines and which is spread by cattle, reached epidemic proportions in South India. A thousand gaur died from it in Periyar. The Forest Department is working out a plan to ensure, through a system of ear tags, that all cattle in adjoining areas are immunized against rinderpest.

A typical sight in Periyar are the **darters** and **cormorants** which bask on the remnant poles of the submerged forest, and allow tourist boats to approach to within yards of them without fear. The depth of the lake excludes wading birds but offers splendid opportunities for anglers such as **ospreys**, **kingfishers** and **kites**. **Otters**, also expert fishermen, are a common sight, fishing in the shallows or bounding along the shore with their wet fur gleaming in the sun.

Both the **great hornbill** and the **gray hornbill** can be easily seen in Periyar. Several fruit trees just around the boat landing area attract these hornbills, **hill mynas**, **orioles** and **racket-tailed drongos**. Very often, the first sign of a great hornbill is the *whoosh, whoosh, whoosh* of its wings as the heavy bird flies overhead. Both hornbills have a somewhat hysterical laughing call, one of the loudest sounds of the forest. Above the forest office at the boat landing, a family of storks have nested for decades in a very tall tree.

Apart from elephants, another herbivore commonly seen is the wild pig. Sounders of 30 or 40 animals are common in Periyar. With its stiff upright mane and disgruntled expression, the pig lends a comic touch to the Periyar scene. The wild pig is an opportunistic feeder and not wholly vegetarian; at Point Calimere on the Tamil Nadu coast, they even dig up and eat the eggs of sea turtles. **Sambar**, **barking deer** and **mouse deer** are the representatives of the deer family in Periyar; interestingly, the spotted deer or chital is absent. An experiment was tried several years ago and a group of chital released on an island in the sanctuary, but they apparently didn't survive. Some of the high hill crests within Periyar are inhabited by the last **Nilgiri tahr** in the area but they are generally too shy and elusive to be seen.

On rocky shelves called *paarai* along the lakeshore one may see a large dark **monitor lizard** basking in the midday sun especially in the cooler months. **Pythons** are fairly regularly seen by the trekking guides and in the evergreen areas an occasional **king cobra** is sighted. Among the smaller reptiles, two spectacular species are the **flying lizard** and the **flying snake**. The flying lizard is hard to see because of its cryptic lichen-like coloration but gliding from one tree to another, its wings are brilliant yellow or orange. An observant naturalist can spot them on a sunny tree trunk by patiently looking for the male, who flaps a tell-tale yellow dewlap or throat flap. The flying snake on the other hand is one of the most colorful snakes in the country with a brilliant pattern of yellow and black, with reddish rosettes. Flying snakes don't really fly, of course, but can launch themselves and flatten their bodies to make an extended "flight" to a lower branch or tree. Yet another flying creature is the incredible **flying frog**, not uncommon in parts of the sanctuary especially during the rains. It "flies," or glides, by extending its toes which are all connected by extra-wide webbing.

Cobra.

Among the predators of Periyar is the **wild dog** or **dhole**, which is fairly commonly seen along the lakeshores and adjoining forests. There are about 50 packs of these carnivores here and they hunt deer, wild pig and other game collectively and alone. Sometimes you may hear the high-pitched, eerie whistle of a wild dog on the hunt. Prey animals typically run to the lake to escape. Wild dogs are much maligned for their so-called "cruelty" and in the past were shot even within sanctuaries, as vermin. In fact, wild dogs are important predators in the food chain of the jungle. As for their cruelty: every carnivore from tigers to spiders must kill for food.

There are several animals which can be seen around the rest houses and other habitations within the sanctuary. After dark, **porcupines** and wild pig scuffle around garbage dumps and vegetable patches. There are four species of monkeys here: the rare and endangered **lion-tailed macaque**, the **Nilgiri langur**, the **common langur** along the eastern boundaries, and the **bonnet macaque** around peripheral areas of the sanctuary. The beautiful **Malabar squirrel** allows fairly close approach at times and one can often hear its loud, excited chatter in the trees. Another large squirrel which lives here is the **flying squirrel** but, being nocturnal, watch and listen for it on bright moonlit nights. It makes spectacular glides between trees which may extend to two to three hundred yards (180 280 meters). Flying squirrels make a fairly loud, plaintive cooing sound which is distinctive if you know what to listen for.

The lucky tourist may even see a **tiger**, which is at the apex of the food chain and which was not long ago in danger of becoming extinct. At the turn of the century there were over 40,000 tigers in India. But sport hunters and commercial interests persecuted the animal so relentlessly that by 1962 less than 200 animals survived. Together with the World Wildlife Fund, the Government of India launched Project Tiger, with a million dollars raised by the WWF to save the animal and its habitat. Project Tiger has been acclaimed one of the most successful conservation campaigns ever undertaken. There are now an estimated 40 tigers in Periyar which seem to be holding their own with little or no increase in numbers.

If you express a particular interest, for example birds, primates etc., the Forest Department is most helpful and the guide provided for trekking, usually a Manan tribal with a vast knowledge of the natural history of the area, will be able to point out things of particular interest. Daytime as well as nighttime periods can be spent on watchtowers, away from the main tourist activity. Shy, timid animals like the gaur, India's largest bovine, prefer the seclusion of the swampy grasslands near Eddapaliyam and other areas associated with watchtowers.

With permission and an accompanying guide, one can trek or boat to the source of the Periyar Lake, the **Periyar river**. This is in the core area of the park, normally not open to visits, and the rest house situated there is known as **Thannikudi**. From here, armed guards patrol a huge 85-sq-mile (220-sq-km) beat to guard against animal and wood poachers. The Periyar is a beautiful, clear river and it is not uncommon to see the dark shapes of yard-long **mahseer**, a game fish made famous by shikar writers such as Jim Corbett, gliding just beneath the surface. Here in Thannikudi the **sloth bear** is common; its signs are everywhere. This is also where tigers can live in peace, away from the main forest activities which are still permitted within the sanctuary.

For those who are anthropologically inclined, there are a few interesting tribal villages near the sanctuary. Among the tribals in this area are the Manans and the Ooralis; the latter still build tree dwellings, these days not so much as residences but as watchtowers to keep animals like wild pig, sambar and elephants from their crops. The Manans are expert fishermen and fish the lake and the clear streams that run into it for mahseer. A few Manans traditionally practice the dangerous exercise of collecting honey of the **hill bees**. These are large and potentially dangerous bees which build massive hives high in the branches of rain forest trees such as the silk cotton, *Bombax*. For climbing to these often 100-foot (30-meter) high honeycombs, they carve bamboo spikes which they hammer into the tree with a wooden mallet. They only do this at night to avoid being stung, and sometimes collect 55 lb (25 kg) of honey at a time from one tree.

Spending a few days in Periyar is a unique and unforgettable experience. Here is one sanctuary where you never travel by road; no traffic noise, no dust, no bumps. Most important, one is not trespassing on the animals' territory.

These are among the many advantages of a sanctuary that is only traversed by boat, and where the thousands of tourists leave no footprints.

Far left: mating damsel flies and star tortoise. *Left*, rhododendron, Horton Plains, Sri Lanka.

SRI LANKA'S UNTAMED TREASURES

Two of Sri Lanka's most precious and purest gems do not lie hidden in that primeval gravel called *illama* that lies beneath the island's layer of alluvial clay; they are found on the surface, spreading over a fair area of her ancient face in a rich and varied pattern. They are her jungle and its denizens.

In its area of 25,000 sq miles (65,000 sq km), Sri Lanka's wild terrain varies from primeval and deep secondary forests down to rolling thornbush plains and the mangrove swamps of the dry zone; from the floodplains of the Mahaveli basin, the home of the great marsh elephant, to the closely knitted steaming jungles of the wet zone and up to the lichen-covered beauty of the mist-draped stark montane forest. One-tenth of Sri Lanka's entire land area is under the jurisdiction of the Department of Wild Life.

The denizens, both feathered and furred, of this diverse habitat, from the treetops to the leaf-covered forest floor are varied and fascinating.

Of her exciting endowment of birds, in excess of 425 different kinds, 251 are resident and the rest are migrant. Among the residents are 21 species and 81 subspecies that are endemic.

Sharing the treetops with the birds is an array of other creatures like the slender loris, five subspecies of monkeys (two of which are confined to the hills), two subspecies of giant squirrel and a flying squirrel.

Treading the forest floor and plain are a single species of wild boar and four species of deer, the commonest of which is the "spotted" which is found in large numbers in all the national parks.

Sri Lanka's "big four" are the elephant, buffalo, leopard and bear, all except the leopard confined to the dry zone and the foothills of the wet zone. The leopard spreads into the hills also, where, in fact, it thrives.

Confined to the floodplains of the Mahaveli are the giant marsh elephants. It has yet to be established whether they are a subspecies or their stature is due to their environment.

In the annals of Sri Lanka's wildlife, only two man-eating leopards have been recorded. The more famous Punani leopard was shot in 1923, after 20 known human kills.

Following the noble traditions of the ancient Buddhist kings, the Department of Wild Life, backed by the State has launched a series of tough and costly measures to protect these untamed treasures against both wanton destruction and "inadvertent" destruction through short-sighted implementation of development projects.

The greatest conservation efforts are being directed towards the elephant. A contiguous system of national parks, jungle corridors where possible, an updated conservation law, with severe penalties, and the translocation of "pocketed herds" to areas of better sustenance, are just a few aspects of this enormous program. These form the base for the overall plan for conservation of all wildlife in the island.

. . . .
***Preceding pages*: leopard yawns at Wilpattu; and large crocodile gapes at a trespasser in a jungle pool at Wilpattu.**

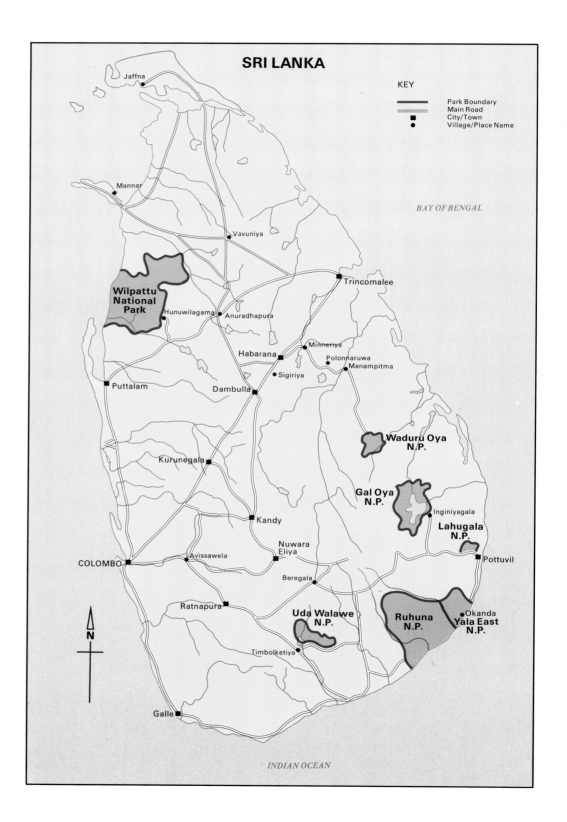

WILPATTU NATIONAL PARK

Eighteen miles (30 km) south along Route A 12 from the ancient Sri Lankan capital of Anuradhapura is a little evergrowing hamlet amidst green surroundings known as Thmbiriwewa. At this spot is the turn-off to one of Sri Lanka's most beautiful national parks, Wilpattu.

Two of the main topographical features of this park are its *villus* and the copper-red, loamy, fine sand. *Villu* is a Tamilized version of the Sinhala word *wila* meaning lake. Most of the Wilpattu *villus* are fairly large, spreading over many acres and do indeed look like lakes; they are not true lakes, however, but rather basin-like pans on the earth's surface. It is interesting to note that Sri Lanka does not have a single natural lake, and all the 11,200 "lakes" or tanks, as they are called, in the north-central area and about 5,000 in the southern sector are man-made, built by ancient monarchs to irrigate the vast agricultural areas.

These crater-like basins of the *villus* are peculiar to this sector of the island, and the greatest concentration of them is to be found within the park. They have no ground-water, only what the rains have brought. In fact, at certain spots, almost by the *villu*, the water table is as far down as 60 feet (20 meters).

Two of the *villus* within the park are saline: **Kokkari** and **Lunuwila**, the latter literally meaning "salt lake." There is still no satisfactory explanation as to how these became salty, but it could be due to a constituent in the soil which becomes progressively concentrated as rain follows drought and so on. The degree of salinity of these *villus* is as high as that of the sea.

Watching at Villus: Almost all the *villus* are surrounded by parkland and are very rich in scenic beauty. They are the finest places in the park to observe animal and bird life, especially in the mornings and evenings. Even on those chance occasions when one does not encounter any animal life at the *villus*, it is still worthwhile to drive around and absorb the beauty and the serene atmosphere.

Another striking characteristic of the park, confined to the western sector, is the red sand, so fine that it will go through the finest of sieves. This sand blankets the western coast of the island from north of Chilaw to about Mannar and is as characteristic to this part of the coast as the white

cliffs are to Dover. It is this coppery loam that prompted the ancient mariners, blown to the west coast by the southwest trade winds, to call the island Tambapanni, the "land of copper sand."

The park has a fairly varied forest pattern. A better part of it is deep secondary forest, but opening out at intervals into sandy glades. The dry thornbush country, reminiscent of Yala, is found in the western sector. Large sand dunes and beds are found throughout the park, where one finds hints of a past submarine land, perhaps during the Middle Tertiary Period.

Leopards: The **leopards** of Wilpattu, for which the park is famous, are not as shy as those at Yala. Often, they walk up to a vehicle. Visitors are, however, well advised to stay as quiet as possible and to avoid any sudden movement when a leopard is in the immediate vicinity. The best time to see these magnificent cats is the early morning hours and the late evenings. Keep a sharp look out in the sandy areas and the edge of the *villus* as you drive around, and let your eyes wander up those magnificent umbrella-shaped trees also.

Though not seen as often as leopard, **bears** too can be observed fairly easily in this park, if conditions are not too dry.

Far left, **tusker and** *left*, **Ceylon hawk eagle.**

However, if one is specially keen on seeing bears, one should plan the visit around late May and June when the palu (*Manilkara hexandra*) and the veera (*Drypetus sepieria*) are in fruit. If you have a sharp shower of rain while you are in the park, get on the track about an hour later and carefully approach the anthills that litter the park, and you are bound to see Mr Bruin sucking up their occupants with his long snout, like a vacuum cleaner. The water holes too are frequented by bears during the late mornings as the sun gets warmer.

Wilpattu is not **elephant** country, yet there is a fair population of these great creatures within the park, and also herds that migrate in and out. But one hardly ever sees them here as they are extremely shy and prefer to stay well under cover during the daylight hours, though, on rare occasions, some lucky visitors have encountered large herds. The occasional loners are known to visit the lodges if there isn't too much disturbance from the occupants. The lodge at Kalli Villu would be the finest place to see elephants from during the dry months, and herds of over 30 have been seen from here. A day spent at **Pomparippu** in the western sector during this period may also bring results.

Wilpattu is best known for its leopards.

The extremely shy and wary **barking deer** and **mouse deer** can both be seen in Wilpattu more easily than anywhere else in the island. This will, however, need a bit of special effort. One will have to spend some time watching quietly at a water hole (your guide will recommend a good one), and your efforts will be rewarded before long.

While touring the *villus*, watch for the **crocodiles** and **water monitors**. Even the two saline *villus* have crocodiles in them, and some of them are exceptionally large.

Birds: During the migratory season, Wilpattu is packed with birds. Even at other times, due to the conditions in the park, almost all avian types in the island, except those that are confined to the hills, can be seen. The best places to observe birds from is the *villus*, and the little water holes which are fairly deep in the jungle but easily accessible. In the deeply forested areas one will come across the more uncommon types such as the **red faced malkoha**, the **Ceylon trogon** and the **shama**. Birds of prey are numerous, and lodge residents should keep a weather-eye open for the magnificent **forest eagle owl**.

There are seven lodges in the park, **Maradanmaduwa, Pannikar Villu, Kalli Villu, Mana Wila, Thala Wila, Manikka**

Pola Uttu and Kokmottai. All except the last are beautifully situated, facing large lotus-filled *villus*. Kokmottai is on the bank of the Modaragam Aru river whose waters offer the visitor a cool, very safe and refreshing dip.

Driving Around: The park is interlaced with about 150 miles (240 km) of dry-weather track. The main track and also tracks to some of the bigger *villus* can be approached and traversed by motorcar during dry times and even after moderate rain, but due to the very sandy terrain the visitor who wishes to see most of the park is advised to use a four-wheel drive vehicle.

Unless one is a very keen wildlife observer or photographer, the best way of seeing game in the park would be to drive around the *villu* areas in a vehicle. For the enthusiast or the wildlife photographer, there is a hide at a water hole named **Danggaha Uraniya** which one can reserve for the day. Sitting there silently and patiently can be very rewarding. There are two other water holes with hides, namely **Cheena Uttu** and **Menikrala Uraniya** accessible by four-wheel drive vehicle. Prior reservation is not required.

Spending the night in any one of the lodges would be an experience, but a night

or two at Thala Wila, Mana Wila or Pannikar Villu could be especially memorable as leopards and bears have been seen just a couple of feet from the verandahs. To encourage these animals to visit, all lamps and conversation should be kept down to the lowest possible level.

FOR THE SPECIALIST

In addition to Sri Lanka's major national parks, a selection of which has been described in this guide, more are at the planning or development stage. Two such are **Lunugamwehera** and **Bundala**.

Even in the suburbs of Colombo there are two bird sanctuaries. One surrounds the House of Parliament and the other is at Bellanvilla.

There are many more national parks, and other protected areas such as strict natural reserves, where no one is permitted to enter except for purposes of scientific research. Among these would be the **Somawathiya** and **Wasgomuwa National Parks**, the **Yala Block 2 Strict Natural Reserve** and the **Weeravila Bird Sanctuary**.

Pannikar Villu, Wilpattu, is one of the many water holes.

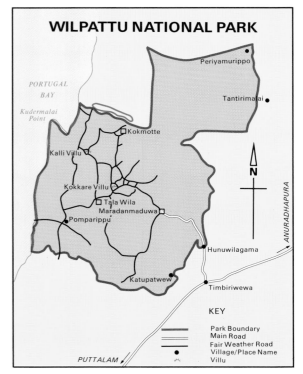

WILPATTU NATIONAL PARK

PORTUGAL BAY

Kudermalai Point

Periyamurippo

Tantirimalai

Kokmotte

Kalli Villu

Kokkare Villu

Tala Wila

Maradanmaduwa

Pomparippu

Hunuwilagama

Katupatwew

Timbiriwewa

ANURADHAPURA

PUTTALAM

KEY
Park Boundary
Main Road
Fair Weather Road
Village/Place Name
Villu

YALA
NATIONAL PARK

Tucked away in the southeast corner of Sri Lanka, almost at the point where the south coast takes its upward curve to the east, is the **Yala National Park**, also known as the Ruhuna National Park, after the ancient name by which the south of Sri Lanka is still known.

The story of this national park goes back to the days of the great kingdom of Ruhuna or Rohana as it was then known. During that period, the area that is now the national park and a vast area surrounding it must have been fairly well developed and populated. The large number of ruins of ancient temples, monasteries and secular buildings that one sees, both within and without the park, bear testimony to this. At one corner of the large Yala plain that gives the park its name, is a fairly large tank, which is today entirely overgrown with tall elephant grass. Archaeologists have identified it as an ancient irrigation tank which supplied water to the surrounding paddy fields, including those in the Yala plain.

Malabar pied hornbill.

As the glory of the Ruhuna kingdom faded, these areas were abandoned and the jungle took over. Many centuries later, under British rule, the area was declared a Residential Sportsmen's Reserve. For a long time after that, hunters, mainly British, enjoyed controlled hunting here. Then on Feb. 25, 1938, the British Government declared it a National Park, thus giving total protection to its fauna and flora. Incidentally, it was on this same day that Wilpattu, on the west coast, was also given the same status.

Another interesting feature in the history of this park is the ancient pilgrim route between Pottuvil and Kataragama that traverses it. Every year, from time immemorial, towards the latter part of July, pilgrims from Pottuvil, an east-coast town, and the surrounding areas start a trek that takes them to the festival at Kataragama, which lies to the west of the park and is the legendary abode of Skanda, the powerful god of war in the Hindu pantheon. The final leg of this route passes through the park, and the pilgrims who walk all the way are permitted to go through without the usual formalities. This practice has caused certain problems for the park authorities but the Government and the Department of Wild Life Conservation are compelled for two weeks each year to turn a blind eye on this disturbance in the even tenor of life in the park. During the 1900s, a man-eating leopard, later called the Pottana man-eater, appeared along this route and many pilgrims fell victim to it.

The Yala "plains": Yala country is generally open, with large grassy areas — the "plains," semi-desert-type brush and gnarled trees, often umbrella-shaped in branch formation; country that strongly reminds one of the African bush.

The term "plains" of Yala, is perhaps a misnomer. These "plains" are really large open glades of many acres that are grassy and dotted with thorny trees and scrub. Most have a couple of water holes in them and are ideal places to see a variety of game and interesting birds. The three best known plains in the park are **Yala**, **Buttawa** and **Uraniya**.

A characteristic feature of the park is the droopy malittan trees (*Saratoga persica*). They are evergreens and even under most severe drought conditions retain their freshness. Another plant that grows in great abundance is the beautiful *Cassia auriculata*, *ranawara* in Sinhala.

As one gets closer to the Menik Ganga (river of gems) which flows along the north-

east border of the park, the dry brush country gives way to vegetation that is more luxuriant in growth and riverine in character. The banks of the river are dominated by the mighty pale-barked kumbuks (*Terminalia arjuna*), whose spreading branches at certain spots form almost a canopy over the murmuring water.

Another feature in the Yala scene is the large rocky outcrops strewn with boulders, favorite haunts of **leopard** and **bear**. The most famous of these is **Vepandeniya**, also known, and for good reason, as **Leopard Rock**. Three other giant megaliths are **Jamburagala**, **Patanangala** and **Akasa Chetiya** (also known as **Elephant Rock** due to its shape). This last one dominates the skyline and Portuguese and Dutch mariners of old used it as a landmark when sailing in these waters.

Elephant Land: Of all the national parks in Sri Lanka, Yala is undoubtedly the finest place to see a variety of species quickly and conveniently. **Elephants** are, of course, its speciality. Except during the very dry months (July — October), a visitor is bound to come across a number of these great creatures even on a half-day tour of the park. The best time to observe them is soon after the rains, when the fresh grasses have

started to grow and the plains have begun to dry again. This period would be from about January to May. Soon after the rains the herds that had migrated northwards during the dry months return to the park and groups of them can be seen scattered over the plains, usually in the evening. Herds of up to 25 or more may be encountered, though this is not common. The usual size of a herd is eight — 10.

Other good places to observe elephants are at the numerous water holes around midday. It has been noticed that certain herds use the same water hole continuously for three or four consecutive days, almost at the same time each day. So, it would be a good idea for a visitor who stays in the park for a few days to observe this and catch the herds at the right place at the right time.

The **tusker** is undoubtedly the most magnificent and also the rarest animal in the Sri Lankan jungles today. Yet, not so long ago, the tusker roamed free and was a common sight before large-scale shooting took a heavy toll of their numbers. Yala could well be proud of its collection of tuskers. Observers have found their numbers in the park have increased during 1984–1986. It is estimated that there are some 18 tuskers in the park, ranging from a

Peacock.

two-foot (60-cm) calf to a nine-foot (three-meter) giant. While this is very encouraging for the wildlife lover, park authorities have a difficult time keeping these tuskers within the park. Despite all their efforts, one of Yala's prime tuskers was shot dead at the beginning of 1986 by poachers just outside park limits, causing a terrific outcry throughout the island. The tusks were recovered following some brilliant police work and the culprits were arrested.

Perhaps it would be fitting to make mention here of Raja, the greatest tusker to ever walk the plains of Yala. He was a majestic bull about nine feet tall and had a pair of great tusks symmetrically curving inwards. At one stage of his life Raja carried a fearful wound near his right armpit, but he totally recovered from this following the administration of a direct antibiotic from a "capture gun." For many years after this Raja was seen in the park, often giving an exhibition of his terrific threat display to any visitor who came upon him unexpectedly at close quarters. When last seen, Raja carried a small wound at the top of his trunk, which nobody realized was a bullet wound, to which before long he succumbed. His skeleton was found within the park long after his death, together with the tusks which were about the heaviest recorded in a Sri Lankan elephant.

Talgasmankade Lodge, Yala National Park.

Most of the elephants at Yala are quite used to vehicles and are easily observed. However, visitors should keep at a fair distance and follow the instructions of their guide very strictly when among these great animals.

Leopard Country: The leopards at Yala are widely distributed and are seen in all sectors of the park. They however favor the more sandy and rocky areas. Ever since the park was established, the Vepandeniya rock has had a pair of resident leopards, perhaps successive generations. Very often visitors see them sunbathing on top of the rock at dawn or dusk. During the mid-morning and early afternoon hours, these cats usually go up the trees and are seen stretched out lazily on the branches of tamarind or wood apple. The leopard here tend to be rather shy and visitors should avoid making any sudden movement when they come across them.

Except during the rains or after a heavy shower, visitors would be very lucky to see a bear. They are not uncommon but not often seen. The best time of the year to look for bear, when one is bound to come across two

or three of them in a day, is late May and June, when their favorite fruits, the palu (*Manilkara hexandra*) and the veera (*Drypetus sepieria*) are ripe.

Among the other animals which may be seen both in Yala and other parks in Sri Lanka are two species of monkey (the **gray langur** and the **torque**), four types of deer (**sambar**, and the **spotted, barking** and **mouse deer**), **buffalo** and **crocodiles**. These last may be seen at all the water holes and along the banks of the Menik river. They are very wary and shy, unlike their more aggressive and larger estuarine counterparts found in the lagoons in the park.

Birds: Yala is a bird watchers' paradise. One of the glorious sights of the park is the mating dance of the **peacock**. Between November and February even a few hours of watching will yield sights of a number of these displays.

Among the numerous avian types found at Yala is the rare **black-necked stork**. It is feared that no more than a dozen survive on the island. When they are sighted, more often than not they are seen as a pair searching for prey in the **Buttawa lagoon**.

Yala offers an interesting range of birds of prey and between September and May the migrants. Visitors who stay at the lodges near the river should keep a look-out for the elusive **Indian paradise flycatcher** and one of the world's greatest songsters, the **Ceylon shama**. Two other common but intriguing birds widely seen are the **Malabar pied hornbill** and the **hoopoe**.

Yala is a well-organized national park with a total extent of 377 sq miles (976 sq km) of which only 52 (135 sq km) are used for game viewing. The park is well roaded and throughout the year most of it can be covered by two-wheel drive vehicles.

There are six lodges in the park: **Mahaseelawa, Buttawa, Patanangala, Yala, Talgasmankade** and **Heenwewa**. They are all superbly situated, two by the Menik river, two looking out to sea, and two overlooking jungle tanks. All these lodges are well-located for seeing animals, especially elephants who at times come up to the doorstep.

For the more outdoor types, Yala offers two campsites, both situated picturesquely by the Menik river. During the dry weather, when almost all the water holes are dry, one can see from these campsites groups of elephants coming down to the almost dry bed of the river and digging for water.

The park is usually closed to visitors from August 1 to October 18 every year.

RUHUNA NATIONAL PARK

YALA EAST N.P.

KEY

Park Boundary
Metalled Road
Unmetalled Road
Path
Water Hole/Tank
Passenger Alight Point
Rest House
Village/Place
Hills/Outcrops

SRI LANKA'S NATIONAL PARKS

Uda Walawe National Park: Lying south of the central hills of Sri Lanka is this 119-sq-mile (308-sq-km) park, established with the prime objective of conserving the catchment area of the Uda Walawe reservoir. Today, a large variety of game, especially elephants from the heavily exploited jungles around have found protection here and have made it their home.

Still under development, the park has 20 miles (32 km) of dry-weather road and six miles (10 km) of jeep track. Due to this area having been heavily exploited in the past for *chena* (slash and burn) farming, a part of the park is devoid of forest cover and, except in the months of June–September, is almost entirely covered by a tall golden grass which makes game viewing in these parts difficult. After September, the grass dies, transforming the whole area into parkland. Close to the river Walawe one encounters fairly heavy forest cover which includes two species of trees not found in other Sri Lankan national parks, the mandorang (*Vatica sinensis*) and daminiya (*Grewia tiliifolia*).

The **elephants** seen here are magnificent specimens and large herds wander along the river and sometimes in the plains. They are very wild and shy and make off at the first whiff of man. Leopards and bears have rarely been sighted. The park is superb for bird-watching, especially for the more uncommon species.

Two campsites are available, both by the river, under a canopy of large trees, amidst scenery that could hardly be bettered.

Lahugala National Park: The lodge at Lahugala is undoubtedly the finest place in Sri Lanka from which to watch wild elephant without much ado and in comfort.

The six square miles (15.5 sq km) encompass two former irrigation tanks, **Lahugala** and **Kitulana**, which are both completely covered by a tall succulent grass called beru (*Oplismenus compositus*), a favorite of the elephants. These two tanks lie slap in the middle of the elephant corridor that connects the Yala region to the Gal Oya region. Thus, one is almost assured of seeing elephants here, throughout the day, every day of the year. Herds in excess of 150 animals have been recorded.

While the two tanks are also famous for their birdlife, mostly aquatic types and birds of prey, the quarter-mile (400-meter) strip of dense forest south of the tanks and north of the Heda Oya (river) offers the visitor some rare species like the elusive **red faced malkoha** and the **blue magpie**.

Leopard and bear are extremely rare here but have been seen on the road leading to the lodge and also by the tank.

The area immediately surrounding the Lahugala lodge and the rocks behind are also fine places to study a variety of uncommon **butterflies**.

Maduru Oya National Park: Established in November 1983, this is Sri Lanka's newest national park and is still at the beginning of its development. It is situated east of ancient Polonnaruwa. It has been established primarily to conserve the catchment area of the three reservoirs — Maduru Oya, Ulhitiya and Ratkinda — and to provide a secure home for the magnificent **marsh elephant** whose environment has been depleted by agricultural development. Also a proposed corridor to Gal Oya will complete the chain of connected National Parks ending at Yala in the south.

At present, the park is fairly open country consisting of mainly bush type vegetation which gives way to fairly dense forest along the Maduru Oya river.

Leopard and bear have been seen while herds of deer and sambar have just started moving in. Birdlife of all kinds is plentiful.

There is still no accommodation or established campsite available within the park.

Yala East National Park: Yala East is one of the most scenic national parks in Sri Lanka and is situated northeast of Yala.

The vegetation here is semi-arid, with large open areas. During the flowering season the yellow blossoms of the *Crataeva roxburgiana* make the park even more attractive.

The 16-mile (25-km) main track starts at Okanda. It is motorable in dry weather. Another 30 miles (48 km) of rough jeep track are also available. Along the main track, one comes across some very picturesque lakelets, plains and four saline lagoons. During the migratory season, the lagoons are filled with **ducks**, mostly **pintail** and **garganey**.

The big game found here are elephants, sometimes in large herds, **leopards** and **bears**, the last found in the more forested areas of the park. Yala East is another place in which to watch out for the red-faced

Spot-billed pelicans, Gal Oya.

malkoha and the blue magpie.

The main attraction of the park however is the **Kumana mangrove swamp**. This is the only place in the island with such large concentrations of resident birds gathered for nesting. This is usually around June and July.

Boating facilities are available at Kumana. Two lodges are available for overnight stay.

Gal Oya National Park: The mighty Senanayake Samudra reservoir in Sri Lanka is totally encompassed by this national park which was established to conserve its catchment area. Today it has become an elephant playground. It lies east of the central hills of the island.

The park has no roads, but boating is available in the reservoir. During the dry season large herds of elephants can be seen cooling off and drinking at the water's edge. This could well be the only place where one can see groups of these great creatures swimming across deep water to the numerous islands to feed on the succulent grass growing on them. When the elephants are swimming in deep water, they can be approached easily by boat.

The reservoir is also the home of millions of birds, all aquatic types, and among them would be the **cormorants**, **darters**, **pelicans** and a variety of **gulls**. During the nesting season, a boat will be literally surrounded by these flocks, as they swim along with it. Birds of prey too are plentiful. This is the best place to observe the majestic **white-bellied sea eagle** and the **tank eagle**, the island's two largest birds of prey.

About a quarter of the park is dry evergreen forest while the rest is tall grassland savanna. An interesting feature of the vegetation here is the extensive areas under medicinal plants. These were first laid by ancient Sinhala monarchs and have survived to this day.

A privately owned spacious hotel and a jungle lodge are available for overnight stay.

Sinharaja Forest Reserve: Though declared a forest reserve and very soon going to be given total protection on being named a "National Heritage," Sinharaja is as yet undeveloped for visitors. However, excursions can be made into the reserve and travel agents should be able to put one in touch with those who can arrange these visits.

Sinharaja is a small belt of forest no more than four miles (6.5 km) at its widest and half a mile (800 meters) at its narrowest point. Its total area is only about 21,000 acres (8500 hectares). Yet what makes Sinharaja unique is that it is the only patch of primeval forest remaining in any significant proportions in Sri Lanka.

The vegetation of Sinharaja is worth looking at. Three-fourths of the total or 125 species of trees there are endemic. An International Union for the Conservation of Nature report states that many of the endemic trees are also dominant components of the canopy, representing an important gene pool found nowhere else in the world.

Though controlled logging which directly threatened this patch of primeval tropical rain forest some years ago has been stopped, illicit logging still continues to a minor extent.

Sinharaja is also the home of all types of the island's wildlife, small and big, excepting the elephant, including some unique insect species.

Horton Plains: At an elevation of 7200 feet (2200 meters) on the Haputale range in Sri Lanka is a saddle of rolling *patnas* or grassland and stark evergreen montane forest known as the Horton Plains. This is one of the most forbidding yet most stupendously beautiful places on the island.

The main attractions here are the two "world's ends," from where one can see the escarpment fall vertically 900 feet (280 meters) from one and a dramatic 2900 feet (900 meters) from the other.

The second and third highest peaks in the island, **Kirigalpotha** and **Thotupola**, are also easily accessible from the plains, while two other eye-catchers are **Bakers Falls** and the **Slab-rock Falls**.

Magnificent specimens of leopard are met with, though rarely, while **sambar** can be seen daily on the plains. Two types of monkeys are also seen, the **purple-faced leaf monkey** and the **highland torque monkey**, both of which are confined to the hills.

Among the reptiles found here are three unique species — the **nose horned lizard** (*Cerataphora stodarti*), the *Calotes nigrilabris* and the *Cophotes ceylonica*.

The **yellow-eared bulbul**, the **dusky blue flycatcher** and the **Ceylon white eye** are endemic birds seen here amongst a host of other birds that are confined to the hills. The most majestic of them is the powerful **mountain hawk eagle**.

Permits for camping and trout fishing can be obtained from the Department of Wild Life.

Far left (above), **pheasant-tailed jacana** *and below,* **mugger crocodile with cormorants.** *Left,* **sambar in velvet.** *Following pages,* **Bandipur water hole.**

TRAVEL TIPS

GETTING THERE

Most visitors arrive by air to one of the main international airports. India: Indira Gandhi International (Delhi), Sahar (Bombay), DumDum (Calcutta) or Meenambakam (Madras); Nepal: Tribhuvan International (Kathmandu); and Sri Lanka: Katunayake International (Colombo).

INDIA

Both Delhi and Bombay are well connected with direct flights from all parts of the world. Calcutta has flights from/to London, Moscow, Kathmandu, Bangkok and Rangoon; Madras with Kuala Lumpur, Singapore and Colombo. Other international airports are Amritsar (flights from Kabul), Patna and Varanasi (flights from Kathmandu), Dabolim Goa (charters from Europe), Trivandrum (flights from the Gulf region), Hyderabad and Bangalore.

The four major airports at Delhi, Bombay, Madras and Calcutta are being constantly improved on and all have left baggage facilities, also porter and licensed taxi services. At Delhi and Bombay a prepayment system for taxis into the city is operated by the police and this saves considerable anguish when the occasional unscrupulous driver takes a long route or tries to overcharge. Delhi and Bombay airports also have restrooms.

Duty-free shops are found in both the arrival and departure halls of all four major airports. Departing passengers pay an airport tax of Rs. 100 per passenger (Rs. 50 if flying to a neighboring country).

Major hotels operate courtesy buses and a public service known as EATS (Ex Serviceman Transport Service) operates in Delhi, Bombay and Calcutta with stops at hotels and major centers enroute to the city center.

NEPAL

Nepal has only one international airport with daily flights from India (Delhi, Patna, Varanasi and Calcutta) and Thailand (Bangkok). There are also frequent connections with Munich, Frankfurt, Dubai, Karachi, Colombo, Rangoon, Singapore and Hong Kong. When traveling to Nepal from the west, sit on the left side of the aircraft to get possible views of the Himalaya.

An airport tax is levied on all departures. There is a duty-free shop in the arrival hall.

SRI LANKA

Colombo has good connections with Europe and Southeast Asia. Air Lanka has an expanding network. For regional travel Colombo has flights from/to Bombay, Trivandrum, Tiruchirapally and Madras in India, Kathmandu and Male in the Maldives. The Katunayake International airport is 21 miles (34 km) from the center of Colombo.

Since the Iraq-Iran war and the Soviet invasion of Afganistan, the overland route to India and on to Nepal or Sri Lanka from Europe has become hazardous and inadvisable. A few European operators do, however, still offer overland tours.

TRAVEL ESSENTIALS

VISAS & PASSPORTS

All visitors to India or Nepal require a valid visa. These are available from embassies or high commissions in most major capitals. (Nepal does not have many representatives so it may be necessary to send the application to another country or obtain a visa in the Nepalese Embassy in Delhi, Bangkok or Colombo.) Any visitor visiting any country more than once on a particular tour should obtain a multiple entry visa.

Indian and Nepalese tourist visas have a lease of up to three months and Indian visas can be extended by another three. Make applications to the Foreigners Registration Offices in major cities or the Superintendent of Police in District Headquarters.

Restricted area and Inner line permits in India can be applied for through embassies and high commissions. In New Delhi, applications are made through the Ministry of Home Affairs (Foreigners Wing), Lok Nayak Bhawan, Khan Market, New Delhi 110003. Allow a minimum of six weeks.

For travel in Nepal outside the *terai*, Kathmandu and Pokhara valleys trekking permits are required. These can be obtained either directly in Kathmandu or through one of the many travel and trekking agencies.

Not all nationals require visas to enter Sri Lanka but the situation is changing and the traveler is advised to contact the local embassy or high commission before departing. Special permits are required to visit the north and these are obtained in Colombo.

For detailed travel information applicable to India, Nepal and Sri Lanka the traveler is directed to the respective *Insight Guide* of each country in publication.

HEALTH

In Nepal, the towns and villages of the *terai* have pharmacies but many of the hill villages do not. In larger towns there are 24-hour pharmacies.

In India and Sri Lanka, private nursing homes and hospitals are found in the larger towns, whose hotels have doctors on 24-hour call as well. Each district-headquarter has its own government hospital or at least a dispensary or health center in smaller towns.

Because of their remoteness, many national parks are without any medical facilites, although some basic aids should be available at each park headquarters. It is therefore advisable that some simple medical aids be carried when visiting remote areas for more than a few days. Longer trips into the Himalaya of course demand a more comprehensive kit.

Malaria is still prevalent in many parks of the subcontinent and some form of anti-malarial should be taken 10 days before, during and for at least six weeks after leaving an infected area. You should consult your doctor as to which type is most suitable for the area you are visiting.

A lot of useful information can be obtained from a number of books. See *Further Reading* for a list of them.

If you are planning to stay in a remote area, many recommend the stocking of (two ampoules) snake antivenom serum. It is manufactured by and can be ordered from the Serum Institute, M.G. Road, Pune, Maharashtra, and remains effective for five years, without refrigeration.

PHOTOGRAPHY

Any recommendations with regard to equipment given by one professional is liable to be disputed by another. There are, though, certain pieces of advice that can be given without fear of contradiction.

Considerable skill is required to photograph insects, flowers and trees in their natural environment and lengthy preparation is often required. Animals, on the other hand, are perhaps surprisingly easier to photograph. Most travelers use one of the many makes of 35 mm SLR cameras, each of which has a facility to change lenses. Unless otherwise stated, all comments refer to this type of equipment.

Unlike the Galapagos islands or Antarctica, nowhere in South Asia are standard lenses adequate for photographing wild animals. Telephoto lenses from 180 mm upward are required for most animal photographs, 35 mm or 28 mm wideangle lenses are extremely useful for striking scenic or environmental pictures. Also, a tripod or monopod is extremely useful, especially when using telephoto lenses.

There are few places in South Asia where prompt and reliable camera servicing can be had, so equipment should be checked before arriving in India. If your equipment is new, it is advisable to shoot a test roll before leaving home to ensure you are familiar with the equipment and that everything is working as expected.

Carrying an extra body not only gives flexibility in using alternative lenses or film types, but also acts as a back-up in case of mechanical or electrical failure.

Film is generally not easily available and when found, may not be of the type you are used to. Carry more film than you think you'll need. Surplus film can be used as presents and is always greatly appreciated.

Having to use telephoto lenses and the poor light conditions of the jungle often means that excellent high-resolution film such as Kodachrome 25 or 64 is not fast enough. Higher speed Ektachrome or Fujichrome lack a certain quality but do give flexibility in poor light. The same applies to print or negative film.

PARKS & RESERVES

INDIA

Much of India's wilderness now falls within areas giving legal protection to the many species and the flora within them. Some of these protected areas are small, obscure and extremely difficult to reach. Many have little or no accommodation and are in no way capable of accommodating visitors. Others have a variety of accommodation ranging from forest bungalows, resthouses and Public Works Department (PWD) bungalows to deluxe tented camps and lodges. The list that follows shortly is as comprehensive as possible within the needs of this volume. Basic information, such as location, status, access and accommodation, is given along with an indication of the major mammals, birds, reptiles and flora that are to be found.

Even when a resthouse is available, the facilities may be limited. In many areas there is only a building with basic furniture—the visitor must bring his/her own food and bedding. A contact address is given wherever possible and bookings can be made by post. Some parks have a wider range of facilities provided by State Tourism Corporations, the Indian Tourism Development Corporation (ITDC) and private companies. Bookings for these can be made through most travel agencies.

All areas are listed alphabetically within an alphabetical listing of states and union territories.

There are 55 national parks and 247 sanctuaries in India constituted under the Wildlife (Protection) Act of 1972 covering a total of approximately 35,000 sq miles (90,000 sq km). This is about 3 percent of the total land area of Indian compared to almost 12 per-

cent in Sri Lanka.

In early 1986, the status of national parks and sanctuaries in India was as follows:
(*In the listing figures not within brackets mean number of national parks and figures within brackets, sanctuaries. For example, Rajasthan has 4 national parks and 19 sanctuaries.*)

Andaman and Nicobar Islands; 6 (5)
Andhra Pradesh; (14)
Arunachal Pradesh; 1 (4)
Assam; 1 (8)
Bihar; (13)
Chandigarh; (1)
Goa, Daman & Diu; 1 (3)
Gujarat; 4 (12)
Haryana; (1)
Himachal Pradesh; 2 (28)
Jammu & Kashmir; 4 (6)
Karnataka; 3 (16)
Kerala; 3 (11)
Maharashtra; 4 (10)
Madhya Pradesh; 11 (31)
Manipur; 2
Meghalaya; (2)
Mizoram; (1)
Nagaland; (3)
Orissa; 1 (15)
Punjab; (5)
Rajasthan; 4 (19)
Sikkim; 1 (3)
Tamil Nadu; 2 (10)
Uttar Pradesh; 4 (13)
West Bengal; 1 (13)

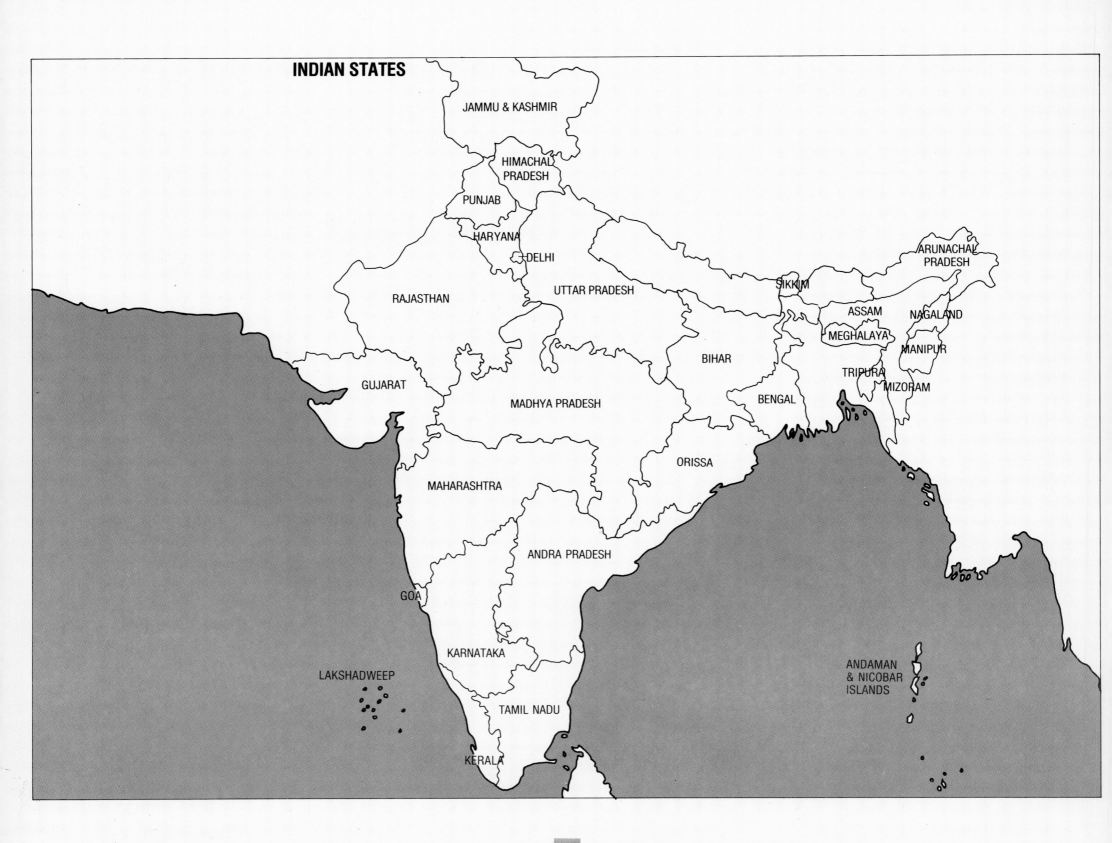

INDIAN STATES

JAMMU & KASHMIR

HIMACHAL PRADESH

PUNJAB

HARYANA

DELHI

ARUNACHAL PRADESH

SIKKIM

RAJASTHAN

UTTAR PRADESH

ASSAM

NAGALAND

MEGHALAYA

MANIPUR

BIHAR

TRIPURA

MIZORAM

GUJARAT

MADHYA PRADESH

BENGAL

ORISSA

MAHARASHTRA

ANDRA PRADESH

GOA

KARNATAKA

LAKSHADWEEP

ANDAMAN & NICOBAR ISLANDS

TAMIL NADU

KERALA

ANDAMAN & NICOBAR ISLANDS:

These islands lying in the Bay of Bengal were once a hill range stretching from Sumatra (Indonesia), 75 miles (120 km) to the south, to Burma. Many of the islands are still covered with rich tropical evergreen and tropical moist deciduous forests and are home to many endemic birds and reptiles. Most of the mammals are introduced species. Not only is the bird and forest life fascinating, but many islands are home to ancient and highly threatened tribes struggling to maintain their traditions and identity despite the pressure from the 20th century. Although the first outside permanent settlement was established by Lieutenant Archibald Blair in 1789, the islands had been recorded in the 9th century by Arab merchants sailing to Sumatra. For a short time prior to Blair's survey the Danes had a settlement in the Nicobars.

Visitors to the islands enter by sea or air from Madras and Calcutta via the capital, Port Blair. Only a few islands can be visited and many sanctuaries are in fact closed. Permits for up to a two-week visit to the "open" areas (Port Blair, Jolly Buoy and Cinque Island) are available on arrival in India but permission to visit Car Nicobar, Neil and Havelock Islands must be applied for locally although the application might be referred to Delhi for clearance.

The temperature of the islands ranges from 68°F-86°F (20-30°C) with the rainy season from June to October.

Middle Button Island N.P. (plus North Button Island N.P. & South Button Island N.P.) Established in 1979 (the southern park was established in 1977), these small island parks have few land mammals. The dolphin and dugong are often sighted near the coast and the water monitor lizard is also found.
Best time to visit: Jan.-Mar.
Accommodation: none
Permission: DFO, Middle Andaman, Long Island, A & N Islands 744203
Nearest town: Long Island (38 miles/60 km)

Mount Harriet N.P. Established in 1979, this small park of only 18 sq miles (47 sq km) is prime habitat for the Andaman wild pig.
Best time to visit: Jan. & Feb.
Accommodation: 1 bungalow (four beds)

Permission: DFO, South Andaman Division
Nearest town: Port Blair (10 miles/16 km)

Saddle Peak N.P. Established in 1979, this park rises from sea level to 2421 feet (738 meters) at the summit of Saddle Peak on North Andaman Island. To be seen are not only a magnificent display of birdlife, including the Andaman hill myna and Andaman imperial pigeon, but also wild pig, salt water crocodile and other reptiles.
Best time to visit: Nov.-Apr.
Accommodation: 2 forest resthouses
Permission: DFO, Middle Andaman, Long Island, A & N Islands 7442203
Nearest town: Diglipur (3 miles/5 km)

Barren Island Sanctuary. Established in 1977, this island of only 3 sq miles (8 sq km) is, as its name suggests, almost barren. The waters around the island are home to dolphins and dugongs.
Best time to visit: Jan.-Mar.
Accommodation: none
Permission: DFO cum W.L. Warden, North Andaman Division
Nearest town: Long Island (38 miles)

Crocodile Sanctuary. Established in 1983, this sanctuary is home to important marine reptiles including green-sea, leather-backed, olive ridley and hawksbill turtles and salt-water crocodiles. The birdlife includes the white-bellied sea eagle, Andaman wood pigeon and Andaman teal.
Best time to visit: Jan.-May
Accommodation: 1 resthouse
Permission: DCF (W.L.), Port Blair
Nearest town: Port Blair (19 miles/30 km)

Narcondum Island Sanctuary. Established in 1977 to protect the sole habitat of the narcondum hornbill (*Rhytidoceros narcondami*) which lives in the forest covering the lower slopes of the main peak.
Best time to visit: Nov.-Apr.
Accommodation: none
Permission: DFO/WL Warden, North Andaman Division
Nearest town: Port Blair (160 miles by sea)

North Reef Island Sanctuary. Established in 1977 on a small island to the west of North Andaman to protect Andaman teal and Nicobar pigeon habitat.
Best time to visit: Nov.-Apr.
Accommodation: none
Permission: DFO/WL Warden, North Andaman Division
Nearest town: Maya Bundar (18 miles)

South Sentinel Sanctuary. Established in 1977 as a marine sanctuary on this island, with an area of only about half a sq mile (1.6 km), as its nucleus. Green-sea, olive ridley and leader-backed turtles all lay eggs here and the white-bellied sea eagle hunts in the surrounding waters.
Best time to visit: Jan.-May
Accommodation: none
Permission: DFO (WL), Port Blair
Nearest town: Port Blair (78 miles/125 km)

ANDHRA PRADESH:

The largest of the four South Indian states, Andhra Pradesh, has a varied terrain with a rich and interesting population of birds and animals. Although it has 14 sanctuaries, including the large Nagarjunasagar Tiger Reserve, it has no area with national park status. While most of the sanctuaries have accommodation, the tourist infrastructure is limited and visitors have to make their own arrangements in most cases. For up-to-date information, contact: The Chief Wildlife Warden, Saifabad, Hyderabad, AP 500004.

Andhra has a long coastline with two great rivers (the Godavari and the Krishna) flowing west to east into the Bay of Bengal. There are mangrove forests along the estuaries, dry deciduous forests inland, and extensive open scrub stretching into the Deccan plateau. The Pulicat Lake is one of South Asia's

largest lagoons and an important center for both resident and migratory waterbirds.

Coringa Sanctuary. Established in 1978, this area of 90 sq miles (235 sq km) in the delta region of the Godavari river is home to otters, fishing cats, the estuarine crocodile (*Crocodylus porosus*) and many water birds.
Best time to visit: Nov.-Mar. (summer temperatures up to 96°F/36°C)
Accommodation: resthouse
Permission: DCF (WL Management), Rajahmundry.
Nearest town: Kakinada (12.5 miles/20 km) with railhead. Accommodation and transport are available in the town.

Eturnagaram Sanctuary. Established in 1953, this large sanctuary covering 313.5 sq miles (812 sq km) of dry deciduous mixed forest near the borders of Maharashtra, Madhya Pradesh and Andhra is the habitat of many mammals (tiger, leopard, sloth bear, chousingha, chinkara, mouse deer, blackbuck and leopard cat) and interesting birdlife. The forest department has both vehicles and *machans* for game viewing.
Best time to visit: Mar.-May (up to 114°F/ 46°C); Nov.-Mar. are cooler months.
Accommodation: 8 guest cottages (22 beds); forest resthouses at Salvai, Tadavai and Eturnagaram town
Permission: DFO Warangal. AP 506010
Nearest town: Eturnagaram (10 miles)
Rail: Warangal (56 miles/90 km)
Airport: Hyderabad (140 miles/225 km)

Kawal Sanctuary. Established in 1965, this sanctuary covering 345 sq miles (893 sq km) of dry deciduous hill forest with dry teak stands over uneven terrain contains tiger, leopard, sloth bear, gaur and chousingha among others.
Best time to visit: Feb.-May (up to 112°F)
Accommodation: 2 resthouses
Permission: DFO (WL), Jannaram, Adilabad Dist. AP 504205
Nearest town: Jannaram (o.5 mile/1 km)
Rail: Mancherial (30 miles/60 km), Hyderabad (175 miles/280 km)

Kinnersani Sanctuary. Established in 1977 with a core area of 86 sq miles (222 sq km) and a buffer zone 160 sq miles (413 sq

km), this undulating sanctuary of mixed forest surrounding the Kinnersani Reservoir has a good range of mammal and bird species, including tiger, dhole, leopard, guar, wild buffalo and sloth bear.
Best time to visit: Nov.-June (summer maximum 120°F/49°C drops to 50°F/10°C in January)
Accommodation: 7 small resthouses
Permission: Wildlife Warden, Poloncha, Khamman Distt., AP
Nearest town: Paloncha (7.5 miles/12 km)
Rail: Bhadrachalam Road (15 miles/24 km)
Air: Vijayawada (106 miles/170 km)

Kolleru Sanctuary. Established in 1963, this large bird sanctuary of almost 347 sq miles (900 sq km) wetland and marsh surrounds the Kolleru Lake, between the Krishna and Godavari deltas. Water, after the northeast monsoon, extends over 232 sq miles (600 sq km). Many migratory ducks and resident water birds and the famous pelicanry at the village of Aredu use the lake for feeding.
Best time to visit: late Oct.-Feb.
Accommodation: 5 huts; PWD resthouse at Eluru
Permission: DCF (WL), Rajahmundry, AP
Nearest town & Rail: Eluru (12.5 miles)
Air: Vijayawada (40 miles/63 km)

Manjira Sanctuary. Established in 1978, this small pocket of riverain forest on the banks of the river Manjira is only 12.5 sq miles (20 sq km) in extent. Many water birds and mugger crocodiles; also two species of freshwater turtles.
Best time to visit: Nov.-Feb.(cool), and Mar.-June
Accommodation: small resthouse

Permission: DFO (WL), Medak, AP.
Nearest town: Sangareddy (2.5 miles/5 km)
Rail: Ramachandrapuram (15.5 miles)
Air: Hyderabad (34 miles/55 km)

Nagarjunasagar Srisailam Sanctuary (Tiger Reserve). Established in 1978, this sanctuary of 1374 sq miles (3560 sq km) is the largest of India's tiger reserves, with a core area of 463 sq miles (1200 sq km). A dam across the Krishna river forms the Nagarjunasagar reservoir. The area is dissected by deep winding gorges which cut through the Mallamalai hills. A range of forest types, from dry scrub and dry mixed deciduous forests on the plateau to the west and south to moist valleys with bamboo and tropical thorn forest to the east. Since the sanctuary came under Project Tiger in 1983 a program to relocate the villages inside the core area is now under way. With the reduction of human interference and the stopping of grazing this sanctuary could soon become a major park. The range of animals includes leopard, sloth bear, palm civet, wolf, striped hyena, in addition to tiger. Also found are barking deer, nilgai, chinkara, chousingha, sambar, chital, langur, bonnet macaque and the Indian pangolin.
Best time to visit: Oct.-June (summer maximum 108°F/43°C).
Accommodation: 3 guesthouses next to temples within the sanctuary.
Permission: Field Director, Project Tiger, Srisailam Dam East, AP 512102
Nearest town & Rail: Machesla (8 miles)
Air: Hyderabad (94 miles/150 km)

Neelapattu Sanctuary. Established in 1976, this small waterbird sanctuary at the coastal village of Neelapattu covers only 1.5 sq miles (4.5 sq km). The focal point is the village tank which, during the winter, becomes a large and mixed heronry.
Best time to visit: Nov.-Mar.
Accommodation: PWD resthouse at Sulurpetta
Permission: ACF (WLM), Sulurpetta, Nellore Dist, AP
Nearest town: Sulurpetta (10 miles/16 km)
Rail: Dorawai Satram (1 km)
Air: Madras (75miles/120 km)

Pakhal Sanctuary. Established in 1952, this sanctuary of 344 sq miles (892 sq km) of forest includes a large lake. Interesting birdlife and an extensive range of mammals.
Best time to visit: Nov.-June
Accommodation: 2 guesthouses
Permission: DFO (WLM), Warangal, AP 506010
Nearest town: Narsampet (6.25 miles)
Rail: Warangal (28 miles/45 km)
Air: Hyderabad (112 miles/180 km)

Papikonda Sanctuary. Established in 1978, 228 sq miles (590 sq km) of mixed forest on the banks of the Godavari as it cuts through the Eastern Ghats, with a core area of 85 sq miles (221 sq km). Many steep slopes of the Papikonda range give the sanctuary its name. Animals include tiger, leopard, chousingha and wolf and waterbirds.
Best time to visit: Nov.-June
Accommodation: 2 resthouses
Permission: DCF (WLM), Rajahmundry, AP
Nearest town & Rail & Air: Rajahmundry (50 miles/80 km)

Pocharam Sanctuary. Established in 1952 on the banks of the Pocharam Lake on 50 sq miles (129 sq km) of scrub and mixed forest. Contains leopard, sloth bear, wolf, wild boar and chousingha with flamingoes and other water birds at the lake.
Best time to visit: late Oct.-May
Accommodation: 2 bungalows
Permission: DFO (WLM), Medak, AP
Nearest town: Medak (5.6 miles/9 km)
Rail: Akkannapet (9.4 miles/15 km)
Air: Hyderabad (72miles/115 km)

Pranahita Sanctuary. Established in 1980 along the river Pranahita on 52 sq miles (136 sq km) of mixed teak forest holding a few gaur, tiger, leopard, sloth bear, chousingha and others and a few water birds.
Best time to visit: Nov.-May
Accommodation: 2 resthouses
Permission: DCF (WLM), Rajahmundry, AP
Nearest town & Rail & Air: Rajahmundry (50 miles/80 km)

Pulicat Sanctuary. Established in 1976, the southeastern mouth of this large lagoon is in Tamil Nadu. Of the 224 sq miles (580 sq km), about 193 sq miles (500 sq km) are in Andhra. Flocks of flamingo, many migrant shore birds, and local residents are seen. Boats are available in the early morning.
Best time to visit: Oct.-Mar.
Accommodation: small guesthouse
Permission: ACF (WLM), Sulurpetta, Nellore Dist, AP
Nearest town & Rail: Sulurpetta (5 miles)
Air: Madras (63 miles/100 km)

Siwaram Sanctuary. Established in 1978, this small sanctuary of undulating forest on the Godavari river near the Madhya Pradesh border holds a wide range of mammals and birdlife.
Best time to visit: Nov.-Mar.
Accommodation: 3 resthouses
Permission: DFO (WLM), Jannaram, Adilabad Dist, AP 504205
Nearest town: Manthani (3 miles/5 km)
Rail: Peddalpalli (19 miles/30 km)
Air: Hyderabad (187 miles/300 km)

ARUNACHAL PRADESH: Being close to the Chinese border, this area is sensitive and most of the region is closed to tourism. Permits for the "open areas" can be applied through Indian embassies and high commissions abroad or from the Ministry of Home Affairs (Foreigners Wing), Lok Nayak Bhawan, Khan Market, New Delhi 110003. Allow at least six to eight weeks for the application to be processed.

The area has a rich and varied tribal culture with the 650,000 population drawn from 82 mongoloid and Tibeto-Burmese tribes. There are reports that a recently discovered community living in caves and eating food raw, has not yet discovered fire. The birdlife of Arunachal, as with most northeastern India is extensive and still little known.

Itanagar Sanctuary. Established in 1978 on 54 sq miles (140 sq km) of semi-evergreen forest with a small tiger population and visiting herds of elephant. The area is hilly with the highest point at 3820 feet (2264 meters).
Best time to visit: Oct.-Apr.
Accommodation: 3 resthouses
Permission: Dy. Chief Wildlife Warden, PO Nahar Lagun, Arunachal Pradesh 791110
Nearest town: Itanagar (9.5 miles/15 km)
Rail: Hamati (13.75 miles/22 km)
Air: Lilabari (42 miles/67 km)

Lali Sanctuary. Established in 1978 at the base of the eastern Himalaya, covering an area of 77.3 sq miles (190 sq km). The sanctuary holds swamp deer and wild buffalo, among other mammals.
Best time to visit: Nov.-Mar.
Permission: ACF (WL), PO Pasighat, Dist: East Siang, Arunachal Pradesh 791102
Nearest town: Pasighat (10 miles/16 km)
Rail: Morkongselak (22.5 miles/36 km)
Air: Lilabari (125 miles/200 km)

Mehao Sanctuary. Established in 1980, this sanctuary of extremely high rainfall (165 inches/419 cm) ranges from 1313 feet (400 meters) to cover 11,500 feet (3500 meters) in the Mishmi Hills. The fascinating range of wildlife here includes clouded leopard, Hoolock gibbon, leopard cat, musk deer, spotted linsang and swamp deer.
Best time to visit: Nov.-Mar.

Accommodation: 5 resthouses
Permission: ACF, PO Roing, Dist: Dibang Valley, Arunachal Pradesh.
Nearest town: Roing (16.25 miles/10 km)
Rail: Tinsukia (175 miles/120 km)
Air: Tezu

Namdapha N.P. Established in 1972, this park and tiger reserve has perhaps the widest diversity of habitats of any of South Asia's protected areas. It is the only area with three major predators: the tiger, leopard and clouded leopard. The snow leopard is a possible fourth. The park's 698 sq miles (1807 sq km) rise from 650 feet (200 meters) to 14,800 feet (4500 meters) above mean sea level and the forest ranges from wet evergreen forest at the lower levels through mixed deciduous forest to temperate alpine forest at the upper reaches. Three major rivers drain the area and run into the Noa-Dehing river and then the Brahmaputra. The diverse habitats and local climates hold a fascinating mix of Indo-Burmese, Indo-Chinese and Himalayan wildlife. The mammals include gaur, goral, takin, musk deer, Hoolock gibbon, slow loris, binturong and red panda, apart from the major predators. Hornbills and pheasants are among the great range of birds. Access to the area is difficult and this has helped keep much of it unspoilt. It is important to Project Tiger as the northeasternmost limit to the Indian tiger's range. The area is a proposed biosphere reserve and extensions are planned.
Best time to visit: Oct.-Mar.
Accommodation: Resthouses at Namchik, Miao and Deban
Permission: Field Director-Project Tiger, PO Miao, Dist: Tirap, AP
Nearest town: Margheritta (39 miles/62 km)
Rail: Ledo (35 miles/56 km)
Air: Dibrugarh (102 miles/163 km)

Pakhui Sanctuary. Established in 1977 in the southwestern part of Arunachal Pradesh over 333 sq miles (862 sq m) of the Dafla Hills at the base of the Eastern Himalaya. The mixed forest includes elephant, tiger, leopard, sloth bear and slow loris.
Best time to visit: Dec.-Mar.
Accommodation: 4 resthouses
Permission: DFO, Pakhui WL Division, PO Seipre, Dist: East Kameng, AP
Nearest town & Air: Tezpur, Assam (41 miles/65 km)
Rail: Rangapara North (32.5 miles/52 km)

ASSAM: Today's state of Assam follows the course of the Brahmaputra river from the point where it leaves the Eastern Himalaya in Arunachal Pradesh until it turns south into Bangladesh. Traditionally known for its tea, its forests and its wildlife, Assam is a fascinating mix of industry (10 percent of India's oil is produced near Duliajan), agriculture, history, religion, and great natural beauty.

Some of Asia's conservation successes have been in Assam. The Indian one-horned rhinoceros was on the brink of extinction 50 years ago but, thanks to proper management and experiments in translocation, its future now seems secure. The swamp deer and Asiatic wild buffalo have in recent years been equally threatened. In 1971 the hispid hare and the pigmy hog were rediscovered in the grasslands to the north after being thought extinct for about 30 years.

Permission for individual visitors to enter Assam is still difficult to get, but groups of six or more are getting permits without too much delay. Applications should be made to any Indian Embassy or High Commission abroad or direct to the Ministry of Home Affairs (Foreigners Wing), Lok Nayak Bahwan, Khan Market, New Delhi 110003. (Allow six to eight weeks.)

Information can also be obtained by writing to 4 Reet Hazarika, Sheeba Travels, G.N. Bordoloi Road, Ambari, Guwahati 781001 (Tel: 22135).

There are two proposed biosphere reserves at Kaziranga and Manas.

Barnadi Wildlife Sanctuary. Established in 1980 to protect one of the few remaining habitats of the extremely elusive hispid hare and pigmy hog, this sanctuary has an area of only 10 sq miles (26 sq km) of grassland, subject to pressure from local villagers cutting grass and cattle grazing. Elephant, tiger and leopard are also seen.
Best time to visit: Nov.-Mar.
Permission: DFO, West. Assam WL Division, PO Tezpur, Dist: Sonitpur, Assam.
Nearest town and Rail: Tangla (25 miles)
Air: Guwahati (87 miles/140 km)

Garamani Sanctuary. Established in 1952, this small sanctuary has a few tigers, leopards, elephants (which cross from the Rengma Hills to the foothills of the Naga Hills) and other mammals.
Best time to visit: Nov.-Mar.
Accommodation: 1 resthouse
Permission: DFO, Golaghat Division, PO Golaghat, Dist: Jorhat, Assam.
Nearest town & Rail: Golaghat (15 miles)
Air: Jorhat (44 miles/70 km)

Kaziranga N.P. In 1908, when the area was declared a forest reserve there were only about a dozen rhinos left in it. In 1926, Kaziranga became a game sanctuary and in 1974 it was declared a national park. It is justly famous, but not only for rhino but also for wild buffalo, the magnificent swamp deer and hog deer. Tiger, wild boar, Hoolock gibbon, capped langur and ratel (hog badger) are among the other animals seen. Mihimukh is a good viewing area. Visitors facilities are available and well-trained elephants can be hired. There is a good network of fair weather roads.
Best time to visit: Nov.-Mar.
Accommodation: forest resthouses and bungalows; Kaziranga Forest Lodge

(ITDC) (airconditioned rooms, bar, restaurant, Cable: RHINOWALK)
Permission: Director, Kaziranga N.P., PO Bokakhat, Dist: Jorhat, Assam 785612
Nearest town: Bokakhat (14miles/23 km)
Rail & Air: Jorhat (59 miles/95 km)

Laokhowa Sanctuary. Established in 1979, this sanctuary has a small population of rhino and wild buffalo. The habitat is similar to Kaziranga, with areas of swampy flats, tall grasses and scattered trees.
Best time to visit: Nov.-Apr.
Accommodation: 1 resthouse with 24 beds
Permission: DFO, Nagaon Division, PO Nagaon, Assam.
Nearest town & Rail: Nagaon (12 miles)
Air: Guwahati (106 miles/170 km)

Manas Sanctuary and Tiger Reserve. Established in 1928 as a small reserve, the area now protected is over 1094 sq miles (2840 sq km), of which 151 sq miles (391 sq km) form the core area and come under Project Tiger. The protected area continues north into the Bhutan foothills. Visitors can cross into the Bhutanese sanctuary. The park lies across two rivers (the Manas and its tributary, the Hakua) with an unparalleled variation of habitat for such a narrow strip.

The scenery of Manas is considered by many the most attractive of any Indian park. To the south are grasslands with the rivers, with their pebble-banks and islands, spreading as they leave the great forests on the Bhutan hills.

On the Indian side, the forests are mixed deciduous with open glades. Manas holds viable populations of 19 of India's most endangered animals. Great herds of elephant (up to 2000 in the area) migrate across the border. Rhino, wild buffalo, gaur, swamp deer, capped langur and clouded leopard are just a few of the mammal species. The tiger population here is perhaps the most dense of all the tiger reserves. Pigmy hog and hispid hare are also found here but rarely seen. On the Bhutan side, the only extant groups of golden langur are found.

The rich birdlife is distinctive and abundant. Transport in the park, riding elephants and boats on the rivers are available.
Best time to visit: Nov.-Mar.
Accommodation: Tourist Lodge and forest bungalow at Mothanguri
Permission: The Field Director-Project Tiger, PO Barpeta Road, Dist: Barpeta, Assam 781315
Nearest town & Rail: Barpeta Road (25 miles/41 km)
Air: Guwahati (116 miles/186 km)

Orang Sanctuary. One of India's oldest protected areas, this sanctuary of swampy grassland on the north bank of the Brahmaputra holds rhino, wild buffalo, swamp deer, elephant and tiger, among others.
Best time to visit: Nov.-Apr.
Accommodation: 1 resthouse
Permission: DFO, West. Assam WL Division, PO Tezpur, Dist: Sonitpur, Assam.
Nearest town & Rail: Tezpur (53 miles)

Sonai Rupai Sanctuary. In the Dooar grasslands at the base of the Dafla hill, this park covers about 67 sq miles (175 sq km). Although not seen since about 1940, the area possibly still holds pigmy hog and hispid hare which are still known to be in the Rowta Reserve Forest to the west and the Balipara Reserve Forest to the east. Tiger, a few swamp deer, buffalo and hog deer are found.
Best time to visit: Nov.-Mar.
Permission: DFO, West. Assam WL Division, PO Tezpur, Dist: Sonitpur, Assam.
Nearest town & Air: Tezpur (47miles)
Rail: Rangapara (34 miles/55 km)

A FLOCK OF PIN-TAILED SANDGROUSE.

BIHAR: Lying at the eastern end of the Gangetic plain, Bihar is a state of extremes. Subject to drought and flood, of great natural wealth but having some of India's poorest villagers, the state has some important and interesting sanctuaries. As in many other parts of India, most of the mammal sanctuaries were once private forests which, with independence in 1947, were subject to over-exploitation by *shikaris* (hunters), villagers and others. Most of the state has long, hot dry summers relieved by moderate rainfall from July to September.

Bhimbandh Sanctuary. 262 sq miles (681 sq km) of mixed deciduous forest—mostly sal on undulating ground south of the Ganga. Potentially a good park if given more protection. Leopards, sloth bear, wolf, chousingha, chital etc.
Best time to visit: Nov.-Mar. (Apr.-June good but hot)
Accommodation: 3 resthouses
Permission: DFO, Munger Forest Division, PO Munger, Bihar.
Nearest town: Munger (31 miles/50 km)
Rail: Jamui (25 miles/40 km)
Air: Patna (132 miles/212 km)

Dalma Sanctuary. Established in 1976 with 74 sq miles (193 sq km) of sal and mixed deciduous forests. Wolf, mouse deer, sloth bear, chital etc.
Best time to visit: Dec.-Mar. (Apr.-June hot)
Accommodation: 3 resthouses
Permission: DFO, Wildlife Div., Ranchi.
Nearest town & Rail: Jamshedpur (7.5 miles/12 km)
Rail: Tatanagar (12 miles/20 km)

Gautam Buddha Sanctuary. Established in the early 1970s and enlarged to 100 sq miles (259 sq km) in 1976. Mainly sal and thorn scrub. Previously protected as a private *shikar* reserve but for 20 years subject to cattle grazing, illegal felling and other disturbances. White tigers have been seen in what was the neighboring forest although the last one to be shot was in 1936. A few tiger, chital, chinkara, sloth bear etc.
Best time to visit: Dec.-Apr.
Accommodation: 1 resthouse
Permission: DFO, Gaya Forest Division, Gaya, Bihar
Nearest town, Rail & Air: Gaya (40 miles)

Hazaribagh Sanctuary. Established in 1954 and covering 71 sq miles (184 sq km) of undulating sal forest. Rich birdlife but few mammals are seen during the day. In the evening and after dusk sambar, nilgai, chital and wild boar are seen on night drives. Also the occasional leopard and a few tigers. The national highway to Hazaribagh passes through the area. It was previously the *shikar* reserve of the Raja of Ramgarh. Vehicles available for night drives.
Best time to visit: Oct.-Apr.
Accommodation: resthouses with food at Rajderwa and Harhad
Permission: DFO, Hazaribagh West Division, Hazaribagh, Bihar.
Nearest town: Hazaribagh (12 miles/20 km)
Rail: Kodarma (31 miles/50 km)
Air: Ranchi (71 miles/115 km)

Kaimur Sanctuary. A large sanctuary of over 338 sq miles (1000 sq km) on the west bank of the Son river near the border with Uttar Pradesh. Extremely hot summers (118°F/48°C). Chinkara, chousingha, wolf, a few leopards.
Best time to visit: Nov.-Mar.
Accommodation: 3 resthouses
Permission: DFO, Shabad Division, PO Sasaram, Dist: Rohtar, Bihar.
Nearest town & Rail: Sasaram (31 miles)
Air: Varanasi (70 miles/112 km)

Lawalong Sanctuary. Established in 1978 to the southwest of Hazaribagh with 81 sq miles (211 sq km) of mixed deciduous forest (largely sal). Leopard, wolf, chital, black panther (melanistic leopards) have been reported.
Best time to visit: Nov.-Mar.
Accommodation: 1 resthouse
Permission: DFO, Chatra South Division, PO Chatra, Dist: Hazaribagh, Bihar.
Nearest town: Hazaribagh (43 miles/70 km)
Rail: Tori (32 miles/52 km)
Air: Ranchi (99 miles/160 km)

Mahuadaur Sanctuary. Established in 1976 to protect the gray wolf. 24 sq miles (63 sq km) of sal forest flanking a remote deep valley cut by the Burha river.

Best time to visit: Nov.-Feb.
Accommodation: 2 four-bed resthouses
Permission: DFO, WF Division, PO Hinoo, Dist: Ranchi, Bihar.
Nearest town: Mahuadaur (7.5 miles/12 km)
Rail: Chhipadwar (31 miles/50 km)
Air: Ranchi (84 miles/135 km)

Palamau (Betla) Sanctuary and Tiger Reserve. Established in 1960 but now extended to cover 377 sq miles (979 sq km) of which 77 sq miles (200 sq km) is the core area. The world's first tiger census took place here in 1932 and in 1973 Palamou was one of the first reserves to be identified for inclusion under Project Tiger.

Lying on the northern edge of the Chota Nagpur plateau, the sanctuary has an undulating landscape of sal forest with pockets of bamboo cut by the Koel river and its tributaries. Two ruined forts stand near the Auranga river. A large range of mammal species and about 1400 species of bird have been identified. Elephant, gaur, chital, sambar, nilgai and, of course, tiger. Good viewing from the watchtower at Hathibajwa (Betla) and during the summer at Madhuchan. Transport is available.
Best time to visit: Oct.—May
Accommodation: tourist lodge and forest resthouses at Betla; resthouses at Kerh, Kechi, Mundu and Barwadih.
Permission: The Field Director, Project Tiger, Palamau Tiger Reserve, Daltenganj, Bihar 822101 (Tel: 350)
Nearest town & Rail: Daltenganj (15.5 miles/25 km)
Air: Ranchi (112 miles/180 km)

Udaipur Sanctuary. Established in 1978 and only 2.5 sq miles (six sq km) in area, this small wetland reserve has a resident waterfowl population and winter migrants.
Best time to visit: Nov.—Mar.
Accommodation: 1 resthouse
Permission: Deputy Director, Champaran Forest Division 2, PO Bettiah, Dist: Champaran, Bihar.
Nearest town & Rail: Bettiah (six miles)
Air: Patna (127 miles/205 km)

Valmiki Sanctuary. Established in 1970 and covering 178 sq miles (461 sq km) of mixed deciduous forest, riverine forest and grassland on the Indo-Nepal border. To the north is the Chitwan National park in Nepal, to the west the Gandak river and the border with Uttar Pradesh and to the east the Kapan river. Animals migrate from Chitwan, especially tiger, rhino, and gaur. Resident species include hog deer, chital, sambar, sloth bear and serow.
Best time to visit: Dec.—Apr.
Accommodation: tourist cottages at Koleshwar, Harnatar and Valmikinagar.
Permission: Deputy Director, Champaran Forest Division 2, PO Bettiah, Dist: Champaran, Bihar.
Nearest town: Bettiah (50 miles/80 km)
Rail: Valmikinagar (3 miles/5 km)
Air: Patna (140 miles/225 km)

Other sanctuaries in Bihar are at Nagi Dam (Munger Dist.), Rajgir (Nalanda Dist.), and Topchanchi (Dhanbad Dist.)

GOA, DAMAN AND DIU: Neither Daman or Diu have any protected area although the flats and narrow channel separating Diu from the mainland have plenty of shore birds.

Goa's protected areas are all in the foothills of the Western Ghats.

Bhagwan Mahavir N.P. and Molem Sanctuary. The sanctuary was established in 1967 and the national park in 1978. Their present areas are 98 sq miles (255 sq km) and 41 sq miles (107 sq km) respectively: the park forms the core area. The forest is mixed and wet deciduous with abundant birdlife and a fair mammal population—leopard, sloth bear, chital, etc.

Best time to visit: Oct.—Mar.
Accommodation: resthouse and tourist cottages
Permission: Range Forest Office (WL), Molem, Goa 403410.
Nearest town: Ponda (18 miles/29 km)
Air: Dabolim (50 miles/80 km)

Bondla Sanctuary. The smallest of Goa's sanctuaries, established in 1969. Sambar, wild boar and a few leopard. Regular buses from Panaji via Ponda.
Best time to visit: Oct.—Mar.
Accommodation: tourist cottages and dormitory food available
Permission: ACF, Bondla, Goa
Nearest town: Ponda (15.5 miles/25 km)
Rail: Madgaon (22 miles/36 km)
Air: Dabolim (44 miles/70 km)

Cotigao Sanctuary: Established in 1968 with 40 sq miles (105 sq km) of undulating hills where the Western Ghats almost touch the coast on the Karnataka border. Sloth bear, sambar, chital, pangolin, leopard etc.
Best time to visit: Oct.—Mar.
Accommodation: resthouse
Permission: Range Forest Officer (WL), Cawacona, Goa.
Nearest town and Rail: Madgaon (30 miles/48 km)
Air: Dabolim (48 miles/78 km)

GUJARAT: The westernmost state of India has many species unique to it. It is the last home of the Asiatic lion and Indian wild ass. Gujarat has little forest but 40 species of animals and over 450 species of birds—some migrant from Africa. Many local subspecies of birds are documented in the excellent and privately published *Birds of Saurashtra* by the late M.K. Dharmakumarsinhji. India's first Marine National Park was established by the Gujarat Government.

Gir N.P. and Lion Sanctuary. Established in 1965, this national park forms a core area of 100 sq miles (259 sq km) with the 444 sq miles (1153 sq km) of the sanctuary providing a buffer zone around it. Only some 10 percent of the total area is forested. The area was originally protected by Junagadh State, and although hunting was banned from 1948 onwards, the greatest pressure was from thousands of cattle that grazed the area. An area of hot humid summers (112°F/44°C) and cool winters. The monsoon brings little rain. The park has a good tourist infrastructure and most of the many species in the park can be seen. Buses and jeeps are available at Gujarat Tourism, Rangmahal, Diwan Chowk, Junagadh (40 miles/65 km).
Best time to visit: Dec.—Apr. (closed during the monsoon to mid-Oct.)
Accommodation: Forest Bungalow, (contact Sanctuary Supervisor, Sasan Gir, Dist: Junagadh. Tel: Visavadar 60; ITDC Forest Lodge, (Tel: 21)—can be booked through any ITDC office or hotel.
Permission: Conservator of Forests, Sardar Baug, Junagadh, Gujarat 362001
Nearest town: Veraval (26 miles/42 km)
Rail: Sasan (0.5 mile/1 km)
Air: Keshod (53 miles/86 km) (Gujarat Tourism Corporation organizes tours from Keshod including a stay at the park).

Barda Sanctuary. Established in 1979 to cover 109 sq miles (282 sq km) of mostly thorn forest north of Porbandar, the area was once a home for lions but it now lacks a corridor to link it to Gir. The area has suffered now from overgrazing and fuel-wood collection. Wildlife is scarce.
Best time to visit: Nov.—Feb.
Accommodation: 1 small resthouse
Nearest town & Rail: Ranavar (5 miles)
Air: Porbandar (14 miles/22 km)

Dhangadhra Sanctuary. Established in 1973 and covering a huge area of 1864 sq miles (4840 sq km) and more often known as the Little Rann of Kutch, this special sanctuary was set up for the Indian wild ass. The Rann is a flat saline wilderness with little vegetation. Other animals in the area include blackbuck, a few chinkara, wolf and desert cat. During the monsoon, part of the area becomes flooded and the wild ass move to elevated grass patches known as *bets*.
Best time to visit: Jan.—June
Accommodation: Desert Cowrsers, Camp Zainabad, Nr. Dasada 382751 (contact Ahmedabad 445068, 448699)
Permission: Sanctuary Superintendent, Dhangadhra, Dist: Surendranagar, Gujarat.

Nearest town & Rail: Dhangadhra (14 miles)
Air: Rajkot (87 miles/140 km); Ahmedabad (129 miles/209 km)

Jessore Sloth Bear Sanctuary. Established in 1978 near the border with Rajasthan this sanctuary covers 69 sq miles of thorn forest and scrub over hilly terrain. Sloth bear, nilgai and leopard are seen.
Best time to visit: Nov.—Mar.
Accommodation: 2 resthouses
Permission: Conservator of Forests, Gandhinagar, Gujarat 382016
Nearest town: Palanpur (17 miles/28 km)
Rail: Iqbal garh (6 miles/10 km)
Air: Ahmedabad (99 miles/160 km)

Khijadaya Sanctuary. Established in 1981, this small bird sanctuary of wetland covers only 2.5 sq miles (6 sq km)
Best time to visit: Nov.—Jan.
Accommodation: large resthouse and an 80-room hotel run by the Gujarat Tourism Corporation
Permission: Conservator of Forests, Pradarshan Ground, Jamnagar, Gujarat.
Nearest town & Rail: Jamnagar (10 miles)

Marine N.P. & Sanctuary (Pirotan). The sanctuary was established in 1980 with an area of 176 sq miles (457 sq. km). The national park was formed in 1982 with an additional area of 62 sq miles (162 sq km) as the core. Green-sea, leather-backed and olive ridley turtles along with other fascinating life can be seen.
Best time to visit: Nov.—Jan.
Accommodation: 2 guest houses (60 beds)
Permission: Director, Marine N.P., Pradarshan Ground, Jamnagar, Gujarat.
Nearest town & Rail: Jamnagar (4.5 miles)

Nal Sarovar Sanctuary. Established in 1969 over 44 sq miles (115 sq km) of wetland to the southwest of Ahmedabad. The lake is extensive and during the winter it is home to migrant geese, ducks, flamingoes etc. Local waterbirds also come here to feed though not to breed.
Best time to visit: Nov.—Feb.
Accommodation: Forest Lodge
Permission: Range Forest Officer, Nal Sarovar Sanctuary, PO Vekaria, Dist: Ahmedabad, Gujarat

Nearest town: Viramgam (22 miles/35 km)
Rail & Air: Ahmedabad (40 miles/64 km)

Velavadar N.P. Established in 1969 to give full protection to the blackbuck in this dry and open (13 sq miles/34 sq km) scrubland. Highest concentration of blackbuck anywhere in India. Also a few wolves. Excellent viewing.
Best time to visit: Nov.—May
Accommodation: Kaliyar Bhawan Forest Lodge
Permission: Range Forest Officer, Velavadar N.P, Velavadar, PO Vallabhipur, Gujarat
Nearest town: Vallabhipur (20 miles/32 km)
Rail & Air: Bhavnagar (40 miles/64 km)

Other sanctuaries in Gujarat include Hingolgarh (Rajkot Dist.), Narayan Sarovar (Kutch Dist.), Ratan Mahal (Panchmahals Dist.), Dhumkhal Sloth Bear Sanctuary (Bharuch Dist.), Vansda N.P. (Bulsar Dist.).

For information contact: Conservator of Forests, Gandhinagar, Gujarat 382016. You may also seek assistance from Tourist Corporation of Gujarat Ltd., HK House, Off Ashram Road, Ahmedabad 380009. Tel: 449683; Tlx: 0121-549 TCGL-IN.

COMMON CRANE.

HARYANA: Although Haryana has only one sanctuary there are some interesting areas west of Hissar where blackbuck and even bustard are found. For further information, contact: The Wildlife Officer, Kothi No. 974, Sector 9, Panchkula Ambala Dist., Haryana.

Sultanpur Jheel. Established in 1971 and in fact developed by the State Tourism Department, this lake is less than a square mile in area and a buffer area needs to be created. There are few local breeding birds, but the main attraction are the migratory birds who come in large numbers during late October and November.
Best time to visit: Nov.—Feb.
Accommodation: Haryana Tourism Lodge with both airconditioned and non-airconditioned rooms, restaurant, bar and cottages. Tel: Farakh Nagar Exchange, 42. Book through Haryana Tourism Bureau, Chanderlok Bldg, 36 Janpath, New Delhi (Tel: 344911).
Nearest town: Gurgaon (9 miles/15 km)
Air: Delhi (Palam), (22 miles/35 km) — Delhi City center, (30 miles/48 km).

HIMACHAL PRADESH: This state rises from the plains of the Punjab to the Great Himalaya and the Tibetan plateau beyond. Because of the range in altitude, the state has a wide range of flora and fauna. 28 areas are protected, including one national park. Most of the sanctuaries are in areas unconnected by public transport. The most enjoyable and in fact the only practical way to visit most of the areas is by trekking. It is possible to trek in much of Himachal and to buy food in many villages, although a couple of days' food should always be carried. One of the threats to Himachal's sanctuaries is the human pressure and continued exploitation of the forests. The birdlife is rich and varied. Most of the sanctuaries are in temperate and subtropical areas of the lower Himalaya.

Chail Sanctuary. Established in 1975, with 42 sq miles (108 sq km) of subtropical pine and temperate forest. Good bird-viewing, including chir pheasants, leopards and martens.
Best time to visit: Mar.—Dec.
Accommodation: resthouses with 14 beds in the sanctuary; Palace Hotel, Chail, HP 173217 (Tel: 3743)
Permission: Chief Wildlife Warden, Shimla, HP.
Nearest town: Shimla (28 miles/45 km)
Rail: Kandaghat (7.5 miles/12 km)
Air: Chandigarh (73 miles/118 km)

Daran Ghati Sanctuary. Established in 1974 with 64 sq miles (167 sq km) of temperate and mixed coniferous forest. Among the mammals are leopards, musk deer, civets, martens, bears and gorals, and monal, kaleej and kokla pheasants.
Best time to visit: Apr.—July, Sept.—Oct.
Accommodation: 4 resthouses
Permission: Chief Wildlife Warden, Shimla, HP
Nearest town: Rampur (37 miles/60 km)
Rail: Shimla (100 miles/160 km)
Air: Chandigarh (172 miles/277 km)

Govind Sagar Sanctuary: Established in 1974 to include the wetland and shore of the Govind Sagar reservoir, (38 sq miles/100 sq km). Migratory water birds.
Best time to visit: Oct.—Dec.
Accommodation: 5 resthouses
Permission: Chief Wildlife Warden, Shimla
Nearest town: Bilaspur (3.5 miles/6 km)
Rail: Kiratpur (16 miles/30 km)
Air: Chandigarh (44 miles/70 km)

Great Himalayan N.P. Established in 1984, this is the largest of Himachal's protected areas covering 669 sq miles (1736 sq km) to the southeast of Kulu. The Sainj and Tirthan valleys are less disturbed than many parts of Himachal and hold good populations of many species. There is also a tremendous variety of birds.
Best time to visit: Apr.—June, Sept.—Oct.
Accommodation: resthouses
Permission: DFO, WL Division, Kulu, HP
Nearest town: Kulu (37 miles/60 km)
Air: Bhuntar (31 miles/50 km)

Kalatop Khajjur Sanctuary. Established in 1958, this small area, 18 sq miles (47 sq km), of mixed temperate forest is a few miles from the hill station of Dalhousie. Ranges from 3888 to 8753 feet (1185 to 2668 meters) above sea level. Monal pheasants, woodland birds and hawks.
Best time to visit: May—June, Sept.—Nov.
Accommodation: 5 resthouses
Permission: DFO, WL Division, Chamba, Himachal Pradesh
Nearest town: Dalhousie (3.5 miles/6 km)
Rail: Pathankot (53 miles/86 km)
Air: Jammu (121 miles/194 km)

Kanawer Sanctuary. Established in 1954 on 2.33 sq miles (6 sq km) of mixed forest with deodar, oak, pine etc, 22 miles (35 km) east of Kulu on the north side of Parbati river. Altitudes range from 5900 to 15,856 feet (1800 to 4833 meters). Tahr, serow, goral, bharal, musk deer and leopard are among the animals, and kokla, kaleej, chir and western tragopan among the pheasants seen.
Best time to visit: May—June, Sept.—Oct.
Accommodation: 4 resthouses
Permission: DFO, WL Division, Kulu, Himachal Pradesh
Nearest town: Manikaran (2.5 miles/4 km)
Air: Bhuntar (Kulu) (22 miles/35 km)

Kugti Sanctuary. Established in 1962 on 45 sq miles (118 sq km) of temperate forest with oak scrub at the higher levels (highest point: 19,600 feet/5975 meters). Musk deer, tahr, ibex, barking deer, leopard are seen.
Best time to visit: May, June, Sept., Oct.
Accommodation: 2 resthouses
Permission: DFO, WL Division, Chamba, Himachal Pradesh
Nearest town: Chamba (54 miles/87 km)
Rail: Pathankot (128 miles/206 km)

Lippa Asrang Sanctuary. Established in 1962 with 68 sq miles (109 sq km) of temperate and coniferous forest. Permission is required for foreign nationals to visit this area. Ibex, musk deer, bharal and leopard are seen.
Best time to visit: Apr.—Oct.
Accommodation: 3 resthouses
Permission: Chief WL Warden, Shimla, HP
Nearest town: Kalppa (16 miles/25 km)
Rail: Shimla (202 miles/325 km)

Manali Sanctuary. Established in 1954 (12 sq miles/31 sq km). Tahr, serow, musk deer, leopard are seen. Snow leopard have also been reported. Tragopan, chir, and monal pheasants are present.
Best time to visit: May, June, Sept., Oct.
Accommodation: 5 resthouses
Permission: DFO, WL Division, Kulu, HP
Nearest town: Manali (2.5 miles/4 km)
Air: Bhuntar (Kulu) (3.4 miles/55 km)

Rakchhalm Chitkul Sanctuary. Established in 1962 and covering 86 sq miles (138 sq km) of Kinnaur district (highest point: 17,933 feet/5466 meters). Permission is required for foreigners to visit this area.
Best time to visit: Apr.— June, Sept, Oct.
Accommodation: 2 resthouses
Permission: Chief WL Warden, Shimla, HP
Nearest town: Rampur (124 miles/200 km)
Rail: Shimla (198 miles/319 km)

While Himachal Pradesh has an impressive list of sanctuaries, many of them were established for shooting in the 1950s and '60s and little, if any, wildlife management has taken place since the introduction of Wildlife Protection Act in 1972. None have been enlarged. The Western Himalaya is a magnificent area with magnificent forests, but with the ever increasing human pressure on the environment, strong administration is required to protect, conserve and develop the remaining natural habitat.

JAMMU AND KASHMIR: In the Central and Western ranges of the Himalaya are the mountains of Kashmir known to most tourists. In fact the state ranges from the Punjab plains to the Tibetan plateau. The north is bounded by the Karakoram mountains, the east by Tibet and the Great Himalayan range. The Indus river cuts through the state as it flows east to west and into Pakistan. Large areas of good wildlife habitat fall outside protected areas: the snow leopard range covers most of Ladakh district; the Tibetan wild ass (kiang) and the black-necked crane survive in fairly secure but extremely small numbers near the Chinese border, east of Leh. The western and southern parts of the state are affected by the monsoon while precipitation beyond the Great Himalayan range is often limited to winter snowfall.

Conservation in Ladakh is fairly recent and there is little tourist infrastructure. Like Himachal Pradesh to the southeast and much of Nepal, the only way to see the area is by trekking. Many travel agencies in Delhi can advise on treks and limited equipment is available in Srinagar. Hiring of warm clothing and sleeping bags is not recommended— bring your own!

For information contact: The Chief Wildlife Warden, Tourist Reception Centre, Srinagar 190001, Kashmir (Tel: 75411).

Dachigam N.P. Originating as a game reserve and then further developed to protect the catchment area for much of the drinking water supply of Srinagar, 13 miles (21 km) to the west, it now covers an area of 54 sq miles (141 sq km). Today the park is famous as the home of the last viable population of hangul. Other species found include both the brown and black Himalayan bear, musk deer and fox and over 150 species of birds. A metaled road links Srinagar with lower Dachigam. Upper Dachigam (14,072 feet/4289 meters) should be reached on foot.
Best time to visit: May—Aug. Upper Dachigam; Sept.—Dec. in lower Dachigam.
Accommodation: 2 lodges and resthouses; hotels and house-boats in Srinagar.
Permission: The Chief Wildlife Warden, Srinagar
Nearest town and Air: Srinagar (20 miles)
Rail: Jammu (196 miles/315 km)

Hemis High Altitude N.P. Established in 1981 and covering 231 sq miles (600 sq km) of the Markha and Rumbak valleys. Most of the area is rocky and sparsely covered. Among the endangered mammals here are bharal, ibex, snow leopard and marmot. Over 50 bird species have been identified. The winters can be extremely cold and drop to -40°F (-40°C).
Best time to visit: May—Sept.
Accommodation: none, camping permitted
Permission: DFO, Hermis N.P., Leh, Ladakh, J. & K
Nearest town & Air: Leh 19 miles/30 km from Nimu

Jasrota Sanctuary. Established in 1984 this extremely small area of 3.75 sq miles (10 sq km) supports a large population of chital, barking deer, wild boar, rhesus macaque. It is situated on the right bank of the Ujh river and has a large area of bamboo.
Best time to visit: Sept.—June
Accommodation: 2 resthouses
Permission: Regional Wildlife Warden, Near Jammu Ashok Hotel, Manda (Ramnagar), Jammu
Nearest town: Kathua (15.5 miles/25 km)
Air: Jammu (40 miles/65 km)

Kishtwar N.P. A new park established in 1981 encompassing almost 154 sq miles (400 sq km) at heights of 5600—15,750 feet (1700—4800 meters). Most of the area is within the catchment area of the Chenab river. The forest is largely coniferous, including neoza pine and deodar. At higher altitudes the forests give way to alpine

meadows and scrub. A few hangul, musk deer, markar, ibex, gray langur and leopard can be seen.
Best time to visit: May — Oct.
Accommodation: 2 resthouses
Permission: Regional Wildlife Warden, Nr. Jammu Ashok Hotel, Manda (Ramnagar), Jammu
Nearest town: Kishtwar (137 miles/60 km)
Air & Rail: Jammu (152miles/245 km)

Overa Sanctuary and Biosphere Reserve. Established in 1981. Although only 12.5 sq miles (32 sq km), the area falls within the proposed Overa-Aro Biosphere Reserve of almost 154 sq miles (400 sq km). The sanctuary is located in the upper Lidder Valley above Pahalgam. The area is largely forested and has a good pheasant population and other birdlife. Mammals include hangul, musk deer, serow, langur, leopard.
Best time to visit: Apr.—Oct.
Accommodation: resthouse, camping sites
Permission: The Chief Wildlife Warden, Srinagar
Nearest town and Air: Srinagar (47 miles)

Other sanctuaries include Lungnag (Kargil Dist.), Nandi (Jammu Dist.), Ramnagar (Jammu Dist.) and Surinsar Mansar (Udhampur Dist.). A second biosphere reserve at Gulmarg covering 112 sq miles (180 sq km) has also been proposed.

KARNATAKA: The forests of southern Karnataka in what was once Mysore State have long been famous for their rich and distinctive wildlife and magnificent forests. The great tracts of forest that remain today as a legacy of the management and concern shown by the Mysore rulers are noted for elephant, gaur and other large mammals. In the northern part of the state the dry thorn forests and scrub are home to different species. In the dry deciduous scrub of Ranibennur, the blackbuck and an increasing number of great Indian bustard are found. The bustard has also returned to the scrub areas north of Bijapur, near the Maharashtra border.

Bandipur N.P. and Tiger Reserve. Established in the early 1930s with an area of 23 sq miles (60 sq km), the area was expanded to 266 sq miles (690 sq km) with a core area of 129 sq miles (335 sq km) in 1974. A further extension is proposed to the northeast. It is bounded on the northwest, west and south by the Nagarahole, Wynad and Mudumalai parks respectively.

It has one of the best-planned road systems among Indian parks which provides excellent opportunities for game viewing, especially for elephant. The gaur population is on the increase after the 1968 rinderpest epidemic. The park is bisected north-south by the Mysore Ootacamund road. The hilly landscape in the shadow of the Western Ghats is intersected by rivers and streams. Forest vehicles are available.
Best time to visit: Mar.—July, Sept., Oct.
Accommodation: forest lodges, cottages; forest resthouses at Kakanhalla, Mulehole, Kalkere and Gopalaswamy (Betta).
Permission: Field Director—Project Tiger, Bandipur Tiger Reserve, Mysore 570004
Nearest town: Gundulpet (12.5 miles/20km)
Rail: Nanjungud (34 miles/55 km)
Air: Mysore (50 miles/80 km)

Bannerghatta N.P. Established in 1974 with 40 sq miles (104 sq km) of undulating terrain with valleys and hills; only 17 miles (28 km) south of Bangalore. Mammal life is poor although the occasional leopard is seen, and also chital, wild boar and sloth bear. A few elephants still migrate through the area. Interesting scenery and good birdlife. Heavily visited, especially during weekends.

Best time to visit: Sept.—June (open all the year round)
Accommodation: forest resthouse
Permission: ACF, Bannerghatta N.P., Bangalore 83
Nearest town: Arekal (12 miles/19 km)
Rail & Air: Bangalore (17 miles/28 km)

Bhadra Sanctuary. Established in 1974 over 189 sq miles (490 sq km) of the Bhadra river valley and ringed by the Bababudan range. Most of the valley is covered with moist deciduous forest. Roads are in poor condition and jeeps are needed. Large gaur population, a few elephant, tiger, chital and sambar. Vehicles and forest guides available at Muthodi.
Best time to visit: Oct.—May
Accommodation: forest resthouse at Sigekhan and Kesave
Permission: ACF Wildlife Preservation, 50 Jayanagar 1st Cross, Shimoga, Karnataka 577 201
Nearest town: Shimoga (19 miles/30 km)
Rail: Tarikere (12.5 miles/20 km)
Air: Bangalore (158 miles/255 km), Mangalore (135 miles/218 km)

Biligiri Rangasamy Sanctuary. Established in 1974 south of Mysore over 125 sq miles (324 sq km). Facilities are limited. Elephant are occasionally seen (migratory), and chital, sambar and an occasional tiger.
Best time to visit: Oct.—May
Accommodation: 2 resthouses
Permission: ACF Wildlife Preservation, SD, Mysore 4 (Tel:21159)
Nearest town and Rail: Chamarajanagar (37 miles/60 km)
Air: Mysore (75 miles/120 km)

Brahmagiri Sanctuary. Established in 1974 in southern Coorg near the border with Kerala. Borders Nagarahole National Park to the east. Hill country with moist and mixed deciduous forest. Elephant, gaur, tiger, mouse deer, chital and sambar are seen.
Best time to visit: Oct.—May
Accommodation: none
Permission: ACF Wildlife Preservation, SD, Vanivilas Road, Mysore 4 (Tel:21159)
Nearest town: Virajpat (24 miles/39 km)
Rail: Cannanore (Kerala) (47 miles/75 km)
Air: Mysore (84 miles/135 km)

Dandeli Sanctuary. Established in 1975 and now covering 220 sq miles (572 sq km) of mostly moist deciduous forest; some teak and bamboo. Fair road system. Large mammals including elephant, tiger, sambar, chital and occasional wolf seen.
Best time to visit: Dec.—May
Accommodation: 6 resthouses
Permission: ACF Wildlife Preservation, SD, Dharwad, Karnataka
Nearest town: Dandeli (1.25 miles/2 km)
Rail: Dharwad (25 miles/40 km)
Air: Belgaum (51 miles/82 km)

Ghataprabha Sanctuary. Established in 1974, a small bird sanctuary of 11 sq miles (29 sq km). Mostly wetland next to the Ghataprabha river north of Belgaum.
Best time to visit: Oct.—Jan.
Accommodation: 4 small resthouses
Permission: ACF Wildlife Preservation, SD, Dharwad, Karnataka
Nearest town & Rail: Gokak Falls
Air: Belgaum (37 miles/60 km)

Mookambika Sanctuary. Established in 1974 on the edge of the Western Ghats with a mixed semi-evergreen forest and tropical evergreen forest at the highest elevations. High rainfall from early June. Tiger, sloth bear, lion-tailed macaque and chital seen.
Best time to visit: Nov.—Apr.
Accommodation: 2 bungalows (10 beds)
Permission: ACF Wildlife Preservation, SD, Jayanagar 1st cross, Shimoga, Karnataka 577201
Nearest town: Bindur (15 miles/25 km)
Air & Rail: Mangalore (56 miles/90 km)

Nagarahole N.P. Established in 1955 and expanded to its present size of 221 sq miles (573 sq km) in 1975. Extremely attractive situation with the Brahmagiri hills in the distance. The Kabini river has been dammed to form a large and attractive reservoir which separates the park from Bandipur National Park to the southeast. The game viewing is excellent and well organized by the Kabini River Lodge. Large groups of gaur, elephant, the occasional tiger and leopard, chital and sambar are seen. Over 250 species of bird recorded. Park vehicles available.
Best time to visit: Oct.—Apr.
Accommodation: 2 forest resthouses (contact ACF-Mysore): Kabini Jungle Lodge, 14 rooms (double), with excellent facilities. Good food and bar. Trained naturalists and staff. Contact: Jungle Lodges & Resorts Ltd., Brooklands, 348/349, 13th Main Road, Raj Mahal Vilas Extn., Bangalore 560080 (Tel: 362820).
Permission: ACF, Wildlife Preservation, SD, Vanivilas Road, Mysore 4 (Tel:21159)
Nearest town: Kutta (2.5 miles/7 km)
Rail & Air: Mysore (60 miles/96 km)

Ranganathittu Bird Sanctuary. Established in 1940 near Tippu Sultan's capital of Srirangapatnam on tiny islands in the Kaveri river 10 miles (16 km) north of Mysore. Boats available for hire. Nesting starts as early as June for many species. Scenically beautiful. A few crocodiles and flying foxes (fruit bats) seen.
Best time to visit: June—Oct.
Accommodation:1 guesthouse
Permission: ACF, Wildlife Preservation, SD, Vanivilas Road, Mysore 4 (Tel:21159)
Nearest town, Rail & Air: Mysore (10 miles)

Ranibennur Blackbuck Sanctuary. Established in 1974 to check the rapid decline of blackbuck in northern Karnataka. The wolf and great Indian bustard are also found. Mostly dry scrub and open ground.
Best time to visit: Open throughout the year.
Accommodation: 2 resthouses
Permission: ACF, Wildlife Preservation SD, Dharwad, Karnataka
Nearest town: Ranibennur (2.5 miles/4 km)
Rail: Bennur
Air: Bangalore (185 miles/298 km)

Sharavathi Valley Sanctuary. Established in 1974 over 166 sq miles (431 sq km) of the Western Ghats with wet tropical evergreen forest and semi-evergreen forest. Has high rainfall from June. Chital, sloth bear, macaques and the occasional tiger seen.
Best time to visit: Nov.—May
Accommodation: 4 resthouses (34 beds)
Permission: ACF, Wildlife Preservation SD, Jayanagar 1st Cross, Shimoga, Karnataka 577201
Nearest town: Kagal (0.5 mile/1 km)
Rail: Talguppa
Air: Mangalore (112 miles/180 km)

Shettihally Sanctuary. Established in 1974 on 152 sq miles (395 sq km) of mixed deciduous and semi-evergreen forest. Tiger, elephant, chital and sambar seen.
Best time to visit: Nov.—May
Accommodation: 4 resthouses (20 beds)
Permission: ACF, Wildlife Preservation SD, Jayanagar 1st Cross, Shimoga, Karnataka 577201
Nearest town & Rail: Shimoga (3 miles)
Air: Mangalore (118 miles/190 km)

Other sanctuaries in Karnataka include: Adichuncha Nagiri (Mysore Dist.), Arabithittu; Melkota Temple (Mandya Dist.); Nugu (Mysore dist.); Someswara (South Kanara Dist.) and Tungabhadra (Bellary Dist.). Information on these and other protected areas can be obtained from: The Chief Wildlife Warden, Aranya Bhawan, 18th Cross, Malleshwaram, Bangalore 560003 (Tel: 31993).

KERALA: Flanked to the west by the Indian Ocean and along the east by the Western Ghats, Kerala is well endowed with dense vegetation supporting a rich and varied fauns. Road communication throughout the state is good and the major airports at Trivandrum (the state capital) and Cochin are connected to all major Indian cities. Both Cochin and Trivandrum are major rail terminuses. The weather throughout the year is pleasant with the monsoon arriving in late May and the wet period continuing up to September.

Eravikulam N.P. Declared a national park in 1978, this area was earlier established as a sanctuary to protect the Nilgiri tahr (the only wild goat south of the Himalaya). The park covers 37 sq miles (97 sq km) of beautiful rolling grass hills and forests in the valleys. It also has the highest peak in South India: Anaimudi (8853 feet/2695 meters). The tahr are often seen near the bordering Rajamalai tea estate. Elephant, tiger, leopard, Nilgiri langur, lion-tailed macaque and giant squirrel are found.
Best time to visit: Nov.—Apr.
Accommodation: resthouse at Rajamalai (separate arrangement needed for food)
Permission: DFO, Munnar Division, PO Devi Kolam, Kerala (Tel: Munnar 37).
Nearest town: Munnar (10 miles/16 km)
Rail & Air : Cochin (89 miles/143 km)

Idikki Sanctuary. Established in 1976 with an area of 27 sq miles (70 sq km) above the Idikki arch dam. Sambar and elephant are usually seen and tiger, sloth bear and gaur occasionally.
Best time to visit: Nov.—May.
Accommodation: inspection bungalows at Kulamaur and Vazhathope
Permission: Asst. Field Director, Idikki Sanctuary, Vazhathope, Idikki, Kerala.
Nearest town: Vazhathope (1.25 miles)
Rail & Air : Cochin (102 miles/164 km)

Neyyar Sanctuary. Established in 1958 it has an area of 49 sq miles (128 sq km) with the Neyyar reservoir covering slightly more than 3.5 sq miles (9 sq km). Boats are available to explore the narrow creeks, channels and islands. Most of the sanctuary is wet tropical evergreen forest although in higher areas the grasslands have tahr. Agasthyadoodam at 6203 feet (1890 meters) is the highest point. A rich bird and insect life. Lion-tailed macaque, Nilgiri langur, gaur, sloth bear and wild boar are seen. Occasional tiger sightings.
Best time to visit: throughout the year
Accommodation: inspection bungalow at Neyyar; 2 guesthouses
Permission: Wildlife Warden, Forest Headquarters, Trivandrum, Kerala 695014 (Tel: 60674).
Nearest town: Kattakada (6 miles/10 km)
Rail & Air : Trivandrum (20 miles/32 km)

Parambikulam Sanctuary. First established as a small sanctuary in 1962, the present area of 110 sq miles (285 sq km) was gazetted in 1973. The sanctuary stretches around the Parambikulam, Thunacadavu and Peruvaripallan reservoirs, each with a good population of crocodile. Most of the area has dense deciduous forests and in one area old teak plantations. Gaur viewing is good with the largest population in Kerala. Sambar, chital, lion-tailed macaque and a few tigers and leopards are seen. Transport and boats available.
Best time to visit: Feb.—Apr.
Accommodation: forest resthouses at Thunacadavu, Thellikkal and Elathode
Permission: DFO, TP Division, Thunacadavu Post, Via Pollachi (Tel: Pollachi 33).
Nearest town & Rail: Pollachi (30 miles)
Air: Coimbatore (62 miles/100 km)

Peechi Vazhani Sanctuary. Established in 1958, over 48 sq miles (125 sq km) to protect the catchment areas of the Peechi and Vazhani dams. Mammal life is poor due to the area's proximity to habitation. Moist deciduous forest with interesting birds.
Best time to visit: Nov.—Apr.
Accommodation: resthouse (4 beds), Peechi
Permission: DFO, Ayyanthol, Trichur, Kerala (Tel: 23268).
Nearest town & Rail: Trichur (9.5 miles)
Air : Cochin (62 miles/100 km)

Peppara Sanctuary. Established in 1983, this hilly area of mixed forest covering 20 sq miles (53 sq km) of the Western Ghats has some fascinating birdlife. Elephant, sambar and lion-tailed macaque are seen and

the occasional leopard.
Best time to visit: throughout the year
Accommodation: guesthouse with 4 beds, tourist complex at Ponmude (7.5 miles/11 km, Tel: Vithura 30)
Permission: DFO, Trivandrum Forest Division, Trivandrum, Kerala 695014 (Tel: 60637).
Nearest town: Vithura (7 miles/10 km)
Rail & Air: Trivandrum (30 miles/48 km)

Periyar Tiger Reserve and N.P. Established in 1934 as the Nelliampatty Sanctuary, it was enlarged in 1950. It now extends over 299 sq miles (777 sq km) and is India's southernmost tiger reserve. The lake covers 10 sq miles (26 sq km). Most of the sanctuary is undulating. The elephant viewing is excellent, although only a few tuskers have avoided the poacher's gun. In 1983 there were 932 elephants in the sanctuary. Tiger sightings are rare. Woodland birds are abundant. Boats and dugouts are available.
Best time to visit: Sept.—May (open all the year round)
Accommodation: forest resthouses at Manakauala, Mullakudi and Thannikudy; at the park entrance and HQ at Thekkady tourist accommodation is available: Aranya Nivas Hotel (Tel: Kumily 23); Edapalayam Lake Palace (Tel: Kumily 24); Periyar House (Tel: Kumily 26)—only Indian food and dormitory accommodation.
Permission: The Field Director, Project Tiger, Kanjikuzhi, Kottayam, Kerala (Tel: Kottayam 8409).
Nearest town: Kumily (2.5 miles/4 km)
Air: Madurai (TN) (90 miles/145 km) or Cochin (118 miles/190 km)

Silent Valley N.P. Established in 1984 after a national campaign to protect the peninsula's last substantial area of primary tropical forest, 35 sq miles (90 sq km) of park hold a valuable reserve of rare plants and herbs. Elephant, lion-tailed macaque and tiger are among the animals seen.
Best time to visit: Sept.—Mar.
Accommodation: resthouse (4 beds)
Permission: DFO, Palghat, Kerala 678009 (Tel: Palghat 8156).
Nearest town: Mannarghat (20 miles/32 km)
Rail: Palghat (47 miles/75 km)
Air : Coimbatore (TN) (96 miles/155 km)

Thattekkad Bird Sanctuary. Established in 1983 as Kerala's first bird sanctuary. Mostly moist deciduous forest on 9.5 sq miles (25 sq km) of land between branches of the Periyar river. Many water and forest birds including rarities such as the Ceylon frogmouth and the rose-billed roller. Also, lion-tailed macaque and flying squirrel.
Best time to visit: Sept.—Mar.
Accommodation: 1 forest bungalow
Permission: DFO, Malyathur Forest Division, Kodanad Post, via Perumbavoor, Kerala.
Nearest town: Kothamangalam (12.5 miles)
Rail: Alwaye (31 miles/50 km)
Air : Cochin (44 miles/70 km)

Wynad Sanctuary. Established in 1973 although a game reserve since the 1920s. Borders Nagarahole and Bandipur in Karnataka and Mudumalai in Tamil Nadu. Area: 132 sq miles (344 sq km). Rich birdlife in remarkable and varied forests. Elephant, chital, gaur, sambar and sloth bear are fairly common. Good roads.
Best time to visit: Dec. — Apr.
Accommodation: resthouses at Manantody and Sultan's Battery
Permission: DFO, Wynad, PO Manantody, Kerala (Tel: 33).
Nearest town: Sultan's Battery (0.5 mile)
Rail: Calicut (68 miles/110 km)
Air : Mysore or Bangalore (155 miles)

WHITE SPOONBILL (¼ nat. size).

MADHYA PRADESH: The heart of India and the country's largest state. With the largest area still under forest and the largest number of protected areas. In fact, a third of India's forest is in Madhya Pradesh. It also has the country's largest national park (Sanjay). The state includes many geographical regions. To the north is the Indo-Gangetic plain. The central plateau with hill ranges interspersed with river valleys creates an attractive landscape. Communications across the state are difficult and it is often easier to begin a journey in Delhi or Bombay than say the state capital, Bhopal.
Most parks in Madhya Pradesh are closed from the beginning of the monsoon till early November.

Achankmar Sanctuary. Established in 1975 on 212 sq miles (551 sq km) of sal and bamboo forest, a few miles to the northwest of Bilaspur. Mouse deer, gaur and tiger are among the animals reported.
Best time to visit: Mar. — June
Accommodation: 5 resthouses
Permission: DFO, Achankmar Sanctuary, PO Kargi Road, Kota, Bilaspur Dist., MP
Nearest town: Bilaspur (35 miles/56 km)
Rail: Kargi Road (16 miles/26 km)
Air: Raipur (107 miles/172 km)

Bagdara Sanctuary. Established in 1978 to protect a 184-sq mile (478 -sq km) area of dry mixed scrub and deciduous forest near the northeastern border with Uttar Pradesh. Blackbuck, chinkara, wolf and the occasional leopard are seen. Extremely hot summers up to 120°F (48°C).
Best time to visit: Dec. — Feb.
Permission: Superintendent, Bagdara Sanctuary, East Sidhi Division, Sidhi, MP
Nearest town: Mirzapur (53 miles/85 km)
Air: Varanasi (88 miles/142 km)

Barnawapara Sanctuary. Established in 1976 on 94 sq miles (244 sq km) of mixed deciduous forest near the border with Orissa. It is still possible to drive for long distances through forest along the state border. This sanctuary is only a small part of this forest area. Leopard, sambar and chital are seen.
Best time to visit: Jan. — June
Accommodation: forest resthouses
Permission: Superintendent, Barnawapara

Sanctuary, PO Pithora, Dist: Raipur, MP
Nearest town & Air: Raipur (62 mile)
Rail: Mahasamund (35 miles/57 km)

Bandhavgarh N.P. Originally the private forest and preserve of the Maharaja of Rewa who encouraged the establishment of a national park in 1968. Recently extended to over 175 sq miles (450 sq km). Undulating terrain with 22 hills of which the main one, rises 1300 feet (400 meters) above its surroundings. Sal and mixed forest with bamboo brakes. Open grassland to the south where village land has been reclaimed. Excellent game viewing and birdlife. Tiger, leopard, gaur, chital sambar, dhole, nilgai, wild boar, sloth bear and chinkara are seen. Elephant riding available.
Best time to visit: Feb. — Jun (the park is open from Nov. 1 each year and closes for the monsoon early in July).
Accommodation: Bandhavgarh Jungle Camp—a deluxe camp opposite the park entrance with excellent food, bar, trained naturalists and vehicles. Book through any travel agent or Tiger Tops India Pvt. Ltd., 1/1 Rani Jhansi Road, New Delhi 55 (Tel: 771075, 731075, 521932, 523057, 7777483; Tlx: 031-63016 TREK IN); White Tiger Lodge (MP state Tourism Development Corpn.)—8 double rooms. Book through Bhopal head office (see below).
Permission: Director, Bandhavgarh N.P., P.O. Umaria, Dist: Shahdol, MP 484661
Nearest town & Rail: Umaria (22 miles)
Rail: Also to Satna (70 miles/112 km)
Air: Khajuraho (131 miles/210 km); Jabalpur (121 miles/195 km)

Bhairamgarh Sanctuary. Established in 1984 to protect one of three small groups of wild buffalo in peninsular India. Acts as buffer to Indravati National Park. Tiger, leopard, chital and sambar are seen. Mixed deciduous forest with a high percentage of teak. Permission to visit Bastar district must be sought, contact M.P. Tourism in Delhi or Bombay for advice.
Best time to visit: Feb. — May
Accommodation: none
Permission: Superintendent, Wild Buffalo Sanctuary, Bhairamgarh, PO Bijapur, Dist: Bastar, MP
Nearest town & Rail: Jagdalpur (96 mile)
Air: Raipur (302 miles/486 km)

Bori Sanctuary. Established in 1977 with 200 sq miles of mixed deciduous and bamboo forest. Part of the Mahadeo range which cuts across southwestern MP. Good viewing but poor infrastructure at present.
Best time to visit: Oct. — June
Accommodation: 4 resthouses
Permission: Superintendent, Bori Sanctuary, 79 Surajganj, Itarsi, MP
Nearest town: Pachmarhi (20 miles/32 km)
Rail: Itarsi (47 miles/75 km)
Air: Bhopal (78 miles/125 km)

Indravati N.P. & Tiger Reserve. Established in 1978 on a core area of 485 sq miles (1258 sq km) with a buffer sanctuary of 594 sq mile (1541 sq km) which includes the Bhairamgarh Sanctuary (see above). Came under Project Tiger in 1983. The park is part of the vast forest belt that stretches across southern Maharashtra, northern Andhra Pradesh, Madhya Pradesh and Orissa. The Indravati river flows through the park.

The importance of this park cannot be underestimated. It holds perhaps the only viable population of wild buffalo in central India and is a possible alternative home for the swamp deer of Kanha. Most of the forest is mixed deciduous with teak and large areas of bamboo. Also open grassland with large groups of chital etc. Other animals seen include sambar, nilgai, chousingha, chinkara, blackbuck, gaur, sloth bear, wild boar, leopard, wolf, hyena and jackal. Very hot summers of up to 48°C.
Best time to visit: late Jan. — Apr.
Accommodation: none
Permission: Director, Indravati N.P., PO Bijapur, Dist: Bastar, MP 49444.
Nearest town & Rail: Jagdalpur (104 miles)
Air: Raipur (302 miles/486 km)

Kanger Ghati N.P. Established in 1982 on 77 sq miles of moist deciduous forest with chousingha, leopard and wolf.
Best time to visit: Feb. — June
Accommodation: none
Permission: Director, Kanger Ghati N.P., Jagdalpur, Dist: Bastar, MP
Nearest town: Jagdalpur (18.5 miles/30 km)
Air: Raipur (205 miles/330 km)

Kanha N.P. Considered by some to be India's greatest national park, the area is certainly an excellent place to see many species in their natural habitat. First declared as a small sanctuary in 1933 and then a national park from 1955, the area under Project Tiger is now 250 sq miles (1945 sq km) of which 362 sq miles (940 sq km) is the core area.

One of India's great conservation sucess stories is from Kanha where the barasingha (swamp deer) population has increased from about 66 in the late 1960s to over 450 by 1985. Attractive forest with bamboo brakes. Grassy plateaus and meadows in the valleys. Elephant riding and Forest Department jeeps available.
Best time to visit: Feb. — June (closed July — Nov.)
Accommodation: forest resthouses at Kisli, Mukki, Supkhar and Garhi; M P Tourism Log Huts at Kisli; bungalow at Mukki; Kanha Safari Lodge (ITDC), Mukki (with AC rooms). Kipling Camp—a deluxe camp and lodge with attached bedrooms. Near the Kisli entrance to the park. Good food and bar. Advance booking to Kipling Camp, c/o Tollygunge Club Ltd., 120 D.P. Sasmal Road, Calcutta 700 003 (Tel: 4691922, 467806).
Permission: Field Director, Project Tiger, PO Mandla, MP
Nearest town: Mandla (40 miles/65 km)
Rail & Air: Jabalpur (104 miles/160 km); Nagpur (153 miles/247 km)

Karera Great Indian Bustard Sanctuary. Established in 1981. Much of the 78 sq miles (202 sq km) is still used by villagers for seasonal grazing. Jheel with excellent water birds including flamingo. Bustard best seen in April-June. Mammals include wolf, fox, blackbuck and chinkara.
Best time to visit: throughout the year.
Accommodation: resthouse at Karera
Permission: Superintendent, Bustard Sanctuary, Karera, Dist: Shivpuri, MP
Nearest town: Karera (7.5 miles/12 km)
Rail: Jhansi (34 miles/55 km)
Air: Gwalior (93 miles/150 km)

National Chambal Sanctuary. Established in 1978 across three states (Rajasthan, UP and MP) to total 1503 sq miles (3902 sq km). Formed to protect the gharial and other freshwater reptiles. The Chambal river forms the border between Rajasthan and MP and then Uttar Pradesh with MP. The sanctuary follows both banks of the river and includes the many dramatic ravines formed by erosion over the year.
Best time to visit: Nov. — Mar.
Accommodation: resthouses
Permission: Project Officer, National Chambal Sanctuary, PO 11, Morena, MP
Nearest town & Rail: Morena (13 miles)
Air: Gwalior (40 miles/65 km)

Madhav N.P. (Shivpuri). Previously the hunting preserve of the Scindia family (Maharajas of Gwalior), this area, lying on the main Bombay Asia road became a national park in 1959. It currently covers 60 sq miles (156 sq km) but a plan to extend it to 130 sq miles (337 sk km) is now in hand. The park lies in low hills with dry deciduous forest and scrub. There is a large perennial lake with an attractive building on its shore (Sakhya Sagar Boat Club). Some of the largest tigers recorded were shot in those forests which have a good network of roads. Nilgai, chinkara, chital, chousingha, sambar, wild boar and some blackbuck are seen and also a few tigers and leopards. Jeeps and boats available for hire.
Best time to visit: Oct. — Apr.
Accommodation: Sakhya Sagar Boat Club (Forest Dept.)—food available; Chinkara Motel (MP Tourism), Shivpuri town (Tel: 297); forest resthouse.
Permission: Director, Shivpuri N.P., Shivpuri, MP.
Nearest town: Shivpuri (3.75 miles/6 km)
Rail: Jhansi (62 miles/100 km)
Air & Rail: Gwalior (72 miles/116 km)

Pachmarhi Sanctuary. Established in 1977 to include the hills and valleys of the Mahadeo range of the Satpura hills around the attractive resort town of Pachmarhi. Covers 177 sq miles (461 sq km) of dry deciduous forest of teak and sal. Some leopard, blackbuck, sambar and nilgai are seen.
Best time to visit: Apr. — June, Oct. — Dec.
Accommodation: forest resthouses— Satpura Retreat (Tel: 97); Amaltas (Tel: 98); both MP Tourism
Permission: Superintendent, Pachmarhi Sanctuary, Pachmarhi, Dist: Hoshangabad, Madhya Pradesh

Nearest town: Pachmarhi (0.6 miles/1 km)
Rail: Piparia (3 miles/5 km)
Air: Bhopal (106 miles/170 km)

Panna N.P. Previously the hunting preserve of the Panna family, the area was declared a national park in 1981. Its 209 sq miles (543 sq km) of good forest is divided by the Ken river flowing north to join the Yamuna. Tiger, sloth bear, wolf, chital, chinkara and sambar are seen.
Best time to visit: Jan. — May.
Accommodation: forest resthouse, good hotels at Khajuraho
Permission: Director, Panna N.P., Panna, Madhya Pradesh
Nearest town: Panna (12.5 miles/20 km)
Rail: Stana (56 miles/90 km)
Air: Khajuraho (35 miles/57 km)

Panpatha Sanctuary. Established in 1983 on 95 sq miles (246 sq km) of mixed deciduous forest with sal and bamboo. Close to Bandhavgarh and with many of the same species in similar, although less undulating, forest. Tiger, chital and sambar are seen.
Best time to visit: Mar. — June
Accommodation: PWD inspection hut
Permission: Superintendent, Panpatha Sanctuary, PO Umaria, Dist: Shahdol, MP
Nearest town & Rail: Umaria (31 miles)
Air: Jabalpur

Pench N.P. and Sanctuary. Both established in 1977 and covering an area of 115 sq miles (299 sq km) and 173 sq miles (449 sq km) respectively. Located in southern MP, the park runs with the Pench National Park in Maharashtra to give a total area of almost

385 sq miles (1000 sq km). The forest is largely teak with some areas of mixed deciduous forest. Tiger, leopard, sloth bear, chinkara and chousingha are seen.
Best time to visit: Mar. — June
Accommodation: forest resthouses
Permission: The Director, Pench N.P., Dist: Seoni, MP
Nearest town & Rail: Seoni (18.5 miles)
Air: Nagpur (58 miles/93 km)

Sanjay N.P. and Sanctuary. This sanctuary, established in 1975 with an area of 140 sq miles (365 sq km) was previously known as Dubari. In 1981, with a further 747 sq miles (1938 sq km), it was set up as a National Park. The forest is largely sal with an attractive river flowing through. Facilities are at present poor, but the area has potential as a major game-viewing area. Tiger, leopard, chital, sambar, nilgai and wild boar, with extensive birdlife, are seen.
Best time to visit: Feb. — May.
Accommodation: foresthouses (one large new building over looking the river)
Permission: Director, Sanjay N.P., Sidhi, Madhya Pradesh
Nearest town: Sidhi (37 miles/60 km)
Rail: Jaora (12.5 miles/20 km)
Air: Khajuraho (168 miles/270 km), Varanasi (149 miles/240 km)

Satpura N.P. Sharing a boundary with the Pachmarhi Sanctuary, this (1983) park covers 203 sq miles (524 sq km) of mixed deciduous forest with sal and teak. Tiger, leopard, gaur, chital and sambar are seen. The park is hilly, with the highest point at 4437 feet (1352 meters). A system of forest roads is being developed.
Best time to visit: Jan. — June
Accommodation: forest resthouse, stay at Pachmarhi
Permission: Director, Satpura N.P., Pachmarhi, 461881, MP
Nearest town: Pachmarhi (0.75 mile/1 km)
Rail: Piparia (33 miles/54 km)
Air: Bhopal (118 miles/190 km)

Son Gharial Sanctuary. Established in 1983 and covering 80 sq miles (209 sq km) along the banks of the Son river.
Best time to visit: Nov. — Apr.
Permission: Superintendent, Son Gharial

Sanctuary, Sidhi, 486661, MP
Nearest town: Sidhi (3.5 miles/6 km)
Rail: Satna (87 miles/140 km)
Air: Khajuraho (147 miles/236 km), Varanasi (142 miles/228 km)

Van Vihar N.P. Established in 1979 to form the nucleus of an extensive zoological park. The existing area consists of dry mixed deciduous forest and has an exciting range of animals.
Permission: Director, Van Vihar N.P., B-Wing, 1st Fl., Satpura Bhawan, Bhopal 462004, MP
Nearest town, Rail & Air: Bhopal (4.5 miles)

Among the other sanctuaries in Madhya Pradesh are: Badalkhol (Raigarh dist.), Gandhi Sagar (Mandsaur dist.), Ghatigaon (Gwalior dist.), Gomradha (Raigarh dist.), Ken Gharial (Panna & Chhatarpur dists.), Kharmore (Dhar dist.), Kheoni (Dewas & Sehore dists.), Narsingarh (Rajarah dist.), Nauradhehii (Sagar dist.), Palpur Kund (Morena dist.), Pamed (Bastar dist.), Phen (Mandla dist.), Ratadani (Raisen dist.), Sailana (Ratlam dist.), Semarsot (Surguja dist.), Singhori (Raisen dist.), Sitanadi (Raipur dist.), Tamore Pingla (Surguja dist.), Udanti (Raipur dist.).
There is also a small Fossil National Park, eight miles (13 km) from Shahpura in Mandla district.
For information on any of the above areas contact the Chief Wildlife Warden, E-2/0 Mahavir Nagar, Bhopal, Madhya Pradesh.

MAHARASHTRA: The widely differing habitats of Maharashtra range from the coast, inland to the rich Western Ghats and the teak, sal, bamboo and scrub areas of the Deccan. Of the 2000 plus species and subspecies of birds in India, the state has records of 540, of which 442 are found in the area of Bombay and the Western Ghats.

Borivali N.P. Also known as the Sanjay Gandhi N.P. (There is another park of the same name in MP.) Now covering 36 sq miles (94 sq km), the area includes a Safari Park (since 1974) and a tourist-orientated deer park. Being only 21 miles (35 km) north of central Bombay, it has perhaps the highest number of visitors of any wildlife area in Asia (1,200,000 people in 1974!). The park has two small lakes and the Kanheri caves with a history of 2000 years. A large variety of birds.
Best time to visit: Oct. — May
Accommodation: 6 bungalows, restaurants
Permission: Divisional Manager, Sanjay Gandhi N.P., Borivali (East), Bombay 400066
Nearest town & Rail: Borivali (1.75 miles)
Air: Santacruz (9 miles/15 km)

Kinwat Sanctuary. Established in 1971. 84 sq miles (218 sq km) of mostly dry teak forest. Although tiger, leopard, chital, chinkara and blackbuck (in the open scrub) are found, game viewing is poor and there is no infrastructure.
Best time to visit: Feb. — June (hot: 45°C)
Accommodation: 5 resthouses
Permission: DFO, Pusad Forest Division, Pusad, Dist: Yavatmal, Maharashtra
Nearest town & Rail: Kinwat (1.75 mile)
Air: Nagpur (144 miles/232 km)

Melghat Tiger Reserve. One of the initial Project Tiger reserves (1973) with a total area of 605 sq miles (1571 sq km), of which 120 sq miles (311 sq km) form the core area. Largely dry teak forest in the Gaurilagarh Hills. The main ridge rises to over 3280 feet (1000 meters). The Tapi river flows along the northern border. The forest is dense and game viewing poor. The wildlife population are all on the increase. At present facilities are limited but park vehicles are available. Tiger, leopard, and wild dog are the main

predators. Sambar, barking deer, chinkara, chital, nilgai, wild boar and gaur all occur.
Best time to visit: Jan. — June
Accommodation: forest resthouses, Kolkaz
Permission: The Field Director, Melghat Tiger Reserve, East Melghat Division, Amravati, Maharashtra
Nearest town: Akot (31 miles/50 km)
Rail: Badnera (77 miles/124 km)
Air: Nagpur (162 miles/260 km)

Nagzira Sanctuary. Established in 1969 on 59 sq miles (153 sq km) of largely teak forest near the Nawegaon N.P. Tiger, leopard, sloth bear, chousingha and chital are present.
Best time to visit: Oct. — June
Accommodation: 6 forest resthouses
Permission: ACF (WL), Nagzira, Sakoli, Maharashtra
Nearest town & Rail: Gondiya (31 miles)
Air: Nagpur (81 miles/130 km)

Nawegaon N.P. Established in 1975 with 52 sq miles (134 sq km) of mixed deciduous forest in the Nishani range, it includes two lakes: Nawegaon and Itiadoh. The highest point is Ambajhar peak. A good system of forest roads. Boats available on Nawegaon lake. Large variety of birds. Tiger and leopard are rarely seen. A few gaur, chousingha, nilgai, sambar and chital are seen.
Best time to visit: Oct. — June (114°F/46°C)
Accommodation: 2 bungalows overlooking Nawegaon Lake; resthouses at Gothangaon and Nawegaon
Permission: DCF (Wildlife), Nagpur (Tel: 22024); or
DFO, Gondiya, 441601 (Tel: 265)
Nearest town & Rail: Gondiya (37 miles)
Air: Nagpur (81 miles/130 km)

Pench N.P. Established on 99 sq miles (256 sq km) of the Satpura Hills due north of Nagpur. The protected area continues across the border into MP where an additional 270 sq miles (700 sq km) has sanctuary or park status. The area is cut north-south by the Pench river. Most of the park is mixed deciduous forest with open meadows in some of the valleys. Most areas are accessible on a good network of fair-weather roads. Tiger, a few leopards, chital, sambar and gaur are seen. Attractively located resthouses on the Pench river at Totladoh and Ranidoh.
Best time to visit: Nov. —June
Accommodation: 5 forest resthouses
Permission: DFO, Nagpur, 440001 (Tel: 22024)
Nearest town, Rail & Air: Nagpur (35 miles)

Taroba N.P. Established as a reserve in 1935, the area was declared a park in 1955. The area became part of Maharashtra with the reorganization of states but retained its status as a park. The focal point is a lake in the midst of mixed deciduous forest and rolling hills. Leopards are sighted more often than the few tigers that come to the area. Wild boar are numerous. Chital, sambar, nilgai and gaur are seen. Good roads.
Best time to visit: Oct. —June (115°F/47°C)
Accommodation: 3 resthouses (with food)
Permission: DFO, West Chanda Division, Mul Road, Chandrapur, Maharashtra
Nearest town & Rail: Chandrapur (28 miles)
Air: Nagpur (98 miles/158km)

The other sanctuaries in Maharashtra include Dor (Nagpur Dist.). Devlagaon Dehekuri Blackbuck Sanctuary

(Ahmednagar Dist.), Dhakua Kolkaz (Amravati Dist.), Great Indian Bustard Sanctuary (Solapur Dist.), Radhanagri (Kolhapur Dist.), Tansa (Thane Dist.) and Yawal (Jalgaon Dist.). For further information on these and other protected areas contact The Chief Wildlife Warden, Pune, Maharashtra.

MANIPUR: There are two national parks in this small mountainous state on the Burma border. The area was a former princely state linked by treaty to India in 1825. Sixty percent of the population are members of a Tibeto-Burmese tribe, the Meitheis. Access to the area is restricted and for foreign tourists extremely difficult.

Keibul Lamjao N.P. Previously an area for waterfowl shoots, the area became a sanctuary in 1954 when a few surviving sangai or Manipur brow-antlered deer were reported. Perhaps the most endangered mammal and most localized in the world. Although the park is now almost 14 sq miles (36 sq km) in area, the sangai live on only about 2.5 sq miles (6 sq km) of floating vegetation known as *phumdi*.

There are possibly more deer in captivity (about 50) than in the wild—the largest group at the Delhi Zoo. The deer is distinguished by its gracefully curved antlers—the brow tines sweep forward and the beams backwards in an almost continuous curve. The park is located at the southeastern end of the Logtak Lake 20 miles (32 km) south of Imphal. Three hills—Pabot, Toya and Chingiao provide vantage points over the *phumdi* and during the monsoon the deer move onto the higher and harder ground. Other animals seen include hog deer, fishing cat and wild boar.
Best time to visit: Dec. — May
Accommodation: forest resthouse at Sendra and Phubala
Permission: ACF, Keibul Lamja N.P., BPO Kha-Thimungei, Manipur
Nearest town and Air: Imphal (20 miles)
Rail: Dimapur (142 miles/229 km)

Sirohi N.P. Established in 1982. Covering a small area of forest near the Burma border. Tigers are reported. Rich birdlife, including pheasants.
Accommodation: none
Permission: Chief Wildlife Warden, Imphal
Nearest town: Ukhrul (3 miles/5 km)
Rail: Dimapur
Air: Imphal (31 miles/50 km)

INDIAN LAND-CRAB (⅓ nat. size).

MEGHALAYA: "The abode of clouds" previously constituted the hill districts of Assam south of the Brahmaputra. Three tribes live in the hill areas of the same name: Garos, Khasis and Jaintias. The capital, Shillong, was previously the capital of Assam. The world's wettest place is Cheera Punji to the southwest of Shillong which receives about 500 inches (1270 cm) of rain each year.

A third of the state is still forested but little of this is reserve forest and enjoys little protection. It is extraordinary that Meghalaya, with its rich animal and birdlife, extensive forest and untold insects has only two absurdly small sanctuaries. The state has a possible population of 2500 elephants but none of its habitat is yet protected. A proposal for a 112 sq mile (292 sq km) sanctuary to be called Balphakram, with a buffer area of a further 115 sq miles (299 sq km) is still pending. This area of evergreen and moist deciduous forest with large tracks of scrub, grass and bamboo, is representative of much of the state.

With its well-forested hills, steep gorges and rivers, it has tiger, leopard, gaur, wild buffalo, golden cat, clouded leopard, capped langur; Hoolock gibbon, leopard cat, black bear, serow and other animals have been recorded. Peacock pheasants are only one among the fascinating bird species seen.

Permission to enter Meghalaya is obtainable. Permits for Shillong are often granted along with permission to visit Manas and Kaziranga Parks and Gwauhati.

Nongkhyllem Sanctuary. Established in 1981 on 11 sq miles (29 sq km) of sal forest containing a good range of species including binturong, clouded leopard, golden cat and leopard cat.
Best time to visit: Oct. — May.
Accommodation: 2 forest bungalows
Permission: Chief Wildlife Warden, Shilong, Meghalaya
Nearest town, Rail & Air: Guwahati (40 miles/65 km)

Siju Sanctuary. This extremely small sanctuary of only 2 sq miles (5 sq km) was established in 1979. The forest is mixed everywhere, with some sal.
Best time to visit: Dec. — Mar.
Accommodation: 1 bungalow
Permission: Chief Wildlife Warden, Shillong, Meghalaya
Nearest town: Tura (25 miles/40 km)
Rail & Air: Guwahati (130 miles/210 km)

A biosphere reserve has been proposed at Nokrek east of Tura in the West Garo Hills.

MIZORAM: In this mountainous state bounded by Bangladesh on the west and Burma to the south and east, there is at present only one wildlife protected area. Much of the state is forested and new sanctuaries need to be developed. Permission for tourists to enter the territory is yet again hard to obtain, but following the 1986 political settlement it is hoped that some restrictions will be lifted.

Dampa Sanctuary. Established in 1976 at the northwestern tip of the Mizo Hills. About 20 percent of the sanctuary is covered with bamboo while the rest is mostly semi-evergreen forest. The area is drained by the Dhaleswari river and its tributaries. Swamp deer are reported in the lower areas. Tiger, leopard, elephant and Hoolock gibbon are among the mammal species seen.
Best time to visit: Nov. — Mar.
Accommodation: 2 resthouses
Permission: FRO, Teiri Range Office, PO Theiri, Via Phaileng, Aizawl, Dist: Mizoram
Nearest town: Phaileng (6.5 miles/10 km)
Rail: Silchar (180 miles/290 km)
Air: Aizawl (56 miles/90 km)

BAR-TAILED GODWIT.

NAGALAND: To the east of Assam in the Naga hills is the small fascinating state of Nagaland, bounded by Burma to the east with the upper reaches of the Chindwin river beyond. Most of the area has a strong tribal culture and travel is restricted.

As with much of northeast India, the Naga hills have a distinctive wildlife and equally fascinating flora. Numerous species of orchid are unique to these hill areas. Most of Nagaland is covered by tropical evergreen forest while in the higher areas subtropical pine and temperate deciduous forest thrive.

Fakim Sanctuary. This small sanctuary in the eastern hills close to the Burma border was formed in 1983. The park rises to almost 9850 feet (3000 meters) and receives high rainfall in June and July, making travel extremely difficult. Tiger is reported in the area. Hoolock gibbons are seen.
Best time to visit: Feb. — Mar.
Accommodation: none
Permission: Wildlife Preservation Officer, PO Dimapur, Dist: Kohima, Nagaland
Nearest town: Kiphire (61 miles/98 km)
Rail & Air: Dimapur (241 miles/388 km)

Itanki Sanctuary. Cover 78 sq miles (202 sq km) of subtropical forest in the southwest corner of the state bounded on the west by the Dhansiri river which also forms the state border with Assam. Most of the sanctuary is low lying with the highest point being only 2216 feet (677 meters). Of the total estimated elephant population in Nagaland of above 250, almost 150 in four or five herds use this sanctuary and the adjacent area. The elephants migrate to/from the North Cachar Hills of Assam to the west.
Permission: Wildlife Preservation Officer, PO Dimapur, Dist: Kohima, Nagaland
Nearest town: Kohima (1.25 miles/2 km)
Rail & Air: Dimapur (44 miles/76 km)

Puliebadze Sanctuary. Established in 1979 on a small area of forest (3.5 sq miles/9 sq km) on the edge of Kohima. Tragopan and kaleej pheasant are among the many fascinating hill and forest birds seen.
Best time to visit: Nov. — Mar.
Accommodation: none
Permission: Wildlife Preservation Officer, PO Dimapur, Dist: Kohima, Nagaland
Nearest town: Kohima (1.25 miles/2 km)
Rail & Air: Dimapur (47 miles/76 km)

ORISSA: With Orissa's long coastline of offshore islands, lagoons (Chilka is India's largest salt-water lake), salt flats and deltas along the Bay of Bengal, it is possible to forget that inland, to the west, there are large areas of hill forest running into Madhya Pradesh and Andhra Pradesh. The varied habitats contain an equally wide-ranging bird and animal life. While the wildlife is rich and in many places exciting, few of Orissa's parks have adequate infrastructure for visitors. The parks are off the beaten track and few have transport for hire or facilities for food.

Baisipalli Wildlife Sanctuary. Established in 1981 in the Eastern Ghats, rising from almost sea level to 2800 feet (855 meters), the sanctuary covers 64 sq miles (166 sq km). Apart from a few elephants and tigers, there are also sambar, mouse deer and fascinating range of birds.
Best time to visit: Dec. — Feb.
Accommodation: 4 resthouses
Permission: Chief Wildlife Warden, Baisipalli Sanctuary, Nayagarh Forest Division, PO Nayagarh, Dist: Puri Dist, Orissa.
Nearest town: Nayagarh (37 miles/60 km)
Rail: Khurda (50 miles/80 km)
Air: Bhubaneshwar (93 miles/150 km)

Balukhand Sanctuary. Established only in 1984, this coastal sanctuary covering 28 sq miles (72 sq km) protects the shoreline nesting sites of the olive ridley and green sea turtle. On land are groups of blackbuck.
Best time to visit: Oct. — May
Accommodation: 8 resthouses
Permission: DFO, Puri Forest Division, PO Khurda, Dist: Puri, Orissa.
Nearest town & Rail: Puri (6 miles/10 km)
Air: Bhubaneshwar (44 miles/70 km)

Bhitarkanika Sanctuary. Established in 1975, this marine sanctuary in the estuary of the Brahmani river covers 250 sq miles (650 sq km). Extensive birdlife, estuarine crocodiles and sea turtles are the attractions.
Best time to visit: Oct. — May.
Accommodation: 3 resthouses
Permission: DFO, Chandabali, Dist: Baleshwar, Orissa.
Nearest town: Chandabali (22 miles/35 km)

Rail: Bhadrakh (48 miles/77 km)
Air: Bhubaneshwar (118 miles/190 km)

Chilka Sanctuary. Established in 1973 over 345 sq miles (900 sq km) of lake, shore and hinterland. The lagoon covers 425 sq miles (1100 sq km) of shallow water separated from the Bay of Bengal by a narrow sand bar. White chital and blackbuck are seen on the scrubby shoreline, it is the extensive birdlife that makes the area important. The migratory birds arrive in early winter and stay till March. Also seen are resident shore birds and birds of prey. Dolphins are occasionally sighted near the mouth of the lagoon. Boats can be hired at Rambha.
Best time to visit: Dec. — Mar.
Accommodation: tourist lodges at Barkul, Rambha and Balugaon
Permission: DFO, Ghunar South, PO Khurda, Dist: Puri, Orissa.
Air: Bhubaneshwar (62 miles/100 km)

Nandankanan Sanctuary and Biological Park. Only 8 miles (13 km) from Bhubaneshwar, this small sanctuary, established in 1979, is in fact a modern zoological park. The species shown in varying habitats give a good introduction to the range and diversity of India's fauna.
Best time to visit: Nov. — Feb. (open throughout the year)
Accommodation: hotel and tourist lodge
Permission: Wildlife Conservation Officer, 145 Sahid Nagar, Bhubaneshwar, Orissa 751007.
Nearest town, Rail & Air: Bhubaneshwar

Satkosia Gorge Sanctuary. Established in 1976 and including a 14-mile (22-km) long gorge where the Mahanadi river cuts through the Eastern Ghats, the total sanctuary area is 306 sq miles (796 sq km). Although established to protect crocodile habitat and support projects for the gharial, the surrounding forests also have leopard, the occasional tiger, wolf and sambar.
Best time to visit: Nov. — May.
Accommodation: resthouses
Permission: DFO, Satkosia WL Conservation Division, PO Angul, Dist: Dhenkanal, Orissa 759122
Nearest town: Angul (36 miles/58 km)

Rail: Talche (47 miles/76 km)
Air: Bhubaneshwar (138 miles/220 km)

Simlipal N.P., Tiger Reserve and Sanctuary. Previously the hunting preserve of the maharajas of Mayurbhanj, the forests of north Orissa are among the most attractive in India. The area was declared a sanctuary in 1957 and the core became a national park in 1980. The total area is 1059 sq miles (2750 sq km), of which the park is only 117 sq miles (303 sq km). One of the first sanctuaries under Project Tiger.

The park has 12 rivers cutting across it and on many there are waterfalls. The largely sal forest is broken up by clearings and green grasslands along the rivers. Many of the rivers have mugger crocodiles. Mammals include tiger, elephant, gaur, leopard, chital, mouse deer, sambar and pangolin. The birdlife is extensive and varied, with the singing hill myna being among the more noticeable. Jeeps are available.

Best time to visit: Feb. — June
Accommodation: forest resthouses
Permission: Field Director, Simplipal Tiger Reserve, PO Khairic-Jashipur, Dist: Mayurbhanj, Orissa.
Nearest town: Baripada (31 miles/50 km)
Rail & Air: Jamshedpur (87 miles/140 km), Bhubaneshwar (217 miles/350 km); Calcutta (150 miles/240 km).

Ushakothi Sanctuary. Established in 1962, this sanctuary of 110 sq miles (285 sq km) is of mixed deciduous forest. Tiger, elephant, sambar, chital and gaur are found but are usually seen only on night drives. The sanctuary is to the east of the Hirakud Reservoir into which the area drains.

Best time to visit: Oct. — May
Accommodation: resthouses, bungalow
Permission: DFO, Ushakothi Sanctuary, PO Bamra, Sambalpur Dist., Orissa
Nearest town & Rail: Sambalpur (22 miles)
Air: Bhubaneshwar (186 miles/300 km)

Among the many other excellent sanctuaries in Orissa are Chandaka Dampadu (Puri dist.), Debrigarh (Sambalpur dist.), Hadgarh (Mayurbhanj dist.), Khalasoni (Sambalpur dist.), Kotgarh (Phulbani dist.), Kuldiha (Baleshwar dist.), and Sunabeda (Kalahandi dist.). Obtain information from the Chief

Wildlife Warden in Bhubaneshwar, Govt. of Orissa Tourist Office, Tourist Bungalow, Bhubaneshwar 751006, (Tel: 50099).

PUNJAB: Between the Himalayan foothills and the desert of Rajasthan lies the fertile land of five rivers—Punjab. The state is now highly developed with extensive irrigation projects to enable intensive agriculture. A consequence of this is that there are few wilderness areas left. The declared reserves are small, with the exception of the Abohar Sanctuary (73 sq miles/188 sq km) which, being in Firozpur district, close to the border with Pakistan, cannot be visited.

The other sanctuaries are Bir Bunar Heri Sanctuary (3 sq miles/8 sq km), Patiala dist; Bir Gurdialpura Sanctuary (0.4 sq mile/1 sq km), Patiala dist.; Bir Motibagh Sanctuary (2 sq miles/5 sq km), Patiala dist; Harike Lake Sanctuary (16 sq miles/41 sq km), Amritsar dist.

Information on all the above can be obtained from Chief Wildlife Warden, SCD 2463-64, Sector 22-C, Chandigarh.

RAJASTHAN: Situated in the northwest of India. The Aravalli Hills form a line across the state and about three-fifths of the state lie northwest of this line, leaving two-fifths in the east. These are the two natural divisions of Rajasthan.

Much of the flora is scrub jungle and towards the west, plants characteristic of the arid zone occur. Trees are scarce, found only sparingly in the Aravallis and in eastern part of Rajasthan.

Bhensrod Garh Sanctuary. Established in 1983 over 88 sq miles (229 sq km) of scrub and dry deciduous forest. The area has been increasingly threatened by illegal grazing

and collecting of fuel wood. Despite these threats, leopards are still seen in the area along with chinkara, sloth bear etc.

Best time to visit: Oct. — May.
Accommodation: resthouses
Permission: Range Forest Officer, Rawatbhuta, Dist: Chittor.
Nearest town: Rawatbhuta
Rail & Air: Kota (33 miles/53 km)

Darrah Sanctuary. Established in 1955 but previously the hunting reserve of Kota State. The former Maharao kept an interesting photographic record of the tigers in the area, part of which is still on display. The sanctuary covers 102 sq miles (266 sq km) of dry deciduous forest (mostly *Anogeissus penduia*). Animals include wolf, sloth bear, chinkara and leopard. Despite the disturbance from local villages it is worth visiting.

Best time to visit: Feb. — May
Accommodation: 1 resthouse
Permission: Range Officer, Darrah Wildlife Sanctuary, via Kamalpura, Dist: Kota
Nearest town & Air: Kota (31 miles/50 km)
Rail: Darrah (5 miles/8 km)

Desert N.P. Established in 1980, this large park of 1220 sq miles (3162 sq km) is only 20 miles (32 km) from Jaisalmer. Although known as a park, much of the area in fact has only sanctuary status but the area as a whole has its own distinct wildlife. Very little of the area is a Sahara type of desert with rolling sand dunes, in fact, much of the area is covered with patchy scrub and even trees and flowers. The shrubs have adapted themselves to the harsh climate and although many are leafless, they provide shelter and shade for many animals.

There are many Bishnoi village in the sanctuary area and environs, and blackbuck and chinkara are usually seen nearby. Other animals seen include wolf, desert fox, hare and desert cat. Many birds of prey such as the tawny eagle, short-toed eagle, spotted eagle, kestrel and laggar falcon are seen. Other birds often seen are flights of sandgrouse in the early morning, gray partridge and great Indian bustard.

Best time to visit: Sept. — Mar. (Summer temp. exceeds 122°F/50°C)
Accommodation: 6 resthouses; some villages have rooms to let.

Permission: Dy. Director Research, Desert N.P., Jaisalmer.
Nearest town, Air & Rail: Jaisalmer (20 miles/32 km)

Jaisammand Sanctuary. Established in 1957, beside the large manmade (62 sq mile/160 sq km) lake from which it takes its name. The lake was built by Maharana Jai Singh in the 16th century and the surrounding hills are dotted with *chhatris*, a marble palace and other buildings. Some of the islands are inhabited by Bhils—a tribe of southern Rajasthan. The sanctuary is small (20 sq miles/52 sq km) but ranges from the lake shore to the open dry deciduous forests on the adjoining hills.

A wide variety of birds is to be seen and the forest holds chital, chinkara, wild boar and a few leopard. Many crocodiles feed on a large population of fish. A boat is available from the Irrigation Department.

Best time to visit: Nov. — June
Accommodation: Jaisammand Tourist Bungalow (RSTDC) on Udaipur—Banswara Rd
Permission: Wildlife Warden (Jaisammand Dist.), Udaipur
Nearest town, Rail & Air: Udaipur (30 miles/48 km)

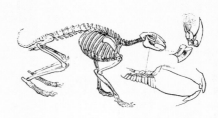

Keoladeo Ghana N.P. Previously known as the Bharatpur Bird Sanctuary, this magnificent park is one of the world's greatest and most important heronries. Originally protected for the occasional duck shot, the area became a sanctuary in the mid-1950s and a national park in 1983.

About a third of its 11 sq miles (29 sq km) is a shallow, freshwater marsh formed by retaining water after the monsoons. The dry areas are mostly scrub, thorn and mixed deciduous forest. Over 12,000 nests produce over 30,000 chicks. Although mainly famous for its waterbirds, many other species, including many raptors, are also to be seen. Mammals include sambar, blackbuck, chital, nilgai, fishing cat, jungle cat, otter and mongoose.

Best time to visit: open throughout the year; breeding season: Aug. —Oct; migrants: Oct. — late Feb.
Accommodation: In the sanctuary: Shanti Kuti forest resthouse; ITDC Forest Lodge (Tel: 2322, 2864) with restaurant, bar, air-conditioned and non-airconditioned rooms. Outside the sanctuary: Saras Tourist Bungalow (RSTDC), Fatehpur Sikri Road, has both airconditioned and non-airconditioned rooms (Tel: 2169); Golbargh Palace Hotel, Agra Road (Tel: 3349).
Permission: Dy. Chief Wildlife Warden, Keoladeo N.P., Bharatpur
Nearest town & Rail: Bharatpur (1 mile)
Air: Agra (3 miles/55 km)

Kumbalgarh Sanctuary. This large sanctuary (222 sq miles/ 578 sq km) in the rugged Aravalli Hills is perhaps the only area in India where the highly endangered wolf is successfully breeding. Other animals seen there include leopard, sloth bear, chinkara, chousingha, ratel and flying squirrel. The Kumbalgarh fort to the east is one of the most impressive in Rajasthan. The sanctuary is dry and apparently barren for much of the year but comes alive during the monsoon and in October when the deciduous trees change color before shedding their leaves.
Best time to visit: Mar. — May (hot days), Sept. — Nov.
Accommodation: Gokul Tourist Bungalow (RSTDC) at Nathwara; Shilpi Tourist Bungalow (RSTDC) at Ranakpur; and Ghanerao Royal Castle at Ghanerao (Tel: 35), only 3 miles (5 km) from the sanctuary.
Permission: Wildlife Warden, Kumbalgarh Sanctuary, Dist: Udaipur
Nearest town: Sadri (5 miles/7 km)
Rail: Falna (15 miles/25 km)
Air: Udaipur (75 miles/120 km)

Mount Abu Sanctuary. A small sanctuary established in 1960 consisting of 110 sq miles (289 sq km) of forested hills to the northeast of Mount Abu. Includes Guru Shikhar which at 4895 feet (1772 meters) is the highest point in the Aravalli Hills. Animals include leopard, chinkars and, in the lower areas, sloth bear, sambar and wild boar. Among the interesting birds is the gray jungle fowl.
Best time to visit: Mar. — June
Accommodation: Shikhar Tourist Bungalow (RSTDC) in Mount Abu; also many hotels; PWD bungalows and Circuit Houses
Permission: Wildlife Warden, Mount Abu
Nearest town: Mount Abu (5 miles/8 km)
Rail: Abu Road (17 miles/28 km)
Air: Udaipur (115 miles/185 km)

National Chambal Sanctuary. Established in 1983 along the Chambal river from Rana Pratap Sagar to the southwest of Kota to its confluence with the Jamuna. It has an area of 211 sq miles (549 sq km) and has sanctuary status to protect the gharial crocodilian. Southeast of Swai Madhopur the Chambal joins the Parbati river which forms the border with MP. The MP bank is also a sanctuary. Blackbuck, caracal, chinkara and wolf are among the many animals that enjoy protection here. Boats can be taken upstream from Kota and in the winter, gharials are often seen basking on the sand banks.
Best time to visit: Oct. — Mar.
Accommodation: Chambal Tourist Bungalow (RSTDC), Kota; forest resthouses at other places
Permission: Warden, National Chambal Sanctuary, Kota
Nearest town, Rail & Air: Kota

Ranthambhore N.P. Established as a sanctuary in 1955 and one of the original areas under Project Tiger. Although the smallest of the Project Tiger reserves, Ranthambhore has an impressive range of animal species including sambar, chital, nilgai, chinkara, wild boar, sloth bear, hyena, jackal, leopard and tiger within its 150 sq miles (392 sq km).

Since coming under Project Tiger management, these arid hills at the junction of the Aravalli and Vindhya ranges have been restored to their full dynamism. Artificial lakes now blend with the forested hills and form the integral part of the park. Excellent birdlife with the crested serpent eagle among the many birds of prey to be seen. Many waterbirds are seen on the lakes. A thousand-year old fort rises 700 ft (214 m) above the park.
Best time to visit: Oct. — Apr.
Accommodation: Jogi Mahal in the park, bookings can be made through the Field Director's office; Castle Jhoomer Baori Forest Lodge (RSTDC), Ranthambhore Road, Sawai Madhopur (Tel: 620)—will arrange vehicles; Maharaja Lodge, Sawai Madhopur, bookings can be made through Ranthambhore Palace Hotel in Jaipur.
Permission: The Field Director, Ranthambhore N.P., Sawai Madhopur
Nearest town & Rail: Sawai Madhopur (9 miles/14 km)
Air: Jaipur (82 miles/132 km)

Sariska N.P., Tiger Reserve and Sanctuary. Originally the shooting area of the Alwar ruling family, Sariska became a sanctuary in 1958. The sanctuary came under Project Tiger in 1979 and the core area of 191 sq miles (498 sq km) became a national park in 1982.

The park also has 9th- and 10th-century ruins of Shiva temples and the Kanokwari fort. Most of Sariska is hilly with a wide valley from the gate to Thana Gazi. It has a good network of roads. Animals seen include leopard, wild dog (first sighted in 1986), nilgai, chital, chousingha, chinkara, ratel and tiger.
Best time to visit: Nov. — June. Very dry summers make June good for game viewing, although hot.
Accommodation: forest resthouse; Tiger Den Tourist Bungalow (RSTDC) has air-conditioned and non-airconditioned rooms (Tel: 42); Hotel Sariska Palace, opposite the park entrance is a converted Royal Palace—has jeep for hire.

Permission: The Field Director, Sariska Tiger Reserve, Dist: Alwar.
Nearest town & Rail: Alwar (22 miles)
Air: Jaipur (68 miles/110 km)

Sitamata Sanctuary. Established in 1979 in the southern forest of Rajasthan over 163 sq miles (423 sq km) of dry deciduous forest and bamboo. The flying squirrel is more often seen here than in most other sanctuaries. Other species seen include leopard, caracal, chousingha, pangolin, sambar, wild boar and chinkara.
Best time to visit: Apr. — July
Accommodation: forest resthouse
Permission: Wildlife Warden, Sitamata Wildlife Sanctuary, Dhariawad, Dist: Udaipur.
Nearest town: Dhariawad
Rail: Bansi (19 miles/31 km)
Air: Udaipur (65 miles/108 km)

Tal Chapper Sanctuary. This small sanctuary covering 27 sq miles (71 sq km) has a large blackbuck population. Chinkara, partridge and sandgrouse are the other animals and bird species usually seen, including the occasional desert fox and cat. Mostly thorn scrub with high summer temperatures and low rainfall.
Best time to visit: Apr. and Oct.
Accommodation: 1 resthouse
Permission: Dy. Conservator of Forest, Churu.
Nearest town: Chapper
Rail: Abu Road (17 miles/28 km)
Air: Jaipur (130 miles/210 km)

Other sanctuaries in Rajasthan include Jamia Ramgarh (Jaipur Dist.), Jawahar Sagar (Kota, Bundi Dist.), Kaila Devi (Sawai Madhopur Dist.), Nahargarh (Jaipur Dist.), Phulwari (Udaipur Dist.), Ramgarh (Bundi Dist.), Shergarh (Kota Dist.), Todgarh-Rad, (Ajmer, Udaipur and Pali Dists.)

and Vanvihar (Dholpur Dist.). Information on all these areas can be obtained from The Chief Wildlife Warden's office, Van Bhawan, Jaipur.

Rajasthan has a reasonable tourist infrastructure with a range of accommodation and public transport. The Rajasthan State Tourism Development Corporation (RSTDC) provides accommodation throughout the state.

SIKKIM: This small, strategically important state is surrounded on three sides by Nepal to the west, Tibet to the north and northeast and Bhutan to the east. The state is only 2818 sq miles (7300 sq km) in area and its only national park occupies 10 percent of this. Compressed into the 70 miles (12 km), from north to south is an incredible range of habitats and diversity of flora. Over a thousand orchids are recorded from Sikkim, and near Gangtok (the capital), is an orchid sanctuary with 250 species which flower prior to the the monsoon (in May and June), while others bloom in December and January.

Travel in much of Sikkim is restricted but permits to visit the western and southern region are obtainable from any Indian Embassy or High Commission abroad or from the Ministry of Home Affairs (Foreigners Wing) Lok Nayak Bhawan, Khan Market, New Delhi 110003.

Kangchendzonga N.P. Established in 1977 on 328 sq miles (850 sq km) of wet temperate and mountain forests at the lower levels, rising to the bare rock, ice and snow of the peaks. The park is bounded by Nepal on the west with some of the world's highest mountains straddling the border: Tent Peak, Nepal Peak, Kabur North, Kabur South and, of course, Kangchendzonga herself (28,179 feet/8586 meters). To the north is the Zemu glacier flowing into the Zenu river and then the Tista. The park has an impressive range of animals and birds: leopard, clouded leop-

ard, tahr, musk deer, Bharal, serow, snow leopard, red panda and binturong.
Best time to visit: Apr. — May, Aug. — Oct.
Accommodation: 4 resthouses
Permission: Asst. Wildlife Officer (KNP), Forest Dept., Deorali, Sikkim 737102
Nearest town: Chungthany (12.5 miles)
Air: Bagdogra

Other sanctuaries developed in the mid-1980s are: Fambung Kho (5.8 sq miles/15 sq km); Kyongnosla Alpine Sanctuary (1.5 sq miles/4 sq km), established to protect the natural flora; and the Singba Rhododendron Sanctuary.

TAMIL NADU: The parks of Tamil Nadu are mostly little-known, although their range is extraordinary—mixed deciduous forests of the Western Ghats, through the hot, dry plains, to the coastal and marine parks. Two biosphere reserves are proposed: one at the Gulf of Mannar and the other in the Nilgiris. Most of Tamil Nadu receives both the monsoons, and the two rainy seasons severely limit game viewing. November to February are pleasant months to travel through the state.

Anamalai Wildlife Sanctuary. Established in 1976, it covers 368 sq miles (955 sq km) of the northern end of the Cardamom Hills and abuts Kerala on its Western border. The focal point, with tourist accommodation, is known as Top Slip. Rich, mixed deciduous forest with large rosewood and teak trees. The main attractions are the lion-

tailed macaque and Nilgiri langur for which it offers a secure home, and both of which tend to stay in the evergreen sholas. Gaur can be seen near the Srichalippallam river. Elephant, chital, sambar, mouse deer and barking deer are all found here. Riding elephants and forest vehicles are available. Also extensive birdlife.
Best time to visit: Feb. — June
Accommodation: 5 resthouses and log huts, food and bedding available.
Permission: Wildlife Warden, 5 Round Rd., Mahalinga Puram, Pollachi, Dist: Coimbatore, Tamil Nadu 642001
Nearest town & Rail: Pollachi (15.5 miles)
Air: Coimbatore (41 miles/65 km)

Kalakad Sanctuary. Established in 1976 on 86 sq miles (224 sq km) of mixed semi-evergreen forest containing a wide range of animals, including elephant, macaques and good birdlife. Core area consists of 31 sq miles (81 sq km), and the rainy season is from October to December.
Best time to visit: Jan. — Mar.
Accommodation: 1 resthouse
Permission: Wildlife Warden, St Peter's Hall, Tiruneveli, Tamil Nadu 627002
Nearest town: Nanguneri (9.5 miles/15 km)
Rail: Tirunelveli (25 miles/40 km)
Air: Trivandrum (Kerala) (88 miles/140 km)

Mudumalai Sanctuary. Established in 1938 and now expanded to cover 124 sq miles (322 sq km) of mixed and moist-deciduous forests. Bisected by the road from Mysore to Ootacamund and bounded to the north by Bandipur National Park in Karnataka and to the west by the Wynad Sanctuary in Kerala. Good game-viewing and facilities. Vehicles and elephant riding available.
Best time to visit: Mar. — June, Sept. — Oct.
Accommodation: resthouses at Masinagudi, Theppakadu, Abhayaranyam and Kargundi; Bamboo Banks Farm, 11 miles (18 km) from the sanctuary has comfortable accommodation and good food. Contact Mrs. S.T. Kotawala, Bamboo Banks, Masinagudi PO Nilgiris, Tamil Nadu.
Permission: Wildlife Warden, Mahalingam Bldg, Coonoor Road, Ootacamund 643001
Nearest town: Gudalur (10 miles/16 km)
Rail: Ootacamund (40 miles/64 km)
Air: Coimbatore (103 miles); Mysore

Mundanthurai Sanctuary. Established in 1962, this large sanctuary covering 219 sq miles (567 sq km) is excellent for viewing examples of India's primates. The facilities are regrettably poor. The area receives almost 120 inches (300 cm) of rain and there are still pockets of virgin rainforest. The bonnet macaque and common langur are found throughout the sanctuary; the Nilgiri langur at Tarucvattampaarai and the lion-tailed macaque near the top of Valaiyar Hill. Tiger, leopard, sloth bear, sambar and chital are also seen.
Best time to visit: Sept. — Dec.
Accommodation: Resthouse overlooking the Tambaravarani river.
Permission: Wildlife Warden, Shengottai, Dist: Tiruneveli, Tamil Nadu 627809
Nearest town: Ambasamudram (6 miles)
Rail: Tirunelveli (28 miles/45 km)
Air: Trivandrum (100 miles/160 km)

Point Calimere Sanctuary. Established in 1967, protecting 6.5 sq miles (17 sq km) of shoreline and hinterland that surround a saline lagoon. Part of the area is tidal swamp. Dolphins are occasionally seen in the lagoon. Also, there are numerous shore birds and waders, large flocks of both greater and lesser flamingoes. Blackbuck, chital, feral pig and bonnet macaques are among the land mammals seen.
Best time to visit: Nov. — Jan.
Accommodation: forest resthouse (14 beds), food available on prior booking
Permission: DFO, 281/1846 West Main St., Thanjavur, Tamil Nadu 613009
Nearest town: Vedaranyam (7 miles/11 km)
Rail: Kodikkarai
Air: Tiruchchirappalli (103 miles/165 km)

Vedanthangal Sanctuary. Protected for over two hundred years, and first legislated protection in 1798 when shooting was prohibited. The sanctuary is small and consists of a grove of trees growing in and around the village tank. There are a number of resident breeding waterbirds and many migrants. Can be visited in a day from Madras.
Best time to visit: Oct. — Feb.
Accommodation: resthouse, food available
Permission: Wildlife Warden, 50 IVth Main Rd, Gandhi Nagar, Madras 600020.

Nearest town: Maduranthakam (9.5 miles)
Rail: Maduranthakam
Air: Madras (50 miles/80 km)

There is a small preserve of only one sq mile (2.7 sq km) at Guindy in Madras city which also has a zoo and the Madras Snake Park. A Marine National Park in the Gulf of Mannar has been proposed as a biosphere reserve. Other sanctuaries are Karikili (Chengalpattu dist.); Nilgiri Tahr Sanctuary, Pulicat (Chengalpattu dist.); and Vettangudi (Ramanathapuram dist.). For further information contact The Chief Wildlife Warden, 50 IVth Main Rd, Gundhi Nagar, Madras 600020.

UTTAR PRADESH: This huge state ranges from the High Himalaya to the Gangetic Plain. It is densely populated, with a population larger than any country in Europe, but it nevertheless has an important and vast range of wilderness areas. The Himalayan region has many peaks between 21,000 and 26,000 feet (6000-8000 meters) high. The central part is a vast alluvial and extremely fertile plain formed by the Ganga and its major tributaries: the Chambal, the Yamuna, the Ramganga and others.

Some of the sanctuaries have been established for specific species such as the gharial, while others are more general, such as Corbett and Dudhwa.

Corbett N.P. Established in 1936 as the Hailey N.P., following the advice of the hunter-naturalist, Jim Corbett. The park in 1986 covered 200 sq miles (520 sq km) and proposed extensions of up to 230 sq miles

(600 sq km) are under consideration. The park is set in the undulating Siwalik foothills of the Himalaya with the Ramganga river flowing through it from east to west.

The diversity of the wildlife and its location in relation to the major cities of northern India have made it perhaps the most famous park in the region. The many pools of the Ramganga have both mugger and gharial. The river also holds mahseer and other sporting fish. The park is closed during the monsoon, till mid-November. Elephants and vehicles are available at Dhikala.
Best time to visit: Feb. — May. Closed from mid-Jun to mid-Nov.
Accommodation: forest resthouses at Khinanauli, Sarapduli, Bijrani and Ghairal, bookings can be made through the Project Tiger Office at Ramnagar or in Lucknow (Chief Wildlife Warden). In Dhikala are forest resthouse, loghuts, tourist huts, tented camp. Lodge is being developed at the park entrance which will eventually take over from Dhikala.
Permission: Field Director, Project Tiger. Corbett N.P., PO Ramnagar, Dist: Nainital, UP. Cable: PROTIGER, Ramnagar, Tel: Office 189; WL Warden 32.
Nearest town & Rail: Ramnagar (12 miles)
Air: Phoolbagh (Pantnagar) (32 miles)

There is a regular bus service from Delhi and Lucknow to the park entrance.

Chilla Sanctuary. Established in 1977 on the east bank of the Ganga, this area (96 sq miles/249 sq km) has traditionally been known for the elephants that migrate through it. A few tiger, bear and small cats are seen along with interesting birds.
Best time to visit: Nov. — mid-June
Accommodation: forest resthouses
Permission: Wildlife Warden, Kotalwara, Dist: Garhwal, UP
Nearest town & Rail: Haridwar (4 miles)
Air: Dehra Dun (20 miles/32 km)

Dudhwa N.P. Established as a sanctuary in 1968 and later upgraded to a national park in 1977. The 189 sq miles (490 sq km) of *terai* jungle were long protected thanks to the efforts of "Billy" Arjan Singh whose farm, Tiger Haven, forms part of the southern boundary. Best known for the leopard

and tiger re-introduction projects Arjan Singh carried out with the support of the WWF and the Government of India during the 1970s. The original sanctuary was established to protect a large population of swamp deer; other species include tiger, leopard, sloth bear, chital and hog deer. Rhinoceros were introduced from Assam in 1985. An excellent range of bird is seen.
Best time to visit: Dec. — June
Accommodation: forest resthouses at Dudhwa and Sathiana; Tiger Haven farm has comfortable facilities and well-organized visits to the jungle are arranged. Write to Tiger Haven, PO Palia, Dist: Kheri, UP
Permission: Director, Dudhwa N.P., Lakhimpur, Kheri, UP
Nearest town: Dudhwa (6.25 miles/10 km)
Rail: Dudhwa
Air: Lucknow (162 miles/260 km)

Govind Sanctuary. Established in 1955 in the upper Tons valley bordering Himachal Pradesh and covering 368 sq miles (953 sq km). The sanctuary includes some interesting mountains including Swarg Pohini, Black Peak and Bandarpunch. The Har-Ki-dun valley forms part of the sanctuary. Animals seen include musk deer, brown bear, bharal serow and leopard.
Best time to visit: May — Oct.
Accommodation: resthouses
Permission: ACF, Purola, Uttarkashi, UP
Nearest town: Mussoorie (100 miles)
Rail & Air: Dehra Dun (119 miles/190 km)

Kaimur Sanctuary. Established in 1982 and covering 193 sq miles (500 sq km) of dry, mixed forest and scrub. Leopard, blackbuck and chinkara are seen. Wolf are also possibly in the area.
Best time to visit: Oct. — Feb.
Accommodation: 3 resthouses
Permission: WL Warden Kaimur Sanctuary, Robertsganj, Dist: Mirzapur, UP
Nearest town & Rail: Robertsganj (2 miles)
Air: Varanasi (20 miles/32 km)

Katerniaghat Sanctuary. Established in 1976, this little-known *terai* sanctuary near the Nepal border covers 154.5 sq miles (400 sq km). A few swamp deer and tiger are seen along with gharial and mugger crocodiles in the Girwa river and its tributaries.

Best time to visit: Nov — Mar.
Accommodation: none
Permission: Wildlife Warden, Katerniaghat Sanctuary, Baharaich, UP
Nearest town: Nanpara (125 miles/40 km)
Rail: Bichua (15 miles/24 km)
Air: Lucknow (119 miles/190 km)

Kedarnath Sanctuary. Established in 1972 on 373 sq miles (967 sq km) of the Garhwal Himalaya. Leopard, tahr, serow and musk deer are among the animals seen. A detailed musk deer study funded by the WWF was undertaken here between 1978 to 1980. Kaleej and monal pheasants are among the many birds seen.
Best time to visit: late Apr. — Oct.
Accommodation: 8 resthouses
Permission: Kedarnath Sanctuary, Gopeshwar, Chamoli, UP
Nearest town: Gopeshwar (2 miles/4 km)
Rail: Rishikesh (133 miles/213 km)
Air: Dehra Dun (143 miles/228 km)

Kishanpur Sanctuary. Established in 1972 over 77 sq miles (200 sq km) of *terai* forests and open meadows similar to Dudhwa to its east. Tiger, a few swamp deer, leopard, sambar and hog deer are seen.
Best time to visit: Feb. — May
Accommodation: 3 resthouses
Permission: Wildlife /Warden, Kishanpur Sanctuary, Lakhimpur-Kheri, U P
Nearest town & Rail: Mailani (2 miles/3 km)
Air: Lucknow (140 miles/225 km)

Nanda Devi N.P. Established in 1980 to include a unique range of both slora and fauna over 243 sq miles (630 sq km) in the vicinity of Nanda Devi Peak (25,675 feet/7816 meters), India's second-highest mountain. The natural sanctuary was first entered in 1934 by the remarkable British mountaineers, Eric Shipton and Bill Tilman.

Apart from Tilman's successful attempt on Nanda Devi in 1936, the area remained virtually undisturbed until the 1950s, when a spate of climbing and trekking expeditions into the area began. Since 1980, access to the area has been restricted and climbing expeditions must first get permission from the Indian Mountaineering Federation (Benito Juarez Marg, New Delhi). When Shipton first entered the sanctuary he gazed on herds of bharal and goral—the numbers are now reduced but they can still be seen. Other animals seen include musk deer, serow and, possibly, snow leopard. The area is a proposed biosphere reserve.
Best time to visit: Apr. — Oct.
Accommodation: none
Permission: DCF, Nanda Devi N.P., Joshimath, Dist: Chamoli, UP
Nearest town: Joshimath (17 miles/23 km)
Rail: Rishikesh (72 miles/276 km)
Air: Dehra Dun (185 miles/295 km)

National Chambal Sanctuary. Established in 1979 and part of a large area co-administered by Rajasthan, MP and UP.
Best time to visit: Nov. — Mar.
Accommodation: 7 resthouses
Permission: DFO, National Chambal Sanctuary, Project 13, Lajpatrai Marg, Lucknow.
Nearest town & Rail: Etawah (11 miles)
Air: Agra (44 miles/70 km)

Rajaji Sanctuary. Established in 1966, this small sanctuary on the edge of the Dehra Dun valley still has a few tiger and leopard in its 95 sq miles (246 sq km). Other animals seen include sloth bear, chital and sambar.
Best time to visit: Oct. — June
Accommodation: 4 resthouses
Permission: Wildlife Warden, Dehra Dun, Uttar Pradesh
Nearest town & Rail: Haridwar (7 miles)
Air: Dehra Dun (20 miles/31 km)

Valley of Flowers N.P. Established in 1981 in one of the most remarkable areas in the Himalaya, this small park of 33.5 sq miles (87 sq km) is now a proposed biosphere reserve. Apart from the remarkable flora, there is an interesting range of birds and animals, including tahr, musk deer and leopard. F. W. Smyth's book *The Valley of Flowers*, published in 1938, gives a dramatic description of the area's discovery.
Best time to visit: July & Aug.
Accommodation: 2 resthouses
Permission: DCF, Nanda Devi N.P., Joshimath Dist., Chamoli, UP
Nearest town: Joshimath (20 miles/33 km)
Rail: Rishikesh (181 miles/290 km)
Air: Dehra Dun (196 miles/313 km)

Other sanctuaries in UP include Chandra Prabha (Varanasi dist.), where lions were unsuccessfully reintroduced in the late 1950s; Mahavir Swami (Lalitpur dist.); Motichur (Dehra Dun dist.); Nawabganj Sanctuary (Unnao dist.); and Ranipur (Banda dist.).

For further information, contact the Chief Wildlife Warden, 17 Rana Pratap Marg, Lucknow (Tel: 46140; Cable: Wildlife, Lucknow). Tourist information can also be obtained from the UP Government Tourist Office, Chandralok, 36 Janpath, New Delhi 110 001 (Tel: 3222-251).

WEST BENGAL: Stretching from the Himalaya to the Bay of Bengal, the narrow strip forming West Bengal includes a range of climates and diversity of habitat. Sharing a language, history and culture with Bangladesh, Bengal is both tradition-bound and in part a symbol of India's progres with industry and booming agriculture.

Ballarpur Sanctuary. Established in 1977 in the grounds of Rabindranath Tagore's university at Santiniketan, this sanctuary of only 0.75 sq mile (2 sq km) area holds captive blackbuck.
Best time to visit: Nov. — Feb.
Accommodation: A tourist lodge at Santiniketan
Permission: Ballarpur Wildlife Sanctuary, PO Santiniketan, Dist: Birbhum, W. Bengal.
Nearest town & Rail: Bolpur (1 mile/3 km)
Air: Dum Dum Calcutta (72 miles/115 km)

Buxa Tiger Reserve. This area came under Project Tiger during the winter of 1982/83. Of a total area of 288 sq miles (745 sq km), 121 sq miles (313 sq km) form the core area. The reserve forms a vital linking corridor for elephants migrating between the forests of Bhutan to the north and the Manas Tiger Reserve in Assam to the east. The eastern boundary is the Sankosh River which in turn forms the western boundary of Manas. Much of the reserve was worked in the recent past and the forest has taken over from the natural reedlands. Much of the forest is sal. The range of animals is large and includes, apart from tiger and elephant, gaur, sambar, muntjac, leopard, leopard cat and sloth bear. Mahseer can still be sought in the Rydak river.
Best time to visit: Nov. — Apr.
Accommodation: forest resthouses
Permission: Field Director, Buxa Tiger Reserve.
Nearest town & Rail: Alipur Duar
Air: Cooch Bihar

Haliday Sanctuary. Established in 1976, this small pocket of mangrove forest in the Hoogly delta is the nesting area of sea turtles and saltwater estuarine crocodiles.
Best time to visit: Oct. — Mar.
Accommodation: none

Permission: DFO, 24 Parganas Division, 35 Gopal Nagar Rd, Calcutta 27
Nearest town: Namkhana (38 miles/60 km)
Rail: Diamond Harbour (56 miles/90 km)
Air: Dum Dum (110 miles/180 km)

Jalpara Sanctuary. Established in 1943 to protect the rhinoceros of which there are now about 50 in the sanctuary. Lying at the foot of the Bhutan hills, the sanctuary covers only 44 sq miles (115 sq km) and is bisected by the river Torsa. The sandy river banks have extensive belts of tall grass. The forest is rich, mixed deciduous and riding elephants is the only way to move through the area. Apart from rhino, there are tiger, gaur, leopard, sambar, muntjac, hog deer and elephant. Among the rich avifauna, the Bengal florican is typical of the area.
Best time to visit: Nov. — Apr.
Accommodation: forest lodge with board and forest resthouses, WBTDC Madarihat Tourist Lodge.
Permission: DFO, Wildlife Division II, PO Jalpaiguri, West Bengal
Nearest town & Rail: Madari Hat (1 mile)
Air: Cooch Bihar (28 miles/45 km)

Lothian Island Sanctuary. Established in 1976, this 14 sq miles (37 sq km) area of mangrove is the nesting area of numerous sea turtles.
Best time to visit: Oct. — Mar.
Accommodation: none
Permission: DFO, 24 Parganas Division, 35 Gopal Nagar Rd, Calcutta 27
Nearest town: Namkhana (19 miles/30 km)
Rail: Diamond Harbour (40 miles/64 km)
Air: Dum Dum (Calcutta)

Mahanada Sanctuary. Established in 1976 it consists of 50 sq miles (130 sq km) of mixed forest on the foothills of the eastern Himalaya. The height ranges from 500 to 4266 feet (150 to 1300 meters) above m.s.l. and this is reflected in the range of animals seen. A few swamp deer on the lower grasslands, the occasional elephant, leopard, and, in the higher forest, serow.
Best time to visit: Nov. — Mar.
Accommodation: 2 resthouses
Permission: DFO, Kurseong Division, Downhill PO, Dist: Darjeeling, West Bengal

Nearest town & Rail: Siliguri (5 miles/8 km)
Air: Bagdogra (14 miles/20 km)

Sajnakhali Sanctuary. Established in 1976 and incorporating 140 sq miles (362 sq km) of the Sunderbans. Tiger and fishing cat are the main mammals seen. Also some olive ridley turtles.
Best time to visit: July — Sept.
Accommodation: tourist bungalow
Permission: Field Director, Sunderbans Tiger Reserve, 24 Parganas, PO Canning, West Bengal
Nearest town: Gosaba (14 miles/20 km)
Rail: Canning (48 miles/76 km)
Air: Dum Dum (Calcultta) (85 miles)

Sunderbans N.P. and Tiger Reserve. Up to independence, a vast region of mangrove swamp, forested islands and small rivers covering over 6526 sq mile (16,907 sq km) stretched from the Hoogly in the west to the Tetulia river in the east. The Reserve is 998 sq miles (2585 sq km), of which 513 sq miles (1330 sq km) is national park and forms the core. Most of the area is estuarine mangrove forest and swamp supporting an ecosystem specially adapted to high salinity. The park holds more tigers than any other tiger reserve. In the area to the east under Bangladesh, slightly more than 400 tigers were recorded in its 2600 sq miles (6736 sq km) during the mid 1980s. Project Tiger has also launched a program to conserve the ridley sea turtle. A motor-launch is available with the park authority.
Best time to visit: Dec. — Feb.
Accommodation: Forest lodge at Sajnakhali
Permission: Field Director, Sunderbans Tiger Reserve, PO Canning, Dist. 24 Parganas, W. Bengal.
Nearest town: Gosaba (31 miles/50 km)
Rail: Canning (66 miles/105 km)
Air: Dum Dum (Calcutta) (104 miles)

Other santuaries in Bengal include Bethvadahari (Nadia dist.), Chapramari (Jalpaiguri dist.), Gorumara (Jalpaiguri dist.)., Narendrapur (24 Parganas), Parmadan (Nadia dist.), Ramnabagan (Burdwan dist.), and Senchal (Darjeeling dist.).

SRI LANKA

Apart from the Wilpattu and Yala National Parks, Sri Lanka has a relatively large area of protected wilderness compared to the other countries of South Asia.

Assistance in booking accommodation in the parks can be obtained at The Wildlife & Nature Protection Society office on Chaitiya Road (Marine Drive, opp, Light House), Colombo 1 (Tel: 25248); from the Tourist Information Desk, Transworks House, Lower Chatham Street, Fort, Colombo 1, or any travel agency.

Information on all areas is also available from the Department of Wildlife Conservation, Anagarika Dharmapala Mawatha (next to Zoological Gardens), Dehiwela, or Transworks House, Lower Chatham Street, Fort, Colombo 1 (Tel: 32698, 34040).

Gal Oya N.P. Established in 1954 on 100 sq miles (259 sq km) of the catchment area of the Senanayake Samudra reservoir. Elephants are the animals most often seen. Excellent waterbirds, including the magnificent white-bellied sea eagle. Boats are available for hire.
Accommodation: Numerous guesthouses at Inginyagala and Ampari: Inginyagala Safari Inn, Inginyagala, reservations can be made in Colombo. (Tel: 26611-9). Ekgal Aru Lodge (14 miles/22 km away).
Nearest town: Inginyagala
Route from Colombo: Via Ratnapura, Wellawaya, Moneragala, Siyambalnduwa and Inginyagala (235 miles/376 km)

Lahugala N.P. Declared a national park as recently as 1980, this small area is of importance far in excess of its size (6 sq miles/15 sq km). Probably the finest place in Sri Lanka to watch elephant. Access to the park is controlled by the lodge management.
Best time to visit: throughout the year
Accommodation: lodge on the park edge; numerous hotels at Pottuvil (14 miles/22.5 km) to the east.
Nearest town: Lahugala
Route from Colombo: Via Ratnapura, Wellawaya and Moneragala (195 miles)

Maduru Oya N.P. Established in November 1983 as one of a series of parks to protect the traditional elephant corridors which stretch south of Yala. It is close to the ancient city of Polonnaruwa where accommodation is available.
Accommodation: none at the park but at Polonaruwa: Hotel Araliya (Tel: 547420); Hotel Serowa (Tel: 23501); and Amaliyan Niwas (Tel: 22232, 22233).
Nearest town: Polonnaruwa
Route from Colombo: Via Kurunegala, Dambulla, Habaranna, Polonnaruwa and Manampitiya (260 miles/416 km)

Ruhuna N.P. (Yala West). Established in 1938. Now covers 377 sq miles (977 sq km) but only 52 sq miles (134 sq km) are used for game viewing. Has good roads. Permits are obtained at the park office at Palatupana, a mile from the park entrance.
Best time to visit: Open mid-Oct. to July
Accommodation: lodges inside the park at New Buttawa, Mahaseelawa, Patanangala, Yala, Talgasmankade and Heenwewa; campsite at Yala and Kosgamankade. Outside the park there are hotels and lodges, many of which organize visits into the park: Brown's Safari Beach Hotel, Yala Safari Hotel, Tissamaharama Resthouse and the Wildlife Protection Society Lodge.
Nearest town: Tissamaharama
Route from Colombo: Via Ratnapura, Pelmadulla, Uda Wellawe, Tanamalvila and Tissamaharama (220 miles/352 km)

Uda Walawe N.P. Established in 1972 surrounding the Uda Walawe reservoir and covering 119 sq miles/308 sq km. Has good fair-weather (dry season) roads.
Accommodation: campsites at Weheramankade and Pransadhara
Nearest town: Uda Walawe
Route from Colombo: Via Ratnapura, Pelmadulla and Thimbolketiya (115 miles/184 km)

Wilpattu N.P. Established in 1938, this is the largest of Sri Lanka's parks, covering 508 sq miles (1316 sq km). Excellent network of fair-weather roads (a four-wheel-drive vehicle is advisable). Within the park are the ruins of Kuwenis Castle at Kudermalai Point and the Roman Catholic Church at Pomparippu.
Accommodation: Lodges in the park at Manikka Pola Uttu, Thala Wila, Mana Wila, Kalli Villu, Kokmottai, Pannikar Villu and Maradanmaduwa. Outside the park the Hotel Wilpattu (organizes visits) and the Wildlife Protection Society Lodge.
Nearest town: Nochchiyagama
Park Office: Hunuvilagama (park gates)
Route from Colombo: Via Chilaw and Puttalam (110 miles/176 km)

Yala East N.P. Established in 1969 as a northeastern extension of Ruhuna. Permits and guides available from the park ofice at Okande. Excellent birdlife, especially in and near the Kumana Mangrove Swamp. Boats are available.
Accommodation: lodges at Okande and Tunmulla
Nearest town: Pottuvil
Route from Colombo: Via Ratnapura, Uda Wellawe, Tanamalwila, Wellawaya, Moneragala, Pottuvil and Panama (240 miles)

Nepal's park and reserves fall in all faunal and geographical zones and because of the physical difficulties of communication, all present problems for the tourist. The grandeur and elegance, the savagery of the Himalaya and the tranquility of the *terai* all make good homes for 300 species of mammals, 800 species of birds, numerous reptiles and amphibians and many thousand species of insects. The central massif of the Himalaya forms the bulk of Nepal. Stretching 500 miles (800 km) east to west and between 90—150 miles (144 — 240 km) north to south, the country is bounded by India to the west, south and east and by the Tibetan region of China to the north.

A lowland area of flat *doons* (valleys) and riverine grasslands called the *terai* forms a belt along the southern borders with India. Over 75 percent of the rest of the country is mountainous and cut by great rivers flowing from the Tibetan plateau or the great ice caps of the Himalaya to the Gangetic plain of northern India.

The country is divided into two distinct zoogeographic zones with the Kali Gandaki river forming a natural division between east and west. The north-south range in altitude complicates the compressed and extensive variety of habitat, but ensures that no part of the country is without interest to the ornithologist, the trekker or in fact to any visitor.

The system of parks and reserves of Nepal was started in 1973 with funds and technical assistance from the United Nations Development Programme and the Food and Agriculture Organisation. Some areas had earlier been set aside as hunting reserves by the Rana regime (1846—1950) and a small rhino reserve was established in Chitwan in 1961 following a 1959 survey by E.P. Gee, the British naturalist who had dedicated his life to the wildlife of the subcontinent.

The National Parks and Wildlife Conser-vation Project offices in Kathmandu can provide information, maps and checklists of birds and animals for most of the areas described below. Most travel companies in Kathmandu can give guidance, and Mountain Travel Pvt. Ltd. (PO Box 170, Kathmandu, Tel: 414505, 411562. Tlx: 2216 TIGTOP NP) can give detailed on the Himalayan and trans-Himalayan areas.

Royal Bardia Wildlife Reserve. Established in 1976 over an area of 134 sq miles (348 sq km) and extended in 1985 to 373 sq miles (968 sq km). The vegetation is mostly sal forest with riverine forest and grassland. Over 350 species of birds have been re-

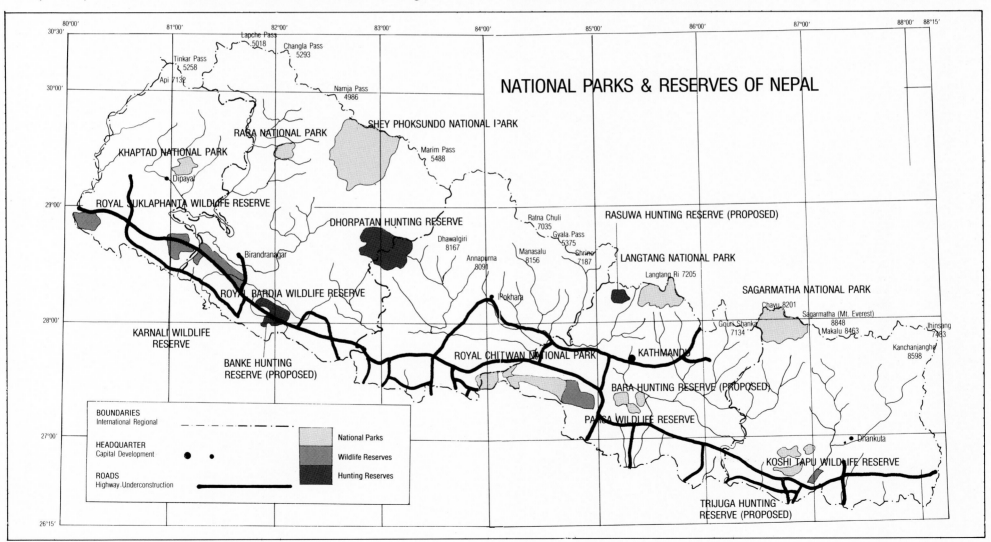

NATIONAL PARKS & RESERVES OF NEPAL

corded here and the main mammal species include tiger, leopard, elephant, sloth bear, wild dog, swamp deer and dolphin (in the Karnali-Girwa river).

Best time to visit: Nov. — May

Accommodation: Karnali Tented Camp a few kilometers south of Chisapani is operated by West Nepal Adventures and reservations can be made through Tiger Tops, Box No. 242, Kathmandu (Tel: 212706; Tlx: 2216 TIGTOP NP). A deluxe camp with accommodation for up to 24 people, qualified naturalists available.

Nearest town & Rail: Nepalganj. A 4-5 hour journey via Thakurdwara and Chisapani (west) by four-wheel drive vehicle. The supposedly daily bus between Nepalganj and Chisapani (West) takes 8-10 hours. Daily flights operate between Kathmandu and Nepalganj (takes one and a half hours) and the overnight bus from Kathmandu via Narayanghat and Butwai takes 20 hours.

Royal Chitwan N.P. Much of the Chitwan valley or *doon* was reserved for shoots by the royal family and Rana prime ministers. In 1962, a small rhinoceros sanctuary was established and in 1973 a national park of 210 sq miles (544 sq km). In 1979 the park was extended to 360 sq miles (967 sq km). The park is mostly sal forest with riverine forest and grasslands. The major river, the Narayani, and two tributaries (the Reu and the Rapti) flow through the park. Considerable research has been undertaken in the park since it was established, and two books (*The Face of the Tiger* by Dr Charles McDougal and *The Heart of the Jungle* by K. K. Gurung) are products of this work.

The most important species in the park is the one-horned rhinoceros which can be easily seen from elephant back. The tiger, leopard, gaur, sambar, chital, hog deer and wild boar are some of the other animals often seen. Mugger crocodile is seen throughout the park and dolphin and gharial along the Narayani. To date, over 450 species of birds have been recorded in the park. The park is scenically very beautiful, with views of Himalayan peaks rising to over 26,000 feet (8000 meters) from only 465 feet (142 meters) above sea level.

Best time to visit: Nov. — May (park inaccessible in July and Aug.)

Accommodation: Chitwan has perhaps the best range and highest standards of accommodation of any park in South Asia. In the western part of the park is Tiger Tops Jungle Lodge on the banks of the Reu river with 20 deluxe rooms in two treetop lodges. Activities include tiger tracking, jungle treks and excellent bird-watching. Tiger Tops Tented Camp or Bandorjhula Island in the Narayani river has 12 comfortable safari tents and organizes nature walks and boat rides to view game and the diverse bridlife. To the west of the park (2 miles/3 km), is the "cultural camp" operated by Tiger Tops called Tharu Village. All bookings can be made through Tiger Tops, Box 242, Durbar Marg, Kathmandu (Tel: 212706, Tlx 2216 TIGTOP NP). The lodge is open from September 1 to mid-June; the Tented Camp and Tharu Village from October 1 through May.

In the Eastern part of the park are Gaida Wildlife Camp on the north bank of Dhungre Khola near Sauraha with 20 rooms. Open throughout the year and bookable through Gaida Wildlife Camp, P.O. Box 2056, Durbar Marg, Kathmandu (Tel: 215840, 410786, Tlx: 2237 GAIDA NP).

Chitwan Jungle Lodge near Khagendramalli has 20 rooms in cottages. Open Oct. through May. Book through Chitwan Jungle Lodge (next to Indian Airlines office), Durbar Marg, PO Box 1281, Kathmandu (Tel: 410918; Tlx: 2263 METRA NP).

The Hotel Elephant Camp near Sauraha is just outside the park (22 rooms in five bungalows). Bookings can be made through Hotel Elephant Camp, PO Box 78, Durbar Marg, Kathmandu (Tel: 213976). In the Sauraha area are also many small-budget operations and elephants can be hired from the government elephant camp at Sauraha.

Nearest town & Air: The western end of the park is serviced by a daily flight operated by RNAC to Meghavli airfield. RNAC also operates a daily flight to Bharatpur which is a short drive from Sauraha. The park is a four- to six-hour drive from Kathmandu and Himalaya. River Exploration (PO Box 170, Durbar Marg, Kathmandu, Tel: 414508, 411562, 212706; Tlx: 2216 TIGTOP NP) operates 3-day raft trips on the Trisuli and Narayani rivers from near Kathmandu to the Tiger Tops Tented Camp.

Karnali Wildlife Reserve. Situated between the Karnali and Babai rivers to the west of the Bardia Wildlife Reserve, much of this park is sal riverine forest and flat grasslands and almost a third of the area consists of stunted sal forest covering the Churia Hills. The wide range of habitats holds tiger, serow, chinkara and blackbuck, with dolphin and gharial in the river.
Best time to visit: Nov — May
Accommodation: Karnali Tented Camp in the Bardia Wildlife Reserve
Nearest town & Air: Nepalganj

Khaptad N.P. Located in the sub-Himalayan region of West Nepal, this small park is slightly south of the Seti river. Much of the park is a plateau at about 9850 feet (3000 meters), with the highest point at 10,830 feet (3300 meters) and the slopes on all sides dropping to about 6500 feet (2000 meters).

The animals seen include leopard, marten, barking deer and black bear.
Best time to visit: Oct. — Nov., Mar. — Apr.
Accommodation: none
Air: Doti

Kosi Tappu Wildlife Reserve This is a small reserve covering 25 sq miles (65 sq km) in the flood plain of the Kosi river in the Eastern Terai. The area is covered with extensive grasslands with swampy areas and waterholes created by monsoon floods. A small population of wild buffalo live in the park. The park includes islands in the Kosi river upstream of the small dam and the area attracts thousand of migratory birds.
Best time to visit: Nov. — May
Accommodation: none
Nearest town & Air: Biratnagar (25 miles)

Lake Rara N.P. One of Nepal's first, this park covers an area of 41 sq miles (106 sq km) with Lake Rara at a height of 9815 feet (2990 meters) and with an area of 4 sq miles (10 sq km), as the focal point. The highest point is Chuchemera Dara at 13,254 feet (4038 meters). Most of the park is forested (mainly conifers) and the animals include black bear, yellow throated marten, musk deer, goral and serow. The many birds include impeyan, kaleej and blood pheasants, and chukar, and in the winter a few migratory species such as mallard, common teal, grebes and pochards visit the lake.
Best time to visit: Oct. — Nov., Feb. — Apr.
Accommodation: camping permitted with permission
Air: Jumla, 2-3 day's walk away (trekking permit required)

Langtang N.P. The largest of Nepal's national parks with an area of 659 sq miles (1710 sq km) lies almost directly north of Kathmandu. The Langtang valley is bordered on the north by the main crest of the Himalaya dominated by Langtang Lirung (23,780 feet/7245 meters). To the south are the Chimse Danda ridge, crossed by the Ganja Lal (16,810 feet/5122 meters) and the Dorje Himalaya culminating in Dorje Lakpa (22,940 feet/6989 meters).

The vegetation ranges from alpine meadow to juniper, birch, rhododendron, fir, blue pine and chir pine as the height descends from 14,750 feet (4500 meters) to 5000 feet (1500 meters) at Syabrobensi. The Langtang river flows through dense deciduous forest to join the Bhole Kosi flowing from Tibet to form the Trisuli river. The forest and alpine pastures are home to barking deer, black bear, leopard, goral in the lower forested areas and tahr, musk deer, and possibly snow leopard in the alpine regions. A wide range of pheasants and other birds are seen.
Best time to visit: Oct. — Nov., Mar. — early May
Accommodation: camping allowed within the park
Air: Kathmandu (three and a half hours drive from Trisuli Bazar). The road from Kathmandu is being extended to Dhunche, trekking permit required.

Sagarmatha N.P. (Everest N.P.). Established in July 1976, this park covering 480 sq miles (1243 sq km) is known as Khumbu in the northeast. The spectacular mountain scenery includes Mount Everest, and it is from the peak's Nepali name that the park gets its name. Sagarmatha means "mother of the universe". In 1979 the park was declared a World Heritage Site and became eligible for additional funds and support from UNESCO. The park's original establishment was assisted by six years' support from the government of New Zealand.

The park is bordered to the north by Tibet and the ridge never drops below 18,700 feet (5700 meters). Apart from Everest at 29,028 feet (8848 meters), two other 8000 meter peaks fall within the park: Choster (27,903 feet/8501 meters) and Chooyu (26,760 feet/ 8186 meters). Much of the park is rugged, with deep gorges and glaciers breaking the terrain. Access to the area is through the Dudh Kosi river valley but is restricted by the narrow gorges.

Unique among South Asia's parks, Sagarmatha has a large and permanent human population. The Sherpa villages are islands within the park but do not fall under its authority. The Sherpa manage through cultivation of some areas, but many now earn their living through tourism, handling treks and assisting climbs. Of the villages in the park, most are located at the southern portion where the Dudh Kosi, Imie Kosi, Kyajo Brahgha and Thengpo Kola valleys meet and the rivers flow south to join the Kosi river and ultimately flow into the Ganga.

The park's forested areas are only a small proportion of the total and these are being subjected to thinning at an alarming rate due to the demand for fuel wood. The main tree species are rhododendron, birch, blue pine, juniper and silver fir, which give way to scrub and alpine plants and then bare rock and snow. The rhododendron forests bloom in the spring (April and May) although many of the flowers are in bloom during the monsoon months of June to August.

The animals in the park most often seen are tahr, goral, serow and musk deer. Black bear, marten weasel, marmot, red panda, mouse hare and langur are also occasionally seen. The presence of snow leopard within the park is doubted by many authorities. At least 118 species of bird are found within the park and many other migrant species probably stop for a sojourn or overfly. Of the pheasants, the impeyan (monal) and blood pheasant are the most common. Both the red-billed and yellow-billed choughs, snow pigeon, skylarks, the Himalayan griffon and lammergier are also fairly common.

The park headquarters is at Nande Bazar on Mendalphu Hill.

Best time to visit: Oct. — May, Dec. — Feb. (day temperatures below freezing)

Accommodation: The Namche, Thyangboche, Pheriche and Lobuche villages all have accommodation and food supplies. There are many tea shops on trekking routes which provide simple food. Above the Shyangbocle airstrip is the Hotel Everest View which can be booked through Kathmandu travel agents.

Nearest town & Air: Lukla is two days' walk and Lamosangu (10-14 days' walk) is the closest road head with regular buses from Kathmandu.

Shey Wildlife Reserve. Covers over 160 sq miles (415 sq km) of secluded Tibetan and trans-Himalayan habitat in Dolpho district of northwestern Nepal. Largely undisturbed the area was made famous by Peter Mattiessen's book, *The Snow Leopard*. The area is extremely barren, with pine, juniper and small bushes in the valleys. The main animals are blue sheep, yak, goral, musk der, tahr, bear, muntjac and snow leopard. The area around Lake Phuksunda has some spectacular scenery.
Best time to visit: Oct. — Nov., Mar. — May
Accommodation: none

USEFUL ADDRESSES

In all countries of South Asia there are private charities, societies and other organizations promoting wildlife conservation and environmental protection. Some are old and revered, such as the Bombay Natural History Society which celebrated its centenary in 1984; others are new and extremely specialized. In mid-1986, the Environmental Service Group of the World Wildlife Fund, India, prepared a directory listing 415 such organizations. Given below is information on some of the most interesting and helpful organizations for travelers.

INDIA

Assam Valley Wildlife Society. A small society with members in Assam, Arunachal Pradesh, Meghalaya and Nagaland. Achieved some success in locating and protecting the white-winged wood duck in the Doom Domma and Dangri Reserve Forests and subsequent captive breeding at Bordubi Tea Estate.
Address: Pertabghur Tea Estate, Post Sootea, Dist. Sonitpur, 784 175, Assam.

The Bombay Natural History Society (BNHS). Despite its name, the BNHS covers the whole of the oriental region. Established in 1883 by a group of concerned sportsmen, it has become the foremost organization of its type in Asia. It collects data and natural history specimens throughout South Asia and Burma. Its museum and library have perhaps the best collections in the continent. Much of its work in recent years has been on bird migration and more recently, a series of studies on certain endangered species and their habitats. It publishes,

three times a year, an important journal (since 1886) which is recognized throughout the world as an authoritative source of information on the flora and fauna of the subcontinent. The society also publishes a popular magazine, *Hornbill*, quarterly. Membership is open to all.
Address: Hornbill House, Opposite Lion Gate, Shahid Bhagat Singh Road, Bombay 400 023.

Centre for Science and Environment (CSE). Founded by Anil Agarwal in 1981 to study the social and economic impact of science and technology. CSE organizes a feature and service for newspapers and publishes a comprehensive report, *The State of India's Environment*, each alternate year.
Address: 807 Vishal Bhawan, Nehru Place, New Delhi 110019.

Himalayan Club. Founded in 1928 to encourage and assist Himalayan travel and exploration. It maintains a reference library in Delhi (at the India International Centre, Lodhi Estate) and publishes *The Himalayan Journal.*
Delhi Branch Address: C-559 Defence Colony, New Delhi 110024

Madras Crocodile Bank Trust. Founded by Romulus Whitaker in 1974 to breed and study the three endangered Indian crocodiles; and to study and breed snakes, turtles and other reptiles. It is located 22 miles (35 km) south of Madras, 9 miles (14 km) before Mahabalipuram.
Address: Vadenemelli Village, Perur PO, Mahabalipuram Road, Madras 603104.

Nilgiri Wildlife Association. Founded in 1877 to conserve and protect the natural resources, wildlife and habitat of the Nilgiri Hills. The association assists tourists in making bookings in Mudumalai, Bandipur and other nearby parks.
Address: Ootacamund, Tamil Nadu 643001 (Tel: Coonoor 453).

Wildlife Association of South India. Founded in 1972 to help enforce game laws and extend reserves. In recent years it has run fishing camps and the Kaveri river each spring in pursuit of the mahseer.

Address: 49 Richmond Rd, Bangalore 560025 (Tel: 578379)

Wildlife Preservation Society of India. For over 20 years the society's journal, *Cheetal*, has published articles and papers on many aspects of India's wildlife.
Address: 7 Ashley Hall, Dehra Dun, UP

World Wildlife Fund—India. Started in 1969. Since 1970 it has undertaken a wide variety of projects for the conservation of nature, for youth education and creating public awareness of conservation needs. WWF-1 also assists and provides technical support for research projects and study. Publishes a regular newsletter for its members.
Address: Secretariat, c/o Godrej and Boyce Manufacturing Co., Pvt. Ltd., Lalbaug, Parel, Bombay 400012 (Tel: 441361, 442927). Note: The national headquarters will soon move to Delhi.
Branch: Bhopal, "Gulnar", Shamla Hills, Bhopal 462013 (Tel: 72939/70191).
Eastern Region, Tata Centre, 43 Chowringhee, Calcutta 700071 (Tel: 449960).
Goa, c/o National Institute of Oceanography, Dona Paula, Goa 403004 (Tel: 3291, 3292, 3294).
Gujarat, "Sundarvan", Jodhpur Tekra, Ahmedabad 380015; 90 Vidyut Electronics, Nr. Fire Brigade Sadar, Rajkot, 360001 (Tel: 46211); 16 Alkapuri, Vadodara 390005 (Baroda) (Tel: 67118).
Hyderabad, 624/1 Road No. 10, Banjara Hills, Hyderabad 500 034 (Tel: 37388).
Kerala, c/o University of Cochin, Dept. of Fisheries, Fore Shore Road, Cochin 682016.
Nagpur, 54 Bajaj Nagar, Central Bazar Road, (Nagpur 440010, Maharashtra (Tel: 25112).
Northern Region, 403 Palika Bhawan, Sector XIII, R. K. Puram, New Delhi 110066 (Tel: 600362).
Pune, c/o Vijay Paranjpye, "Durga", 99/2/ Erandawne, Pune 411004 (Tel: 52448).
Southern Region, "Hamsini", 1, 12th Cross Rajmahal Extension, Bangalore 560008 (Tel: 362574, 360400).
Tamil Nadu, c/o Dr. C. P. Ramaswami Aiyar Foundation, 1 Eldams, Madras 600018 (Tel: 446249).
The World Wildlife Fund, India, has two

important subsidiary organizations managed and run by scientists:

Data Centre for Natural Resources, 18 Spencer Road, Fraser Town, Bangalore 560005 (Tel: 566506).

Environmental Services Group (ESG), B-1 L.S.C. (1st floor), J. Block Saket, New Delhi 110017 (Tel: 656714).

ESG is the environmental research, analysis and consultancy wing of WWF-1.

NEPAL

International Trust for Nature Conservation (ITNC), c/o Tiger Tops Pvt. Ltd., PO Box 242, Durbar Marg, Kathmandu (Tel: 212706).

King Mahendra Trust for Nature Conservation, National Parks Building, Barbar Mahal, PO Box 3712, Kathmandu (Tel: 215850, 215912; Tlx: NP 2203).

International Centre for Integrated Mountain Development, P.O Box 3226, Kathmandu.

SRI LANKA

Wildlife and Nature Protection Society of Sri Lanka. Established in May 1894 as the Ceylon Game and Fauna Protection Society, it has published a journal, *Loris*, since 1936. The society has bungalows in Wilpattu and Yala National Parks. It also has an extensive library.
Address: Chaitiya Road (Marine Drive), Colombo 1 (Tel: 25248).

The Ceylon Bird Club. Founded in 1934, the club organizes regular outings and conducts surveys throughout the island. Publishes monthly *Club Notes*.
Address: PO Box 11, Baurs Building, Upper Chattam St., Colombo 1.

FURTHER READING

NATURAL HISTORY

Allen, Hugh. *The Lonely Tiger*. London: Faber 1960. Enjoyable account of Central Madhya Pradesh in the 1950s.

Ali, Salim. *The Moghal Emperors of India as Naturalists* and *Sportsmen*. Bombay: Journal BNHS 31 (4) 833-61.

de Alwis, Lyn. *National Parks of Ceylon*. Colombo: 1969. A detailed although now out of date description of the many parks. Useful maps.

Alvi, M.A. & A. Rahman. *Jahangir—The Naturalist*. Delhi: 1968.

Bedi, Rajesh & Ramesh Bedi. *Indian Wildlife*. New Delhi. 1984.

Bhatt, Dibya Deo & T.K. Shrestha. *The Environment of Sukla Phanta*. Kathmandu: 1977.

Brandar; A. Dunbar. *Wild Animals of Central India*. London 1923, Indian reprint 1982. A classic account of the forests and animals of central and southern Madhya Pradesh.

Booth, Martin. *Carpet Sahib—A Life of Jim Corbett*. London: Constable 1986. A good biography of the great hunter-conservationist.

Burton, R.G. *The Book of the Tiger*. London: Hutchinson. 1933.
Sport and Wildlife in the Deccan. London: Hutchinson 1928. An interesting account of what is now northern Andhra Pradesh.

Champion, F. *In Sunlight and Shadow*. London: Chatto & Windus 1925.
With a Camera in Tiger Land. London: Chatto & Windus 1927. Two excellent books with pioneering wildlife photography in the Kumraon and what is now Corbett National Park.

Cooch Behar, Maharaja of. *Thirty-seven Years of Big Game Shooting*. Bombay: 1908.

Corbett, Jim. *Man Eaters of Kumaon*. Bombay: OUP 1944.
The Man Eating Leopard of Rudraprayag. Bombay: OUP 1948.
The Temple Tiger: OUP 1954. Exciting and well written accounts of life in Kumaon and northern Uttar Pradesh in the first 40 years of this century.

Cubitt, Gerald & Guy Mountfort. *Wild India*. London: Collins 1985. Good text and a splendid range of photographs.

C.S.E. *The State of India's Environment*. Biannual citizen's report published by the Centre for Science and Environment, New Delhi. Excellent material.

Flemming, Robert, L. Jr. *The Ecology, Flora* and *Fauna of Midland Nepal*. Kathmandu: 1977. A useful survey of, and introduction to, the accessible parts of Nepal.

Fletchar, F.W.F. *Sport on the Nilgiris* and in the *Wynad*. London: 1911. Includes the area of Mudumalai and Wynad Sanctuaries in Tamil Nadu and Kerala.

Forsyth, J. *The Highlands of Central India*. London: 1889. Indian reprint 1975. Covers northeastern Maharashtra and Central Madhya Pradesh.

Ganhar, J.N. *The Wildlife of Ladakh*. Srinagar: 1979.

Gee. E.P. *The Wildlife of India*. London: Collins 1964. A fascinating introduction by a pioneer conservationist.

Ghorpade. M.Y. *Sunlight* and *Shadows*. London: Gollanez 1983.

Gurung. K. K. *Heart of the Jungle: The Wildlife of Chitwan, Nepal*. London: Andre Deutsch 1983.

Hardy, Sarah B. *The Langurs of Abu*. Harvard: 1977. A controversial scientific study of the langur monkey communities in Mount Abu, Rajasthan.

Jefferies, Margaret. *Sagarmatha. The Story of Mount Everest National Park*. Auckland (NZ): 1986. A detailed and well illustrated handbook.

Krishnan, M. *India's Wildlife in 1959-70*. Bombay: BNHS 1975. A detailed study of the mammals of Peninsular India.
Handbook of India's Wildlife. Madras: 1983.

Kurt, Fred. *Zoo Inde*. Zurich: Editions Silva 1976.

Lekagul, Dr. & J.A. McNeely. *The Mammals of Thailand*. Bangkok: 1977.

McDougal, C. *The Face of the Tiger*. London: Andre Deutsch 1977. The classic study of the tiger.

Matthiseen, Peter. *The Snow Leopard*. London: Chatto and Windus 1979. Descriptions of travels with field biologist George Schaller in Dolpo, Nepal.

Medway, Lord. *The Wild Mammals of Malaya*. Kuala Lumpur: OUP 1969, 1978.

Mishra, Hemanta & Dorothy Mierow. *Wild Animals of Nepal*. Kathamandu: 1976. In both English and Nepali.

Mountfort, Guy. *Tigers*. Newton Abbot: David & Charles 1973.
  Saving the Tiger: London: Michael Joseph 1981. A detailed survey of the tiger conservation by the initiator of Project Tiger.

Mukherjee, Ajit. *Extinct* and *Vanishing Birds* and *Mammals of India*. Calcutta: 1966.

Oliver, William. T*he Pigmy Hog*. Jersey: 1980. A detailed survey of both pigmy hog and hispid hare habitat.

Osmand, Edward. A*nimals of Central Asia*. London: 1967. Includes many species found in Ladakh and the trans-Himalayan region of India & Nepal.

Powell, A. *The Call of the Tiger*. London: Hale 1957.

Prater, S. *The Book of Indian Animals*. Bombay: BNHS 1948, 1971. Still the foremost reference book on the sub-continent's animals.

Roonwul, M.L. & S.M. Mohnot. *The Primates of South Asia*. Harvard 1977. A comprehensive study of the ecology and distribution of all primates in the region.

Schaller, G.B. *The Deer and the Tiger*. A study of *Wildlife in India*. Chicago: UP 1967.
  Mountain Monarchs: *Wild Sheep and Goats of the Himalaya*. Chicago: UP 1967.
  Stones of Silence: Journeys in the Himalaya. London: Andre Deutsch 1980.

Sankhala, Kailash. *Tigerland*. London: Collins 1975.
  Tiger! The Story of the Indian Tiger. London: Collins 1978.

Saharia, V.B. *Wildlife in India*. Dehra Dun: Natraj 1982. A collection of papers prepared for the 1981 C.I.T.E.S. conference which was held in Delhi.

Singh, Arjun. *Tiger Haven*. London: Macmillan 1973.
  Tara, A Tigress. London: Quartet. 1981.
  The Prince of Cats. London: Cape 1982.
  Tiger, Tiger. London: Cape 1984. Four books are the result of a lifetime's study and work in the jungles of Uttar Pradesh and the Dudwa National Park.

Singh, Samar. *India's Rhino Re-Introduction Programme*. New Delhi: 1984.
  India's Wildlife Heritage. Dehra Dun: Natraj. 1986.

Smythies, E.A. *Big Game Shooting in Nepal*. Calcutta: Thacker, Spink & Co.1942.

Sanderson, G.P. *Thirteen Years among the Wild Beasts of India*. London: 1896 (many editions). The Mysore forests—what is now Nagarahole N.P. and the Wynad.

Stacey, P.D. *Wildlife in India — its conservation and control*. New Delhi: 1983.
  Tigers. London: 1963.

Sheshadri, B. *The Twilight of India's Wildlife*. London: 1969.
  India's Wildlife and Reserves. New Delhi. Sterling 1986.

Sahai, S.P. *Backs to the Wall: Saga of Wildlife in Bihar*. Delhi: 1977.

Thapar, Valmik. *Tiger—Portrait of a Predator*. London: Collins 1986.

The journal of the Bombay Natural History Society has now been published for over 100 years and is the most comprehensive source of information available. In 1983 an anthology was published (*A Century of Natural History*, Edited by J.C. Daniel. Bombay: BNHS 1983).

BIRDS

Ali, Salim. *The Book of Indian Birds*. Bombay: Bombay Natural History Society (BNHS) 1941. Many editions and recently revised and expanded with new plates. Excellent descriptions.
  Birds of Kerala. Bombay: Oxford University Press (OUP). Excellent coverage of Southwest India.
  Birds of Kutch. Bombay: 1945.
  Birds of Sikkim. Bombay: OUP 1962.
  Indian Hill Birds. Bombay: 1949, 1979.
  The Fall of a Sparrow. Bombay: OUP 1984. Fascinating autobiography of one of the world's greatest ornithologists.
  Field Guide to the Birds of the Eastern Himalayas. Bombay: OUP 1977. Combines plates and information from *Birds of Sikkim* with new material to give excellent coverage of Bhutan and Arunachal Pradesh.

Ali, Salim & S. Dillon, Ripley. *The Handbook of the Birds of India and Pakistan*. 10 vols. Bombay: OUP 1968-74. The ultimate and definitive work now available in a single volume (1984) covers all the birds in South Asia with maps, illustrations and plates.

Baker, E.C. Stuart. *Fauna of British India—Birds*. 8 vols: 1922-30. An interesting early study to which Ali & Ripley refer for detailed plumage descriptions.
  Indian Ducks and Their Allies. Bombay: BNHS 1908.
  Indian Pigeons and Doves. Bombay: 1913.
  The Gamebirds of India, Burma and Ceylon. Bombay: BNHS 1921.

Banks, John & Judy. *The Birds of Sri Lanka*. Colombo: 1980. An introductory pamphlet.

Bates, R.S.P. & E.H.N. Lowther. *Breeding Birds of Kashmir*. OUP 1952. A useful book with excellent photographs.

Bates, R.S.P. *Birds in India*. 1931.

Detacour, J. *The Pheasants of the World*. London: 1957, 1977. Detailed descriptions of all Galliforms, many of which are found in Eastern India and the Himalaya.

Dewar, Douglas, *Glimpse of Indian Birds*. 1913.
  Himalayan and Kashmir Birds. London: 1923.

Dharamkumarsinhji. R.S. *The Birds of Saurashtra*. Bombay: 1957. An excellent book with photographs (poor color plates) specific to part of Gujarat but relevant to much of western India.

Fleming, R.L. Snr. & Jnr. & J. Bangdel. *Birds of Nepal:* Khatmandu. 1976. A good field guide with over 700 color illustrations facing the text on each species.

Fleming, Robert L., Jr. *Comments on the Endemic Birds of Sri Lanka*: Colombo 1977.

Finn, F. *How to Know the Indian Waders*. Calcutta: 1920. Interesting line drawings of various species with head details.
  Indian Sporting Birds. London 1915. With over 100 color plates.
  The Water Fowl of India and Asia. Calcutta: 1909.

Henry, G. M. *A Guide to the Birds of Ceylon*. OUP: 1955, 1971. A well written and well illustrated book.

Hutson, H.P.W. *The Birds about Delhi*. 1954.

Dick, John Henry. *A Pictorial Guide to the Birds of the Indian Sub-continènt*. Bombay: OUP/BNHS 1963. Unique guide giving illustrations for all the bird species. A companion to Ali & Ripley's *Handbook*.

Ganguli, Usha. *A Guide to the Birds of the Delhi Area*. New Delhi: 1975.

Glenister, A.G. *Birds of the Malay Peninsula*. Singapore: OUP 1971, 1985. Includes species in the Andaman and Nicobar Islands, Burma and parts of Eastern India.

Hume, Allan, O. *The Nests and Eggs of Indian Birds*. 3 vols 1889-90.

Jerdon, T.C. *The Birds of India*. 3 vols 1862-64. The first comprehensive work.

King, Ben, E.C. Dickinson & Martin Woodcock. *The Birds of South-East Asia*. London: Collins 1975. A well illustrated and comprehensive guide to continental South-East Asia with many references to Eastern India and the Himalaya.

Lekagul, Boonsong & E.W. Cronin. *Bird Guide of Thailand*. Bangkok: 1974. Good illustration—covers many species common in Eastern India.

Lowther. E.H.M. *A Bird Photographer in India*. OUP: 1949.

Macdonald, Malcolm. *Birds in My Indian Garden*. London: Cape 1960. A general text illustrated with excellent photographs by Wan Tho Loke.

Philips, W.W.A. *Checklist of the Birds of Ceylon*. Colombo: 1977 (Revised).
  Birds of Ceylon. 4 vols 1949, 52, 55, 61.

Ranasinghe, Douglas. *A Guide to Birdwatching in Sri Lanka*. Colombo: 1977.

Ripley, S. Dillon. *Search for the Spiny Babbler*. 1952.
A Synopsis of the Birds of India and Nepal, 1961. The basis of the *Handbook*.
A Bundle of Feathers. Delhi: OUP 1978. A festschrift proffered to Salim Ali on his 75th birthday.

Saxena, V.S. *Bharatpur Bird Sanctuary*. Jaipur 1975. An introductory study of the flora and fauna of this important National Park.

Smythies, B.E. *The Birds of Burma*. London 1953.

Vauries, Charles. *Tibet and its Birds*. London: 1972. Covers the trans-Himalayan areas of India and Nepal. An excellent study of the history of ornithological exploration and the zoogeography of this little known area.

Whistler, Hugh. *The Popular Hand Book of Indian Birds*. London: 1949 (4th edition). Good descriptions of over 500 species.

Wikramanayake, E.B. *Go to the Birds*. Colombo: 1977. Reflections of a lifetime in ornithology in Sri Lanka.

Woodcock, Martin. H*andguide to the Birds of the Indian Sub-continent*. London: Collins 1980. Excellent illustrations and useful text. The best single volume.

Woodcock. M.W. & M. Gallagher. *The Birds of Oman*. London: Quartet 1980. Excellent illustrations. Many species common to western India and Pakistan.

REPTILES

Daniel, J.C. *The Book of Indian Reptiles*. Bombay: BNHS. 1983. An excellent single volume with useful plates and drawings. Gives detailed information on crocodile, turtles, tortoise, lizards, snakes and their various groupings.

Deoras, P.J. *Snakes of India*. Delhi: NBT 1965, 78.

Fleming, R.L. Sr. & Jr. *Some Snakes from Nepal*. Bombay: BNHS Journal. 1974. Pamphlet reprinted 1975.

Ghorpurey, K.G. *Snakes of India*. Bombay: 1937.

Nicholson, E. *Indian Snakes*. Madras: *Higginbotham 1870*.

Smith, M.A. *Fauna of British India. Reptiles and Amphibia*. 3 vols. London: 1931-1943.

Wall, Major F. *Poisonous Terrestrial Snakes of British India*. Bombay: BNHS 1928.

Whitaker, Romulus. *Common Indian Snakes*. New Delhi: Macmillan 1978.

INSECTS

Antram, Chas, B. *Butterflies of India*. Calcutta: Thaickar, Spick & Co. 1924.

Mani, M.S. *Insects*. New Delhi: NBT 1971. A useful introduction to India's insect life from one of her foremost entomologists.

Smith, C. *Commoner Butterflies of Nepal*. Kathmandu: Natural History Museum 1976.

Wynter-Blyth, M.A. *Butterflies of the Indian Region*. Bombay: BNHS 1957. The most detailed and well illustrated account.

FLOWERS & TREES

Bharucha, F.R. *Plant Geography of India*. Delhi: OUP.

Blatter, E.X. *Beautiful Flowers of Kashmir*. 2 Vols. London, 1928-9.
Palms of British India. Bombay: OUP.

Blatter, E & Walter S. Millard. *Some Beautiful Indian Trees*. Bombay: BNHS 1937, 1977.

Bole, P.V. & Yogini Vaghani. *Field Guide to the Common Trees of India*. Bombay: WWF/OUP 1986.

Bor, N.L. & M.B. Raizada. *Some Beautiful India Climbers and Shrubs*. Bombay: BNHS 1954, 1982.

Brandis, D. *Indian Trees*. London: Constable 1906. Recently reprinted in India. This detailed work remains a standard work for the subcontinent.

Champion, F & Seth. *The Forest Types of India*. Delhi 1962. The most comprehensive classification of the subcontinent's trees.

Coventry, B.O. *Wild Flowers of Kashmir*. 3 vols London: 1923-30.

Collett, H. *Flora Simlensis Calcutta*: 1920. Reprinted in 1984. Useful for the Simla region.

Hara, H. *Enumeration of the Flowering Plants of Nepal*. 3 vols. London: British Museum 1978-82.
Spring Flora of Sikkim Himalaya. Hoikusha, Japan 1963.
Plants of the Eastern Himalaya. Tokyo 1968.

Hooker, Joseph. *The Flora of British India*. 7 vols. London: 1872-97 (reprinted in 1980). Although very out of date, it remains the most comprehensive work in the region.

Kingdom-Ward, Frank. *Assam Adventure*. London: 1941.
The Land of the Blue Poppy. London: 1913, 1973.
Plant Hunting on the Edge of the World. London: 1930-1973.
Plant Hunter in Manipur. London 1952. Kingdom-Ward's books are excellent introductions to the remote areas of Eastern India and the Himalaya.

Mierow, M. & T.B. Shrestha. *Himalayan Flowers and Trees*. Kathmandu 1978. A useful pocket size guidebook with 170 pages of color photographs.

Nasir, E. & S.I. *Flora of (West) Pakistan*. Karachi 1970.

Polunin, Oleg and Adam Stainton. *Flowers of the Himalaya*. Oxford and Delhi: OUP 1984. Detailed descriptions of over 1500 species found from Kashmir to Sikkim. Over 690 color photographs and 315 drawings.

Rau, M.A. I*llustration of West Himalayan Flowering Plants*. Calcutta: BSI 1963.

Santapau, H. *Common Trees*. New Delhi: NBT 1966.

Stainton, Adam. *Forest of Nepal*. London: John Murray 1972. A detailed classification of forest types following 20 years of field work. Over 150 color photographs.

Stewart, R.R. Flora of Ladakh, *Western Tibet*. 1916. Delhi reprint 1973.